Umweltrechtliche Studien
Studies on Environmental Law

Herausgegeben von / edited by
Professor Dr. Sabine Schlacke
Professor Dr. Claudio Franzius

Band 54
Volume 54

Tasso Alexandre Richetti Pires Cipriano

Waste prevention through product ecodesign regulation in Brazilian and EU environmental law

Nomos

This publication was printed with the financial support from
the Alexander von Humboldt Foundation.

The Deutsche Nationalbibliothek lists this publication in the Deutsche Nationalbibliografie; detailed bibliographic data are available on the Internet at http://dnb.d-nb.de

a.t.: Bremen, Univ., Diss., 2018

ISBN 978-3-8487-7837-9 (Print)
978-3-7489-2247-6 (ePDF)

British Library Cataloguing-in-Publication Data
A catalogue record for this book is available from the British Library.

ISBN 978-3-8487-7837-9 (Print)
978-3-7489-2247-6 (ePDF)

Library of Congress Cataloging-in-Publication Data
Cipriano, Tasso Alexandre Richetti Pires
Waste prevention through product ecodesign regulation in
Brazilian and EU environmental law
Tasso Alexandre Richetti Pires Cipriano
316 pp.
Includes bibliographic references.

ISBN 978-3-8487-7837-9 (Print)
978-3-7489-2247-6 (ePDF)

Onlineversion
Nomos eLibrary

1st Edition 2023

FOREWORD

This publication is the book format of my *cotutelle* dissertation submitted to, and approved by, both the University of São Paulo (Brazil) and the University of Bremen (Germany) for the obtaining of a doctoral degree in laws (*doutor em ciências* and *doctor iuris*, respectively). The dissertation was submitted in early May 2017 and approved by the doctoral jury in mid-January 2018.

Since then, relevant regulatory modifications in product and waste legislation have abounded both in the European Union (EU) and Brazil.

In the EU, Directive 2008/98/EC on waste, the Waste Framework Directive, along with a couple of other directives on the management of certain products and packaging at end of life have been considerably amended. Several implementing measures laying down ecodesign requirements for energy-related products under Directive 2009/125/EC, the Ecodesign Directive, have been revised, while new ones have also been introduced. Self-regulatory measures under the Ecodesign Directive have been updated. Not to mention the adoption of Directive (EU) 2019/604 on single-use plastic products.

In Brazil, plastics and single-use plastic products are being particularly and increasingly targeted by legislation seeking to ban or phase them out, at times to regulate their design and material composition as well, especially at the municipal level, as the result not only of a spill-over effect of EU efforts to tackle plastics but also the challenges that those products pose to waste management.

These and other developments made until December 2019 have been acknowledged in the present version of the dissertation.

São Paulo, January 2020.

Inhaltsverzeichnis

ABSTRACT

The present study deals with the issue of waste prevention in Brazilian and European environmental law. Prevention, understood as the taking of action before a problem arises, is unquestionably the cornerstone of environmental law. In waste law, this is no different. Yet, much as the best waste is repeatedly described as being that which is never produced, it is commonplace both in theory and in practice of environmental law that waste prevention remains wishful thinking. The focus of this dissertation lies on quantitative, as opposed to qualitative, prevention of waste materials (i.e. matter as opposed to energy) by improving the ecodesign of products. By drawing on the relationship between law and economics to explain the insufficiency of the traditional approach to the environmental and waste problems, an alternative theoretical framework providing a more adequate account of, and effective solutions to, those problems are searched for. At the centre of such a framework are the contributions of ecological economics and the adoption of the integrated (i.e. metabolic and life cycle) perspective in environmental regulation. Based on this theoretical reconstruction, a comparative and dogmatic legal analysis of Brazilian and EU waste law as well as product-related environmental law is performed. After the functions of waste law and the very legal concept of waste are revisited in light of the integrated waste management paradigm, waste prevention is defined by changes in the production and consumption of products so that fewer materials (i.e. resources) are consumed. Improvements in product ecodesign are instrumental in bringing about such changes and they are best addressed by product-related regulation. A few attempts to regulate the ecodesign of products are found in the European setting, from which Brazilian environmental law could learn.

Keywords: environmental law, waste law, waste prevention, product regulation, ecodesign, European Union, Brazil.

RESUMO

O presente estudo trata da prevenção de resíduos no direito ambiental brasileiro e europeu. Prevenção, entendida como a tomada de ação antes do surgimento de um problema, é inquestionavelmente a pedra angular do direito ambiental. No direito dos resíduos, isso não é diferente. No entanto, por mais que se repita ser o melhor resíduo aquele que nunca é gerado, é um lugar comum tanto da teoria como da prática do direito ambiental o fato de a prevenção de resíduos ainda ser uma utopia. O foco do presente trabalho é a prevenção quantitativa (em contraposição à qualitativa) de materiais residuais (portanto, de matéria, em contraposição a energia) por meio de melhorias no ecodesign dos produtos. Recorrendo à relação entre direito e economia para explicar a insuficiência da abordagem tradicional dos problemas ambientais e dos resíduos, busca-se um arcabouço teórico alternativo a fornecer uma explicação mais adequada e soluções mais efetivas para esses problemas. No centro desse arcabouço estão a contribuição da economia ecológica e a adoção da chamada perspectiva integrada (isto é, metabólica e de ciclo de vida) na regulação ambiental. Com base nessa reconstrução teórica, procede-se a uma análise jurídica dogmática e comparada do direito dos resíduos e do direito ambiental dos produtos brasileiros e europeus. Após uma revisitação das funções do direito dos resíduos e do próprio conceito de resíduos à luz do paradigma da chamada gestão integrada de resíduos, a prevenção de resíduos é definida em função das mudanças na produção e no consumo de produtos de modo a diminuir o consumo de materiais (ou seja, de recursos). Melhorias no ecodesign dos produtos conduzem a tais mudanças e elas são melhor endereças por uma regulação de produtos. Algumas tentativas de regular o ecodesign dos produtos são encontradas no contexto europeu, com as quais o direito ambiental brasileiro poderia aprender.

Palavras-chave: direito ambiental, direito dos resíduos, prevenção de resíduos, regulação de produto, ecodesign, União Europeia, Brasil.

ZUSAMMENFASSUNG

Die vorliegende Arbeit befasst sich mit der Frage der Abfallvermeidung im brasilianischen und europäischen Umweltrecht. Prävention, verstanden als Maßnahmen, die dem Entstehen eines Problems vorbeugen, ist zweifellos der Grundstein des Umweltrechts. Im Abfallrecht ist dies nicht anders. Auch wenn stets jener als der bester Abfall bezeichnet wird, der gar nicht erst produziert wird, ist es in der umweltrechtlichen Theorie und Praxis eine Binsenweisheit, dass Abfallvermeidung nach wie vor Wunschdenken bleibt. Der Schwerpunkt dieser Dissertation liegt auf der quantitativen (im Gegensatz zur qualitativen) Vermeidung von Abfallstoffen (d.h. Materie im Gegensatz zu Energie) durch die Verbesserung des Ökodesigns von Produkten. Die Arbeit untersucht die Beziehung zwischen Recht und Ökonomie, um die Unzulänglichkeiten des traditionellen Ansatzes zur Lösung von Umwelt- und Abfallproblemen zu erklären und einen alternativen theoretischen Rahmen zu entwickeln, der eine angemessenere Berücksichtigung dieser Probleme sowie wirksame Lösungsansätze ermöglicht. Im Mittelpunkt eines solchen theoretischen Rahmens stehen der Beitrag der ökologischen Ökonomie und der sogenannte integrierte (d.h. metabolische und lebenszyklusbezogene) Ansatz zur Umweltregulierung. Auf der Grundlage dieser theoretischen Rekonstruktion wird eine vergleichende und dogmatische Analyse des brasilianischen und europäischen Abfallrechts sowie des produktbezogenen Umweltrechts durchgeführt. Nachdem die Funktionen des Abfallrechts sowie des rechtlichen Abfallbegriffes im Lichte des sogenannten integrierten Abfallwirtschaftsparadigmas erneut überdacht werden, wird Abfallvermeidung als jene Veränderung in der Produktion und dem Verbrauch von Produkten definiert, die den Verbrauch von Materialien (d.h. Ressourcen) verringert, definiert. Verbesserungen im Ökodesign von Produkten tragen maßgeblich dazu bei, solche Veränderungen herbeizuführen. Sie werden am besten durch eine produktbezogene Regulierung vorgenommen. Im europäischen produktbezogenen Umweltrecht finden sich Beispiele für die Regulierung des Ökodesigns von Produkten, von denen das brasilianische Umweltrecht lernen könnte.

Stichwörter: Umweltrecht, Abfallrecht, Abfallvermeidung, Produktregulierung, Ökodesign, Europäische Union, Brasilien.

ACKNOWLEDGEMENTS

I could have never completed this study were it not for the academic, professional and personal support of many.

Professor Ana Maria de Oliveira Nusdeo opened the doors of environmental law for me in my very first year of undergraduate legal studies at the University of São Paulo (Brazil) and has always believed in me more than I do myself. She is an example of ethics and dedication to teaching in a country like Brazil where an academic career is still undervalued.

Professor Maria Alexandra de Sousa Aragão, in my opinion the most authoritative expert in environmental law in the Portuguese-speaking world, has been one of my main sources of inspiration for environmental-legal research. In 2009, she welcomed me at the Faculty of Law of the University of Coimbra (Portugal), on which occasion she drew my attention to the topic of this dissertation. Since then she has helped me whenever I have needed.

Professor Gerd Winter welcomed me with open arms at the University of Bremen (Germany) at the end of 2013 and has ever since been an inexhaustible fountain of knowledge and guidance. During my stay in Bremen, he was a true father in the sense of the word *Doktorvater* and, together with Antje Spalink at *Forschungsstelle für Europäisches Umweltrecht*, spared no effort to let me work on my doctoral studies. Thanks to him I have learnt not only that the most intelligent are the humblest but also how to ride a bicycle.

The three of them are certainly responsible for my decision to pursue an academic career in legal research and professorship.

Fabricio Dorado Soler has been my accomplice in environmental lawyering in São Paulo and the professional experience gained with him has showed to me that theory and practice must go hand in hand, even more so in legal 'science'. Maria Alfa Canaes has always been on our side, taking care of us as her children. And reconciling personal, professional and academic life would have been impossible without the invaluable assistance of Karen Cristine Rodrigues Sant Anna.

The *Sociedade de Estudos Jurídico Brasil Alemanha* (São Paulo), especially thanks to the mobilisation made by Professor Fábio Nusdeo, as well as the *Alexander von Humboldt Stiftung* (Germany) provided me with financial support during my stay in Bremen in the academic years of 2013/2014 and 2014/2015, respectively.

Anna Nowak, whom I first met in 2009 as an exchange student at the University of Munich (Germany) during my undergraduate legal studies, is not only responsible for me actually completing this dissertation by helping me find focus every time I lost it, but she has also taught me that friendship has no barriers, be they spatial, temporal or linguistic.

With Günther (*in memoriam*) I have learnt that love is not exclusive to the human species and this has only reinforced my commitment to striving for a better environment.

My two cherished sisters, Thyelle Caroline and Priscilla Kimberly, in addition to teaching me the meaning of sharing, complicity and love, have held the forts during my stay abroad.

Last, but by no means least, my beloved mother Vera, whose unconditional love has made her always sacrifice herself for my sisters and me, is my greatest example in life. She is the sole reason for all that I am and have become.

To you all, my heartfelt and affectionate *thanks*!

LIST OF ABBREVIATIONS

AbfallR	*Zeitschrift für das Recht der Abfallwirtschaft*
ACP	*ação civil pública*
ADI	*ação direta de inconstitucionalidade*
Ag. Reg.	*agravo regimental*
AI	*agravo de instrumento*
ANEC	European Association for the Coordination of Consumer Representation in Standardisation
BGBl.	*Bundesgesetzblatt*
BMU	*Bundesministerium für Umwelt, Naturschutz und Reaktorsicherheit*
CDC	*Código de Defesa do Consumidor*
CEDOUA	*Centro de Estudos de Direito do Ordenamento, do Urbanismo e do Ambiente*
CEN	*Comité Européen de Normalisation*
CENELEC	European Committee for Electrotechnical Standardization
Conama	*Conselho Nacional do Meio Ambiente*
Des.	*Desembargador(a)*
DfE	design for environment
DOC	*Diário Oficial da Cidade de São Paulo*
DOESP	*Diário Oficial do Estado de São Paulo*
DOU	*Diário Oficial da União*
DVBl.	*Deutsches Verwaltungsblatt*
EABS	European Association for Bioeconomic Studies
EAP	Environmental Action Programme
EC	European Community
ECJ	European Court of Justice
ECOS	European Environmental Citizens Organisation for Standardisation
ECR	European Court Reports
ED	*embargos de declaração*
EEA	European Economic Area
EEB	European Environmental Bureau
EEC	European Economic Community
EEE	electrical and electronic equipment
EIA	environmental impact assessment

elni	Environmental Law Network International
EN	European norm (standards)
EPA	Environmental Protection Agency
EPEAT	Electronic Product Environmental Assessment Tool
EPR	extended producer responsibility
ErP	energy-related product
ETSI	European Telecommunications Standards Institute
EU	European Union
EUI	European University Institute
EuP	energy-using product
EurUP	*Zeitschrift für Europäisches Umwelt- und Planungsrecht*
IEC	International Electrotechnical Commission
IEEP	Institute for European Environmental Policy
inpEV	*Instituto Nacional de Processamento de Embalagens Vazias*
IPP	Integrated Product Policy
IPTS	Institute for Prospective Technological Studies
IWM	integrated waste management
JEEPL	Journal of European Environmental & Planning Law
JEL	Journal of Environmental Law
JIE	Journal of Industrial Ecology
JRC	Joint Research Centre
ISO	International Organisation for Standardization
MCT	*Ministério da Ciência, Tecnologia, das Inovações e Comunicações*
MDIC	*Ministério da Indústrica, do Comércio Exterior e dos Serviços*
MEErP	methodology for the ecodesign of energy-related products
Min.	*Ministro(a)*
MME	*Ministério de Minas e Energia*
MOU	Memorandum of Understanding
MPSP	*Ministério Público do Estado de São Paulo*
n.d.	no date
NLF	New Legislative Framework
No.	number
n/a	not applicable
n.p.	no place or no publisher
NVwZ	*Neue Zeitschrift für Verwaltungsrecht*
OECD	Organisation for Economic Co-operation and Development
OJ	Official Journal of the European Union
OWiG	*Gesetz über Ordnungswidrigkeiten*
p.	page

PAYT	pay as you throw
PNRS	*Política Nacional de Resíduos Sólidos*
POPs	persistent organic pollutants
PRO	producer responsibility organisation
RE	*recurso extraordinário*
RECIEL	Review of European Community & International Environmental Law
rel.	*relator(a)*
Rn.	*Randnummer*
RoHS	restriction of (the use of certain) hazardous substances
SMEs	Small and Medium-sized Enterprises
STF	*Supremo Tribunal Federal*
STJ	*Superior Tribunal de Justiça*
TAC	*termo de ajustamento de conduta*
TEC	Treaty establishing the European Community
TEU	Treaty on the European Union
TFEU	Treaty on the Functioning of the European Union
TJPR	*Tribunal de Justiça do Estado do Paraná*
TJSP	*Tribunal de Justiça do Estado de São Paulo*
UBA	*Umweltbundesamt*
UNEP	United Nations Environment Programme
UPR	*Umwelt- und Planungsrecht*
U.S.	United States of America
vol.	volume
WEEE	waste electrical and electronic equipment
WFD	Waste Framework Directive
ZAU	*Zeitschrift für angewandte Umweltforschung*
ZfU	*Zeitschrift für Umweltpolitik & Umweltrecht*
ZUR	*Zeitschrift für Umweltrecht*

INTRODUCTION

The present study deals with the issue of waste prevention from a legal perspective.

Prevention, understood as the taking of action before a problem arises, is unquestionably the cornerstone of environmental law. In waste law, this is no different. Prevention emerges as the preferred solution to the problematic of waste as soon as it ceases to be seen exclusively as, firstly, a sanitation and, secondly, pollution issue, thus having to be eliminated (i.e. disposed of),[1] and starts to be regarded as being a symptom of a larger problem, namely the depletion of resources resulting from ever-increasing production and consumption patterns.[2]

Much as the best waste is repeatedly described as being that which is never produced, and much as this is reflected in the so-called waste hierarchy[3] adopted by waste law in most nations worldwide, it is a commonplace both in the theory and in practice of environmental law that waste prevention still remains wishful thinking.

In Brazil, this is arguably attributable to the relative novelty of waste law, as illustrated by the enactment of Federal Law No. 12,305 establishing the National Solid Waste Policy only in August 2010. This statute was strongly inspired by waste law of the European Union (hereinafter 'EU'), which now enjoys over four decades of existence and whose protagonism is widely well known. A decision has thus been made to look at and compare both Brazilian and EU environmental law as regards waste prevention with a view to discovering whether and to what extent Brazilian law should look up to EU law.

European efforts to foster waste prevention are found not only in waste law but also and especially in product-related environmental law. Product regulation is of the essence of the EU for the obvious reason of establishing and ensuring the functioning of the integrated internal market. Environmental concerns indeed motivate European product-related environmental regulation, but whether this regulation effectively handles waste prevention is questionable.

---

1 See chapter 1, section C, *infra*.

2 See chapters 2 and 3, *infra*.

3 See chapter 3, section A, *infra*.

The main research questions may then be enunciated as follows: What is waste prevention and how is it to be achieved in the wider context of environmental law? Are Brazilian and EU environmental laws really concerned with waste prevention? What lessons can Brazilian environmental law learn from EU environmental law, if any?

Answers to these questions are sought based on a legal-economic approach to environmental problems. The approach is economic in that legal analysis feeds on the knowledge provided by economics,[4] which is not surprising given that environmental law is, by definition, economic law.[5] Besides, interdisciplinarity, of which the dialogue between law and economics engaged in by this dissertation is an example, is fundamental for a better comprehension and tackling of environmental problems. This is particularly true when finding answers to the first research question, 'What is waste law and how is it to be achieved in the wider context of environmental law?', as shall be seen in different parts of this work.

The legal approach consists of a comparative dogmatic analysis of Brazilian as well as EU positive and case law plus a review of the relevant legal literature. Much as comparison is made between Brazilian and EU law, analysis rests heavily on legal commentary made by German scholars on both German and EU waste law. Reasons are threefold. Firstly, German waste law is widely known to have shaped EU waste law. Secondly, to my knowledge, including the fact that I do not know all the official languages of the EU, legal scholarship on waste law has been most developed in Germany. Thirdly and lastly, the present dissertation is part of a *cotutelle* doctoral study involving a German university. As such it is directed primarily, albeit not exclusively, at a German audience. The proposed comparative-dogmatic legal analysis is instrumental in seeking answers to the second and third research questions. Particularly in relation to the second question ('Are Brazilian and European environmental law really concerned with waste law?'), the hypothesis provides a negative answer as concerns Brazil and a positive answer as concerns the EU.

This study concentrates on consumer waste as opposed to production waste, that is, waste arising from the use of end products instead of that resulting from production activities. The choice to focus on consumer waste is explained by the fact that environmental law has traditionally

4 See chapter 2, section A, *infra*.
5 See Nusdeo, 2010 and 1975. Similarly, see Robbers, 2017, p. 102.

paid more attention to production activities than to products,[6] and the operational conceptualisation of waste[7] corroborates this finding.

Prevention of waste shall refer to preventing the squandering of materials as opposed to that of energy. In physical terms, this means that attention is directed at matter as opposed to energy. Much as energy aspects play a central, if not superordinate, role in environmental protection,[8] it constitutes a topic that is alien to, and therefore usually examined separately from, that of waste law.

A distinction must be made between quantitative and qualitative waste prevention.[9] Whilst the former is concerned with reducing the amount of materials becoming waste, the latter deals with the reduction of their hazardousness. Qualitative aspects are much more familiar to, and have thus far been more frequently and satisfactorily addressed by, environmental law. This is because hazardousness concerns connect more directly with human health protection issues. This is true in relation to both production-related, pollution-oriented environmental law[10] and product-related law[11]. Environmental law hesitates to make use of quantitative regulations,[12] which is explained in part by the fact that they do not fit in the liberal mould of the traditional economic approach.[13] Quantitative prevention lies at the centre of the present study because it is less explored than qualitative prevention.

As for the addressees of waste prevention law (i.e. stakeholders), and based on the *summa divisio* between production and consumption that marks both legal and economic systems of our industrialised society,[14] it is the decisions made by producers as to the design of the products they place on the market that the investigation conducted herein proposes to address. A model for identifying producer decisions in the context of waste prevention strategies as well as the reasons for concentrating on them are elaborated on in chapter 3, section D, and chapter 4, section A, *infra*.

Being so delimited, this dissertation is composed of five parts.

---

6 See chapter 1, section C, *infra*.
7 See chapter 3, section C, *infra*.
8 See chapter 2, section C, *infra*.
9 See chapter 3, section D, *infra*.
10 See chapter 1, section C, *infra*.
11 See chapter 3, section D, *infra*.
12 See chapter 3, section D, chapter 4, and chapter 5, sections A and B, *infra*.
13 As expressly noted in chapter 2, section C, *infra*.
14 See Comparato, 1974, p. 90.

Chapter 1 explores how economics and law have traditionally dealt with environmental problems in general and the waste problem in particular. It provides a description of the main features of the conventional economic and legal approaches individually while drawing attention to the parallels existing between them, including as regards their insufficiency.

In light of this inadequacy, chapter 2 looks at alternative, unorthodox theoretical references providing a more comprehensive account of environmental and waste problems. Such theories are situated in the context of the debate on sustainable development, which, in turn, is also contextualised. Special attention is turned to ecological economics and the seminal contribution of economist NICHOLAS GEORGESCU-ROEGEN. Chapter 2 continues with the interdisciplinary dialogue between law and economics engaged in chapter 1 by building on the analogies that ecological economics makes between the ecological and economic systems in order to draw parallels with environmental law in general and overcome the shortcomings of the traditional legal approach.

Chapter 3 bridges the theoretically reconstructed economic-legal approach to the environmental and waste problems with the more practical, comparative and dogmatic legal analysis of Brazilian and EU environmental law in connection with waste prevention. It does so by examining waste law of both legal orders thoroughly. In light of the concept of integrated waste management, central issues in waste law such as waste hierarchy, the functions of waste law, the legal concept of waste as well as the notion and legal operationalisation of waste prevention are discussed by analysing the relevant legislation, case law and legal commentary.

Chapter 4 provides an in-depth theoretical and practical examination of the main incentive-based instrument provided by waste law to promote waste prevention, namely extended producer responsibility (EPR).

Chapter 5 looks at waste prevention beyond waste legislation. Based on the findings that waste prevention is best grasped and operationalised by changes to the production and consumption of products, four examples of product-related environmental law are scrutinised, namely the product ecodesign mandates found in Brazilian and EU end-of-life (i.e. EPR) legislation; the Ecodesign Directive; the regulation of plastic bags and single-use plastic products in both the EU and Brazil; and the regulation of mobile phone chargers in the EU.

The study concludes with the enunciation of the main theses in summation and the ensuing identification of needs for future research.

Chapter 1 – The traditional economic-legal approach to the environmental and waste problems

This chapter explores how economics and law have traditionally dealt with environmental problems in general and the waste problem in particular. It argues that there is a parallel between the traditional economic and legal approaches and that both are insufficient.

A. *The economic-legal approach*

The so-called 'environmental issue', which can be broadly understood as the set of all environmental problems, can be studied from different perspectives, including economic and legal.

From a system theory viewpoint,[15] the economic system is embedded in – or, strictly speaking, constitutes a subsystem of – the ecological system, for the economic system acts as a mere intermediary between the environment in its source and sink functions[16].

---

15 On system theory, see von Bertalanffy, 1968.

16 Source and sink functions are to be understood within the ecological context of the interactions – in the sense of exchange of matter and energy – between the environment and the biological entities it encompasses. In ecology, 'biological (i.e. living) entities' comprise not only individual organisms, but also the populations and communities that they form in nature (see Begon, Townsend and Harper, 2006, p. 499). They all need matter for their construction and energy for their activities (see Begon, Townsend and Harper, 2006, p. 499). 'Source function' means that matter and energy leave the environment and enter biological entities, whereas 'sink function' means the opposite, namely that matter and energy leave biological entities and enter the environment. (The environment and biological entities are taken here as independent, albeit interacting, systems.) Put another way, to say that the environment acts as a source means that it provides matter and energy to biological entities, whereas to say that the environment acts as a sink means that it receives matter and energy from biological entities. The importance of both energy and matter fluxes to the intrinsic processes of biological entities points to the close linkage between said entities and the abiotic (i.e. non-living), physicochemical environment in which they are set (see Begon, Townsend and Harper, 2006, p. 499).

From an economics standpoint, the economic system means an organic set of institutions through which society tackles the so-called economic problem, which revolves around the notion of scarcity: due to the infinitude of human needs and the finitude of resources to satisfy those needs, decisions as to what, how and to whom to produce – in short the best utilisation of scarce resources – must be made.[17]

However varied in space and time real-life economic systems are, they can be simplified for theoretical purposes into three models – in the sense of Weberian ideal types – depending on whether they have tradition, authority or autonomy as their guiding principle of decision-making.[18] Underlying each of these three models is, so to speak, a different assumption of a psychological-behavioural characteristic, that is, a mental attitude or beliefs engendering a supposedly coherent set of behaviours that are regulated by the institutions proper to each system.[19]

The autonomy model emerged and has since prevailed in the so-called western world, which comprises Western Europe, the USA and the American countries that gradually became independent from their respective European metropoles, and has been later adopted in many other regions of the globe as well.[20] It is ideally and fundamentally marked by a separation of the political and economic decision-making spheres: whilst political decisions are made by the State, economic decisions are left to the individuals, whether acting individually or collectively in groups (e.g. families).[21] Each individual, generically referred to as an 'economic agent', is considered an independent decision-maker. Economic decisions are made based on the agent's autonomous will and are therefore decentralised in relation to the political power, hence the name 'autonomy' or 'decentralised' system. It rests on the assumption that each and every economic agent always behaves with a view to maximising the results of his or her actions or self-interest.[22]

Economic agents display their self-interested behaviour and make their economic decisions in an ideal place known as 'the market', the reason for which reference is also made to the 'market system'. The market is nothing but an abstraction: a virtual place that is enabled by a set of institutions,

17 See Nusdeo, 2010, p. 97.

18 See Nusdeo, 2010, p. 99. On each of these three models, see Nusdeo, 2010, p. 100 *et seq*.

19 See Nusdeo, 2010, p. 99-100.

20 See Nusdeo, 2010, p. 123-124.

21 See Nusdeo, 2010, p. 113.

22 See Nusdeo, 2010, p. 114-115.

including legal ones, and where agents' willingness to trade economic goods – that is, those goods having utility – is manifested.[23] Since no one can produce everything one needs, division of labour and trade happen as two sides of the same coin. Manifestation of agents' willingness to trade occurs through the price mechanism, which is nothing but a theoretically constructed way to valuate (i.e. assess the scarcity and thus the importance of) the economic goods to be traded.

Despite the dispersion of decision-making, the behaviour of all agents is driven by result maximisation so that each and every one of them decides correctly as to how best handle scarcity. In this sense, the pursuit of one's own interests is said to promote that of society as a whole. The market therefore works as a resource allocation mechanism. This capacity of the market to coordinate societal interests – the 'the invisible hand' of which Adam Smith spoke – is another assumption of the model at stake.[24]

Historically, the establishment of the market as a model of economic system in the western world occurred in the last quarter of the eighteenth century as the ideals of political liberalism that had emerged in the seventeenth century in opposition to what the French have termed the *ancien régime* were transplanted into the economic field.[25] Intellectually, freedom and reason became the building blocks of western culture and the fundamental values upon which societal reorganisation took place. One pivotal contribution to the consolidation of economic liberalism was the very emergence of economics as a discipline as a result of the work of the 'classical' economists, which was initiated at the end of the eighteenth century by Adam Smith and continued to be developed until the mid-nineteenth century, followed then by the scientific, mathematical elaboration of economics by the 'marginalists' from the second part of the nineteenth to the early twentieth century, and, more recently, by the 'neoclassical synthesis' carried out by contemporary economists since the twentieth century.[26]

Neoclassical economics, which builds upon both the classical and marginalist schools, constitutes the mainstream of economic thought. Reference is made hereinafter to 'traditional economics' to allude to mainstream economics in the sense of neoclassical economics plus its classical

23 See Nusdeo, 2010, p. 115.
24 See Nusdeo, 2010, p. 118.
25 See Nusdeo, 2010, p. 124.
26 An overview of the classical, marginalist and neoclassical schools is provided by Beinhocker, 2006, p. 24-43.

and marginalist theoretical roots.[27] Since the 'marginalist revolution', traditional economics has had mechanics, a branch of physics, as its scientific paradigm.[28] This entails a worldview revolving around the idea of systems in equilibrium[29], from which follows the ability to explain the functioning of the economic system in precise, mathematical terms and thus to predict economic results.[30]

Legally, the reorganisation of the economic system based on the liberal ideals was enabled by two phenomena. Firstly, the emergence of the 'classical (or liberal) Constitutions', which, on the one hand, recognised individual rights such as life, freedom and private property and, on the other hand, limited State power to police and security functions intended to protect those individual rights, thereby separating the political and economic spheres. Secondly, the codification of private law, which sought to provide a logical and consistent body of rules regulating individual rights, especially property rights, so that economic agents could have legal certainty to use their economic goods.[31]

Some parallels to economics can be drawn. Firstly, just as the market naturally reaches and stays in equilibrium unless provoked by an external factor, so too there is a natural order to be legally maintained, namely that of economic freedom and limitation of State power as provided for by the Constitution.[32] Secondly, just like economics, private law also underwent a process of rationalisation and 'scientification'.[33] Thirdly, legal certainty has to do with – or, to be more precise, enables – predictability of economic results.

Probably for having gained predictability, traditional economics has undeniably played a central role in real-life decision-making,[34] thus being able to influence all realms of social life, including environmental law and policy, if not to prescribe behaviour (normative aspect). Hence the economic approach adopted herein.

---

27 Similarly, see Beinhocker, 2006, p. 23, who uses the term 'traditional economics to refer to the set of ideas that have dominated economic theory for the past century'.
28 See Beinhocker, 2006, p. 17-18, 29-36.
29 Much as scarcity entails tensions in the economy (for instance, between supply and demand), at some point – an *optimal* point – the market reaches equilibrium.
30 See Beinhocker, 2006, p. 29-36.
31 See Nusdeo, 2010, p. 128-136.
32 See Nusdeo, 2010, p. 130-131.
33 See Ferraz Junior, 2003, p. 65-81.
34 See Beinhocker, 2006, p. 43.

Yet, in the past century and a half, which is a rough estimate of the duration of the liberal era,[35] many of the assumptions of both the liberal doctrine and the ideal market-based model pictured by traditional economics[36] have not materialised and the market has, so to speak, 'failed' in various ways. Precision and predictability have been attained at the cost of realism. Within mainstream economic theory, the study of market failures has been undertaken by so-called welfare economics, which 'attempts to provide a framework in which normative judgements can be made about alternative configurations of economic activity'.[37] Correction of the so-called market failures – in other words, rectification of the malfunctioning of the economic system under the liberal regime – has justified State (i.e. legal) intervention in the economy, a contraposition to the separation of the political and economic spheres typical of the liberal mould.

Given the background outlined above, the next section delves into the traditional *economic* approach to environmental problems, which are explained in terms of market failures for which correction is necessary through the law. The section following it then examines the traditional *legal* approach to environmental problems, which are regulated on a rather piecemeal fashion. The ensuing section addresses the main limitations of both approaches.

B. Environmental economics

In the face of environmental problems, most notably pollution in industrialised nations, traditional economics has been called upon to provide an account of the ecological consequences of the malfunctioning of the economic (i.e. market) system. In economics parlance, the branch of neoclassical economics taking on such a task is known as 'environmental economics'. It explains the causes of, and proposes solutions to, environmental problems in light of the mainstream, market-based framework. In this sense, environmental economics is an economic reading of ecology.[38] Analytically, it is divided into economics of natural resources, on the one

35 See Nusdeo, 2010, p. 134.
36 Such a model has become known as 'perfect competition', the assumptions of which are summarised by Nusdeo, 2010, p. 167.
37 See Perman *et al.*, 2011, p. 7-8.
38 See Cavalcanti, 2010, p. 56.

hand, and economics of pollution, on the other hand. It is within the latter sub-branch that economics of waste is localised.

As anticipated in the previous section, traditional economics rests upon three important features: methodological individualism, utilitarianism and the paradigm of equilibrium imported from mechanics. In this sense, in order to explain social phenomena in general and the economic system in particular, mainstream economics has as its central unity of analysis rational individuals driven by self-interest and making decisions in a world of finite resources with a view to maximising their satisfaction (i.e. utility), which is expressed by individual preferences (which are, in turn, a 'given' element of analysis), thereby leading the economy to a single, stable, socially optimal result.[39]

Considering the traditional economic theoretical framework above, environmental economics revolves around what could be named the optimal use of the environment in both its source and sink functions. Regarding each of these two functions, environmental economics is analytically divided into two branches, namely and respectively the economics of natural resources and the economics of pollution. Each of these two sub-disciplines has, despite their commonality, 'largely distinct roots in the core of modern mainstream economics. The former emerged mainly out of neoclassical growth economics[40], the latter out of welfare economics and the study of market failure'[41].[42]

The economics of natural resources concerns the use of the environment as a source. It deals with the optimal extraction of naturally occurring resources, both renewable and non-renewable, or exhaustible[43]. Just as the

39 See Amazonas, 2001, p. 15.
40 Economic theoretical considerations about growth and the environmental problem are found in chapter 2, *infra*.
41 See Perman *et al.*, 2011, p. 8.
42 A very concise, albeit very informative, exposition of both branches is provided by Earp and Romeiro, 2015, p. 641-642.
43 The distinction between renewable and non-renewable resources is all but straightforward and definitions vary considerably in the literature. Fundamentally, a resource may be classified as being renewable if it has the capacity of reproducing (in the case of biotic resources) or replenishing (in the case of abiotic resources) – and thus increasing – over time. In this sense, renewable resources are said to be infinite (i.e. present use does not *prima facie* affect future availability) whereas non-renewable resources are said to be finite (i.e. present use does *prima facie* affect future availability). For some, '[e]ven renewable resources are ultimately finite because their renewability depends on energy from the sun and the sun is expected to serve as an energy source for only the next five or

economics of natural resources and the economics of pollution share the same neoclassical background but are studied separately under different ramifications within mainstream economics, so too are the economics of renewable and non-renewable resources analysed as two distinct sub-branches of resource economics despite their common theoretical framework.[44] One central question to the economics of natural resources is the 'intertemporal problem', that is, the optimal allocation of natural resources over time. It revolves around the issue of time preference – the trade-off between extracting or harvesting natural resources today and saving them for future exploitation.[45] The optimal rate of extraction or har-

---

six billion years' (see Tietenberg and Lewis, 2015, p. 152). For others, conversely, 'all natural resources are renewable', for the distinction between renewability and non-renewability is based on 'the length of time it takes a particular resource to be reproduced [or replenished]' (see Hartwick and Olewiler, 1986, p. 2). The divergence of opinions lies in the differing time frames adopted as reference (in the first case and explicitly, the solar lifespan; in the second case and rather implicitly, the human lifespan). Indeed, renewability only makes sense if defined in relation to a human time horizon, for it revolves around the notion of present and future availability of naturally occurring resources to mankind. It is therefore an anthropomorphic concept. More specifically, resource renewability has to do with the time frame for resource reproduction/replenishment *vis-à-vis* a meaningful human time frame or, to put it another way (in more economic terms), the reproduction/replenishment occurring 'on a relevant economic time scale' (see Conrad, 2010, p. 1) or 'within a reasonable period of time' (Anderson, 2010, p. 334). 'For example, how should we classify a stand of old-growth coast redwood or an aquifer with an insignificant rate of recharge? Whereas the redwood tree is a plant, and can be grown commercially, old-growth redwoods may be 800 to 1,000 years old, and their remaining stands might be more appropriately viewed as a non-renewable resource. Whereas the water cycle provides precipitation that will replenish lakes and streams, the water contained in an aquifer with little or no recharge might be more economically similar to a pool of oil (a non-renewable resource) than to a lake or reservoir that receives significant recharge from rain or melting snow' (Conrad, 2010, p. 1-2). Of course, defining 'meaningful', 'relevant' and/or 'reasonable' is somewhat arbitrary, so that the classification of a resource as renewable or non-renewable is made on a rather practical, argumentative, case-by-case basis (see, for instance, Hartwick and Olewiler, 1986, p. 2). Lastly, renewable resources may be regarded as being non-renewable if they are harvested/extracted at a rate exceeding their reproduction/replenishment rate (see, for instance, Perman *et al.*, 2011, p. 12; Hartwick and Olewiler, 1986, p. 2). This makes the distinction between renewable and non-renewable resources even less clear-cut.

44 See Mueller, 2007, p. 336.

45 See Conrad, 2010, p. 3 and 11; Amazonas, 2001, p. 28; Hartwick and Olewiler, 1986, p. 3.

vest of a given resource is obtained based on HOTELLING's formulation[46].[47] Other key issues in the economics of natural resources include the role of technology in providing substitutes for non-renewable resources[48] as well as market failures, notably externalities, and property rights.[49] Since the latter two topics are also central to the economics of pollution, which is the focus here and examined below, the economics of natural resources is not looked at in more depth.

The economics of pollution concerns the use of the environment as a sink. It deals with the optimal level of environmental degradation, or pollution, which is explained as an instance of market failure for which correction is necessary. More specifically, pollution represents a negative externality, which is a market failure.

Externalities can be understood as costs that are not borne, or benefits that are not reaped, by the economic agents generating them, thereby falling on third parties, whether individually identifiable or not. Externalities may be positive or negative. Pollution is a typical example of a negative externality. To illustrate, consider a factory next to a laundry and upstream from a fishermen community.[50] Smokestack emissions from the factory that are deposited on the clothes hanging outdoors in the neighbouring laundry's property create an additional cost to the laundry, for it is compelled to either re-clean its clothes or protect them from the smoke. Effluents discharged by the factory into the river reduce water quality, cause fish mortality and hinder fishing activities in the downstream fishermen community. Furthermore, air and water emissions affect the local popula-

46 See Hotelling, 1931.

47 Since the economics of natural resources is not the focus of the present analysis, the economic-mathematical discussion on the optimal rate of resource exploitation in general, and Hotelling's formulation in particular, need not be explored in further detail. Suffice it to say that the decision as to whether to exploit a given resource in the present or in the future as well as how much of it to extract and/or harvest over time is based on an analysis of, and comparability between, the present and future market values of the relevant resource, with prices being calculated on the basis of a mathematical technique known as 'discounting' (for a brief explanation on discounting, see Hartwick and Olewiler, 1896, p. 5-7). For a more elaborate, but still short, account of the intertemporal issue, including the limitations of Hotelling's formulation, see, for instance, Amazonas, 2001, p. 28-32.

48 See Amazonas, 2001, p. 30.

49 See, for instance, Gopalakrishnan, 2000, p. 3-7, and Hartwick and Olewiler, 1986, p. 8-19.

50 The example is taken from Nusdeo, 2010, p. 153-154, and Nusdeo, 2006, p. 359.

tion, which incurs health expenses arising from breathing problems as well as water treatment costs. Externalities may thus fall on single individuals (e.g. the laundry), a group of people (e.g. the fishermen community) or an indeterminate collective (e.g. the local population). Positive externalities can be exemplified by the planting and/or maintaining of a forest, which brings several environmental benefits to bordering properties, the surrounding area and society as a whole, including, respectively, soil protection, regulation of rainfall and biodiversity preservation.

Externalities occur due to a divorce between private property and scarcity:[51] in the absence, or non-exercise, of property rights[52],[53] the market is not able to signal the full price, and hence the importance (in economic terms: the scarcity), of a given economic good, the use and/or provision of which entails costs and/or benefits that are unaccounted for by those agents using and/or providing it. In the case of pollution, the environment – a scarce good given today's population figures[54] – is used as if it were a free (i.e. superabundant) good,[55] the reason why it is degraded. Costs and benefits that would remain private – in the sense that they would be, respectively, borne and reaped by the economic agents creating them – if it were not for the absence of property rights are thus socialised. Social costs (negative externalities or diseconomies) and social benefits (positive

---

51 See Nusdeo, 2010, p. 157.

52 Even though property rights are best conceptualised as a bundle of separable, albeit interrelated, actions that a rule authorises one to take in relation to a thing with enforceable authority (see, for instance, Ostrom, 2000, p. 339; Ostrom and Schlager, 1996, p. 130; Schlager and Ostrom, 1992, p. 250), in the theoretical-economic context of externalities the term 'property rights' usually refers to 'exclusion' (see Ostrom and Ostrom, 1999, p. 76; Nusdeo, 1975, p. 57) or 'exclusivity' (Hartwick and Olewiler, 1986, p. 8), that is, the possibility of denying access to goods (see Ostrom and Ostrom, 1999, p. 76). Yet, exclusion is only *one* trace of the legal discipline of economic goods (see Salomão Filho, 2012, p. 46) and only *one* criterion – alongside that of jointness (or subtractability) of use – to classify such goods (see Ostrom and Ostrom, 1999). The parallels between law and economics are once again striking.

53 See Hardin, 1968. See also Nusdeo, 2010, p. 158.

54 See Hardin, 1968.

55 In fact, most environmental goods correspond to what economists call 'collective goods' or, more precisely, 'common-pool resources', that is, goods displaying a low degree of exclusion (i.e. difficulty to deny access to them) and a high degree of subtractability (i.e. use or consumption by one person precludes use or consumption by another person). A high degree of subtractability, which is also a characteristic of private goods, renders scarcity a more serious problem (see Salomão Filho, 2012, p. 48).

externalities or economies) are called externalities because they circulate – that is, they are transferred from one unit to another within the economic system – externally to the market and hence cannot be captured by the price mechanism.[56] Negative externalities tend to be much more common than positive externalities since it is of the essence of the market system – given the psychological-behavioural assumption underlying it – that costs are socialised and benefits remain private.[57]

In these terms, externalities must be internalised, as the jargon has it. Two proposals for doing so stand out within mainstream economic theory.[58] The first one has been put forward by ARTHUR CECIL PIGOU[59], whose systematic analysis of externalities suggests that the State must tax, in an economic sense, activities generating negative externalities and subsidise activities generating positive externalities.[60] Another solution to the problem has been formulated by RONALD COASE[61], for whom in the absence of transaction costs[62] – a rather unrealistic assumption – externalities would be better (i.e. more efficiently) internalised through bargaining between the parties involved, that is, those causing the externality and those suffering and/or benefiting from its effects,[63] than through governmental intervention in the economy as proposed by the Pigouvian solution.[64] This economic debate has influenced environmental law and policy significantly, of which the debate on, and the adoption of, so-called economic instruments[65] aimed at environmental protection is one of the most illustrative examples.

56 See Nusdeo, 2010, p. 153, and Nusdeo, 1975, p. 49. In other words, externalities 'are situations where, because of the structure of property rights, relationships between economic agents are not all mediated through markets' (Perman *et al.*, 2011, p. 8).
57 See Nusdeo, 2010, p. 156, and Nusdeo, 1975, p. 48-49.
58 See Nusdeo, 2006, p. 360-362; Gopalakrishnan, 2000, p. 3-5.
59 See Pigou, 1920.
60 See Nusdeo, 2006, p. 360-361, and Nusdeo, 1975, p. 53.
61 See Coase, 1960.
62 Coase (1960, p. 15) defines transaction costs as those involved in carrying out a market transaction.
63 Transaction costs and distributional effects aside, Coase's bargaining solution seems feasible only where externality is an exclusively bilateral situation. That is, however, not the case of pollution, which is a rather diffuse, multilateral externality situation.
64 See Nusdeo, 2006, p. 361.
65 On the notion of economic instruments, see footnote 422, *infra*.

The economics of waste can be understood as a particular instance of the economics of pollution. Product prices fail to reflect full social cost, including the cost of the pollution caused to the environment as a result of disposal (in the sense of landfilling and/or incinerating) of waste materials,[66] which is an activity that has been traditionally carried out as a public service by municipal authorities in lieu of the economic agents – producers and consumers – generating them. The environment's limited waste assimilation capacity is under-priced and the use of the environment as a sink is congested,[67] thereby reducing air, water and soil quality.

C. *The legal parallel: managerial, single-point, pollution-oriented, production-related environmental law*

Although the law has always regulated the relations between man and nature in one way or another, environmental law as we know it today, that is, as a response of the legal system to the negative consequences caused by the economic system to the ecological system or, in short, as the law of environmental protection, emerged in the western world in the late 1960s and throughout the 1970s in reaction to the so-called first generation of environmental problems. These comprise fundamentally the *pollution* caused to environmental media, namely, air, water and soil,[68] by large production processes such as resource extraction sites and industrial

66 See Ayres and Kneese, 1989, p. 95-96.

67 See, for instance, Porter, 2002, p. 4 *et seq.* and p. 122 *et seq.*; Pearce and Turner, 1992, p. 6; Turner and Powell, 1991, p. 6-7.

68 In the environmental literature, including the legal one, these three components of the abiotic environment – air, water and soil – are usually referred to as 'environmental media' (*Umweltmedien*). An 'environmental medium' may be defined as an *abiotic* (i.e. non-living) component of the natural environment that not only surrounds, contacts and serves as habitat for living organisms but also can receive and 'store' pollutants and through which these pollutants can move and reach those organisms. In sum, it is that which serves as a *means of communication between pollutants and living organisms*. This is clearly an anthropocentric, pollution-driven notion that focuses the environment exclusively in its 'sink function'. By contrast, some sectors of environmental law face the environment also in its 'source function', as is the case of abiotic and biotic resource regulation (e.g. mining law, fauna and flora protection law).It is based on the concept of 'environmental media' that one speaks of media-related (*medienbezogen*) environmental law as opposed to facility-related (*anlagenbezogen*), product-related (*produktbezogen*) and/or substance- and/or material related (*stoffbezogen*) environmental law. The distinction lies in the target environmental regulation and each of the four

facilities, for which state control has become necessary.[69] Yet, with respect to *natural resources*, at the time environmental protection law emerged the law was – as it had hitherto been – concerned less with their protection (in order to ensure future availability) than with their exploitation and efficient allocation (intra-generationally). The first-generation of environmental regulation therefore corresponds to the second and third phases of WINTER's periodisation of environmental law[70] as regards the environment's source and sink functions, respectively.[71]

That being so, first-generation environmental protection law, hereinafter simply traditional environmental law, is marked by an eminently *sectoral* approach for two main reasons. Firstly, it regulates environmental media *in isolation*, the same happening in relation to the emission of pollutants and the use of hazardous substances. Secondly, it focuses on production facilities, as epitomised by the law of environmental permitting. Despite its focus on *point sources*, i.e. easily identifiable/controllable, individual media, pollutants, substances, facilities, traditional environmental law has been successful to some extent, after all air and water – media in relation to which pollution is most visible as opposed to soil – are cleaner. Nevertheless, at least three criticisms of the traditional legal approach to environmental problems can be made.

The first problem concerns its *fragmentary character*.[72] Due to the sectoral approach[73] mentioned above, traditional environmental law allows pollution to be shifted from one form to another; that is, from one environmental medium to another,[74] instead of reducing or eliminating its total amount.

Secondly, by assuming that it is possible to concentrate and contain, or rather dilute and disperse, pollution until it no longer constitutes a threat,

---

categories implies a specific regulatory technique. See, for instance, Schenkel and Reiche, 1993, p. 184-185.

69 See Cipriano, 2016, p. 159, footnote 9 and the extensive references cited therein. See also Tojo and Lindhqvist, 2010, p. 1; Oosterhuis, Rubik and Scholl, 1996, p. 46-49.

70 See Winter and Blazek, 1989.

71 This description of first-generation environmental law clearly parallels the analytical division of environmental economics.

72 See Powers and Chertow, 1997.

73 Of course, the compartmentalisation of environmental problems makes them easier to understand and address (see Powers and Chertow, 1997, p. 20).

74 See the examples provided by Powers and Chertow, 1997, p. 21; Redclift, 1996, p. 44; Faber, Niemes and Stephan, 1995, p. 75; Ayres, 1994, p. 17; Schenkel and Reiche, 1993, p. 186.

traditional environmental law is concerned more with the mitigation of already existing environmental problems, i.e. with the *management of the consequences of pollution*, than with its prevention.[75] In economic and legal parlance, this is known as *end-of-pipe* environmental regulation.

Thirdly and lastly, large *production processes*, notably resource extraction sites and industrial facilities, constitute, if not the only, at least the main target of traditional environmental law, which neglects other increasingly important sources of environmental degradation, be they non-industrial (e.g. agriculture, services) or non-point/diffuse – thus less visible and more difficult to control – and only in isolation less environmentally impactful (e.g. product use/consumption).

Waste law, especially in its origins, is particularly illustrative of traditional environmental law.

At first, from a purely anthropocentric perspective, waste constituted a problem because of its harmfulness to human beings and their health. The problematic of waste was identified as a *sanitation* issue only, with local governments being in charge of cleaning the urban space and subsequently disposing of the collected waste as a way to circumvent the harmful consequences of the physicochemical and/or biological deterioration of waste materials for *public health*. Historically,[76] disposal occurred in locations far from the urban space by means of deposition, burial (landfilling) and/or combustion (incineration) of waste materials.

However, disposal of waste into the environment initially and conventionally occurred – and in many places still occurs – without any planning or monitoring of the negative effects of waste materials to the environmental media receiving them. In other words, no control of the *pollution* arising from the environmentally unfriendly disposal of waste took place. This is where waste law as environmental protection law came in. As environmental awareness increased, local authorities were faced with the task of making waste 'disappear' by adopting disposal techniques that are considered appropriate from both a public health *and* an environmental perspective. It is within this context that legal rules on waste *management* emerged.

Yet, even though waste management law started to aim to protect the environment *in addition to* public health, for a long time it continued to revolve around *disposal* operations carried out as local public services.

---

75 See Harsch, 1999, p. 551-552; Redclift, 1996, p. 47.

76 On the evolution of waste law, see, for instance, Smeddinck, 2016; Kloepfer, 2012; Ormond, 1998; Kunig, 1994b.

Waste law in its origins (or 'classical waste law'[77]) is therefore labelled as 'waste disposal law' (*Abfallbeseitigungsrecht* in German).

In this sense, waste *management* law is no more than a reflex of the *managerial*, end-of-pipe solutions offered by first-generation environmental law. Waste is seen as something inevitable for which technical solutions – namely disposal operations – are to be mandated and controlled. Above all, waste law is the very epitome of the shifting of pollution that is typical of traditional environmental law: filters, which are the most illustrative means to mitigate air and water pollution emissions, must eventually be disposed of as wastes, either by means of landfilling (pollution is shifted from air or water to soil) or incineration (pollution is shifted from water to air, or merely transferred back to air).

D. *The insufficiency of the traditional approach*

Several criticisms can be levelled at the traditional economic and legal approaches to the environmental and waste problems. The most important ones are pointed out below.

In that *environmental economics* is the response of mainstream economics to environmental problems, it is not surprising that said problems are regarded as being something external to the market, that is, as something that does not *per se* connect with the functioning of the economic system, after all said system is seen as a closed one[78]. Price as an individual-utilitarian-based mechanism for evaluating the importance of the environment as an economic good is methodologically transgressive[79] and short-sighted, since it does not necessarily, automatically and truly reflect the collective, i.e. societal preference for such goods, nor does it account for the future importance thereof. In addition, scarcity regarding environmental goods is of an absolute rather than a relative nature: it imposes itself upon the market and there is no way to circumvent it despite the technological optimism inherent to environmental economics. Finally, the analytical separation of the environment's source and sink functions is obviously artificial: resource extraction may also represent a social cost, especially

77 To use KUNIG's words (see Kunig, 1994a, p. 97).

78 For now, a closed system may be defined as one that does not interact (i.e. engage in any kind of exchange) with its surroundings.

79 See Amazonas, 2001, p. 54-55.

to future generations, and pollution also has an intertemporal dimension, whether cumulative or dissipative.[80]

Precisely in this respect, the main shortcoming of *waste economics* is that it sees wastes only as outputs from the economic system, thereby concentrating on the congestion in the use of environmental quality (in short, on the overuse of the environment as a sink), and neglecting the fact that wastes are still materials and thus resources. It is precisely the waste of resources (*desperdício* in Portuguese, *Verschwendung* in German) that generates scarcity, even though this issue is not addressed by mainstream economics.[81] Not surprisingly, one economist observes that

> 'Although depletion of resources has also been going on with increased intensity all times, it ordinarily is a volume phenomenon below the earth's surface, where no one can see it truly. Pollution, on the other hand, is a surface phenomenon, the existence of which cannot possibly be ignored, much less denied. [...] Because pollution is a surface phenomenon which also strikes the generation which produces it, we may rest assured that it will receive much more official attention than its inseparable companion, resource depletion.'[82]

As already anticipated, *environmental law* has been traditionally piecemeal. In concentrating on pollution control (i.e. limits on the amount of more easily visible emissions) over resource consumption (i.e. limits on the amount of resources extracted) and neglecting product regulation, it has adopted a sectoral approach focused on point sources of pollution and the single media affected by it, relying on end-of-pipe solutions that manage the symptoms of environmental problems – of which pollution shifting is illustrative – rather than prevent and/or solve them altogether.

As a reflex of traditional environmental law, the main drawback of *waste law* as waste disposal law is that it regards waste as something inevitable and, just like waste economics, tackles waste as a *pollution* problem, not as a *resource* problem. That being so, given that in the economic process the input of natural resources and the output of waste are two sides of

80 See Amazonas, 2001, p. 16.

81 On the contrary, mass (and often monopolised) production enables economies of scale and makes it much cheaper to dispose of than to recover waste materials, after all recovery requires investment and is labour-intensive. Besides, structural changes in the whole production-consumption system such as the actual physical approximation of production and waste management facilities would be necessary. See Salomão Filho, 2012, p. 56.

82 See Georgescu-Roegen, 1975, p. 364 and 377, respectively.

the same coin, with the latter being nothing but the mirror of the former both quantitatively and qualitatively, it is not surprising, firstly, that ever-increasing production and consumption levels entail ever-increasing amounts of waste and, secondly and most importantly, that waste *disposal* law not only eventually encounters limitations such as declining landfilling capacity, but it is also incapable of tackling the problem of waste *generation*, which is at the heart of the issue.

E. Summary

In the western world, the market-based system of economic activities prevails. Intellectually and ideologically, it rests upon the liberal doctrine. The emergence of economics as a discipline has been a major step in the consolidation of economic liberalism. Probably due to the predictability of results it claims to achieve, economics has, as a scientific field of knowledge, played a central role in real-life decision-making and indeed influenced the realm of environmental law and policy. The law has played a role not only in the implementation of the market (autonomous or decentralised) model, but also in the correction of the malfunctioning of the economic system, including, but not limited to, environmental degradation.

Environmental economics is the response of neoclassical economics to environmental problems. It is analytically divided into the economics of resources, on the one hand, and the economics of pollution, on the other. Based on the utilitarian-individualistic rationale of mainstream economics, environmental economics and its sub-branches argue that environmental degradation – resource depletion and pollution – may occur at a socially and intra-generationally optimal level that can be calculated. Being localised in the economics of pollution, the economics of waste explains the waste problem as market failure, namely as a negative externality, for which correction through State intervention in the economy (i.e. regulation) is necessary. More specifically, waste economics argues that the environment's capacity to serve as sink for the disposed waste materials is under-priced and thus overused.

Traditional environmental law regulates the relationship between mankind and its environment differently depending on whether the environment is seen as a source of natural resources or as a sink for pollution, a division that is similar to that between resource and pollution economics in environmental economics. Whilst in the former case the law is concerned less with the protection of natural resources than with their exploitation and efficient intra-generational allocation, in the latter situation it governs the control of pollution with a view to protecting humans against the negative effects thereof. Traditional environmental law concentrates on pollution control rather than resource depletion. In doing so, it adopts a rather piecemeal approach: focus lies on managing pollution from large point sources, most notably productive processes, affecting single environmental media. Traditional waste law, which revolves around the disposal of waste materials by local public services, is particularly illustrative of the managerial, end-of-pipe, pollution-shifting approach of traditional environmental law.

Both the traditional economic and legal approaches are insufficient for two main reasons. Firstly, both approaches to environmental problems in general are marked by a methodological split, for they address those problems from two different perspectives of the environment, namely as a source on the one hand, and as a sink on the other. Secondly, in doing so, both approaches fail to adequately tackle the specific waste problem, namely the increase in waste generation, for it is also a *resource* problem despite being treated as if it were a pollution problem only.

This calls for a more comprehensive theoretical framework, both economic and legal.

Chapter 2 – Theoretical reconstruction: sustainable development and its legal implementation

This chapter explores unorthodox economic and legal approaches and provides a more comprehensive account of the environmental and waste problems. The greater comprehensiveness of the theoretical framework analysed in this chapter in comparison to the traditional approaches discussed in the previous chapter lies fundamentally in the adoption of a systemic view that not only addresses the problem of resource depletion *in tandem with* that of pollution but also understands the degradation of the environment (both as a source and as a sink) as a function of economic growth. Both issues – resource depletion and economic growth – are central to the debate on sustainable development, in which the heterodox economic and legal theories explored hereinafter are situated.

A. *Sustainable development in context*

In mainstream economics, focus on allocation and the utilitarian-individualistic approach entail the prevalence of a microeconomic perspective to economic analysis, one that revolves around economic agents and their behaviour,[83] as shown in the previous chapter. Apart from wealth distribution, another central question in economics, which is of a more macroeconomic nature and with which the discussion on sustainable development directly connects, is that of wealth creation or, in short, economic growth.[84]

The discussion on economic growth, which takes place in the context of that on economic development, attracted the attention of economists in the mid-1940s and gained political prominence in the 1950s during the post-World War II period.[85] Back then, the benefits of industrialisation

83 See Nusdeo, 2014, p. 233.

84 See Beinhocker, 2006.

85 See Nusdeo, 2002, p. 11. Similarly, see Georgescu-Roegen, 1975, p. 347: 'Search all economic periodicals of the English-speaking world before 1950 [...] and you will hardly find any mention of "economic development"'. As shall be seen below, because development is a time-related process of qualitative change, it

were – and have so far still been – confined to a minority of rich (i.e. developed) countries and the gap existing between them and the vast majority of poor (i.e. underdeveloped or developing) countries in terms of income level and quality of life posed a threat to the world peace that had just been achieved.[86] Economic development – whether understood broadly as material progress or more precisely as dynamic efficiency (the ability to expand productive capacity) as opposed to the notion of static efficiency (the ability to fully utilise productive capacity) that had prevailed in economics in the 1930s[87] – became a major goal of the international community, one intrinsic to all conventional ideologies from the liberal to the socialist.[88]

Economic development has also occupied a central role in the scientific debate in economics. Yet it was initially reduced to the notion of economic growth[89] in the sense of a greater availability of goods and services, and in more tangible terms, as a continuous increase in *per capita* income at a rate superior to demographic growth.[90] This approach has failed not only to contextualise underdevelopment, which since the Industrial Revolution and despite country particularities corresponds to a specific condition of the periphery of the capitalist system, but also to account for the need of structural changes in the economic system.[91] Economic development is a qualitative rather than a purely quantitative process that results in the betterment of quality of life. It presupposes societal improvements in realms other than simply the economic, including, but not limited to, the cultural and political fields.

Once said improvements are *politically* desired, economic development becomes one, if not the main, goal of economic policy and the State is called on to promote the desired qualitative changes. The attainment of economic goals, including that of development, has therefore been anoth-

was at the time off the radar of the mechanistic epistemology of neoclassical economics.

86 See Nusdeo, 2002, p. 11, and Nusdeo, 1975, p. 1-6.

87 See Nusdeo, 2010, p. 349, and Nusdeo, 2002, p. 11-14.

88 See Gillespie, 2001, p. 16.

89 'Search as search can through the entire economic literature no one could find a single paragraph in which the meaning of "development" is dissociated from that of "growth"; on the contrary, constantly "development" is used interchangeably with "growth" [...]' (see Georgescu-Roegen, 1991a, p. 12).

90 See Nusdeo, 1975, p. 6-8.

91 See Nusdeo, 2014, p. 228-229.

er justification for the presence of the State in the economy alongside market failure correction as discussed in the previous chapter.

To speak of economic goals naturally entails a discussion not only on the means of achieving them but also on the conflicts between different economic goals as well as between economic and non-economic goals. It therefore connects with a discussion on economic policy and governmental concern with the performance and the results of the economy. This is where economic law (also law and economics) comes in, whether understood as a branch of law comprised of all legal rules undertaking a given economic policy or as a method of legal analysis and interpretation that feeds on the knowledge provided by economics.

One goal of economic policy that is in direct dialogue with that of economic development is environmental protection. On the one hand, economic development and environmental protection are conflicting goals of economic policy in that economic activity impacts the environment. On the other hand, the increasing importance of environmental protection has been such that it has transformed the debate about *economic* development into a debate about *sustainable* development.

Industrialisation – at bottom a *technological* revolution – and the progress resulting therefrom have negated the pessimistic analysis of classical economists that nature would impose an absolute limitation to economic growth due to the inelastic supply of land as a factor of production.[92] Nature has been relegated to the background in neoclassical economics, which has focused on the other two factors of production, namely capital and labour, as improved by technology.[93] To be sure, '[t]he only environmental factor which appears in the standard theory of production is land in the Ricardian sense, that is, indestructible space'[94].

Material progress led to an intensive consumption of natural resources and high levels of pollution. At the time it became synonymous with economic development as a strategy to overcome the gap existing between developed and developing countries, the environmental degradation resulting from economic growth was more than ever justified.

Ironically, however, said gap has not narrowed, it has in fact widened, and environmental degradation has been felt in both developed and developing countries as a problem affecting quality of life, an issue that is central to the notion of economic development as a qualitative rather

92 See Nusdeo, 1975, p. 5.
93 See Nusdeo, 1975, p. 5.
94 See Georgescu-Roegen, 1977, p. 267, footnote 1.

than purely quantitative phenomenon. At this point, criticism starts to be expressed against the dominant economic model in respect of its negative ecological consequences, most notably due to the threat that certain environmental problems pose to the survival of the human species. The discussion on a *sustainable* development then arises in connection with the idea of conditioning present actions in order to maintain something constant over time for the sake of future generations.[95] What is to be maintained constant is controverted, though, as shall be seen in the following sections.

If, then, material progress had been responsible for the degradation of the environment, in order to advance an ecologically sound (i.e. sustainable) development one had to decouple the idea of development from that of growth. Initial discussions about the unsustainability of the economic system centred precisely on the environmental limits to the economic growth, as epitomised by the publication of 'The Limits to Growth' and its catastrophic prediction that 'if […] growth trends […] continue[d] unchanged, […] the most probable result [would] be a rather sudden and uncontrollable decline in both population and industrial capacity'[96].

Amongst the many reactions to the attacks on economic growth in general and the Malthusian-like report commissioned by the Club of Rome in particular[97] has been the criticism that such apocalyptic, anti-growth theories disregard a twofold injustice underlying the use of the environment both as a resource and as a sink by developed and developing countries. Firstly, developed countries have developed *inter alia* thanks to the use of the environment and it would be unfair to prevent developing countries to use the environment to develop. Secondly, developed countries continue to use the environment as a source thanks to the natural resources that are provided to them by developing countries; yet, the international division of labour creates inequity in the trade of such resources, which are exchanged from the latter to the former at low costs.

The refusal of developing countries to accept any restraints on their development process along with the fear of developed countries of changes in both the capitalist mode of production and the distribution of power in the international economic order have prevented a deeper and more fruitful discussion about sustainable development.[98] With reason, the notion

95 See Nusdeo, 2014, p. 227.

96 See Meadows *et al.*, 1972, p. 23.

97 For a critical account of the attacks made by mainstream economists on the report, see Georgescu-Roegen, 1975, p. 364-365.

98 See Nusdeo, 2014, p. 232.

of sustainable development that has been coined by the 'Brundtland Report'[99] is marked by vagueness and is devoid of polemical aspects, in a way very similar to that which may be labelled 'three-pillar sustainability' or 'sustainable development in a broad sense', namely the aspiration for the compatibility of economic development, social justice and environmental protection as well as the balancing of the interests of both developed and developing countries.

Much as the notion of sustainable development has reached the international political arena as well as spread and become familiar to many different fields of knowledge, it originated as criticism to the prevailing model of economic development, which is eminently an *economic* discussion. Therefore, the debate on sustainable development is, at least from the perspective of its origin and content, also and predominantly an economic one.[100]

Perhaps running the risk of simplification,[101] the main strains of economic thought addressing the issue of sustainable development are environmental economics and ecological economics. As shall be discussed below, the former is too optimistic, whereas the latter, at least in the version adopted herein, is too pessimistic. Most fundamentally, they offer completely different answers to the question of what constitutes the constancy that is to be transmitted to the next generations, which, as anticipated above, is behind the very concept of sustainable development. Whilst environmental economists advocate maintenance of the capacity to provide utility, for ecological economists it is the existence of ecosystems as well as their adaptive capacity to provide ecological functions that should be transmitted to future generations.

B. Sustainable development in environmental-economic theory

Considering that the main contours of environmental economics have already been outlined in the previous chapter, this section focuses on the specific debate on sustainable development at the aggregate level. For the purpose of such a discussion, more important than the social and

99 'Sustainable development is development that meets the needs of the present without compromising the ability of future generations to meet their own needs'.
100 See Cipriano, 2011.
101 As acknowledged by Nusdeo, 2014, p. 233.

intertemporal (i.e. intergenerational) optimality in both resource depletion and pollution is the technological optimism on which environmental economics is based. According to the mainstream economic paradigm, innovation (or technical progress) – an element that is as exogenous to the economic system as the environment – is able to compensate for the loss of environmental resources and quality (substitution effect) and therefore overcome environmental scarcity.

In environmental economics, this optimism is manifested in the discussion on strong versus weak sustainability. The common point of both versions is that sustainable development implies that utility (i.e. well-being) should be kept constant or growing for future generations.[102] They only differ as to the criteria according to which such constancy is to be achieved.

Borrowing from Neumayer, 'for the analysis that follows, those items that form the capacity to provide utility are called capital. Capital is defined here broadly as a stock that provides current and future utility'[103]. This aggregate stock can be also termed total capital, or K_t, and it consists of three items, namely man-made capital (i.e. machinery, infrastructure etc.), K_m; human capital (i.e. knowledge), or K_h; and natural capital (i.e. the environment in its entirety or, more simply, nature), or K_n. In short, $K_t = K_m + K_h + K_n$.

Weak sustainability refers to the idea that what is to be maintained constant or increasing over time is the total capital (K_t). The three items composing it are completely substitutable amongst themselves so that consumption of either type of capital can be compensated by investment in another one. Therefore, in order for economic development to be sustainable natural capital needs not necessarily be kept constant: any decrease in the amount or quality of environment is perfectly in tune with the precept of sustainable development as long as an increase in man-made or human capital is provided for.

Conversely, in strong sustainability it is the stock of natural capital that should be kept constant or growing for present and future generations. It refutes the idea of perfect substitutability between natural capital and the other two types of capital. As one ecological economist points out, '[…] they are basically complementary and only very marginally substitutable'[104]. The only possible kind of compensation is that operated within

102 See Amazonas, 2001, p. 40.
103 See Neumayer, 2013, p. 8-9.
104 See Daly, 1990, p. 3.

natural capital itself,[105] that is, it is only possible to substitute non-renewable K_n for renewable K_n, even though this also faces physical and technical limitations.

Whether weak or strong, environmental economists' view of sustainable development is imbued with great optimism about the perpetuity of the human species in the face of the environmental problems that threaten it. For, ultimately, mankind will always be able to compensate for the loss of environmental resources and quality that economic activity causes. As a result, the economy can develop indefinitely. Put another way, there is no such a thing as ecological limits to the growth of the economic system. It is this that is the core idea challenged by ecological economics.

C. *Sustainable development in ecological-economic theory and the contribution of Nicholas Georgescu-Roegen: 'matter matters'*

Ecological economics corresponds to a heterodox strain of economic thought consisting of a myriad of widely ranging propositions the common ground of which is the acknowledgement of biophysical limits to the economic system, in stark contrast to environmental economics.

Unlike environmental economics, ecological economics regards the economic system as being a subsystem of the ecological system, from which follows that the economic system is governed by the laws of physics and biology and not only by the laws created by men, including the laws of economics. Ecological economics is an ecological reading of economics.[106]

Based on a metabolic perspective that is typical of the biological sciences, ecological economics refutes the neoclassical idea that the economic system consists of a closed, circulatory system composed exclusively of monetary flows.[107] Instead, ecological economists argue that the economic system is surrounded by, or embedded in, a larger system, namely the natural environment, from which it draws the resources (input) necessary to its functioning (throughput) and to which it returns waste in the form of degraded matter and energy (output). The economic system is therefore an open one due to the energy and material exchanges with the environment. Metaphorically speaking, the economic system may be seen as a living

105 See Amazonas, 2001, p. 47-48.
106 See Cavalcanti, 2010, p. 58.
107 '[...conventional economics] is a one-eyed discipline which sees only the market carried out by money' (see Georgescu-Roegen, 1986, p. 4).

organism endowed with a digestive system and not only a circulatory system.

It then follows that the economic system is inexorably dependent upon a biophysical basis that sustains it. To put it another way, all economic activity has an energetic correlate as well as a material substratum and hence the emphasis on the existence of environmental constraints on economic activity. This being so, in order to be able to sustain itself over time, the economic system must conform to the ecological system.

Amongst the different strains of thought that make up ecological economics is the pioneering, albeit not criticism-free, work of GEORGESCU-ROEGEN (1906-1994)[108], who was critical of the conventional representation of the economic process and whose contribution represents a rupture in the paradigm of traditional economics. He is often considered to be the father of ecological economics.[109]

For him, neoclassical economics is based on the epistemology of mechanics, the central figure of which is locomotion, and consequently it has predictability (and hence calculability), reversibility, atemporality and static equilibrium as its main features, thus allowing a description of the economic system as one that is free from any qualitative change. In this sense, the economic process could be metaphorically depicted as a pendulum.

In contrast, GEORGESCU-ROEGEN proposes an economic analysis from the perspective of thermodynamic physics and metaphorically depicts the economic process as an hourglass that can never be turned upside down. This being so, the economic process is seen as an irreversible and temporal one that tends to a state of dynamic equilibrium and is marked by truly qualitative transformations.

According to GEORGESCU-ROEGEN, under a thermodynamic view the economic system constitutes an *open* system, which he defines as one that exchanges energy and matter with the larger system surrounding it, namely the planetary environment. The Earth, in turn, is a *closed* system, which he defines as one that exchanges only energy, but not matter, with the larger system surrounding it, namely the universe. Finally, the universe

---

108 See Georgescu-Roegen 1991a, 1991b, 1986, 1980, 1977, 1975 and 1971, the core ideas of which are summarised in the following paragraphs.

109 See, for instance, Mayumi, 2001, p. 1.

is an *isolated* system, which he defines as one that exchanges neither energy nor matter.[110]

If the economic system is an open system and surrounded by, or embedded in, the ecological system, then the laws of nature, and not only the laws created by man, apply. Accordingly, the economic process is necessarily ruled by the laws of physics (thermodynamics) and invariably conditioned by the biophysical limits that those rules impose. For the purposes of the present discussion, two of such rules merit attention: the second and fourth laws of thermodynamics, the latter having been expressed by GEORGESCU-ROEGEN himself.[111]

As per the second law of thermodynamics, the entropy of any *isolated* system (e.g. the universe) continuously and irrevocably increases and inevitably tends to a maximum. Entropy, which is involved in every transformation process, may be defined as an index of the amount of *unavailable energy* of a given system at a particular point in its evolution.[112] The greater the entropy of a system, the lower the availability of energy in it. In *isolated* systems, entropy can only be created, never destroyed. Hence, at some point every isolated system will inescapably reach an irreversible state of complete unavailability of its total energy. However, the entropy law is not capable of making predictions in quantitative terms, that is, it can determine neither the magnitude of the increase in energy unavailability at any given future moment nor the corresponding entropy pattern.[113]

---

110 'Whether truly isolated natural systems exist at all is an open question. Real systems on Earth always exchange at least energy with their environment, albeit only in small amounts. The universe as a whole could be an isolated system, but that conjecture is beyond testing in physical experiments. However, let us suppose, for the sake of this discussion, that the universe is an isolated system' (see Faber, Manstetten and Proops, 1996, p. 99).

111 According to the first law of thermodynamics, known as the law of conservation of energy, energy can be neither created nor destroyed, so that the total energy of a given closed system is always constant. The third law of thermodynamics, in turn, states that it is impossible to reach absolute zero (measured in Kelvin).

112 For a succinct but very elucidative explanation of the notion of entropy as well as its heuristic usefulness for economics in general and the comprehension of environmental problems in particular, see Faber, Manstetten and Proops, 1996, p. 95-135.

113 'Because of this fact, there is an entropic indeterminateness in the real world which allows not only for life to acquire an endless spectrum of forms but also for most actions of a living organism to enjoy a certain amount of freedom. Without this freedom, we would not be able to choose between eating beans or meat, between eating now or later. Nor could we aspire to implement economic plans (at any level) of our own choosing' (see Georgescu-Roegen, 1975, p. 363).

As GEORGESCU-ROEGEN points out, the concept of entropy is essentially anthropomorphic, for both the unavailability of energy and the related unidirectionality – i.e. the amount of unavailable energy *increases over time*, never the reverse – are referenced to the finite and limited nature of the human being. In other words, energy unavailability means energy unavailable to mankind, the same occurring in relation to increasing entropy: one speaks of an increase in the unavailability of energy because the time horizon of human consciousness is taken into account.[114]

Based on the ideas of unidirectionality and irreversibility of the phenomenological concept of entropy, GEORGESCU-ROEGEN's contribution lies in the demonstration of the entropic nature of the economic process: '[...] the economic process is entropic: it neither creates nor consumes matter or energy, but only transforms low into high entropy'[115].

The functioning of the economy, which is an *open* subsystem of the ecological system, may be then described from the perspective of its biophysical metabolism, that is, by understanding the material and energy flows between economy and environment in light of the entropy law. The economic process, according to GEORGESCU-ROEGEN, corresponds to a qualitative transformation phenomenon, one consisting of the input into the economic system of low-entropy (i.e. high-quality, available) energy in the form of natural resources as well as the output from the economic system of high-entropy (i.e. low-quality, unavailable) energy in the form of waste plus dissipated, hence also unavailable, energy, that is, energy lost to the environment in the form of heat, radiation etc.

Even though the economic process inevitably results in an increase in the total amount of entropy of either the economic system or the ecological system surrounding it, the end product of the economy is not the generation of entropy, but the immaterial flow it provides, namely the enjoyment of life.

This being so, low entropy is a *necessary*[116] *but insufficient* condition for the formation of economic value. For, in addition to being *available*, energy must be equally *accessible* in order to be used by man. For GEORGESCU-ROEGEN, accessibility seems to refer not only to the fact that energy can

---

114 See Georgescu-Roegen, 1986, p. 4. Put another way, '[...] the entropic transmutation occurs in the same direction as the stream of our consciousness, i.e., parallel with our lives' (see Georgescu-Roegen, 1977, p. 267).

115 See Georgescu-Roegen, 1971, p. 281.

116 '[...] the entropy law is the root of the basic economic scarcity [...]' (see Georgescu-Roegen, 1991b, p. 188).

actually be used but also to the fact that the amount of energy we may want to obtain must be greater than the amount of energy we spend to obtain it. As regards the former aspect (usability), he cites the example of the nourishing energy contained in a poisonous mushroom, which may be available but is unusable because of the poison. Another instance is the large-scale use of nuclear energy, which is to be regarded as being unusable (and thus inaccessible) due to the risks involved. As for the latter aspect (efficiency), GEORGESCU-ROEGEN writes that

> 'Solar energy and its by-products are accessible to us with practically no effort, no consumption of additional available energy. *In all other cases, we have to spend some work and materials in order to tap a store of available energy*. The point is that even though we may land on Mars and find there some gas deposits, that available energy will not be accessible to us if it will take more than the equivalent energy of a cubic foot of gas *accessible on earth* to bring a cubic foot of gas from that planet. [...] The distinction regards efficiency in terms of energy, not in terms of economics. Economic efficiency implies energetic efficiency, but the converse is not true. [...]'[117]

Since the economic system is an *open* one, strictly speaking its entropy could be reduced, for example, through the recovery of energy availability, that is, by transforming high-entropy (i.e. low-quality) energy (waste) into low-entropy (i.e. high-quality) energy (secondary raw materials). Yet, as GEORGESCU-ROEGEN points out, this can only occur *at the expense of increasing the total entropy of the surrounding system*, as low-entropy energy is required for every recycling process to be performed.

GEORGESCU-ROEGEN identifies three important sources of low-entropy energy: 'the free energy from the sun, on the one hand, and the free energy and the ordered material structures stored in the bowels of the earth, on the other'.[118] Both of these two categories have their own advantages and disadvantages.[119]

Solar energy reaches us without fail and the amount of its flow is immensely greater than the size of the stock of terrestrial energy. In addition,

117 See Georgescu-Roegen, 1975, p. 354. He notes that '[...] *from the point of view of the long run* it is only efficiency in terms of energy that counts in establishing accessibility'.

118 See Georgescu-Roegen, 1975, p. 369.

119 Said advantages and disadvantages are summarised based on Georgescu-Roegen, 1975, p. 369-372.

it is pollution-free. Yet, solar radiation comes to us with an extremely low intensity, which hinders the industrial utilisation thereof, and its flow rate is beyond human control.

As for terrestrial stocks, the fact that they are available in very concentrated forms allows enormous amounts of energy to be almost instantaneously obtained from them. In other words, they display greater ease of use. However, as GEORGESCU-ROEGEN notes,

> 'The terrestrial energies on which we can rely effectively exist in very small amounts, whereas the use of those which exist in ampler amounts is surrounded by great risks and formidable technical obstacles. [...] From the viewpoint of the extreme longrun [sic.], the terrestrial free energy is far scarcer than that received from the sun. The point expresses the foolishness of the victory cry that we can finally obtain protein from fossil fuels! Sane reason tells us to move in the opposite direction, to convert vegetable stuff into hydrocarbon fuel [...].'[120]

Since energy cannot be transformed into matter, at least on a human scale, 'accessible material low entropy is by far the most critical element from the bioeconomic viewpoint'[121]. This criticality is further reinforced by what GEORGESCU-ROEGEN, borrowing from biologist LOTKA, terms the exosomatic addiction of the human species, that is, our addiction to using exosomatic organs. 'Exosomatic organs' are to be understood in opposition to 'endosomatic organs', which, in turn, may be defined as those belonging to the individual's soma.[122] Although other species also use exosomatic organs,

> '[...] we are the only creatures on this planet to produce exosomatic organs by which to produce exosomatic organs in a progressive sequence. As Joseph Schumpeter used to put it wittily, we make machines to make machines, to make machines, ... which is the quintessence of the economic process'[123].

Therefore, unlike other species, mankind's exosomatic addiction makes it dependent on terrestrial stocks of natural resources.[124]

---

120 See Georgescu-Roegen, 1975, p. 371.

121 See Georgescu-Roegen, 1975, p. 369.

122 See Georgescu-Roegen, 1991b, p. 184.

123 See Georgescu-Roegen, 1991b, p. 185.

124 A long-term solution would be an energy revolution, one that would increase the use of solar energy, for instance. Even overcoming technological limits and

Finally, in GEORGESCU-ROEGEN's view, the impossibility of perfect recycling is also true in relation to matter in *closed* systems. For him, just like energy, matter exists in two states, namely available and unavailable, and 'it degrades continuously and irrevocably from the former to the latter state'[125]. Dissipation, which is present in every transformation process, including the economic one, occurs in relation to both energy and matter.[126] By analogy with the second law of thermodynamics, which applies to *isolated* systems, he postulates that in *closed* systems (e.g. the Earth) material entropy continuously and irrevocably increases and inevitably tends to a maximum.[127] It is from the applicability of the entropic phenomenon to matter that he asserts that 'the entropic process is entropic in all its *material* fibers'[128] or, more briefly, that 'matter matters'.

In light of all the above, GEORGESCU-ROEGEN refutes many theses supported by economists, including ecological economists, that he considers to be myths, for they are not capable of resisting the entropy law in both its energetic and material versions. Four such myths stand out: the immortality of the human species, the possibility of a steady-state economy, the possibility of complete environmental protection and pollution prevention and, as already mentioned, the possibility of perfect recyclability. It goes without saying that this is too pessimistic a view.

---

the conflicts of interests involved in the implementation of such a revolution, the entropy law would remain intact, which means that any energy revolution would at best prolong the existence of the human species on the planet.

125 See Georgescu-Roegen, 1986, p. 7.

126 '[...] because no conversion of energy is achieved without material support, friction dissipates not only energy but also matter' (see Georgescu-Roegen, 1977, p. 268). It should be made clear, however, that according to Georgescu-Roegen '[…] that what we can actually recycle is not *unavailable* matter – the rubber molecules dissipated over the highways or the imperceptible bits of glass from breakages – but only *available* matter that no longer is in a useful form: pieces of broken glass, old newspapers, old motors, etc., that is, what we find in garbage cans and in junk yards' (see Georgescu-Roegen, 1991b, p. 197).

127 See Faber, Manstetten and Proops, 1996, p. 106, emphasis added: '[Georgescu-Roegen] accepts the Second Law [of thermodynamics] only in its phenomenological formulation […]. However, phenomenological thermodynamics describes only transformations of available (free) energy into non-available energy; it does not make any statement about the availability of matter. […] By analogy with the Entropy Law in *isolated* systems, he argues that in *closed* systems there exists "material entropy" which always increases. […] It is important to note that [Georgescu-Roegen]'s Fourth Law attempts to extend classical thermodynamics.'.

128 See Georgescu-Roegen, 1986, p. 3.

Even though he acknowledges that 'it would be foolish to propose a complete renunciation of the industrial comfort of the exosomatic evolution' or the return of mankind 'to the cave or, rather, to the tree',[129] he lists some points that he considers would make up a 'minimal bioeconomic program', one that would protect the future generations from the excessive consumption of resources and hence cease the dictatorship of the present over the future.

Among such points is, of course, environmental protection. In this respect, GEORGESCU-ROEGEN is of the opinion that, in general, 'the greatest we can do is to avoid any unnecessary depletion of resources and any unnecessary deterioration of the environment, without stating that we know the precise meaning of "unnecessary" in that context'[130]. More specifically, he recommends *inter alia* the following:[131]

- '[...] man should gradually lower its population to a level that could be adequately fed only by organic agriculture';
- '[...] until either the direct use of solar energy becomes a general convenience or controlled fusion is achieved, all waste of energy – by overheating, overcooling, overspeeding, overlighting, etc. – should be carefully avoided, and if necessary, strictly regulated';[132]
- '[...] we must cure ourselves of the morbid craving for extravagant gadgetry, splendidly illustrated by such a contradictory item as the golf cart, and for such mammoth splendors as *two-garage* cars [sic.] [...]';
- '[....] we must also get rid of fashion [...]';
- '[...] closely related to the preceding point [...] is the necessity that durable goods be made still more durable by being designed so as to be repairable'.

It is precisely in connection with the ideas above, in particular the benefits of solar energy as well as the recommendations of both environmental conservation (avoidance of unnecessary resource depletion and pollution) and decreasing population that GEORGESCU-ROEGEN states his view on sustainable development:

> 'Sustainable Development, as presented by almost all its advocates, is in essence an economy fuelled by the solar energy harnessed by green plants. This necessarily means that tractors, trucks, and other agricul-

129 Both quotations are from Georgescu-Roegen, 1975, p. 377.
130 See Georgescu-Roegen, 1975, p. 363.
131 See Georgescu-Roegen, 1975, p. 378.
132 Similarly, see Georgescu-Roegen, 1991a, p. 20: '[...] we should economize by ceasing to overheat, overcool, overspeed, and many other such overdose'.

tural machinery should be replaced by beasts of burden. And this is the hitch that has bothered (so it seems) no advocate of that economic prescription. *The beasts of burden are no perpetual motions of the first kind.*[133] To live and pull loads they must be supplied with energy, viz. fodder. Fodder, in turn, needs some land on which to grow. The final conclusion of this simple concatenation is that all humans must divide the agricultural land between the production of food and that of fodder (a point confirmed by the wisdom of Romanian peasants who used to say "the horse eats people", flabbergasting the uncongenial town-dwellers). Since there is some necessary minimum of daily food intake for the average human, the human's number [sic.] in the world must be reduced drastically not only for a sustainable development but even for a stationary economy. But as we know by now no community would accept such a demographic programme, save if forced at the gun point, as it was, perhaps it still is, the practice in China. However, the issue of overpopulation has not been viewed yet in its dismaying dimension. Think of it, if [the] United States were populated as thickly as Bangladesh, it would have a population as large as that of the whole world now. If it could support itself in that condition, it should be able to support now the world['s] population – which, of course, is an absurd speculation.

By a careful unravelling it will be seen that the actual target of Sustainable Development is "Conservation" which must not be even whispered because it has no alluring power for a lullaby, nor can it suggest to be the product of a sophisticated analysis. That conservation in its basic meaning is the only valid ecological programme is what I have tried to bring it home. But I also showed that a sine qua non of conservation is a *negative population growth*. For surprising though as it may seem, Malthus was not Malthusian enough. His solution for the food scarcity was a steady population, the same as the earliest of the current lullabies. For the good of their own species, humans will eventually accept a steadily decreasing population.'[134]

---

133 Perpetual motion of the first kind refers to the notion of a hypothetical machine that can perform work indefinitely without any energetic input or producing more energy than consumed, in clear violation of the first law of thermodynamics, which states that energy can never be created, only transformed.

134 See Georgescu-Roegen, 1991a, p. 14-15.

Nevertheless, GEORGESCU-ROEGEN is sceptical as to whether mankind would be willing to reduce its exosomatic (i.e. material) comfort and accept any of his proposed radical changes:

> 'Perhaps, the destiny of man is to have a short, but fiery, exciting and extravagant life rather than a long, uneventful and vegetative existence. Let other species – the amoebas, for example – which have no spiritual ambitions inherit an earth still bathed in plenty of sunshine'[135].

Be the case as it may, as anticipated at the beginning of this section, GEORGESCU-ROEGEN's ideas are not free from criticism. In fact, some physicists have pointed out some flaws in his work.[136] The main one is that his fourth law of thermodynamics, an extension of the second law of thermodynamics, has no standing in physics. The assertion that perfect recycling of matter is impossible even if solar energy is constantly available,[137] while corroborated by the depletion of natural resources, is challenged by the fact that the biosphere recycles many natural elements utilising solar energy.[138] As one expert explains,

> '[...] what does follow from [Georgescu-Roegen's] proposition [that materials can never be recycled with 100% efficiency because there are

---

135 See Georgescu-Roegen, 1975, p. 379.

136 See, for instance, Ayres, 1999; Ayres, 1997; Faber, Manstetten and Proops, 1996; 115-135.

137 Although GEORGESCU-ROEGEN does acknowledge that the Earth receives a constant supply of low-entropy energy from the sun, he argues against the possibility of perfect recyclability of dissipated matter mainly because this would occur on a much slower and thus longer time than the time horizon of human life. See, for instance, Georgescu-Roegen, 1986, p. 7 '[P]erhaps, we could recycle everything if and only if we could dispose not only of a limitless amount of energy but also of an infinite time [...]' and Georgescu-Roegen, 1977, p. 269 '[A]ll processes moving with infinitely small speed are reversible, because with infinitely small speed there is practically no friction. However, such a slow motion takes a practically infinite time. This is in fact the analytical reason why reversibility is not possible in actuality. It also is the analytical reason why matter cannot be recycled completely'.

138 In a paper dealing exclusively with the topic of matter and thermodynamics, Georgescu-Roegen refutes the argument that matter can be completely recycled as instanced by the natural cycles of oxygen, carbon, nitrogen etc. For him, '[t]hese "cycles" are not complete cycles. It suffices to observe, for example, that not all carbon deposited on the bottom of the oceans as calcium carbonate will return to the cycle. If we continue to believe in the natural cycles, it is because the actual departures from a true cycle are hard to estimate' (see Georgescu-Roegen, 1980, p. 81).

> always entropic losses] is the following: even the most efficient conceivable process will generate some high entropy wastes. These wastes will accumulate over time in a storehouse or "wastebasket", which might be the earth's crust, or just a tank in a spaceship. It follows further that, in the absence of any further recovery, the useful materials or products in circulation would be diminished in every period by the amount lost to the wastebasket. Under these circumstances the economy would, indeed, "run down" as [Georgescu-Roegen] asserted. However, there is a fundamental flaw in this reasoning. It is simply that, given the postulated availability of energy (exergy), there is no barrier to treating the 'wastebasket' as an ore pile and recovering materials from it. It is true that the secondary recovery process will never be 100% efficient, due to the second law [of thermodynamics]. So, there will always be some waste from the recovery process itself. However, this waste merely goes back into the wastebasket. But as long as the waste pile is big enough, regardless of grade, it is possible to compensate for the losses. Thus, the correct implication of [Georgescu-Roegen's] proposition [about the impossibility of perpetual and perfect recycling] is just that not all of the materials in the earth (or in a spaceship) can be in "active service" at any given time because the wastebasket can never be eliminated altogether. The size of the wastebasket compared to the size of the active inventory is a function (as will be seen) of the efficiency of recycling, the rate of depreciation and the rate of waste mining. If the exergy flux is limiting (which could be the case) then the maximum sustainable concentration ratio will also depend on the available exergy.'[139]

This misunderstanding aside, the laws of physics remain extremely relevant to economics for several reasons. Firstly, they make it evident that the expansion of the economic system – in other words, economic growth – requires more energetic and material inputs (increase in resource depletion) and entails more energetic and material outputs (increase in pollution). Secondly, they pinpoint limits on capital-resource substitution imposed by mass-energy balance considerations,[140] in stark contrast to environmental economics. Thirdly, any decrease in entropy in open and/or closed systems, the economy and the natural environment, respectively, can only be achieved at the cost of an increase in entropy of the larger, surrounding

139 See Ayres, 1999, p. 475.
140 See Faber, Manstetten and Proops, 1996, p. 123.

system, the environment and the universe, respectively. This is the point GEORGESCU-ROEGEN made.

Even though the laws of thermodynamics in general and the entropy law in particular only shed light on rather than provide solutions to environmental problems, they form the basis for a much more comprehensive account of such problems, reason for which the theoretical framework of ecological economics is superior to that of mainstream economics and is followed herein.

Interestingly, ecological economics in general and its 'entropic school' in particular make a strong case in favour of resource conservation, which lies at the heart of the sustainability and waste issues, as shown above. In this respect, for example, GEORGESCU-ROEGEN contends that

> 'Because pollution is a surface phenomenon which also strikes the generation which produces it, we may rest assured that it will receive much more official attention than its inseparable companion, resource depletion. But since in both cases there is no such a thing as the cost of undoing an irreparable harm or reversing irrevocable depletion, and since no relevant price can be set on avoiding the inconvenience if future generations did not have the choice, *we must insist that the measures taken for either purpose should consist of quantitative regulations*, notwithstanding the advice of most economists to increase the allocation efficiency of the market through taxes and subsidies. The economists' plank will only protect the wealthy or the political protégés. Let no one, economist or not, forget that the irresponsible deforestation of numerous mountains took place because "the price was right" and that it was brought to an end only after quantitative restrictions were introduced. But the difficult nature of the choice should also be made clear to the public – that *slower depletion means less exosomatic comfort* and that greater control of pollution requires proportionally greater consumption of resources.[141] Otherwise only confusions and controversies at cross-purposes will result.'[142]

Following the economic-legal parallel outlined in the previous chapter, the implications of the ecological-economic approach for environmental law are several-fold. Above all, and methodologically speaking, it invites jurists

---

141 According to Georgescu-Roegen (1975, p. 358), '[...] like recycling, disposal of pollution is not costless in terms of energy. Moreover, as the percentage of pollution increases, the cost increases even more steeply than for recycling'.

142 See Georgescu-Roegen, 1975, p. 377, emphasis added.

to regard resource depletion and pollution as two sides of the same coin, thereby expanding their regulatory horizons beyond the end-of-pipe management of pollution caused by large, single-point productive processes of single environmental media towards the reduction in the use of materials and substances and their transformation into products. The next section elaborates on that reconstruction.

D. *The 'ecologisation' of environmental law and its methodological corollaries*

So far, attention has been drawn to the analogies existing between the biological and the economic systems. To sum this up, it has been posited that the economic system – at bottom a materials processing system driven by a flow of available energy – is not only entropic,[143] but also a mechanism of metabolic regulation.[144]

The analogy can be explored a step further by looking at how materials are processed – in the biological jargon: metabolised – by a given open system, be it a biological community or the economy.[145] A typology may be created based on whether metabolisation – or, to put it another way, the exchange of materials between the system and its environment – occurs in a linear or circular fashion. One may speak of closed cycles if the system has the capacity of (re)cycling the materials it takes from and returns to its environment, as is the case of natural cycles. Conversely, one may speak of open cycles if the system does not have the capacity of (re)cycling the materials it takes from and returns to its environment, as is the case of the existing industrial cycles. The higher the linearity – or the lower the circularity – of material flows, the more reliant on the environment the system is. The cycling of resources in biological systems points to the importance of closing material cycles in the economic system, especially in the industrial one.[146] Industrial ecology is the interdisciplinary field of knowledge that studies the ecologisation of industrial metabolism.[147]

---

143 See the previous sections in this chapter as well as all the references therein made to Georgescu-Roegen.

144 See Ayres, 1994, p. 5.

145 For the considerations of this paragraph, see Lifset and Graedel, 2002, p. 4-5, as well as Ayres, 1994, p. 4-6.

146 See Lifset and Graedel, 2002, p. 4.

147 On industrial ecology, see, for instance, Lifset, 2009; Lifset and Graedel, 2002; Ehrenfeld, 1997; Ayres, 1994. On industrial ecology and waste, see, for instance, Chertow, 1998, and Frosch, 1996.

Such a metabolic outlook can be applied to environmental regulation as well. Borrowing from Breen[148], environmental law can be described from the perspective of what he names the 'resource to recovery cycle'. For him, environmental law is divided into three categories or groups of laws, namely those; (1) governing resource extraction, (2) governing resources as they are transformed into products and (3) governing damage to the environment and the reintegration of resources into the environment. The first group comprises laws; (1.1) excluding areas from extraction (e.g. protected areas law), (1.2) allocating resources for extraction (e.g. mining, water, forest and/or fisheries law) and (1.3) governing the extraction process (e.g. environmental permitting law). The second group consists of laws; (2.1) governing the manufacturing process (e.g. environmental permitting law), (2.2) governing the products manufactured (that is, the results of the manufacturing processes) and (2.3) regulating information about the product. The third group is made of laws governing; (3.1.) damage caused to the environment as well as (3.2) the reintegration into the environment of resources that have been extracted and transformed into products, including the regulation of waste.

Traditional environmental law has concentrated on stages (1.3), (2.1) and (3.1), laid relatively less emphasis on stages (1.1), (1.2) and (3.2) and virtually neglected stages (2.2) and (2.3), thereby incurring several criticisms, as discussed in the previous chapter. One way of tackling such criticisms is to broaden the regulatory horizon of environmental law so that it addresses the quantitative and qualitative ecological aspects associated with the use of substances[149] and materials[150] throughout the entire life cycle of products *in addition to* the mere control of the negative impacts caused

148 See Breen, 1993.

149 Borrowing from the legal definition provided by point 1 of Article 3 of Regulation EC 1907/2006 on chemicals (OJ L 396, 30 December 2006, best known and hereinafter referred to as the 'REACH Regulation'), 'substance' means 'a chemical element and its compounds in the natural state or obtained by any manufacturing process'.

150 'Material' is a more comprehensive term than 'substance'. It may be understood roughly in contrast to the atomic and molecular level at which 'substance' has been defined herein (see previous footnote), so that materials would comprise of a combination of substances, or more broadly as matter (as opposed to energy) that is or can be used for a purpose. In this latter and much more general sense, substances are materials as well. See, for instance, Mitchell, 2004, p. 2. Because materials encompass substances, the word 'material' is hereinafter slightly preferred over the word 'substance', although both terms may be used interchangeably when used in isolation.

by large productive facilities to environmental media. Put another way, in order to overcome the shortcomings of the traditional legal approach to ecological problems a regulatory reorientation towards an environmental law that is *not only* facility-related or media-related *but also* material-related *and* product-related is called for.

An approach focusing also and especially on products and materials may be regarded as a reaction to the drawbacks of first-generation environmental law in that it seeks to address diffuse-sources (as opposed to point-sources) of environmental degradation, as epitomised by the consumption of products, and prevent (rather than manage and/or shift) ecological problems by adopting a holistic (in substitution of a fragmentary) way of looking at them. The so-called product life cycle perspective brings all these features together. Still by analogy of the biological systems and their metabolic cycles, the life cycle of a product may be understood as the series of stages starting from the obtainment of materials from the environment, going through their transformation and/or incorporation into products followed by consumption via product use and ending with their reintegration into the environment as wastes.

Even though attention is turned to the life cycle of the *product*, the life cycle perspective makes it possible to address the environmental effects of all processes, installations and services associated with it, whether at stages upstream, downstream or coinciding with the product use phase. As has been noted, '[…] addressing the product captures the process as well, whereas the converse is not true'[151]. For instance, a life cycle approach allows one to look at activities having an immaterial (i.e. non-physical) dimension, such as product design or even at the environmental impacts of services, including those of transport and distribution activities. Consumption becomes amenable to environmental regulation as well. These examples show that under a life cycle perspective virtually no human activity escapes the regulatory eyes of environmental law.

Of course, looking at the bigger picture is not an easy task and demands much more from jurists. These are required *inter alia* to work both inter- and intra-disciplinarily, that is, to dialogue with non-legal disciplines, including but not limited to, (ecological) economics, industrial ecology, materials science and engineering, as well as with other branches of law, in particular other sub-branches of economic law such as trade law and consumer protection law. By setting the scene for the imposition of concrete legal duties questioning all production and consumption decisions in

151 See Ehrenfeld, 1997, p. 91.

terms of the amount of environment they deplete, such a comprehensive approach also calls for an ecological re-dimensioning of the proportionality test[152] in all those cases involving restrictions to the economic freedom to decide whether, what, how much and how to produce and consume.

Finally, a terminological note is necessary. The entropic and life cycle perspectives to ecological economics and environmental law, respectively, reflect the adoption of a systemic view to environmental problems. In environmental law, an early attempt to implement such a systemic view is the so-called *integrated* approach to pollution prevention and control. This integrated approach, sometimes referred to integrated environmental protection (*integrierter Umweltschutz*[153]) or simply *integrated environmental law* (*integriertes*[154] or *integratives*[155] *Umweltrecht*), emerged within a context where efforts were made to advance preventive[156] (as opposed to end-of-pipe), cross-media (*medienübergreifend, übermedial*) environmental protection against all the impacts of production facilities, most notably industrial ones.[157] Although this original version of the integration proposal is rightly about looking at the environment as a whole, that is, as a set of functionally interconnected components instead of the mere sum of its constituent parts,[158] so that impacts on one part of the environment are prevented or reduced from the outset in order to avoid impacts to the environment as a whole,[159] it is confined to the impacts caused by production processes,

152 Such endeavour has been made by Winter, 2013.

153 See, for instance, Breuer, 2008, p. 625-630; Masing, 1998, and Röckinghausen, 1998.

154 See, for instance, Schröder, 2000.

155 See, for instance, Wagner, 1999, and di Fabio, 1998.

156 For di Fabio (1998, p. 330), the integrative approach is a further development of the prevention principle.

157 In the European Union, such efforts are epitomised by Council Directive 96/61/EC (OJ L 257, 10 October 1996, p. 26), concerning integrated pollution prevention and control, known as the 'IPPC Directive', later repealed by Directive 2008/1/EC (OJ L 24, 29 January 2008, p. 8), which has now been replaced by Directive 2010/75/EU on industrial emissions (OJ L 334, 17 December 2010, p. 17).

158 See Masing, 1998, p. 550, and Röckinghausen, 1998, p. 40.

159 See Röckinghausen, 1998, p. 45-46. In environmental legal commentary, the term 'integration' is also often used to refer to the consideration and/or incorporation of environmental concerns into other sectoral, non-environmental policies (see, for example, Aragão, 2015, and Dhondt, 2003). Breuer (2008, p. 625-630) speaks of 'concurrent integrated environmental protection' (*konkurrierend integrierter Umweltschutz*) to refer to the balancing of conflicting ecological and non-ecological (i.e. economic) concerns, which is best manifested in

much as all impacts of facilities – from material and energetic input to waste output – are addressed.[160]

The bridge between this narrow, production-oriented notion of integration focused on single processes and integration in the broader sense of paying attention to societal metabolism (i.e. the amount of energy and matter exchanged between the ecological and the economic systems), which is typical of the entropic perspective, and therefore to the set of all human activities in the economic circuit, which is typical of the life cycle perspective, is built by looking at the results of production processes, namely the products leaving said processes and further connecting with other processes, whether production or consumption. It is this product perspective that allows one to notice and realise the additive connectedness of all isolated production processes and thus arrive at the aggregate perspective of the production-consumption chain (i.e. the entire economic process).[161] For one author, this paradigmatic shift from a process-oriented to a product-based approach represents a move away from an anthropocentric approach to environmental regulation towards an ecological approach.[162]

---

planning law (*Recht der Raumplannung*), in particular in environmental impact assessment. This notion of integration is sometimes referred to as 'external integration' as opposed to 'internal – or substantive (see Faure, 2000, p. 177) – integration', which is the sense of the term adopted herein, namely that of having regard to the environment as a whole (see, for instance, D'Oliveira, 2015, p. 15-16; Anker, 2002, p. 199-201; Falke, 2001, p. 200; Faure, 2000, p. 177-179; Schröder, 2000, p. 481-482; Wagner, 1999, p. 4). Both internal and external integration may be subsumed under the heading 'material integration' as opposed to 'formal (or procedural) integration', which refers to the coordination of and cooperation between the various competent authorities responsible for single environmental aspects with a view to ensuring that material integration takes place (see Falke, 2001, p. 200; Schröder, 2000, p. 482; Wagner, 1999, p. 4). Formal or procedural integration is also referred to as 'cross-agency integration', which can be horizontal (coordination and interaction between agencies across sector or policy areas) or vertical (coordination and interaction between agencies amongst all levels of government, i.e. international, national, regional and local) (see Anker, 2002, p. 201).

160 Similarly, see Malcom, 2005, p. 143 ('[...] it represents a salami approach where environmental control focuses on a fixed point, ignoring the rest of the chain. IPPC still ignores all other stages other than processing and production'); Rose and Knighton, 1999, p. 266.

161 See di Fabio, 1998, p. 331, 336.

162 See Malcom, 2005, p. 143.

Waste law is the field of environmental law where the integrated approach – in the sense of internal integration under this broader, product-oriented perspective – has been first adopted,[163] precisely because it attempts to 'connect a disconnected chain of actions from the development of a product to its departure from the economic cycle'.[164] It is spoken of as *integrated* waste management, which shall be examined in the next chapter.

E. Summary

More comprehensive economic and legal theories to the environmental and waste problems are found in the context of the sustainable development debate, which is *par excellence* an economic one, and its legal implementation. Economically speaking, the debate is situated within the more macroeconomic discussion about economic growth as opposed to the more microeconomic focus of traditional economics on allocation. Economic growth, in the merely quantitative sense of material progress, represents the means that economics and the international community have found to bridge the gap existing between a minority of rich (i.e. developed) countries and a majority of poor (i.e. underdeveloped or developing) countries that started to threaten world peace in the post-war period. Such a gap has nonetheless not only persisted but also widened as a result of the failure to contextualise underdevelopment as a specific condition of the periphery of the capitalist system and to bring about structural changes in the economy. Economic development is not limited economic growth because it is a qualitative rather than a purely quantitative process that results in the betterment of quality of life. One problem affecting the quality of life in both developed and developing countries, mainly as a result of material progress, is the degradation of the environment both as a source and as a sink. Changes in the economy must therefore also be made with a view to environmental protection, which poses limits to growth. It is in this sense that the debate about economic development becomes a debate about sustainable development.

---

163 Implicitly suggestive in this sense is Rose and Knighton, 1999, who see the so-called integrated product policy (see chapter 3, section D, *infra*) as originating from the so-called extended producer responsibility (see chapter 4, *infra*) introduced by waste legislation.

164 See di Fabio, 1998, p. 331.

In environmental economics, sustainable development is a matter of compensation. Based on technological optimism, for environmental economists it is always possible to compensate for the loss of environmental resources and quality that economic activity engenders. The important thing, ultimately, is to keep utility (i.e. well-being) or, more precisely, the capacity to provide utility, constant in the long run. The stock of all those items forming the capacity to provide present and future utility is termed 'total capital' (K_t). It is composed of three different types of capital, namely man-made (K_m), human (K_h) and natural (K_n) capital. There are two versions of sustainable development. The first one is 'weak sustainability'. It requires that K_t be kept constant, so any decrease in K_n may be compensated for with an increase in K_m and/or K_h. Briefly put, the environment need not be preserved in order for economic development to be ecologically sustainable. The second version is 'strong sustainability', which requires conservation of the natural capital. In this sense, the only possible kind of compensation is that of non-renewable K_n for renewable K_n, although this encounters physical and technical limitations.

Ecological economics lays emphasis on the fact that the economic system is a subsystem of the ecological system and thus focuses on the exchanges of energy and matter between the two systems. It follows from this systemic view and the embeddedness of the economic system in the ecological system that the economic system is governed not only by the laws created by men, including the laws of economics, but also by the laws of physics and biology. One of such laws is the second law of thermodynamics, also known as the entropy law. The importance of the entropy law for the comprehension and explanation of the economic system and its interactions with the surrounding natural environment has been best explored by GEORGESCU-ROEGEN, who is often considered to be the main exponent, nay, the father of ecological economics. His main contribution has been to assert the entropic nature of the economic process. Entropy, which is created in every transformation process, is the amount of unavailable energy of a given system at a particular point in its evolution. The entropy law states that the entropy of any isolated system increases continuously and irrevocably. In isolated systems, entropy can only be created, never destroyed, and it inevitably tends to a maximum. For GEORGESCU-ROEGEN, the economy is an open system (i.e. it exchanges both energy and matter with its surrounding system, namely the planetary environment), the Earth is a closed system (i.e. it exchanges energy but not matter with its surrounding system, namely the universe) and the universe, in turn, is an isolated system (i.e. it exchanges neither energy nor matter with its surrounding system, whatever that might be). By analogy with the second law of thermodynamics, he enunciates the so-called 'fourth law of thermodynamics', according to which the entropic predicament also applies to matter in closed systems. The conversion of high into low entropy (e.g. by means of recycling) is a transformation process that also requires low entropy to be carried out. Therefore, a decrease in entropy of a given system can only occur at the expense of an increase in entropy of its surrounding system. This being so, given the entropic nature of the economic process, the functioning and the expansion of the economic system can only take place indefinitely with the sacrifice of the planetary natural environment and (ultimately) the universe, which are nonetheless materially and energetically finite, respectively. Consequently, ideas such as the immortality of the human species, the possibility of a steady state economy, the possibility of complete environmental protection and pollution prevention and the possibility of perfect recyclability are nothing but myths. The strong pessimism and the flaws of the 'fourth law' aside, Georgescu-Roegen makes a strong case in favour of environmental protection in general, and resource conservation in particular, which according to him lie at the heart of sustainable development. Among his concrete recommendations is the use of regulation, including quantitative measures, as a means of avoiding the waste of energy and resource depletion as well as the design of products that are less resource-intensive, more durable and repairable.

The adoption of a systemic view to environmental law is somewhat unusual and renders the legal tackling of ecological problems much more challenging due to the comprehensiveness it entails. By analogy of the metabolic functioning of biological systems and the cycling of materials in nature, environmental regulation may be best grasped from the so-called product life cycle perspective. By looking at the series of stages, starting from the obtainment of materials from the environment, going through their transformation and/or incorporation into products followed by consumption via product use and ending with their reintegration into the environment as wastes, life cycle thinking is not only a reaction to the drawbacks of first-generation environmental law but it also paves the way for addressing a number of economic activities that have extremely relevant environmental repercussions but which so far have not been adequately dealt with, such as product design, services and consumption, just to mention a few examples. Decisions as to whether, what, how much and how to produce and consume, most of which still remain untouched due to the mantle of economic freedom, become therefore amenable to environmental regulation.

Waste law is the protagonist of such a systemic view to environmental regulation, also known as integrated environmental law, as shall be discussed in the next chapter.

Chapter 3 – Integrated waste management as the protagonist of integrated environmental law

This chapter explores the adoption of the integrated approach to waste law. It delves into the notion of integrated waste management (section A) and its consequences for the understanding and reformulation of the functions of waste law (section B), the legal concept of waste (section C) and the notion of waste prevention (section D).

A. Integrated waste management

In the previous chapters it has been shown that one of the negative corollaries of the fragmentation of traditional environmental law is 'problem shifting' rather than 'problem solving', as illustrated by the case of filters: pollution is shifted from air or water into soil in the case of landfilling or even back to air in the case of incineration.[165] The 'integrated approach' proposes to tackle this particular issue by looking at the bigger picture, that is, by adopting a metabolic, life cycle perspective to environmental impacts.

As regards the waste problem, this implies understanding that waste is nothing but natural resources that were once obtained from nature, then transformed by human activity and ultimately discarded back to the environment once they cease to be of interest to their holder. Waste of materials when they become uninteresting things happens in relation to both resources that are directly transformed or incorporated into products ('consumer waste') and all those other materials that are otherwise mobilised for the production – from manufacturing to distribution – of products at upstream stages of their life cycle ('production waste').

Looking at all product life cycle stages preceding the waste phase allows one to realise that in the socioeconomic system different economic agents use different materials in different economic activities, which results in the generation of different wastes. Therefore, unlike the traditional approach

165 As Tufet-Opi (2002, p. 53) puts it, '[...] waste is increasingly produced as an attempt to solve other environmental problems such as water and air pollution'.

to the environmental and waste problems, according to which waste was seen as a homogeneous mass of materials that should be collected, compacted, and then disposed of (i.e. burnt or buried), the integrated approach recognises the heterogeneity of the waste generated by society in terms of both its composition and the solutions thereto.[166]

The idea that waste is not a mere bulk to be taken care of, but rather made up of different components relates directly to the very first sense in which 'integrated waste management' (hereinafter 'IWM') can be understood: a system for waste management that should embrace *all types of (waste) materials from all types of activities (waste sources)*[167].[168]

Once this diversity in the composition of waste is acknowledged, a variety of solutions to managing it emerges as the other side of the same coin. In other words, addressing different waste streams entails different types of waste management methods. The choice for one method over another depends therefore on the characteristics of the material to be handled, both intrinsic (e.g. physicochemical composition) and extrinsic (e.g. technical and economic conditions of the respective management method). In view thereof, it has been put forward that some parts of the waste stream should not be generated whatsoever, whilst other parts could be somehow 'recovered' (or 'reclaimed'), either materially (e.g. by means of recycling or composting) or energetically (energy production from waste), instead of only disposed of (e.g. landfilled or incinerated).[169] It is precisely in this second sense of a *plurality of solutions* to a likewise heterogeneous universe of waste materials that reference is made to IWM.[170]

Interpretation as to the meaning and extent of IWM in this second sense has led to two opposing positions.[171] The first one sees the myriad of possible solutions to the different waste streams as a 'menu of options',

166 See Schall, 1992, p. 1.

167 Material type (paper, glass, plastic, metal etc.) and origin (households, agriculture, industry, governments etc.) are only two of the possible criteria to classify waste.

168 See McDougall *et al.* 2001, p. xxiii and 18. See also Aragão, 2006, p. 315-316.

169 See Schall, 1992, p. 1.

170 See McDougall, 2001, p. 17; Tchobanoglous and Kreith, 2002, p. 1-8. See also Aragão, 2006, p. 316. This shift of perspective away from homogeneity under the traditional approach towards heterogeneity under the integrated paradigm is reflected into the legislative call for *separate* waste collection. For 'separating the materials in waste will generally increase their value if uses are available for those recovered materials' (see McDougall *et al.*, 2001, p. 1).

171 See Schall, 1992, p. 1.

each of which being 'equally appropriate under the right set of conditions addressing the right set of waste stream components'[172].

The second, and predominant point of view, in contrast, argues for a 'hierarchy of options': waste management should be carried out in a predetermined order whereby waste prevention[173] takes precedence over waste recovery[174], which, in turn, takes precedence over waste disposal[175]. This idea has been incorporated into waste legislation both in the EU and in Brazil under the so-called 'waste hierarchy'.

In the EU, even though Article 3(1) of the original version of Directive 75/442/EEC[176] on waste already referred to prevention and 'recovery' (e.g. recycling, extraction of energy) as options for managing waste, it did not rank them.[177] The idea of hierarchising solutions was first posited by the Commission of the then European Communities to the Council and to European Parliament in its communication on a waste management strategy[178].[179] Leaning on the 'Fourth Environmental Action Programme'[180], the communication spoke of a 'threefold [waste] policy approach' having waste prevention as its first strategic guideline, followed by waste recycling and reuse as the second guideline, and ultimately by disposal as the third and last guideline.[181]

---

172 See Schall, 1992, p. 1. See also McDougall *et al.*, 2001, p. 13.

173 On the concept of waste prevention, see section D, *infra*.

174 For now, 'recovery' shall be understood as the secondary use of things. It is elaborated on in section C, *infra*.

175 By 'disposal' landfilling and/or incineration is meant.

176 OJ L 194, 25 July 1975, p. 39.

177 Nor did it define the terms 'prevention' and 'recovery'.

178 See SEC (89) 934 final, 18 September 1989.

179 See Versmann, 2015, p. 2.

180 Resolution of the Council of the European Communities and of the representatives of the Governments of the Member States, meeting within the Council of 19 October 1987 on the continuation and implementation of a European Community policy and action programme on the environment (1987-1992), OJ C 328, 7.12.1987, p. 1 (see p. 32-33, paragraphs 5.3.3 to 5.3.6). The 4th EAP recalled the three waste policy headings set out in the 2nd EAP, namely, and in this order, 'the reduction of waste arisings, the increase of recycling and reuse, and the safe disposal of unavoidable wastes', but still did not clearly establish an order of precedence, at least not as clearly as the 1989 waste management strategy.

181 In response to (and support of) the Commission's communication in general, and the then embryonic waste hierarchy in particular, see Council Resolution of 7 May 1990 on waste policy, OJ C 122, 18.5.1990, p. 2 (paragraph 6), and European Parliament Resolution of 19 February 1991 on a Community strategy on waste management, OJ C 72, 18.3.1991, p. 34.

Article 1(1) of Directive 91/156/EEC[182] amended Directive 75/442/EEC and replaced Article 3, the new wording of which expressly embraced the waste hierarchy. It prescribed that Member States should take appropriate measures to encourage – firstly – the prevention or reduction of waste production (quantitative prevention) and its harmfulness (qualitative prevention)[183] and – secondly – the recovery of waste[184], either 'materially' (i.e. extraction of secondary raw materials from waste by means of, for instance, recycling) or 'energetically' (i.e. use of waste as a source of energy). Disposal of waste[185], although not explicitly mentioned, was left as the last waste management[186] option. This follows from a systematic reading of Directive 75/442/EEC as amended by Directive 91/156/EEC.

This three-tier waste hierarchy was confirmed in 1996 by the Commission in its revision of the 1989 communication on waste management strategy[187] and maintained with the same wording by Directive 2006/12/EC[188], which repealed Directive 75/442/EEC with its successive amendments. More recently, it has been fine-tuned into a five-tier hierarchy by Directive 2008/98/EC, known as the Waste Framework Directive (hereinafter 'WFD'), which repealed Directive 2006/12/EC.

Article 4 of the WFD lays down a new, refined priority order that shall apply in EU waste prevention and management[189] legislation and policy:

---

182 OJ L 78, 26 March 1991, p. 32.

183 Neither Directive 91/156/EEC nor the other posterior amendments to Directive 75/442/EEC provided a definition of waste prevention or reduction.

184 Directive 91/156/EEC defined 'recovery' in a practical, exemplifying manner by referring to the activities described in Annex IIB, which contained a list of recovery operations 'as they [were] carried out in practice'.

185 Just like 'recovery' (see previous note), 'disposal' was defined by Directive 91/156/EEC by means of allusion to the disposal operations listed in Annex IIA.

186 Directive 91/156/EEC defined '[waste] management' as 'the collection, transport, recovery and disposal of waste, including the supervision of such operations and after-care of disposal sites'.

187 COM (96) 399 final, 30.7.1996 (see p. 6, paragraph 20). See also European Parliament Resolution of 14 November 1996 on the communication from the Commission on the review of the Community strategy for waste management and the draft Council resolution on waste policy, OJ C 362, 2 December 1996, p. 241, especially 4(a).

188 OJ L 114, 27 April 2006, p. 9.

189 Article 3, point 9, of the WFD defines 'waste management' as 'the collection, transport, recovery and disposal of waste, including the supervision of such operations and the after-care of disposal sites, and including actions taken as a dealer or broker'.

prevention[190], preparing for reuse[191], recycling[192], other recovery[193] (e.g. energy recovery), and disposal[194]. 'Prevention' and 'disposal' remain at the top and the bottom of the hierarchy, respectively, with the latter being expressly enunciated as the last hierarchical level for the first time. Modifications have thus been confined to the recovery tier, which comprises the three other intermediate waste management options.

'Preparing for reuse' has been inserted in the hierarchy as the first preferable recovery option. While, concerning the two subsequent alternatives, namely material recovery (e.g. recycling) and energy recovery, clear preference has been given to the former over the latter.[195] Therefore, the main change to the waste hierarchy has been the prioritisation of the three solutions provided for within the middle, recovery category.

---

190 Article 3, point 12, of the WFD defines 'prevention' as 'measures taken before a substance, material or product has become waste, that reduce: (a) the quantity of waste, including through the reuse of products or the extension of the life span of products; (b) the adverse impacts of the generated waste on the environment and human health; or (c) the content of harmful substances in materials and products'. Reuse is defined by article 3, point 13, of the WFD as 'any operation by which products or components that are not waste are used again for the same purpose for which they were conceived'. These definitions are further discussed in section D, *infra*.

191 Article 3, point 16, of the WFD defines 'preparing for reuse' as 'checking, cleaning or repairing recovery operations, by which products or components of products that have become waste are prepared so that they can be reused without any other pre-processing'.

192 Article 3, point 17, of the WFD defines 'recycling' as 'any recovery operation by which waste materials are reprocessed into products, materials or substances whether for the original or other purposes. It includes the reprocessing of organic material but does not include energy recovery and the reprocessing into materials that are to be used as fuels or for backfilling operations'.

193 Article 3, point 15, of the WFD defines 'recovery' as 'any operation the principal result of which is waste serving a useful purpose by replacing other materials which would otherwise have been used to fulfil a particular function, or waste being prepared to fulfil that function, in the plant or in the wider economy. Annex II sets out a non-exhaustive list of recovery operations'.

194 Article 3, point 19, of the WFD defines 'disposal' as 'any operation which is not recovery even where the operation has as a secondary consequence the reclamation of substances or energy. Annex I sets out a non-exhaustive list of disposal operations'.

195 The revised waste management strategy communicated by the Commission of the then European Communities to the Council and to Parliament in 1996 (see footnote 187, *supra*) already endorsed the view of material recovery taking precedence over energy recovery.

By the same token, in Brazil Article 9 of Federal Law No. 12,305/2010[196], which establishes the National Solid Waste Policy (*Política Nacional de Resíduos Sólidos* in Portuguese, hereinafter 'PNRS'), stipulates that waste is to be managed according to the following priority order: non-generation, reduction, reuse[197], recycling[198], treatment, and environmentally sound final disposal[199]. Energy recovery from urban waste[200] may be allowed if – firstly – it is proven technically and environmentally viable and – secondly – a programme to monitor toxic gas emissions is approved by the environmental authority and then implemented (Article 9, paragraph 1). However, the PNRS is not clear as to the place that energy recovery should have in the priority order established in the chapeau.

---

196 DOU 147, Section 1, 3 August 2010, p. 3.

197 Article 3, point XVIII, of the PNRS defines 'reuse' as 'the process by means of which waste is used without its biological, physical or physicochemical transformation, [which is] subject to the conditions and standards set by the competent [environmental authority] and, if applicable, by the [competent agricultural health and/or human health surveillance authorities]'.

198 Article 3, point XIV, of the PNRS defines 'recycling' as 'the processing of waste that involves changing its physical, physicochemical, or biological properties in order to transform it into inputs or new products, [which is] subject to the conditions and standards set by the competent [environmental authority] and, if applicable, by the [competent agricultural health and/or human health surveillance authorities]'.

199 Article 3, point VIII, of the PNRS defines 'environmentally sound final disposal' as the 'orderly distribution of *final waste* in landfills in compliance with specific operational rules in order to avoid damage or risks to public health and safety as well as to minimise adverse environmental impacts' (emphasis added). 'Final waste' (or 'waste for disposal'), in turn, means 'waste for which there are no other possibilities but the final environmentally sound final disposal after every treatment and recovery possibility that is technically available and economically viable has been exhausted' (article 3, point XV, of the PNRS). The circularity of definitions is evident.

200 In Brazil, 'urban waste' comprises waste arising from both urban households (domestic waste) and public cleaning services (article 13, point I, subpoint c), of the PNRS).

The waste hierarchy is presented graphically in the figure below:

<table>
<tr><td rowspan="2">(1) + (2)
Circular (or closed loop) economy
(Kreislaufwirtschaft)</td><td></td><td>(1) Prevention (non-generation, reduction, reuse)</td><td>No waste</td></tr>
<tr><td rowspan="3">(2) Recovery sensu lato or reclaim
(Verwertung)</td><td>(2.1) Preparing for reuse</td><td rowspan="4">Waste

Waste management (Abfallbewirtschaftung), including, but not limited to, collection, sorting, transport, and treatment activities</td></tr>
<tr><td rowspan="3">(2) + (3)
Elimination
(Entsorgung)</td><td>(2.2.) Material recovery (i.e. recycling)</td></tr>
<tr><td>(2.3) Other recovery (e.g. energy recovery)</td></tr>
<tr><td></td><td>(3) Disposal
(Beseitigung)</td></tr>
</table>

Figure 1 – The waste hierarchy in terminological context

In any case, and regardless of the content of the hierarchy, reaching solutions to the various waste streams, hierarchising these solutions, and making this hierarchisation binding law all involve an assessment of different options in relation to the generation and management of waste. The waste hierarchy ultimately reflects a specific policy decision made from these options, one according to which waste is best coped with by preventing its generation as much as possible, then recovering what cannot be prevented, and finally disposing of only the remainder.[201]

Of course, the waste hierarchy itself is quite abstract, since the ranking of waste management methods is done aprioristically, that is, without taking into consideration the concrete advantages and disadvantages of each of the available options for tackling each of the specific waste streams.[202]

201 See Schall, 1992, p. iii.
202 See Aragão, 2009, p. 32.

Behind it, there is an implicit assumption that it is environmentally best to handle waste in the prescribed hierarchical order.[203]

However, this assumption has serious limitations and lacks scientific justification: it is not possible to explain *a priori* why one option is *always* the better option.[204] Cases exist in which, for several reasons, a lower-ranked option might be preferable than a higher-ranked one. For instance, the reuse of certain types of sewage sludge in agriculture is prohibited both in the EU[205] and Brazil[206] because of the hazards it poses to human and/or animal health and/or to the environment.

This example illustrates that relativising the waste hierarchy may indeed be desirable, after all there is not a ubiquitous, universally ideal solution to the waste problem. This is because any waste management system – and the waste hierarchy is just one instance of it – is context-dependent, that is, it necessarily varies in space and time according to factors such as the composition and the amount of waste generated, as well as the conditions (geographical, technical, economic, environmental etc.) for the management thereof.[207]

Yet, such relativisation only makes sense within a life cycle perspective, at least (and especially) when it is made due to environmental considerations. To put it another way, only by means of a life cycle assessment is it possible to assert that a solution, despite being a lower-ranked option in the waste hierarchy, is nonetheless more environmentally suitable for a specific waste stream in a concrete case.[208]

In the EU, this call for flexibility in the application of the waste hierarchy is acknowledged in Article 4(2) of the WFD, which allows specific

---

203 See Schall, 1992, p. 1.

204 See Bortoleto, 2014, p. 23. See also McDougall *et al.*, 2001, p. 17 (noting that the waste hierarchy is not based on any scientific or technical evidence) and Schall, 1992, p. 1 (noting that the assumption behind the waste hierarchy was never subjected to a technical, economic and environmental validation, and simply became the politically dominant position).

205 See Directive 86/278/EEC (OJ L 181, 4 July 1986, p. 6), as amended by Council Directive 91/692/EEC (OJ L 377, 31 December 1991, p. 48), Council Regulation (EC) 807/2003 (OJ L 122, 16 May 2003, p. 36), Regulation (EC) 219/2009 (OJ L 87, 31 March 2009, p. 109), and Decision (EU) 2018/853 (OJ L 150, 14 June 2018, p. 155).

206 See Resolution No. 375/2006 of Brazil's National Environmental Council (*Conselho Nacional do Meio Ambiente*, hereinafter 'Conama') (DOU 167, Section 1, 30 August 2006, p. 141). On Conama, see footnote 405, *infra*.

207 See Bortoleto, 2014, p. 24; McDougall *et al.*, 2001, p. 13 and 21.

208 See Aragão, 2009, p. 34.

waste streams to depart from the hierarchy provided that this delivers the best overall outcome based on life cycle thinking on the overall impacts of the generation and management of such waste. However, the WFD provides no examples of such deviation, let alone a definition of (product) life cycle (thinking).

In this sense, the waste hierarchy should be read more as a starting point than a strict order. In legal terms, this means interpreting the waste hierarchy norm as conveying a presumption of a relative nature (*praesumptio iuris tantum*), and thus rebuttable on the grounds of concrete life cycle studies, as provided for by the European WFD, rather than of an absolute nature (*praesumptio iuris et de iure*), like the Brazilian PNRS.

Be that as it may, it is in connection with the idea of life cycle thinking, and the flexible hierarchy stemming therefrom, that IWM takes on a third meaning:[209] a system for managing material flows[210] 'from cradle to grave', that is, from the obtaining of resources from nature, through their transformation into products, to their final disposal after consumption.[211] It is by taking into account the whole life cycle of products[212], and not only the disposal stage, that the solution to the waste problem is to be found.[213] IWM will be used henceforth in this third sense.

Such an understanding of IWM might seem a mere shift away from the predominant, hierarchical interpretation of IWM in its second meaning towards the 'menu-of-options' interpretation, largely as a result of the practical failure to enforce the waste hierarchy in general, and to implement waste prevention measures in particular.

209 See Aragão, 2006, p. 316.

210 Materials flows can be understood as the exchanges of matter between the ecosphere and the technosphere. Ecosphere is used here as a synonym of biosphere (or the planetary ecosystem), that is, the biological communities (all living beings on Earth) together with the abiotic environment in which they are set. On the notion of 'ecosystem', see Begon, Townsend and Harper, 2006, p. 499. The term 'technosphere' means the artificial environment resulting from man-made technology that is employed for the satisfaction of human needs and has effects upon the ecosphere.

211 Modernly, it is spoken of 'cradle to cradle'. See McDonough and Braungart, 2003.

212 Article 3, point IV, of the PNRS defines 'product life cycle' as 'the series of steps involving product development, obtainment of raw materials and inputs, the production process, consumption and final disposal'.

213 Of course, a life cycle approach enables tackling *all other* environmental problems as well.

Nevertheless, whilst the inability to move up the waste hierarchy in practice is true, replacing the hierarchical model of waste management for a life-cycle-based one is not so much about reviving the 'menu-of-options school of IWM' and its attacks on the 'hierarchy school of IWM' in favour of more economical (i.e. less costly), market-based disposal solutions.[214]

In fact, in the life cycle approach to IWM, waste prevention is still the most preferable solution ('the best waste is that which is not produced'),[215] albeit subject to relativisation in the face of a concrete life cycle study. Put another way, waste prevention remains the top priority in waste legislation and policy, though it only *prima facie* enjoys preference over other waste management options.

What follows from the third meaning of IWM adopted herein – but *not* from the hierarchical reading of IWM in its second sense – is that, in order for a *prevention-oriented* waste management system to be successful, it must be also a *resource* management system. In other words, it must address the waste problem 'from both a [...] waste *and* production system perspective, as a part of an overall *materials policy*'[216]. This is made possible only by means of an integrated approach.

However subtle the nuances of meaning of the three versions of IWM might seem, the implications of the third, truly metabolic and life-cycle-driven notion of IWM to waste law are several-fold.

Firstly, and most importantly, it gives rise to a revision of the functions of waste law, which are seen to extend beyond the scope of human health and environmental protection to embrace the objective of resource conservation as well (section B, *infra*). Secondly, reviewing the functions of waste law in the broader context of an integrated environmental law spotlights not only the need to abandon the concept of waste but also the corollary trend to dispense with waste law itself (section C, *infra*). Thirdly and consequently, once the role(s) and the necessity of waste regulation are challenged, the concept of waste prevention, if it still makes sense at all, needs at least to be re-defined (section D, *infra*). Also in need of re-definition is the question of whether there is a legal duty to prevent waste and, if so, against whom and how it can be enforced (section D, *infra*).

214 See Schall, 1992, p. 3.
215 See Bortoleto, 2014, p. 24.
216 See Schall, 1992, p. 4, emphasis added.

B. The functions of waste law: a dichotomy

It follows on the heels of the previous section that waste law is, or at least should be, the body of environmental law that governs IWM. If this is true, then *integrated* waste law is by definition *anti-waste* law, for IWM is prevention-oriented, thus focused more on the upstream, *pre-waste* stages of the life cycles of materials. In this sense, one can only anticipate the conclusion that waste law might have no function whatsoever if the environmental repercussions of materials throughout their life cycle are already legally addressed elsewhere, as shall be discussed in the next section. Yet, waste regulations abound both in the EU and in Brazil[217]. What is waste law needed for after all?

Waste law is basically law on materials (*Stoffrecht*). It is built neither on a concrete substance or material nor on a specific legally protected good (*Schutzgut*), like the law on the protection of environmental media (air, water and soil)[218], but on the abstract fact of materials following a particular path, namely and redundantly the 'waste path' (*Abfallpfad*), on which their potential to cause damage increases *or* by virtue of which resources are prematurely depleted.[219] In light of these problems, legal commentary, notably in Germany, acknowledges waste law as serving dual purposes.[220]

On one side, it is contended that waste law differs from the law on materials by the greater degree of danger that the thing's taking the 'waste path' poses to human health and environmental media, that is, by the usually higher probability that pollution risks to said legally protected goods materialise.[221] Rules on waste management are necessary to ensure that those in control of the conditions that give rise to pollution[222], *in casu* the unaccountable getting rid of pollutant-releasing things, act responsibly so as to prevent human health and the environment from being endangered

217 Soler and Silva Filho (2013) note that after the enactment of the PNRS there has been a 'normative explosion' on waste at the federal, state, *and* municipal levels.

218 On the definition of 'environmental media', see footnote 68, *supra*.

219 See Engel, 2002, p. 33, 35-36, 41-42, 306, and 315. See also Krieger, 1995, p. 409-410.

220 In Germany, see, for instance, Engel, 2002; Rehbinder, 1994, p. 17. Amongst English-speaking scholars, see, for instance, Tromans, 2001, p. 133-134. Similarly, but somewhat confusing, see Scotford, 2007, p. 370-371.

221 Engel, 2002, p. 33-37, 41-43. See also Cheyne, 2002, p. 62; Cheyne and Purdue, 1995, p. 151-152.

222 See Aragão, 1997, p. 136 *et seq.*, especially p. 140 and p. 142.

by the things they get rid of[223] as well as to bear the costs of their preventive actions. Here, waste law is a section of the law on harmful materials.

On the other, waste law is accredited with promoting resource conservation as well. It seeks to counteract the dissipation of raw materials by influencing decisions on the handling of such materials, or the products in which they are contained, after their use. This is the case of waste recovery, by means of which secondary raw materials are obtained, thereby replacing the need for raw materials, as well as waste-prevention rules aimed at prolonging and/or renewing the primary use of products, thereby conserving the materials they contain, to cite two examples. Of course, there are several other strategies to avoid, reduce, and/or close material flows.[224] Waste law is just one – accessory[225] – part of the law on resources.[226] In any case, regulation of waste is made with a view to saving resources for the future. In this perspective, it connects with the sustainable development debate.[227]

As already discussed, historically speaking, waste law first pursued the goal of human health and environmental media protection.[228] Only in its modern facet does it encompass the task of resource conservation as well. Whereas in its former function waste law set out to address a more qualitative problem (i.e. the increased harmfulness of materials), the challenge behind its latter function is of a more quantitative nature (i.e. the dissipation of resources). Waste law as the law on *harmful* materials views the environment as a sink whereas waste law as the law on *raw* materials (or resources) views it as a source.

The objectives described above interact with one another in a complementary[229] rather than conflicting[230] manner, which means that the adop-

223 In this sense, waste law protects human health and environmental media only *mediately*.

224 On the categories avoidance, reduction, and/or closure of materials flows, see Aragão, 2006, p. 139-143, 301-431, 585-652. *Non-waste*, e.g. product-related strategies aimed at resource conservation are discussed in chapter 5, *infra*.

225 See Engel, 2002, p. 248.

226 See, for instance, Lee, 2005, p. 223.

227 See chapter 2, *supra*.

228 See chapter 1, section C, *supra*.

229 See Rehbinder, 1994, p. 17; Engel, 2002, p. 36, 311-312.

230 See Engel, 2002, p. 304-305. The author provides four examples of the conflictual relationship between the aims of human health and environmental protection and resource conservation, three of which seem not to hold. *Firstly*, he argues that whilst waste prevention is usually the best solution in terms of resource conservation, it is problematic if it results in an increase of the

tion of a waste-related measure pursuing one aim is likely to be conducive to the other aim as well. The problem of plastic waste is illustrative of the synergy existing between both goals. Plastic is a material consisting of synthetic or semi-synthetic organic-based polymers. Conventionally, it is made from oil, which is a non-renewable resource, and contains other additives. These chemicals hinder the recyclability of plastic, which is con-

---

thing's polluting potential. Nonetheless, he does not illustrate or elaborate on this argument. Concerning waste recovery, assuming that material recovery (i.e. recycling) is unfeasible, he writes that from a resource conservation point of view waste storage – in the implied sense of landfilling – would be better than energy recovery or incineration because the latter operations only allow for the energetic content of waste to be utilised, after all they 'destroy' – or, more accurately, disperse into the environment – the materials involved. Still, because waste materials are normally not inert, waste storage (i.e. landfilling) contradicts the human health and environmental protection goal. The storage of potentially valuable materials for future need may make sense indeed, but it requires not only that we abandon the disposal logic underpinning landfilling – and ultimately the idea of pollutant dispersion/dilution embedded in it – but also that we develop better technologies for the characterisation, labelling and packaging of the materials to be stored (see Frosch, 1996, p. 205, 207). *Secondly*, after noting that under the auspices of the resource conservation goal renewable resources are frequently preferred over non-renewable ones, he posits that most renewable resources consist of organic matter, which, owing to the fact that they decompose, present – presumably in comparison to inorganic matter – a higher polluting potential once in the 'waste path'. The first assertion deserves caution and the second one is fallacious. Renewability is a relative, anthropocentric concept relating to the natural reproduction/replenishment of a given resource occurring at a rate relevant to a meaningful economic time scale. See footnote 43, *supra*. The rate of natural reproduction/replenishment is what determines the degree of availability of renewable resources. It may be affected by the rate of human consumption of said resources, as in the case of water (inorganic matter), biological communities (organic matter) and soil (organic and inorganic matter), or not, as in the case of energy resources such as solar radiation, wind, and tides. Organic matter, in turn, is *not* intrinsically and necessarily more polluting than inorganic matter, as in the case of heavy metals, especially because the harmfulness of a material or substance depends on the use that is made of it as well as the (living and/or non-living) receptors thereof. *Thirdly*, he points out that due to technological advancements new electrical and electronic equipment (hereinafter 'EEE') almost always consume less energy than old EEE. For this reason, the much-praised reuse of old EEE (*Weiterverwendung gebrauchter Geräte*) frustrates the aim of saving energy, which is a resource in a broad sense. Even if true, this is an issue of conserving matter (i.e. the materials contained in old EEE) versus conserving energy, hence a conflict that occurs solely *within* the objective of resource conservation, and *not between* it and the objective of human health and environmental protection.

sidered to be great. Because of their hazardous properties, additives can, even in small quantities, trigger toxic reactions when the plastic product comes into contact with an environmental medium.[231] In addition to not being inert, plastic persists in the environment, particularly in the marine environment. Waste-related measures intended to enhance the recycling of plastics, for instance, contribute to the conservation of the resources that would otherwise be necessary for the production of virgin plastic as well as to the diversion of plastic waste from (legal and illegal) disposal, thus alleviating its environmental impacts.[232]

The same result could be achieved by means of alternative measures, though. A product-related ban on plastic or, less drastically, design requirements on biodegradability are two examples. This indicates that waste law is not the only body of law aimed at protecting human health and environmental media *along with* saving resources. Other sectors of environmental law also serve one or both such purposes, although each of them does so in its own fashion.

In terms of *regulatory technique*, environmental law tackles ecological problems in different ways depending on the *object of regulation*. Such problems are typically regulated on the basis of the facilities, materials (substances included) and/or products causing them or the environmental media they affect. One can therefore speak of environmental regulations that are facility-related (e.g. permitting and environmental impact assessment laws), substance-related (e.g. laws on chemicals), product-related (e.g. laws on motor vehicles), and media-related (e.g. laws on the protection of air, water and/or soil), respectively.[233] Of course, these approaches intersect.[234] For instance, quality, or ambient, standards establish the maximum amounts of specific *substances* allowed to be present in a specific environmental *medium*. Another example is emission standards, which set quantitative limits on the permissible amount of specific *substances* that may be released (into a specific environmental *medium*) from specific sources over specific time frames. Sources, in turn, can be either *facilities* or *products*. Emission levels are then enforced, in the former situation, within the environmental permitting process, as illustrated by the control of the effluents

231 See the European Commission's "Green paper on a European strategy on plastic waste in the environment", COM (2013) 123 final, 7 March 2013, p. 5-6.

232 If the environmental trade-offs of recycling are taken into consideration, the correctness of this assertion may be reversed.

233 See Schenkel and Reiche, 1993, p. 184-185; Krieger, 1995, p. 408-412; Friege, 1995, p. 242; Reese, 2000.

234 See Schenkel and Reiche, 1993, p. 184.

discharged by a factory, or, in the latter case, via design requirements such as the limits on motor vehicles emissions[235] or the content of volatile organic compounds (VOCs) in paints[236].

At first glance, waste law differs from the four approaches to environmental regulation mentioned above in that its scope is defined not in relation to an environmental medium, a facility, a substance and/or a product but instead by reference to the last stage of a thing's life cycle, whether this thing is a product or a substance leaving a facility.[237] It is exactly this mismatch between regulatory criteria that appears to engender the legislative overlaps that are behind the debate on the concept of waste, which is dealt with in the next section.

C. *Waste: a legal creation*

The discussion on the concept of waste is the keystone in any scholarly legal work on waste law, for it determines what falls or not within the ambit of waste regulations. In short, waste law is only applicable where

---

235 In the EU, see Directive 2007/46/EC (OJ L 263, 9 October 2007, p. 1) establishing a framework for the approval of motor vehicles and their trailers, and of systems, components and separate technical units for such vehicles; Regulation (EC) 715/2007 on type approval of motor vehicles with respect to emissions from light passenger and commercial vehicles (Euro 5 and Euro 6) and on access to vehicle repair and maintenance information (OJ L 171, 29 June 2007, p. 1); and Regulation (EC) 595/2009 on type-approval of motor vehicles and engines with respect to emissions from heavy duty vehicles (Euro VI) and on access to vehicle repair and maintenance information and amending Regulation (EC) No 715/2007 and Directive 2007/46/EC and repealing Directives 80/1269/EEC, 2005/55/EC and 2005/78/EC (OJ L 188, 18 July 2009, p. 1). In Brazil, see Conama Resolution No. 18/1986 (DOU 112, Section 1, 17 June 1986, p. 8792) on the Vehicle Air Pollution Control Program and its successive amendments. On Conama, see footnote 405, *infra*.

236 In the EU, see Directive 2004/42/CE on the limitation of emissions of volatile organic compounds due to the use of organic solvents in certain paints and varnishes and vehicle refinishing products and amending Directive 1999/13/EC (OJ L 143, 30 April 2004, p. 87) and its successive amendments. Brazil does not yet regulate VOCs from paints.

237 'Things', obviously, can only be either *materials/substances* or, more commonly, *products made of materials/substances*. For this reason and in this sense, it has been argued that waste law is nothing but law on materials (or substances), though related not to a specific one, but rather to a specific phase at which materials/substances (or products containing them) find themselves in the economic circuit.

there is waste. The importance of defining waste lies in distinguishing it from non-waste, since for the former there is a specific legal regime that is usually stricter than the one applicable to the latter.

Evidently, any specific legal regime, *in casu* that for which is considered waste, is set up in order to reach one or more objectives. As discussed in the previous section, waste law has traditionally been aimed at preventing people from getting rid of things without making sure that these things do not endanger or damage legally protected goods, namely human health and the environment, and without bearing the costs of the proper reintegration of the discarded things – or, more precisely, of the materials and substances contained in them – back into the environment upon disposal operations (i.e. incineration or landfilling). From this perspective, waste is viewed as something that has a negative value, for it is no longer interesting to its holder (and, implicitly, to no one else), and that requires control due to the risks it poses.

With the expansion of the functions of waste law so as to also promote resource conservation, any use other than disposal of the discarded, hitherto uninteresting thing – or, again, of the materials, substances or energy contained in it – is clearly preferred. Here, waste is seen as something with a positive value. Furthermore, waste is no longer thought of 'retrospectively', that is, in relation exclusively to the previous end use (*Zweckverwendung*) of the thing or the previous holder's disinterest towards it, but 'prospectively' with regard to other socio-economic agents that are or may be interested in further using the thing no matter for what purpose. This dichotomy between goals is reflected in the debate on the concept of waste, as shall be discussed below.

The European WFD and the Brazilian PNRS have very similar definitions of waste.[238],[239] In general terms, waste is defined in both legal orders

238 Article 3, point 1, of the WFD defines 'waste' as 'any substance or object which the holder discards or intends or is required to discard'. As per article 3, point 6, '"(waste) holder" means the waste producer or the natural or legal person who is in possession of the waste'. The WFD does not, however, provide a definition of 'discard'.

239 Article 3, point XVI, of the PNRS defines 'waste' as any 'material, substance, object or discarded good resulting from human activities in society to whose final destination one proceeds or intends or is required to proceed, [which can be] in a solid or semi-solid state as well as gases in containers and liquids whose characteristics either render their discharge into the public sewage system or water bodies unfeasible or require for such a purpose solutions that are technically or economically unfeasible in light of the best available technology'. 'Final destination' (or, literally, 'environmentally sound final destination'), in turn,

as something that someone destines (or intends or is required to destine) for a purpose. Firstly, this 'something' is loosely referred to as an object, a material, or a substance. Secondly, 'someone' is any natural or legal person that has a factual or a legal relationship to the thing.[240] Thirdly, lastly and most complicatedly, there is the question as to the purpose for which the thing is destined as well as the circumstances in which the destining takes place.

The end for which the thing is destined concerns the question of what exactly happens to the thing once the holder no longer has interest in it, or, more specifically, the *operations* (or processes) to which the uninteresting thing is (or is intended or required to be) subjected. It is in this context that one speaks of an 'operational' conceptualisation of waste.[241] The traditional operation was always disposal in the sense of landfilling or incineration, but it has been broadened at the European level to include recovery[242] as well. A likewise broad, operational, recovery-embracing, definition of waste is found in Brazil.

In fact, in the European setting, point b of Article 1 of the original version of Directive 75/442/EEC on waste already defined 'disposal' as encompassing recovery,[243] even though some Member States had restricted said definition to mean only landfilling or incineration operations in their national law. Directive 91/156/EEC amended Directive 75/442/EEC and

---

means 'destining waste for reuse, recycling, composting, recovery, including energetic recovery, or other operations that are permitted by the competent environmental, agricultural health and/or human health surveillance authorities, including final disposal [see footnote 199, *supra*], in any case in line with specific operational rules in order to avoid damage or risks to public health and safety as well as to minimise adverse environmental impacts' (article 3, point VII, of the PNRS).

240 Whilst the European WFD identifies the subject who destines the thing for a purpose as the 'waste holder' (see footnote 238, *supra*), the Brazilian PNRS only specifies the subjects to whom it applies, namely all 'natural or legal persons, of a private or public law nature, that are directly or indirectly responsible for the generation of waste as well as to those who engage in any waste-management-related activity' (article 1, paragraph 1). The term 'holder' shall be used henceforward to refer to the second, personal (or subjective) element of the definition of waste provided herein ('someone').

241 See Grosz, 2011, p. 19.

242 'Recovery' shall be understood as any kind of use of things that differs from the original use made by their original holder *and* that is not disposal (landfilling or incineration) either.

243 *In verbis*: "'[D]isposal' means [...] the transformation operations necessary for [the] reuse, recovery or recycling [of waste]".

modified the concept of waste by, at least in its English version, excluding the 'operational element' from the definition and mentioning instead only the undefined act of 'discarding', thereby trying to leave aside the question of the precise future of the thing for the purpose of considering it waste.[244]

This alteration is actually to be seen as an attempt to sidestep the circularity of definitions[245] of the European waste legislation, which is present also in Brazilian waste law. While waste is defined as that which is disposed of or recovered, disposal and recovery operations are defined by reference to waste, that is, they consist of waste management activities.

If the 'new' definition of waste is to be centred around the notion of 'discard' in the sense of any act of getting rid of a thing regardless of its destination, that is, as the mere abandonment of the previous use (*Zweckverwendung*) of the thing,[246] not only is the interpretation on the legal concept of waste to revolve around the meaning and reach of the term 'discard',[247] but the concept itself also and inevitably becomes comprehensive, since whatever happens to the discarded thing – that is, whatever new use is assigned to it – is *prima facie* irrelevant for preventing it from being considered waste.[248] Illustrative hereof is the case law of the European Court of Justice (hereinafter 'ECJ'), which has been heavily criticised for having repeatedly ruled in favour of an all-encompassing and hence inoperable concept of waste.[249]

It is precisely in connection with this conceptual amplitude that an attempt to differentiate between waste and non-waste according to the intrinsic characteristics (i.e. the physicochemical properties) of the thing

244 The replacement of the verb 'to dispose of' for the verb 'to discard' is found only in the English version of Directive 91/442/EEC and sought "to provide for the widest possible inclusion of acts of getting rid of substances and objects" (see Cheyne and Purdue, 1995, p. 155). In other languages, the verb remained unchanged (*'sich entledigen'*, in German; *desfazer-se'*, in Portuguese; *'se défaire'*, in French; *'desprenderse'*, in Spanish; *'disfarsi'*, in Italian; *'usuwać'*, in Polish, to cite a few examples). The definition of 'disposal', however, was narrowed and juxtaposed with the definition of 'recovery' in all of the aforementioned languages. Krämer (2001, p. 261, 263) notes that the word 'discard' has been adopted as the hypernym of 'recovery' and 'disposal', the reason for which he believes the modification to be "more of linguistic nature than of substance".

245 See Birn, 1992, p. 419; Reese, 2009a, p. 1074.

246 See Reese, 2009a, p. 1074.

247 See de Sadeleer, 2005, p. 460; Tromans, 2001, p. 141.

248 See Cheyne and Purdue, 1995, p. 155.

249 On the ECJ's case law on the concept of waste, see van Calster, 2015, p. 5-39. See also Jans and Vedder, 2012, p. 474-479 as well as Aragão, 2006, p. 465-469.

is found. Such a 'substance-based' concept of waste[250] is, nevertheless, almost unanimously – and rightly – rejected by academic commentary. As previously explained, the distinction between waste and non-waste has the purpose of applying to that which is considered waste a specific legal regime with a view to, firstly, protecting human health and the environment against the negative effects that the decomposition of, or any sort of human action involving, waste materials can produce, and, secondly, reducing the need for, and/or fostering the circularity of, materials in the technosphere. Given that situations exist in which, in respect of the first goal, the use of wastes is just as impacting as, or less impacting than, the (same) use of raw materials,[251] or, in respect of the second goal, the same economic result or operation can be obtained or carried out from the use of either wastes or raw materials,[252] the criterion of material composition is of no utility.

The irrelevance of the inherent features of a thing for considering it waste is explained by the fact that waste is socially defined.[253] A thing can be regarded as being waste only *in relation to* a person's, or group's, attitude towards it, never in itself. Being a relative concept,[254] waste varies in space and time. Therefore, the physicochemical properties of a thing – or, more accurately, its increased, yet not maximal, entropy[255] – may be

---

250 See Scotford, 2007, p. 375.

251 The handling of hazardous goods such as chemicals, for example, entails much more risks to the environment than the management of many wastes. Krämer (2001, p. 275) mentions the possibility of the emissions from a production plant being higher than a landfill or an incineration plant.

252 For instance, there is no difference between grinding old, used rubber and grinding new rubber from latex to make new rubber products (Aragão, 2006, p. 535).

253 See Thompson, 1998, p. 58: 'Waste [...] is a quality that is bestowed on various materials by a process that is wholly social'. On the social process of 'wasteness', see Thompson, 1979.

254 See de Sadeleer, 2005 p. 459, and Grosz, 2011, p. 11-15.

255 "[...] it is important to distinguish between high entropy waste in the form of heat and in the form of waste materials. [...] It is only the latter that accumulates in the biosphere, thus causing major environmental problems. Waste materials, however, might cause environmental problems not because of their high entropy, but – just the opposite – because entropy is not yet maximal. In other words, it is the exergy still contained in waste materials, i.e. the potential to initiate chemical reactions and perform work, which makes these wastes potentially harmful to the natural environment" (Baumgärtner, 2002, p. 30).

a necessary but insufficient condition for 'wasteness'[256], which is a social construct.

The legal definition of waste embraces this relativity by referring to the holder's behaviour towards the thing, regardless, at least for now, of whether 'behaviour' means the more generic, undefined act of 'discarding' or the more specific act of 'destining for an operation'. The law contemplates three different modes in which such behaviour is manifested.

First of all, there is the situation in which the behaviour has already occurred. Whether the thing is waste or not can only be ascertained in hindsight in order to assess compliance with waste regulations (and impose the applicable sanctions in case of non-compliance).[257]

Secondly, the holder may be required to behave, which means that he or she is obliged by law to act in relation to the thing even against his or her will. Examples of things that are considered waste *ope legis* include polychlorinated biphenyls and polychlorinated terphenyls (PCB/PCT) in Europe, and healthcare waste in Brazil, both of which *must* be treated and disposed of by virtue of Directive 96/59/EC[258] and Conama Resolution No. 358/2005[259], respectively. Legal scholars talk about an objective concept of waste, one that German commentators correctly observe to be grounded in, or represent a particular instance of, the danger-averting (*Gefahrenabwehr*), nuisance-removal general clause deriving from German police law (*Polizeirecht*).[260]

In the third and last case, the holder is considered to have the intention to behave. In tune with liberal concerns,[261] the 'wasteness' of a thing, here, depends on the holder's will, i.e. he or she can determine whether the thing is to become waste or not by deciding to act in relation to it or not. For this reason, a subjective concept of waste is spoken of[262]. As it is conceived in connection with something as unstable as human will,[263] the

256 See Baumgärtner, 2002, especially p. 25.

257 See Aragão, 2006, p. 454.

258 OJ L 243, 24 July 1996, p. 31, as amended by Regulation (EC) 596/2009 (OJ L 188, 18 July 2009, p. 14).

259 DOU 84, Section 1, 4 May 2005, p. 63. See also Resolution No. 306/2004 of Brazil's National Sanitary Surveillance Agency (DOU 237, Section 1, 10 December 2004, p. 49).

260 See Birn, 1992, p. 420; Engel, 2002, p. 36. On German police law, see, for instance, Schenke, 2016; Götz, 2013; Drews *et al.*, 1986. In Brazil, see Sundfeld, 1993.

261 See Birn, 1992 p. 420; von Lersner, 1981, p. 1.

262 See Cheyne and Purdue, 1995, p. 152.

263 See von Lersner, 1981, p. 2.

subjective concept of waste is, amongst the three 'behavioural variants', the one that raises the most challenges and is therefore focused on henceforth.

The law clearly adopts an 'action-based'[264] (as opposed to a 'substance-based') concept of waste, around which revolves the issue about what actions that the holder intends to take in relation to the thing shall fall within the specific legal waste regime or not in light of the objectives to be reached[265]. This being so, the discussion on the legal concept of waste can be reformulated as follows.

Questioning which actions shall be subjected to the waste regime evinces that the 'operational element' remains central to the definition of waste despite the 'discard-bypass' attempt introduced by Directive 91/156/EEC and maintained by the WFD. In this sense, the debate can be framed as a matter of whether waste regulations should apply only to disposal operations or to recovery operations as well, the former comprising landfilling and incineration, and the latter meaning any use of a thing that is identical to neither its primary use nor its disposal. The underlying idea is that not every secondary use of things should be subjected to waste regulations.[266]

In favour of the first solution, which entails a more restrictive concept of waste, it is submitted that leaving recovery operations outside the cumbersome realm of waste requirements and control would stimulate the recovery market. To put it another way, recovery activities would be fostered due to the fact that a less stringent (i.e. 'non-waste') legal regime would apply to them.[267] This perspective is in line with the resource conservation goal.[268] In favour of the second option and the corollary ampler notion of

---

264 See Scotford, 2007, p. 375.

265 See Scotford (2007, p. 375) refers to a purposive interpretation of the waste definition.

266 See Koch and Reese, 2006, p. 13.

267 In this sense, see Lee and Stokes, 2008, p. 179. Similarly, see Nash, 2009, p. 142.

268 The privileging of recovery operations builds upon the idea that the secondary use of things – from reuse to the utilisation of the materials and/or energy contained in them – is better than their 'elimination' back into the environment by means of disposal operations, since this secondary use replaces the need for the primary use of new, to-be-produced things or to-be-extracted raw materials that would otherwise have arisen if the secondary use did not occur (the so-called 'substitution effect', see Koch and Reese, 2000, p. 304). It follows from this 'substitutive perspective', which has been incorporated into the definition of 'recovery' in article 3, point 15, of the WFD, that most of these secondary uses constitute economic activities just like the primary ones. For this reason, in pure economic terms, things that are subject to a secondary use are considered

waste is the argument that both disposal *and* recovery operations have impacts on the environment and are therefore worth regulatory attention.[269] Such a viewpoint accords with the aim of human health and environmental protection.

The first approach is confronted with the problem that a subjective concept of waste allows the holder to willingly deviate from the waste regime, for he or she, neither having discarded the thing yet nor being required to do so, can simply state that recovery is intended to take place but then proceed to disposal instead. This is further enhanced by the fact that all parties in waste transactions are interested in being spared from the yoke of the burdensome waste regime.[270] The second approach, in turn, fails to recognise that waste operations, including recovery activities, are also already covered by other facility-, media-, and substance-related environmental regulations, a fact that raises questions as to the role and real necessity of waste law in protecting the environment within the broader context of environmental law.[271]

The interpretative dispute as to the breadth of the legal definition of waste is therefore marked by a dichotomy that parallels, and is linked with, that of the functions of waste law: recovery should be *either* included in the concept of waste (thereby falling within the waste regime) in order to protect human health and the environment *or* excluded from the scope of the definition (thereby escaping the waste regime) so as to promote

---

'goods' and should consequently "be left to the market", at least in market-oriented economies such as the European Union (see article 3(3) of the TEU) and Brazil (see articles 170 *et seq.* of the Brazilian Constitution). Of course, within the socio-scientific domain of political economy, "leaving to the market" implies a more liberal concept of market as an unregulated or less regulated – i.e. free(r) –locus of exchanges and that should be kept so, as opposed to economic dirigisme and/or interventionism of the State. The discussion on the legal definition of waste in general, and the recovery-disposal debate associated with it in particular, ultimately represents a matter of more or less economic freedom of – or, conversely, of more or less restriction on – trade and movement of goods. In the EU, this tension is well illustrated by the conflicting relationship between the single (internal) market, on the one hand, and the self-sufficiency and proximity principles (see article 16 of the WFD), on the other hand. On this topic, see, for example, Chalmers, 1994, p. 280-296; Koch and Reese, 2006, p. 56-61 and 85-99; Dieckmann and Reese, 2014, p. 383 and 387-389.

269 In other words, not only negatively valued things (e.g. waste for disposal), but also things with positive, economic value (e.g. waste for recovery, products) impact on the environment and should therefore be regulated and controlled.

270 See Birn, 1992, p. 420.

271 See Reese, 2000, p. 95, 173-174 *et. seq.*

resource conservation. *A contrario sensu*, it is contended that *not* moving recovery into the realm of waste law allows some secondary uses of things to impact on the environment, whereas *not* keeping recovery out of the clutches of waste law may result in less resource-saving secondary uses of things (e.g. disposal) crowding out more resource-saving uses (e.g. recovery). One commentator speaks of an environmental risk (*Umweltrisiko*), in the former case, and a resource risk (*Ressourcenrisiko*), in the latter case.[272]

The solution to this dilemma begins by recognising that, as regards the need to cope with the negative effects of waste materials to human health and the environment (first function of waste law), activities involving waste are normally already subject to other facility-, media-, and substance-related environmental regulations apart from waste-related ones. For example, permitting and environmental impact assessment (hereinafter 'EIA') rules, which specify which installations and/or processes dealing with which materials and/or substances shall be assessed and/or controlled by environmental authorities due to their potential of impacting on the environment, list – and therefore impose duties on – activities both generating and managing waste. In other words, waste generating and, most importantly, waste management facilities are subject to environmental permitting. If this is true, then media- and substance-related environmental standards, which are enforced by facility-related provisions, already address the harmfulness of both waste materials produced as part of an installation's emissions, at least for the activities covered by permitting and EIA regulations[273], and waste management operations (recovery and disposal). In this sense, so far as the hazards posed by waste are still concerned, there is no regulatory difference between, for example, the transport of waste and the transport of dangerous goods, or even between secondary materials, which are the very results of recovery operations, and raw materials: all these instances involve environmental risks which, being associated with the composition of the things to be transported and/or processed, can be legally managed by a product and/or a substance approach to environmental law.[274]

272 See Reese, 2009a, p. 1075, and Reese, 2009b, p. 139-140.

273 In the European Union, see Directive 2010/75/EU and Directive 2011/92/EU (OJ L 26, 28 January 2012, p. 1). In Brazil, see Federal Law No. 6.938/1981 (DOU 167, Section 1, 2 September 1981, p. 16509), Conama Resolution No. 237/1997 (DOU 247, Section 1, 22 December 1997, p. 30841) and Conama Resolution No. 1/1986 (DOU 32, Section 1, 17 February 1986, p. 2548). On Conama, see footnote 405, *infra*.

274 See Koch and Reese, 2000, p. 303-306.

It follows from the considerations above that in respect of *environmental risks* waste law does have a subsidiary role within the broader context of environmental law, for waste regulations are only needed if and where other facility-, media-, substance- and/or product-related environmental legal standards fail to provide sufficient protection ('regulatory holes').[275] In this sense, reducing the scope of waste law in favour of a more product- and substance-based regulation of *resource risks* seems quite plausible.

Yet, in order to exempt things from the waste regime (or, more accurately, to dispense with such a regime at all), one *has to know exactly* what the future, secondary use of things is going to be.[276] In practice, however, this is an unfeasible task, especially in light of the subjective concept of waste and the corollary possibility of the holder evading the applicable environmental rules with a view to proceeding to *uncontrolled disposal* once the thing fulfils no purpose for him or her anymore.[277] It is precisely this risk of loopholes that, on the one hand, justifies *waste*-related controls *in addition to* facility-, media-, product- and/or substance-related ones, as illustrated by the regulation of illegal export of waste, and, on the other hand, explains the generic, discard-based definition of waste as '*any*thing that *any*one intends to destine for *any* purpose'.[278]

Whilst this *evasion risk* (*Ausweichrisiko*[279]) gives ground for the creation of a waste regime in spite of both its 'counterproductive discrimination of recovery'[280] when it comes to tackling *resource risks* and its subsidiarity in relation to facility-, media-, product- and substance-related regulation of *environmental risks*, waste law must necessarily cease to apply whenever and as soon as uncertainty as to the secondary use of a thing is removed,[281] even if removal can only take place on a case-by-case basis due to the relative nature of waste.

This solution is put forward by some academic commentary[282] and has more recently found its way into legislation in the European Union, albeit

---

275 See Reese, 2009b, p. 137.

276 Reese, 2009a, p. 1074; Aragão, 2006, p. 520.

277 See Birn, 1992, p. 420; Cheyne and Purdue, 1995, p. 151-152.

278 Similarly, see Aragão, 2006, p. 520; Koch and Reese, 2005, p. 446.

279 Reese, 2009a, p. 1074; Reese, 2009b, p. 139.

280 Koch and Reese, 2000, p. 305.

281 Reese, 2009a, p. 1074.

282 Aragão (2006, p. 471-568), in a thorough study of Portuguese environmental and waste law made over a decade ago, examined the *waste* duties imposed on both waste producers and managers *vis-à-vis* the overall *environmental* duties imposed on waste producers, whence she concluded that the *certainty* of recovery

in slightly less precise terms, perhaps owing to the fact that it represents a codification of ECJ's case law.[283] The WFD sets forth two cases in which a thing is not to be subjected to waste law, namely when it may be regarded as not being waste but as being a by-product (Article 5), and when it shall cease to be waste (Article 6).

The first situation deals exclusively with things resulting from a production process (i.e. 'production waste'). Article 5(1) of the WFD sets out four conditions that such things must meet in order to be able to escape the waste regime: further use of the thing is certain; the thing can be used directly without any further processing other than normal industrial practice; the thing is produced as an integral part of a production process; further use is lawful, i.e. the thing fulfils all relevant product, environmental and health protection requirements for its specific use and will not lead to overall adverse environmental or human health impacts.

As for the end-of-waste status, Article 6(1) of the WFD prescribes that the thing must not only have undergone a recovery operation but also satisfy specific criteria that are to be developed in accordance with the following conditions: the thing is used for specific purposes; a market or demand exists for such a thing; the thing fulfils the technical requirements for the specific purposes and meets the existing legislation and standards applicable to products; the use of the thing will not lead to overall adverse environmental or human health impacts.

In terms of content and structure, both provisions are very similar in respect of the requirements they impose for a thing to no longer be considered waste. The conditions and criteria laid down by Article 5(1) and Article 6(1) of the WFD revolve around the two aspects behind the erosion of the concept of waste discussed above, namely certainty as to

---

of materials shall be *presumed*, with the consequent *inapplicability of the waste regime*, in any of the following situations: firstly, if the *transport* of a thing is either unnecessary and occurs internally within a facility (cleaner production) or takes place 'privately' between two economically and legally distinct companies via contiguous pathways belonging to them, i.e. to which third parties (can) have no access (industrial endosymbiosis); secondly, if there is a *contract* filed before the commercial registrar between those producing waste and those recovering/managing it, whereby the latter binds themselves to either recover the waste generated by the former in a way that is eco-compatible (industrial ectosymbiosis) or find a third party to do so (industrial ecosystem). Because waste law does not apply in these four situations, the author coherently refers to materials (or things) not as waste, but as internal sub-products, endogenous sub-products, exogenous sub-products, and secondary raw materials, respectively.

283 van Calster, 2015, p. 45-49 and 64-66.

the future use of the thing and the subsidiarity of waste law in relation to environmental law.[284]

The precept of certainty of use[285] in order for the inapplicability of waste law to take effect is basically enunciated by point (a) of Article 5(1) and reinforced by point (a) of Article 6(1). Point (b) of Article 6(1) illustrates that the existence of use for the thing can be ascertained in economic terms ('existing market or demand').

Articles 5(1)(d), 6(1)(c) and 6(1)(d) of the WFD, in turn, refer to the use of the thing fulfilling all other environmental-legal requirements in force, notably product-related ones,[286] and not leading to overall adverse environmental or human health impacts. In this sense, the unnecessity of *waste*-related standards in the presence of other facility-, media-, product- and substance-related environmental provisions is admittedly accounted for.

So far, end-of-waste criteria under Article 6 of the WFD have been established for scrap metal (iron, steel and aluminium)[287], glass cullet[288] and

284 An exception is the conditions established in points (b) and (c) of Article 5 on by-products, which limit themselves to make it clear that said provision is applicable only to things resulting from production processes (i.e. 'production wastes').

285 Similarly, see Lee, 2005, p. 218.

286 To be sure, Article 6(5) of the WFD, as amended by Directive (EU) 2018/851, prescribes that the natural or legal person who either uses, for the first time, a material that has ceased to be waste and that has not been placed on the market or places a material on the market for the first time after it has ceased to be waste shall ensure that the material meets relevant requirements under the applicable *chemical and product related regulation*.

287 See Council Regulation (EU) 333/2011 (OJ L 94, 8 April 2011, p. 2).

288 See Commission Regulation (EU) 1179/2012 (OJ L 337, 11 December 2012, p. 31).

copper scrap[289].[290][291] In order to be exempted from the waste regime, such materials must, in a nutshell, be recoverable and not hazardous, be treated and satisfy certain quality conditions after recovery. More elaborately, end-of-waste regulations for these three materials stipulate the following: which wastes may and which may not[292] 'lose their wasteness'; which properties, namely recoverability and non-hazardousness, materials must have[293] and to which treatment they must have been previously subjected[294] before undergoing a recovery operation; which quality requirements the so-called recovery product (*Verwertungsprodukt*), that is, the secondary raw material (i.e. ex-waste) resulting from the recovery operation, must meet[295] to be apt for further use (as input in production processes).

---

289 See Commission Regulation (EU) 715/2013 (OJ L 201, 26 July 2013, p. 14).

290 In the wake of article 6(2) of the WFD prior to the amendment made by Directive (EU) 2018/851 (OJ L 150, 14 June 2018, p. 109), which called for end-of-waste specific criteria to be considered, among others, at least for aggregates, paper, glass, metal and tyres, technical studies have been conducted by JRC's Institute for Prospective Technological Studies (IPTS) also for waste paper, biodegradable waste and waste plastic. See information available at <http://susproc.jrc.ec.europa.eu/activities/waste/index.html>, last accessed on 15 February 2016. Council Regulation (EU) 333/2001, Commission Regulation (EU) 1179/2012, and Commission Regulation (EU) 715/2013 shall be henceforth collectively referred to as 'end-of-waste regulations'.

291 Directive (EU) 2018/851 amending the WFD requires the EU Commission to monitor the development of national end-of-waste criteria in Member States, and to assess the need to develop Union-wide criteria (Article 6(2) of the WFD). Where criteria have not been set at Union level, Member States may establish national criteria and notify the EU Commission thereof (Article 6(3) of the WFD). Where criteria have not been set at either Union or national level, Member States decide whether waste has ceased to be waste on a case-by-case basis and such decisions need not be notified (Article 6(4) of the WFD).

292 The materials referred to in point 2.3 of Annexes I and II of Council Regulation (EU) 333/2011 as well as the ones referred to in points 2.2 and 2.3 of Annex I of Commission Regulation (EU) 1179/2012 and Commission Regulation (EU) 715/2013, respectively, may not be used as input for recovery operations, and therefore lose their waste status, since they are considered as being 'waste for disposal' under EU waste law.

293 See section "waste used as input for the recovery operation" of the annexes of the end-of-waste regulations.

294 See section 'treatment processes and techniques' of the annexes to the end-of-waste regulations.

295 See section 'quality of [scrap, glass cullet and/or copper scrap, as the case may be] resulting from the recovery operation' of the annexes of the end-of-waste regulations.

The rules above govern both the upstream and mainly the downstream stages of recovery operations by establishing product- and most notably substance-related standards on the 'waste-to-product' materials. In fact, some of these standards are made in reference to requirements from other EU legislative acts.[296] Recovery operations themselves, which are regulated by other facility- and media-related provisions,[297] are not covered by end-of-waste regulations.

End-of-waste regulations are practical illustrations of the subsidiary role of waste law in relation to environmental law: *prima facie* the more things and their use are subjected to substance-, product-, media- and facility-related environmental legal standards, the less they need to be regulated *once again* as they reach the final stage of their life cycle, the more they can be assigned a secondary use, and the less primary uses of (to-be-produced) things or (to-be-extracted) materials are necessary. It is an attempt – albeit casuistic, for it only applies to concretely specified things the use of which is certain – of *integrating* environmental regulation to maximise the attainment of both aims of human health and environmental protection, on the one hand, and resource conservation, on the other hand.

---

296 References to other EU legal requirements are found in all three end-of-waste regulations. For instance, for all the three materials concerned, the recovery product (i.e. the secondary raw material resulting from recovery or ex-waste) must neither display any of the hazardous properties listed in Annex III of the WFD nor exceed the concentration limits imposed by Article 2 of Commission Decision 2000/532/EC establishing a list of hazardous waste. In addition, the recovery material must comply with the limit values for persistent organic pollutants (hereinafter 'POPs') laid down in Annex IV to Regulation (EC) 850/2004 (OJ L 158, 30 April 2004, p. 7, amended by Commission Regulation (EC) 756/2010, OJ L 223, 24 August 2010, p. 20). Another example is the treatment requirements in the case of both scrap metal and copper scrap: the waste material to be used as input for the recovery operation, if originating from end-of-life vehicles or waste electrical and electronic equipment (hereinafter 'WEEE'), must undergo all treatments required respectively by article 6 of Directive 2000/53/EC on end-of-life vehicles (OJ L 269, 21 October 2000, p. 34) and article 8 of Directive 2012/19/EU on WEEE (OJ L 197, 24 July 2012, p. 38) before being subjected to recovery. Both provisions, in turn, make further reference to minimum technical requirements set out in annexes to the two directives.

297 See Directive 2010/75/EU on industrial emissions (integrated pollution prevention control), especially point 5 of Annex I.

On top of that, the subsidiarity of waste law points out that the very concept of waste is a legal creation,[298] for the attribute 'waste' is a regulatory artifice with the sole purpose of indicating that things *de lege lata* shall – but *de lege ferenda* only might – fall within a specific, *additional* environmental legal regime.

D. *Waste prevention through product ecodesign*

If waste is a legal artifice and if in truly integrated environmental law the regulation of waste is redundant since other environmental laws already properly apply at the different stages of the economic circuit preceding the final (i.e. waste) stage, then one may consider abandoning the very concept of waste, dispensing with waste law altogether and focusing instead on product-, material- and substance-related environmental law. After all, before a thing becomes waste it is nothing but a product composed of materials and substances. *Anti-waste law*, better known as *waste prevention law* and which is at the core of IWM, is by definition product-, material- and substance-related environmental law, at least as regards consumer waste.

With reason, Article 3, point 11, of the WFD defines waste prevention by referring to a substance, material or product. The Brazilian PNRS provides no such definition. It only enunciates prevention as one of the guiding principles of the Brazilian waste policy (Article 6, point I). A distinction must be made between *quantitative* prevention (Article 3(12)(a) of the WFD), which is the focus of the present study,[299] and *qualitative* prevention (Article 3(12)(c) of the WFD). The former concerns the reduction in the *amount* of substances, materials or products becoming waste whereas the latter concerns the reduction of their *hazardousness*. Both categories must be distinguished from the prevention of the impacts of the generated waste on the environment and human health (Article 3(12)(b) of the WFD), which is improperly included by the WFD in the legal definition of 'waste prevention'.

Whilst waste prevention is defined negatively, that is, as something that is not wanted, it is best grasped and implemented positively, that is, as that which is wanted instead. For, at least from the point of view of making

---

298 In this sense, see Krämer, 2015, 370. See also Klöck, 2001, p. 102 (reporting Schenkel's reference to waste as a legal category).

299 For this reason, unless otherwise specified, the expression 'waste prevention' shall hereinafter refer to quantitative prevention.

waste prevention an operable notion, it is conceptually and practically much easier to take positive actions with a view to attaining a desirable state of affairs than simply stating what is not desirable.[300] In this sense, it has been stated that 'waste prevention is [...] defined by changes'[301], more specifically by modifications in the production and consumption of materials and products so that no or less waste is generated. Illustrative of this finding is the fact that Article 3(12)(a) of the WFD mentions product reuse and extension of product lifespan as two examples of how to reduce the amount of waste generated. The underlying idea is that durable and reusable products need not be discarded and thus do not become waste.[302]

Waste prevention revolves around a discussion on alternative ways of producing and consuming things – that is, products and the materials needed to make products – *before* we get rid of them, so that less things end up being got rid of. From a *product* life cycle perspective, one is automatically forced to look upstream of the discarding of things. Before things are discarded, they are used. Things go out of use (and are hence discarded) for different reasons, including and most frequently, but not limited to, when they break down or wear out.[303] If things are repairable (and factually repaired), then they may be reused[304] instead of being discarded and therefore do not become waste. Product reparability is thus the

300 I thank my German supervisor, Prof. Dr. Gerd Winter, for insistently drawing my attention to this point.

301 See OECD, 2000, p. 40.

302 But durability and reparability also diminish the need for new products and consequently the need for materials to make them. Strictly speaking, preventing things from becoming waste (quantitative waste prevention) may be distinguished from preventing things from being used (quantitative material prevention). Similarly, see Aragão, 2006, p. 370.

303 This is known as obsolescence of quality (or physical obsolescence). Two other situations are obsolescence of function (or functional obsolescence) and obsolescence of desirability (or psychological obsolescence). The former takes place when a new thing is introduced that performs the same function(s) of the existing thing, only better. The latter occurs when a thing, despite being sound in terms of performance or quality, 'wears out in our minds' because styling (i.e. fashion) changes make it less desirable. See Packard, 1960.

304 Reuse may be defined as 'the multiple use of a [thing] in its original form, for its original purpose or for an alternative, with or without reconditioning' (see OECD, 2000, p. 39). This definition is broader than that provided by the WFD (see footnote 190, *supra*) and somewhat similar to the one provided by the PNRS (see footnote 197, *supra*). A typical instance of re-using things that are functionally or psychologically obsolete (see previous footnote) is the so-called 'second-hand use'. See also Prelle, 2008.

first waste prevention strategy. Of course, the more durable things are, the longer they may be used and the longer it takes for them to break down or wear out. Product durability is the second waste prevention strategy. Taking one step further but still focusing on the product use stage, another waste prevention strategy is what could be called the collective use of things as opposed to individual use. Apart from being reparable/repaired and lasting/being used longer, a product may serve more than one person, that is, it may be used collectively, as illustrated by communal washing centres and cars as well as tool sharing schemes.[305] Whether as a result of servicing business strategies (i.e. the provision of a product's function rather than the material product itself, that is, the selling of services instead of products) or collaborative consumption schemes (e.g. sharing, exchanging, swapping, bartering), collective use reduces the number of products required to deliver a given function (waste prevention) and consequently alleviates the consumption of materials (materials prevention) while satisfying human needs.[306] Much as fewer products might be needed under collective use patterns, some products are still necessary. A further waste and materials prevention strategy is then to reduce the material intensity of the products needed. Lightweighting and miniaturisation are examples of making products less resource intensive. Beyond this strategy the only way the consumption of products can be virtually eliminated is through total dematerialisation[307] (e.g. the replacement of print with digital media) or if the need for the product or the function it provides ceases to exist (e.g. by eliminating interim packaging such as toothpaste cartons or simply renouncing consumption). Of course, all these strategies intersect. For example, durability is clearly coadjutant of collective use, which, in turn, has a dematerialisation aspect.

This five-step model may be summarised by asking (1) whether there is a *need* to be satisfied; if so, (2) whether the existing need can be satisfied by a *service* instead of a product; if not, (3) whether the needed product can

---

305 See, for instance, Mont, 2004.

306 See, for instance, Edbring, Lehner and Mont, 2016; Plepys, Heiskanen and Mont, 2015.

307 Broadly speaking, dematerialisation may be understood as the decoupling of economic development from the use of the environment as a source, that is, the de-linking of production and consumption activities from the use of natural resources. In this broad sense, the prevention strategies mentioned above are all examples of dematerialisation, for they entail a reduction in material consumption. In a narrower sense, it means the virtual elimination of the material (i.e. physical) substrate of a given economic activity. See, for instance, Aragão, 2012.

be *made less resource-intensive*; in any case, whether the product can be *used* (4.1) collectively instead of individually as well as (4.2) for a longer period of time, both/either (4.2.1) because it lasts longer and/or (4.2.2) because it can be repaired when it breaks down or wears out; and finally (5) whether the product need be discarded. Graphically:

The outlined model looks at *products* backwards from their discard through their use to their making, including the question of whether they are needed in the first place. Waste prevention strategies thus comprise extremely wide-ranging measures affecting both the production and the consumption of products and materials. Very illustrative of this extensive range is Annex IV of the WFD, which contains many examples of waste prevention measures that can affect different stages of a product cycle, including the design, production (i.e. manufacturing), distribution and consumption/use phases.

Annex IV of the WFD is to be understood in connection with the so-called waste prevention programs. In the EU, Articles 29(1) and 29(2) of the WFD require Member States to establish waste prevention programs setting out waste prevention measures[308] with a view to breaking the link between economic growth and the environmental impacts associated with the generation of waste.[309] Such programs may be integrated into the national waste management plans, which set out an analysis of the waste management situation in each Member State as well as the measures to be taken to improve it (see Article 28(2) of the WFD), or into other environmental policies and programs. The first option seems to fall short of the waste prevention objectives since product- and material-related measures affecting production and consumption decisions reach far beyond the purview of *waste management* plans. Waste prevention programs should rather integrate a product and/or materials policy.

308 Pursuant to Article 9(1) of the WFD, among the objectives of waste prevention measures are *inter alia* the following: promotion and support of sustainable production and consumption models (point (a)); encouragement of the design, manufacturing and use of products that are resource-efficient, durable (including in terms of life span and absence of planned obsolescence), reparable, re-usable and upgradable (point (b)); encouragement of both the reuse of products and the setting up of systems promoting repair and reuse activities (point (d)); encouragement of the availability of spare parts, instruction manuals, technical information, or other instruments, equipment or software enabling the repair and reuse of products (point (e)).

309 No such obligation exists under Brazilian waste law.

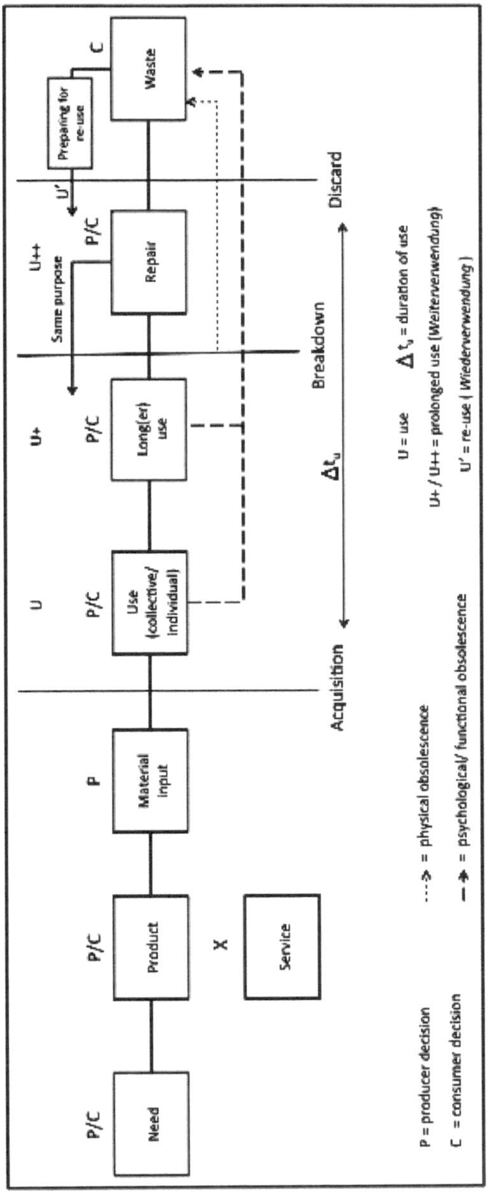

Figure 2 – Waste prevention from a product perspective

In the EU, there has been an attempt on the part of the European Commission to carry out an integrated product policy (hereinafter 'IPP'),[310] albeit not a successful one. The European Commission's green paper on IPP speaks of an approach seeking to reduce the life cycle environmental impacts of products based on various instruments and counting on the involvement of all stakeholders.[311] Despite referring to a variety of instruments, it favours market-based, non-binding and informative ones ('facilitation rather than direct regulation'). In a rather vague and short-sighted communication following the green paper,[312] the European Commission reiterated the core elements of an IPP[313] and elaborated on the reasons for a product approach to environmental problems[314] as well as on the implementation of an IPP. This latter topic is divided into two parts. The first part deals with the mechanisms to establish the economic and legal framework conditions for implementing an IPP, that is, the policy tools.[315] In this regard, direct regulation ('other legislation'), including product design obligations, is addressed only marginally in comparison to the favoured market-based and/or voluntary tools[316] and relates to a few aspects such as the hazardousness of chemicals and the energy use of electrical and electronic equipment.[317] The second part proposes not only a pilot project exercise to demonstrate the advantage of IPP in a practical way before applying it to a number of products individually but also the development of a

310 On IPP, see, for instance, Malcom, 2005; van Rossem, Kogg and Mont, 2004; Schliessner, 2001; Rose and Knighton, 1998.

311 See COM (2001) 68 final, 7 February 2001.

312 For a critical review of the IPP in general and the 2003 follow-up communication in particular, see van Rossem, Kogg and Mont, 2004.

313 Namely life cycle thinking, working with the market, stakeholder involvement, continuous product improvements and a variety of policy instruments. See, COM (2003) 302 final, 18 June 2003, p. 4-5.

314 Firstly, the overall quantity of products is increasing; secondly, the variety of products and services is increasing; thirdly, innovation constantly creates new types of products; fourthly, products are traded globally; fifthly, products are becoming more complex; sixthly, the product can be designed perfectly, but inappropriate use and disposal will cause significant environmental impacts; seventhly and lastly, products now involve a greater variety of actors throughout their life cycle. See COM (2003) 302 final, 18 June 2003, p. 3-4.

315 See COM (2003) 302 final, 18 June 2003, p. 7-14.

316 Preference for incentive-based mechanisms is expressed in Article 4(3) of the WFD, as amended by Directive (EU) 2018/851, which requires Member States to make use of economic instruments to move up the waste hierarchy, such as those indicated in Annex IVa.

317 See COM (2003) 302 final, 18 June 2003, p. 9-10 and 11-12.

methodology to identify specific products having the greatest potential for environmental improvement and hence standing as candidates for the application of the IPP. Krämer notes that the European Commission '[...] published in 2005 and 2006 the results of two pilot projects on mobile phones and teak garden chairs; [but] there was no follow-up on these projects. Since then, the whole discussion on [IPP] largely came to a standstill, as also proven by the Commission's poor implementation report of 2009[318] and a new communication of 2010[319] [that] is full of commonplaces'[320].

IPP's lack of success is understandable, in part, because of the recency of product-related environmental law, at least in comparison to traditional environmental law. The scarcity of legal commentary dealing exclusively with the environmental repercussions of products illustrates this assertion.[321] Legislative efforts to address the environmental impacts of products are negligible in Brazil. In the EU, product-related measures are of the essence of EU law since they are meant to form common rules for the establishment and functioning of the internal market. Internal market concerns aside, the environmental aspects of products have been tackled in a rather unsystematic, patchwork fashion.[322] Three main areas of concern have been identified in product-related environmental regulation, namely 'making products more energy efficient [during use], banning [and/or phasing out] hazardous substances [whether considered as products themselves or incorporated into products], and making sure [products are] disposed of in an appropriate way at its end-of-life'.[323] Reminiscent, and perhaps as a remnant, of the pollution-orientedness of traditional environmental law, emphasis of product-related environmental law has nonetheless lied on the hazardousness of products and the corollary nega-

318 See COM (2009) 693 final, 21 December 2009.

319 See COM (2010) 614 final, 28 October 2010.

320 See Krämer, 2015, p. 224.

321 See Maitre-Ekern, Dalhammar and Bugge, 2018a; Krämer, 2015, p. 223-267; Malcom, 2011; Tojo and Lindhqvist, 2010; Dalhammar, 2007b; Onida, 2006 and 2004; Führ, 2000; Oosterhuis, Rubik and Scholl, 1996.

322 See Krämer, 2015, p. 223; Krämer and Winter, 2015, p. 1607; Dalhammar, 2007a, p. 374; Onida, 2006, p. 243-244. Maitre-Ekern, Dalhammar and Bugge (2018b, p. 2) speak of product-oriented environmental law following 'a long and tortuous path'.

323 See Dalhammar, 2016, p. 155. Similarly, see Faure and Dalhammar, 2018, p. 60; Dalhammar, 2014, p. 148; Tojo and Lindhqvist, 2010.

tive effects to the environment and human health,[324] whether as a result of their composition, as epitomised by the regulation of chemicals, or use, as illustrated by the regulation of emissions from vehicles.[325] This shows a clear prevalence of qualitative concerns over quantitative ones. Curiously, however, this finding does not accord with the entropic lessons from ecological economics that use of quantitative regulations should be made in order to conserve the environment for future generations.[326]

Quantitative concerns are slightly more present in some EU official documents striving for a *materials/resource* policy. The first one is the European Commission's communication on a thematic strategy on the sustainable use of natural resources, which was published in 2005.[327] It draws attention to the fact that the absolute increase in production and consumption levels has outpaced the relative improvements of traditional environmental law, from which follows the need for an integrated, life cycle approach to the use of materials and energy. The strategy has explicitly chosen not to set quantitative targets for resource efficiency and the diminished use of resources due to a lack of knowledge, data and indicators at the time of its publication. It ends by calling for the development of the necessary knowledge database and indicators as well as the taking of action at both national and international levels. The European Commission's communication on the raw materials initiative published a few years later is a second document worth mentioning.[328] It recalls the importance of raw materials for the sustainable functioning of modern societies and exhorts the promotion of resource efficiency, recycling, substitution as well as the increased use of renewable raw materials as a way to ease the critical dependence of the EU on primary raw materials, reduce import dependency, and improve the environmental balance while meeting industrial needs for raw materials. The design of resource-efficient products is cited as a means of achieving resource efficiency. A follow-up document was published in 2011.[329]

The topic of resource efficiency was given political priority by the European Commission's strategy for smart, sustainable and inclusive growth,

---

324 See Dalhammar, 2007a, p. 375; Onida, 2006, p. 236 and 243. Similarly, see Malcom, 2011, p. 494.

325 See Krämer, 2015, p. 223-267 for the best account of product-related regulations in the EU.

326 See chapter 2, section C, *supra*.

327 See COM (2005) 670 final, 21 December 2005.

328 See COM (2008) 699, 4 November 2008.

329 See COM (2011) 25 final, 2 February 2011.

the so-called 'Europe 2020 strategy'[330]. Two key documents on resource efficiency have been published on the heels of said strategy with a view to fostering a resource-efficient Europe: the flagship initiative[331] and the roadmap to resource efficiency[332]. The former sets out a framework supporting long-term, cross-sectoral initiatives conducive to a resource-efficient economy. It calls for a series of coordinated roadmaps to *inter alia* 'define medium and long-term objectives and the means needed for achieving them to decouple economic growth from resource use and its environmental impact'[333]. This is done by the latter document, which '[...] builds upon and complements the other initiatives under the flagship [...] and takes into account progress made on the 2005 Thematic Strategy on the Sustainable Use of Natural Resources and the EU's strategy on sustainable development'[334], thereby being 'a first step towards designing a coherent action framework that cuts across different policy areas and sectors'[335]. Product improvement towards resource-efficient products represents an action falling within such a framework.[336]

In legal scholarship, proposals to reform environmental law with a view to regulating societal metabolism (i.e. the fluxes of matter and energy between the biological and economic systems) in an integrated manner, including a reduction in the total amount of materials that the economy uses, were put forward by German scholars during the 1990s and early 2000s.[337] They spoke of a 'law on (the management of) material flows' (*Stoffstromrecht*). This has been mostly a theoretical endeavour calling for quantitative targets and envisioning the introduction of several material and product-specific concrete duties conducive to those targets. Criticism against such an endeavour is motivated, and failure to implement a law on the management of material flows in practice is explained, mainly by the enormous complexity and dirigisme it entails.[338] More recently, after a

330 See COM (2010) 2020 final, 3 March 2010.
331 See COM (2011) 21, 26 January 2011.
332 See COM (2011) 571 final, 20 September 2011.
333 See COM (2011) 21, 26 January 2011, p. 5.
334 See COM (2011) 571 final, 20 September 2011, p. 2-3.
335 See COM (2011) 571 final, 20 September 2011, p. 23.
336 See COM (2011) 571 final, 20 September 2011, p. 5.
337 See, for instance, Krämer, 2003; Führ, 2001; Brandt and Röckeisen, 2000; Schenkel, 2000; Friege, Engelhardt, and Henseling, 1998; Zundel *et al.*, 1998; Brandt *et al.*, 1996; Friege, 1995; Rehbinder, 1995a and 1995b; UBA, 1995; Kunig, 1994b; Gebers, Führ and Wollny, 1993; Schenkel, 1993.
338 See Ladeur, 1998.

decade of such efforts and due to the emergence of resource efficiency in the political agenda, a few studies conceiving of a resource protection law as a discipline are found once again in German legal scholarship.[339]

Concerns over the utilisation of resources throughout the economy started to be vented in the EU's political agenda under the heading 'circular economy'. In a communication in 2014,[340] the European Commission acknowledged that better use should be made of valuable materials leaking from economies. To this end, changes to value chains, product design as well as business and market models would be necessary, which calls for a policy framework that enables waste prevention, ecodesign, reuse and similar measures not relying solely on solutions at the end of life of a product. In this sense, modernisation of waste – not product or materials – legislation was proposed as a means of moving towards a circular, as opposed to a linear, economy. Proposals included, but were not limited to, the setting of clear recycling targets and a resource productivity target along with the simplification of the waste *acquis*, in an admittedly waste-to-resource approach to 'closing the loop'.

The 2014 communication paved the way for, but was later replaced by, another communication published a year later adopting 'an EU action plan for the circular economy',[341] whereby the European Commission announced the ambitious intention to take a series of measures, including legislative, to promote changes into the whole economy, from product design (e.g. regulation of issues such as durability, reparability, upgradability, recyclability on a product-by-product basis), through production processes (e.g. clarification of rules on by-products so as to facilitate industrial symbiosis) and consumption patterns (e.g. improvement of information mechanisms such as product labelling), to waste management systems (e.g. increasing of recycling targets), so that 'the value of products, materials and resources is maintained in the economy for as long as possible'[342]. More specifically, the 2015 action plan proposed *inter alia* to:

- Impose, on a product-by-product basis, mandatory product design and marking requirements under the framework of the Ecodesign Direc-

339 See, for instance, Reimer, 2016; Reimer and Tölle, 2013; Herrmann *et al.*, 2012; Rehbinder, 2012a; Sanden, Schomerus and Schulze, 2012; Smeddinck, 2012.

340 See COM (2014) 398 final/2, 25 September 2014.

341 See COM (2015) 614 final, 2 December 2015.

342 Idem, p. 2.

tive (Directive 2009/125/EC),[343] with focus on electrical and electronic equipment;

- differentiate the financial contribution paid by producers to producer responsibility organisations under extended producer responsibility schemes based on the end-of-life costs of their products ('eco-modulation') as an incentive to better product design;[344]
- increase recycling targets to ensure high-quality recovery of materials back into the economy;
- adopt EU-wide quality standards for secondary raw materials;
- pay attention to the link with legislation on chemicals, since the promotion of non-toxic material cycles and better tracking of chemicals of concern in products facilitate recycling and improve the uptake of secondary materials;
- address five sectors as priority areas due to the specific challenges they face in the context of the circular economy, including:
  - plastics, which pose challenges throughout the value chain and are thus to be tackled taking into account their entire life cycle, in follow-up to the Green Paper on plastic waste[345];
  - critical raw materials, the recovery of which is to be increased, especially through high-quality recycling of electronic devices.

Despite the envisaged waste prevention measures, the action plan was accompanied by legislative proposals on waste, *not on product or materials*, in revision of the proposals that had already been made with the first communication in 2014 but were later withdrawn. The revised proposals resulted in amendments to waste legislation, including the WFD,[346] the directives on the management of certain end-of-life products[347] and packaging[348], and the directive on landfilling[349], which entered into force in mid-2018.

Early in the same year, the European Commission launched a 'circular economy package', including, but not limited to, the following policy documents: an 'EU strategy for plastics in the circular economy';[350] a

343 See chapter 5, section B, *infra*.
344 See chapter 4, section D, *infra*.
345 See COM (2013) 123 final, 7 March 2013.
346 See Directive (EU) 2018/851, OJ L 150, 14 June 2018, p. 109.
347 Namely vehicles, batteries and accumulators, and electrical and electronic equipment. See Directive (EU) 2018/849, OJ L 150, 14 June 2018, p. 93.
348 See Directive (EU) 2018/852, OJ L 150, 14 June 2018, p. 141.
349 See Directive (EU) 2018/850, OJ L 150, 14 June 2018, p. 100.
350 See COM (2018) 28 final, 16 January 2018.

report on critical materials;[351] a communication on the interface between chemical, product and waste legislation;[352] and a monitoring framework for the circular economy.[353] A report on the implementation of the 2015 circular economy action plan was released in March 2019.[354]

Also in March 2019, a staff working document titled 'Sustainable products in a circular economy – towards an EU product policy framework contributing to the circular economy'[355] was made available. In an illustrative, rather than exhaustive, analysis of the EU product policy, it reached the following conclusion:

> 'It is clear that *no overarching, integrated* EU policy instrument exists that covers the sustainable production and consumption of all products and/or the availability and reliability of information on these products to consumers. Instead, the EU product policy framework consists of a wide range of EU legislative instruments and other policy tools. The policy tools contribute, through varying approaches, to ensuring safety of products and/or promoting sustainable production,

---

351 See SWD (2018) 36 final, 16 January 2018.

352 See COM (2018) 32 final, 16 January 2018. The document explores the four most critical issues identified in the way chemical, product and waste regulations work together and how they are hampering the development of a circular economy: (1) information on presence of substances of concern is not readily available to those who handle waste and prepare it for recovery; (2) waste may contain substances that are no longer allowed in new products; (3) EU's rules on end-of-waste are not fully harmonised, making it uncertain how waste becomes a new material and product; (4) rules to decide which wastes and chemicals are hazardous are not well aligned and this affects the uptake of secondary raw materials. For each of these issues, key questions on how they can be overcome along with planned actions are presented. The communication, which is accompanied by a staff working document containing policy options short and longer terms (see SWD (2018) 20 final, 16 January 2018), concludes by pointing out to the European Parliament, the Council and the Committee of the regions, as well as interested stakeholders that there are legal challenges to achieving full coherence between chemical, product and waste policies and by inviting them to take positions on the identified challenges so that a path towards to a truly circular economy can be defined. A public consultation on the matter was conducted between July and October 2019 (See the information available at <https://ec.europa.eu/info/consultations/public-consultation-addressing-interface-between-chemical-product-and-waste-legislation_en>, last accessed on 31 December 2019).

353 See COM (2018) 29 final, 16 January 2019.

354 See COM (2019) 190 final, 4 March 2019.

355 SWD (2019) 91 final, 4 March 2019.

consumption, reuse, repair, remanufacturing and/or recycling of products, in different phases of the product life cycle. Together they form a *patchwork* providing a substantial contribution to circular economy. [...]
The deployment of different policy tools allows for tailoring them to the specificities of the products they cover and the way they do this. However, to optimize their efficiency and contribution to circular economy, it requires regular consideration of overall consistency of the policy interventions. This begins with considering which products to cover, and how. When multiple policy tools apply to the same products, there should be consideration of possible synergies and avoidance of overlap or inconsistencies.'[356]

The European Commission's recognition of (i) the patchwork character of EU product-oriented environmental law, as acknowledged by legal scholars,[357] (ii) the need to make it consistent with chemicals and waste regulations and (iii) the absence of a comprehensive, integrated materials policy show that there is still a long way for the EU to go to fully transition to a circular economy, as intended by the 2015 action plan. In this sense, efforts to promote waste prevention through product ecodesign regulation, as shall be discussed in the following chapters, may be seen as a positive, albeit incipient, step only in comparison with jurisdictions like Brazil, where discussions on waste prevention at the legal and policy levels simply do not exist, let alone on product regulation.

If waste prevention and product regulation are two faces of the same coin, to speak of a duty to prevent waste in legal terms only makes sense if it takes the form of material-, substance- and product-related legally binding prescriptions (1) not to produce and/or consume, (2) to produce and/or consume less, and (3) to produce and/or consume materials and/or products that (3.1.) are less resource-intensive, (3.2) may be used collectively, (3.3) last longer and (3.4) are repairable. Waste prevention duties therefore entail legal restrictions on the economic freedom to produce and consume, that is, on decisions as to whether, what, how much and how to produce and consume.

Given the *summa divisio* between production and consumption that is typical of the law of our industrialised society,[358] focus is given hereinafter

356 Idem, p. 59, emphasis added.
357 See footnote 322, *supra*.
358 See footnote 14, *supra*. Such a division is nonetheless artificial from a metabolic perspective.

to producer decisions and in particular to their product design decisions. Much as consumer decisions are also central to achieving material and waste prevention (e.g. the success of any durability strategy depends heavily on how the consumer actually uses the product, after all durable products last less if used carelessly), leaving such decisions out of the present analysis is explained in part by the political and legal unwillingness to question them and in part by the economic power exercised by producers.

In a capitalist, consumer society, consumption – whether by individuals, organisations or the State – is seen as a right and this recognition automatically bars any legal duty not to consume. If a licit product is (no longer) socially undesirable, it is the production, not the consumption, thereof that is prohibited or restricted by law. Legal concerns about consumption revolve more around the question of how well we consume, as epitomised by consumer protection law, than with duties to consume better from an ecological point of view. In addition, even if such duties are imposed on consumers, their fulfilment is conditional on the fulfilment by producers of their own duties to produce better from an ecological point of view, for consumers cannot be required to choose services over products and/or to use products for longer periods of time and/or to have them repaired after they break down if services as well as durable and/or repairable products are not available. Moreover, consumers must also know (i.e. be informed) about such availability. Because production precedes and conditions consumption,[359] it is assumed that consumer decisions can only indirectly contribute to the 'greening' of the economy in general and of products in particular.

This assumption about the dependence of consumer decisions on producer decisions is particularly justified by the economic power exercised by producers, of which the creation of consumption needs (for example through advertising strategies) is perhaps the most perverse example. The consumer will get what he or she finds on the market.[360] This power is also particularly reflected in the decisions made by producers as regards the design of their products: from the time a product is thought of and conceived, decisions are made by the producer as to which materials are

359 See Aragão, 2006, p. 587.

360 Consumption decisions made by the State seem to be an exception. That is, the State as a consumer appears to be as powerful as producers in economic terms, thereby being capable of influencing producer decisions towards the supply of environmentally friendlier products. This suggests that legal attention should be drawn to 'public procurement' rules as a means of 'greening' the economy. This is of course beyond the scope of the present study.

to be transformed into which products and how these are to be manufactured, distributed and used.

Considering the five-step model sketched above, attention is directed hereinafter at the design decisions made by producers as to the material composition of the products they place on the market ('step 3') in connection with the problem of resource depletion (producers addressed as users of materials). Modifications in the material composition of products contributing to the reduction in the amount of materials used and waste generated include, but are not limited to, making products less resource-intensive and increasing their content of secondary (i.e. recycled) materials.

A final legal-technical observation merits consideration: just as the waste regime applies only to that which is regarded as being waste, any product or material regime is applicable only to that which is regarded as being a product or a material. Therefore, a legal definition of product and material is necessary for product- and substance-related duties to apply. Brazilian environmental law defines neither materials nor products. In European environmental law, the REACH Regulation on chemicals provides a broad legal definition of substance – namely 'a chemical element and its compounds in the natural state or obtained by any manufacturing process'[361] – for the purpose of protecting human health and the environment against the hazards of substances, whether on their own, in mixtures[362] or in articles[363]. In contrast, such a broad definition does not exist in relation to products. A definitional attempt is found in the environmental code bill proposed by the German Federal Ministry of Environment (*Umweltgesetzbuch*, hereinafter 'UGB').[364] § 116 of the UGB defines products as 'any movable object manufactured for use or obtained from nature, including substances, mixtures and articles'[365]. This wording clearly and intentionally renders the notion of product all encompassing, one that embraces

---

361 See article 3(1) of the REACH Regulation. See also footnotes 149 and 150, *supra*.

362 Article 3(2) of the REACH Regulation defines 'mixture' as 'a mixture or solution composed of two or more substances'.

363 Article 3(3) of the REACH Regulation defines 'article' as 'an object which during production is given a special shape, surface or design which determines its function to a greater degree than does its chemical composition'.

364 See BMU, 1998.

365 The original version in German reads: *'Produkte: alle bewegliche Sachen, die zur Verwendung hergestellt oder aus der Natur gewonnen werden, einschließlich Stoffe, Zubereitungen und Erzeugnisse'*.

practically everything from substances and materials to end products.[366] Whilst this comprehensiveness has the advantage of making it possible to impose legally binding duties on anyone having a legal or factual relationship with absolutely anything (i.e. whether a substance, material or a product), the concrete imposition of such duties only make sense if they are substance-, material- and/or product-specific. Put another way, the decision as to which substances, materials and/or products should be subjected to an environmental-protection legal regime must be made on a rather practical, case-by-case basis depending on the impacts the thing has on the environment both as a source and as a sink.

The first instrument of environmental law looking at specific products with significant environmental burden and seeking to address the decisions made by producers as to their design *vis-à-vis* material and waste prevention is extended producer responsibility, which is examined in the following chapter.

E. Summary

IWM is the protagonist of integrated environmental law. There are three senses in which IWM may be understood. In a first sense, IWM means the management of all types of waste materials from all types of waste generating activities (waste sources). In a second sense, IWM means the plurality of solutions to the heterogeneous universe of waste materials. There are two opposing views as to IWM in this second meaning. The first view considers all solutions as being equally appropriate, with the choice for one instrument over another depending on 'the right set of conditions' to address the 'right set of waste stream components'. In contrast, the second and predominant view ranks solutions aprioristically, culminating in the so-called 'waste hierarchy' adopted in both the EU and Brazilian waste legislation: prevention takes precedence over recovery, which, in turn, takes precedence over disposal. This abstract order may be relativised in a concrete case, but only on the grounds of a life cycle assessment. It is in this connection that IWM takes on a third meaning, namely the life cycle management of materials from cradle to grave. IWM in this third sense paves the way for the reformulation of the functions of waste law as well as the legal concept of waste and waste prevention.

---

366 See BMU, 1998, p. 681-682.

If under an integrated, life cycle perspective wastes are materials, then waste law is law on materials. It does not apply to a specific material, but to the abstract fact of materials following a particular path on which their potential to cause damage increases (waste law as law on harmful materials) or by virtue of which they are prematurely depleted (waste law as law on resources). Waste law therefore serves two purposes. Firstly, waste law is needed to ensure that those getting rid of materials act responsibly so as to protect both human health and the environment against the pollution potential of the things got rid of. Secondly, waste law is needed to counteract the dissipation of materials by influencing decisions on the handling of such materials (or the products in which they are contained) after their use. Human health and environmental protection, on the one hand, and resource conservation, on the other hand, are complementary rather than conflicting functions of waste law.

Waste is a legal artifice used to indicate that materials should fall within a specific legal regime. Waste is legally defined in both the EU and Brazil as something that someone destines, intends to destine or is required to destine for a purpose. This is an operational, action-based concept of waste, one that revolves around the question about which actions (that the waste holder takes, intends to take or is required to take in relation to a thing) should fall within the specific legal waste regime or not in light of the dual objectives to be reached by waste law. More specifically, the question is framed as a matter of whether waste law should apply to recovery operations in addition to disposal operations. The goal of human health and environmental protection answers this question positively, whereas the resource conservation goal provides a negative answer. In IWM law, the first goal can be attained without the need for waste law as long as other facility-, media-, materials/substance- and/or product-related standards apply. In other words, waste law plays a subsidiary role within the broader context of environmental law. Yet, the unnecessity of waste law for the protection of human health and the environment requires certainty as to the secondary use of things. Because this is not always possible in principle, waste is defined broadly as anything that anyone discards, intends to discard or is required to discard for any purpose and waste law applies alongside and in addition to other facility-, media-, materials/substance- and/or product-related environmental law. Waste law can and must cease to apply only, and as soon as, uncertainty as to the secondary use of a thing is removed, even if removal can only take place on a case-by-case basis. This solution has found its way into European waste legislation, as illustrated by Article 5 (by-products) and Article 6 (end-of-waste status) of the WFD.

Waste prevention is best defined positively by changes in the production and consumption of products and the materials/substances needed to make them. It may refer to a reduction in either the number of products and materials/substances becoming waste (quantitative prevention) or their hazardousness (qualitative prevention). Focusing on quantitative prevention, a duty to prevent waste exists only insofar as material and product-related duties are imposed on producers and consumers so that (1) less human needs exist to be satisfied, (2) more needs are satisfied by means of services instead of products, (3) products are made less resource-intensive, (4) products are used (4.1) collectively instead of individually as well as (4.2) for a longer period of time besides (4.3) being repaired and reused when they break down or wear out, thereby not needing to be (5) discarded. Quantitative concerns have usually been neglected in product-related environmental law, which is a relatively recent phenomenon in comparison to traditional environmental law. They are more present in a theoretical endeavour made by German scholars in the 1990s and early 2000s envisioning a comprehensive and systematic regulation of material flows with a view to reducing societal metabolism. Such an effort has not materialised in practice, because of the enormous complexity and dirigisme that such a proposal entails. In the past few years, especially considering the priority given to resource efficiency in the EU political agenda, studies on the development of a 'resource protection law' are found in German scholarship. More recently, concerns about the utilisation of resources throughout the economy started to be vented in the EU's political efforts to transition to a circular economy.

Chapter 4 – Indirect product design regulation: extended producer responsibility

Extended producer responsibility (EPR) has been conceived as a response to the insufficiency of waste disposal law[367]. For this reason, it is often depicted as the central instrument of modern waste law. Despite this centrality, EPR is less about waste than it is about products,[368] even if it focuses on the end-of-life stage of a product. More specifically, EPR is aimed at improving product design and consequently contributing to the prevention and the recovery of waste. For this reason, EPR is regarded as the first attempt to put waste prevention into practice, although it is only one means of doing so. In essence, EPR reallocates responsibility for the environmental consequences arising at the last phase in the product life cycle.[369]

Many conceptual misconceptions and practical challenges about EPR as an instrument of product-related environmental and waste law still abound, both in jurisdictions where it has been explored for over two decades now, as is the case with the European Union, and in jurisdictions where the introduction of EPR is more recent, including Brazil. This chapter provides an outline of the theoretical underpinnings as well as the practical challenges of EPR by answering the following question: who must do what in relation to which (end-of-life) products, how and why?

A. *EPR as incentive-based environmental policy: origins and rationale*

EPR originated in European environmental policy in the late 1980s and early 1990s in the context of the insufficiency of traditional, i.e. disposal waste law. More specifically, it resulted from the aggregate of different ideas that had been gestating in the minds of many people dealing with waste and other product-related problems since the mid-1970s.[370] Its theoretical contours are considered to have been first traced back to a report to

367 See chapter 1, section D, *supra*.
368 See Thomsen, 1998, p. 24-25.
369 EPR only makes sense within a life cycle perspective. See Lifset, 1993, p. 165.
370 See Lindhqvist, 2000, p. 29.

the Swedish Ministry of Environment[371]. In practice, EPR was pioneered by Germany's Packaging Ordinance[372].

From its original conception, EPR meant that responsibility for the management of certain products at their end of life, that is, when they become waste, was to be assigned to the producers[373] thereof. This duty to manage some post-consumer waste[374] streams has been accompanied worldwide by the imposition of numerical targets for the collection and consequent recovery of end-of-life products.[375] Promoting waste recovery, with emphasis on recycling, represents the very first and most obvious goal of EPR.

In that producers started to be made responsible for certain waste streams in lieu of local authorities, which until the introduction of EPR had been alone in charge of the management of all post-consumer waste,[376] government budgets have been relieved of the financial burden

---

371 See Lindhqvist and Lidgren, 1991.

372 *Verordnung über die Vermeidung von Verpackungsabfällen (Verpackungsverordnung – VerpackV) vom 12. Juni 1991* (BGBl. 36, 20 June 1991, p. 1234).

373 At the time EPR was first conceived, 'producers' were understood restrictively as the manufacturers. On the concept of producer, see section C.II.1, *infra*.

374 For the purposes of this chapter, unless otherwise specified, post-consumer waste shall be understood as synonymous with end-of-life products and packaging.

375 See Lifset, 1993, p. 166.

376 In legal terms, hazardous waste aside, the introduction of EPR altered the then-existing dual waste management regime. Before the adoption of EPR, waste generated by production activities – of the primary, secondary and tertiary sectors of the economy – was to be managed by the producer (i.e. the activity operator and waste generator), whereas waste generated by households (i.e. domestic waste) was to be managed by local waste management authorities. Only exceptionally, depending on the legal order and according to certain criteria (e.g. composition and amount of the generated waste), some production waste streams could be regarded as being equivalent to domestic waste, thereby leaving the first legal regime and falling within the second one. Both categories – production as opposed to domestic waste – and their respective legal regimes are thus distinguished based on the *origin* of the waste, that is, according to the *type of activity* generating it. EPR does not rely on this criterion and therefore deviates from the distinction made between production and domestic waste. Instead, it looks simply at the *product* (and its becoming waste at end of life), regardless of the activity within which it is used. By doing so, it introduces a third option into the hitherto dual waste management regime, one that is at the same time *additional and exceptional to* the two existing options. More specifically, this third option consists of having the *producers of the product* – not the waste generator (i.e. user of the product) or local waste management authorities – manage (or at least finance the management of) the end-of-life products covered

associated with the management of those streams now under the responsibility of producers. Such a relief constitutes a *consequential*, second aim of EPR.

Because both goals – improvement of waste management and cost shifting away from public authorities towards producers – focus on the end-of-life stage of products, they are usually referred to as the downstream objectives of EPR.

Less obviously, but more importantly, EPR is expected to pursue upstream goals as well. As producers are made responsible for the management of the products they place on the market once these reach their end of life, it is hoped that they will (re-)design their products so as to facilitate future waste management and hence reduce the costs incurred with said management. Altering producer behaviour towards 'greener' product design is thus another goal of EPR.

This last point deserves elaboration. Firstly, underlying EPR is the implicit assumption about the central role of the design decisions made by producers in determining the environmental problems arising at later phases in the product life cycle.[377] It is commonplace that the ecological fate of a product is fixed at the moment its design is decided upon by the producer. This idea not only calls for an integration of environmental concerns into product design but also paves the way for addressing other environmental problems, both quantitatively and qualitatively, beyond the waste issue. It is in this connection that the so-called 'design for environment' (DfE) comes in.[378] Because product design and other related upstream decisions involve specialised expertise (often proprietary information) that is crucial to waste (i.e. end-of-life) management but to which the hitherto responsible public waste management authorities have no access, EPR serves as a way to bridge the technological knowledge gap between production and downstream activities without having to give government authority over those upstream decisions.[379]

---

by EPR. On the concept of producer and user, see section C.II.1, *infra*. It should be noted, however, that neither waste generators – producers in relation to production waste and consumers in relation to consumer waste – nor public waste management authorities are barred from participating in and/or collaborating to waste management under the EPR regime. See sections C.II.2 and D, *infra*.

377 See, for instance, Webersinn, 2010, p. 269; Kloepfer, 2001, p. 18; Lifset, 1993, p. 170.

378 DfE is not an objective in itself. For it depends on what we want to improve or achieve through better design.

379 See Lifset, 1993, p. 170. Similarly, see Wilts, 2013, p. 1.

Secondly, EPR is aimed at decisions made by producers, not by consumers. As one expert points out, a key premise of EPR is the disbelief in consumer sovereignty. Due to the concentrated economic power exerted by producers,[380] both consumer behavioural change and the ability of consumer purchase decisions in influencing the supply of ecologically improved products are treated with scepticism by EPR.[381] In that consumption is chronologically posterior to and materially conditioned by production,[382] it is argued that consumers, whose economic activities are considered more or less normal and inevitable,[383] only actualise and, so to speak, 'update' (*aktualisieren*) the environmental problems already present in the products that they obtain in the market and which could not be prevented at the production stage.[384] In this sense, the origin of the waste problem is considered to lie in the manufacturing of products and their placing on the market.[385]

Thirdly, EPR can be seen as a form of incentive-based regulation, for it does not prescribe any specific technology or particular product design changes, but rather provides producers with freedom to choose the means of best attaining the desired objective(s).[386] Put another way, EPR represents an indirect[387], 'weak'[388] intervention in the design of products, resembling a performance standard[389].

Even though EPR serves several, interrelated functions, there is usually a lack of clarity around them, which contributes to the obscuring of the existing dispute amongst academics as to the aims of EPR.[390] Proponents of EPR acknowledge it as pursuing both upstream and downstream goals, as do both European and Brazilian regulations,[391] but they contend that the

380 On a legal perspective of economic power and its deleterious effects on the environment, see Salomão Filho, 2012, especially p. 213-215.

381 See Lifset, 1993, p. 169-170.

382 See Aragão, 2006, p. 587.

383 See Aragão, 1997, p. 141. After all, we live in a consumer society.

384 See Frenz, 2008, p. 27.

385 Similarly, see Thomsen, 1998, p. 23.

386 See Lifset, 1993, p. 166.

387 See Kloepfer, 2001, p. 19; Schenkel and Reiche, 1993, p. 187.

388 See Rehbinder, 1994, p. 25.

389 See Lifset, 1993, p. 166. On performance standards, see chapter 5, section B.II.1, *infra*.

390 See Lifset and Lindhqvist, 1998, p. 6.

391 In Europe, see recital 27 of the WFD. In Brazil, see article 30, sole paragraph, of the PNRS.

paramount focus is on DfE,[392] with waste management-related aspirations playing a secondary role.[393] Yet, many deny the ability of EPR to bring about design improvements. One leading specialist in the field advocates that ecodesign ought to be accomplished by other means rather than EPR, which is argued to be best conducive to downstream results in general, and to the diversion of waste from disposal (landfilling and/or incineration) in particular.[394]

The crux of the matter is therefore whether DfE is attainable through EPR. It is in light of this goal that EPR is further analysed below.

B. Products covered by EPR

Which products are covered by EPR varies according to the legal order. The decision to subject a product to the EPR regime is a political one and depends essentially on the degree of contribution the product makes to the total waste streams, if one looks at downstream goals, and the extent to which the product is to be improved, if one looks at the upstream goal.

In the EU, secondary legislation mandates EPR for the following products: packaging, end-of-life vehicles, batteries and accumulators, waste electrical and electronic equipment (hereinafter 'WEEE'), and certain single-use plastic products.[395] Directive 75/439/EEC[396] on the disposal of waste oils has been repealed by the WFD, which now leaves it up to Member States to regulate the management of such a stream.[397] Member States may establish EPR for other products in their national law as well.[398]

Under the Brazilian PNRS, EPR is compulsory for pesticides packaging, batteries and accumulators, tyres, lubricating oils and their packaging, fluorescent sodium-vapour, mercury-vapour and mixed-light lamps, and

392 See Lifset and Lindhqvist, 1998, p. 7; Lifset and Lindhqvist, 1997, p. 6-7.

393 See Lindhqvist, 2000, p. 129.

394 See Walls, 2003, p. 6.

395 See, respectively, Directive 94/62/EC (OJ L365, 31 December 1994, p. 10), Directive 2000/53/EC, Directive 2006/66/EC (OJ L 266, 26 September 2006, p. 1), Directive 2012/19/UE, and Directive (EU) 2019/904 (OJ L 155, 12 June 2019, p. 1).

396 OJ L 194, 25 July 1975, p. 23.

397 See article 21 of the WFD.

398 For a list of products subjected to EPR under the national law of Member States in addition to the four (or five) ones covered by European legislation, see Monier *et al.*, 2014, p. 40.

EEE.[399] Prior to the PNRS, EPR had already been in place at the national level for the former four products except lubricant packaging.[400] After the PNRS, EPR was negotiated and introduced by means of sectoral agreements[401]for lubricant packaging[402], fluorescent lamps[403] and EEE[404].

399 See article 33, points I to VI, of the PNRS. EPR applies *ope legis*.

400 See Federal Law No. 7.802/1989 (DOU 235, Section 1, 12 July 1989, p. 11459) on pesticides, Conama Resolution No. 362/2005 (DOU 121, Section 1, 27 June 2005, p. 128) on lubricating oils (but not on their packaging), Conama Resolution No. 401/2008 (DOU 215, Section 1, 5 November 2008, p. 108) on batteries and accumulators, and Conama Resolution No. 416/2009 (DOU 188, Section 1, 1 October 2009, p. 64) on tyres. By incorporating these already existing EPR schemes, the PNRS has conferred legality to the ones laid down by Conama Resolution No.s, which are *infra-legal* normative acts. See footnote 405, *infra*.

401 Article 3, point I, of the PNRS defines sectoral agreements as "contracts entered into by public authorities [on the one hand] and manufacturers, importers, distributors and sellers [on the other hand] with a view to implementing [their] shared responsibility for the product life cycle".

402 See the Sectoral Agreement on Lubricant Packaging (DOU 27, Section 3, 7 February 2013, p. 124), available (in Portuguese only) at <https://sinir.gov.br/images/sinir/Arquivos_diversos_do_portal/ACORDO%20SETORIAL%20SISTEMA%20LOGISTICA%20REVERSA%20EMBALAGENS%20PLASTICAS%20LUBRIFICANTES>, last accessed on 28 December 2019.

403 See the Sectoral Agreement on Fluorescent Mercury-Vapour, Sodium-Vapour and Mixed-Light Lamps (DOU 48, Section 3, 12 March 2015, p. 150), available (in Portuguese only) at <https://sinir.gov.br/images/sinir/Acordos_Setoriais/02%20-%20Acordo%20Setorial%20de%20L%C3%A2mpadas.pdf>, last accessed on 28 December 2019.

404 See the Sectorial Agreement on Household Electrical and Electronic Equipment (DOU 223, Section 3, 19 November 2019, p. 116), available (in Portuguese only) at <https://sinir.gov.br/images/sinir/Acordos_Setoriais/Eletroeletr%C3%B4nicos/Acordo_Setorial_-_Eletroeletr%C3%B4nicos__sem_anexos.pdf>, last accessed on 28 December 2019.

Implementing acts (*regulamentos*)[405], sectoral agreements or commitment agreements[406] may also impose EPR on other products in addition to the six mentioned above. So far, this has happened at the national level

405 In Brazilian law, implementing acts are legal acts issued by the Executive on the basis of and with a view to elaborating on (and thus ensuring the uniform application of) the laws enacted by the Legislative, which are often referred to as 'laws in a formal sense' (or 'formal laws'). Only formal laws may introduce an innovation into the legal order. They rest directly and immediately on the Constitution. Implementing acts, in turn, are subordinate to and dependent upon a formal law. They are usually labelled 'infra-legal normative acts'. See Bandeira de Mello, 2013, p. 35-36 and 347. That a formal law must exist in order for an implementing act to be issued is a requirement following from the principle of legality laid down by article 5, point II, of the Brazilian Constitution, which reads 'no one shall be obliged to do, or refrain from doing, something except by virtue of law'. Implementing acts are normally, but not exclusively, issued by the chief executive, case in which they are called decrees. An example is Federal Decree No. 7.404/2010, which implements the PNRS. (In fact, though, it confines itself to repeating the PNRS, without really elaborating on it). In the environmental field, Federal Law No. 6.938/1981 grants the National Environmental Council (*Conselho Nacional do Meio Ambiente*, shortly 'Conama'), which is a consultative and deliberative body (article 6, point II), normative powers to, *inter alia*, decide on (i.e. set) environmental protection standards in the sense of quantitative and/or qualitative limits on pollution and/or resource use (article 8, points VI and VII) as well as to establish standards and criteria for the environmental permitting of actually or potentially polluting activities (article 8, point I). In practice, however, many Conama Resolution No.s, including and especially those introducing EPR regimes before the enactment of the PNRS, have innovated in the legal order without being supported by an existing formal law, in flagrant violation of the constitutional principle of legality. The lack of legality of said resolutions has never been challenged before Brazilian courts, though. Be the case as it may, at present, for the purposes of the PNRS, both decrees and Conama Resolution No.s may be considered implementing acts.

406 The PNRS does not provide a legal definition of commitment agreements. Nevertheless, article 32 of Federal Decree No. 7.404/2010 allows public authorities to enter into a commitment agreement with manufacturers, importers, distributors or sellers of products with a view to implementing EPR in two situations, namely (i) when there is no sectoral agreement or implementing act governing EPR for a given product and/or (ii) for setting more demanding targets than those already established by sectoral agreements or implementing acts.

with regard to packaging in general[407], steel packaging[408] and lead-acid batteries[409]. Negotiations on a nationwide sectoral agreement on household medicines are in progress.

C. *What does EPR stand for?*

I. Extended producer responsibility

From a life cycle perspective, law has traditionally dealt with environmental problems *directly* at the stage at which they occur,[410] arguably because in this *stage-specific* approach there is a closer connection between those problems and the solutions to them.[411] Problems at the production stage – for instance, the input-related and output-related environmental impacts of energy generation, mining, agricultural and manufacturing activities – are particularly illustrative of such a *same-point* strategy, since they are addressed by controlling productive activities exactly at the time and place in which these activities create those impacts.

Handling environmental problems at the same point in the product life cycle in which they arise may be seen as an expression of the long-sought policy priority of rectifying environmental impairment at source, which, despite appearing as an established principle of European environmental law pursuant to Article 191(2) of the TFEU, has remained of no practical relevance.[412]

---

407 See the Sectoral Agreement on Packaging in General (DOU 227, Section 3, 27 November 2015, p. 169), available (in Portuguese only) at <https://sinir.gov.br/images/sinir/Embalagens%20em%20Geral/Acordo_embalagens.pdf>, last accessed on 28 December 2019.

408 See the Commitment Agreement on Steel Packaging (DOU 248, Section 3, 27 December 2018, p. 168), available (in Portuguese only) at <https://sinir.gov.br/images/sinir/Termo_de_Compromisso.pdf>, last accessed on 28 December 2019.

409 See the Sectoral Agreement on Lead-Acid Batteries (DOU 188, Section 3, 27 September 2019, p. 115), available (in Portuguese only) at <https://sinir.gov.br/images/sinir/Acordos_Setoriais/Baterias_Chumbo_Acido/Acordo_Setorial___Baterias_Chumbo_Acido___assinado.pdf>, last accessed on 28 December 2019.

410 Suggestive in this sense is Goddard, 1995, p. 192.

411 See Lifset, 1993, p. 166.

412 See Krämer and Winter, 2015, p. 1566. See Krämer, 2015, p. 26, emphasis added: "The principle that environmental damage should, as a priority, be rectified at source […] *represents wishful thinking rather than reality*". In Brazilian

The principle of rectification at source, sometimes referred to as the 'source principle' (*Ursprungsprinzip*), answers the question of when and where to best fight environmental degradation.[413] According to the principle, environmental protection measures should preferably be adopted at the time and place in which negative environmental effects directly originate *or* be imposed on an earlier participant of the chain of causation.[414] It is in connection with this second alternative, which assumes the existence of a vertical causal chain of contributions to the degradation of the environment, that the principle of rectification at source can be enunciated as the prevention of environmental problems at the earliest possible stage in the product life cycle. In this sense, it represents nothing but a refinement of the prevention principle in reaction against end-of-pipe technologies.[415]

However commonsensical and straightforward the principle of rectification at source may be, as one commentator points out, it is unclear what 'rectification' exactly means.[416] How are environmental problems to be corrected? May it imply, for example, the cessation of the activity regarded as the source of degradation? If environmental impairment can hardly ever be staunched completely, to what extent can one consider it to have been rectified? Difficulties also arise with regard to the notion of 'source': how is an activity to be ascertained *the* cause of an environmental problem?

Such a lack of clarity connects immediately and invariably with the polluter pays principle in general[417] and the interrelated discussions as to

---

environmental law, there is no single reference in legislation, case law or legal commentary to the idea of correcting environmental problems at source.

413 See Epiney, 2013, p. 151.

414 See Meßerschmidt, 2011, p. 305.

415 See de Sadeleer, 2014, p. 68; Jans and Vedder, 2012, p. 48; Webersinn, 2010, p. 266.

416 See Krämer, 2015, p. 26: 'Indeed, to rectify environmental damage from cars – air pollution, land use, noise, traffic congestion, waste generation, etc. – at source would mean that cars would have to be abolished or at the very least absolute priority should be given to public transport, the price of fuel be increased in order to reduce the use of cars, restrictions on the making of cars – maximum fuel consumption, maximum speed and so on – be imposed or other measures taken. This would have implications on production, employment, and investments for which no country in the world seems to be prepared. The present technology of catalytic converters for cars is clearly an end-of-pipe technology, but it is not seriously challenged. Similarly, examples could easily be given for measures regarding climate change, waste generation, forest decline, acidification or marine pollution.'.

417 The polluter pays principle deals with the questions of distributing the financial burden of, and selecting the instruments for, environmental protection (see

the concept of polluter ('source') as well as for what the polluter should pay ('rectification') in particular.

Pollution, herein understood broadly as any negative effect on the environment in its resource or sink function, can occur at either the production or the consumption stage. By 'occur' the *materialisation* of pollution as a *direct* result from either production or consumption activities is meant. Under the very first rule of thumb, the person carrying out the polluting activity should be the one in charge of coping with pollution or, more precisely, bearing the costs of pollution, regardless of whom is responsible for dealing effectively with it. It is easier to justify and apply this rule when the polluting activity concerns production for self-consumption or consumption of natural, untransformed goods (e.g. natural resources), but less so regarding production for the market or consumption of transformed goods, which are undoubtedly the most frequent situations in practice.[418]

In both latter cases, besides the person from whose behaviour or thing the pollution directly emerges,[419] the so-called direct or material polluter, there is another agent without whose behaviour the direct polluter would neither have (had) interest in polluting (pollution at production) nor be (or have been) able to pollute even if he or she wanted to (pollution at consumption), the so-called indirect or moral polluter.[420] Accordingly, if production is polluting, then the producer is the direct polluter and the consumer is the indirect polluter; conversely, if consumption is polluting, then the consumer is the direct polluter and the producer is the indirect polluter.

Underlying this distinction is the acknowledgement that, in a world of multiple polluters, it might be desirable to deviate from the rule, accord-

---

Rehbinder, 2012b, p. 196). The latter issue is particularly and closely tied with the principle of rectification at source, for any choice of instrument must take into account the matter of where and when to best address the environmental problem at stake.

418 The distinction is made by Aragão (1997, p. 139-140). She cites the burning of wood for heating to illustrate pollution associated with the consumption of natural resources. As for pollution deriving from production for self-consumption, she observes that, while possible in theory, it is unlikely in practice. An example would be the homemade production of soap from lard for household use, although this situation may be regarded as polluting only in a very broad sense.

419 See Bullinger, 1974, p. 84. The power of a person over a thing can be either factual or legal.

420 See Aragão, 1997, p. 139-140.

ing to which the direct polluter *alone* should pay for pollution.[421] Who exactly is to carry the burden of paying for pollution (i.e. whether the direct or the indirect polluter or both) is then a matter of debate and any assignment of pollution costs to one instead of the other through the imposition of environmental protection measures[422] has to be justified in the concrete case in light of different criteria. These include, but are not limited to, the efficacy of the measure in achieving the desired environmental policy goal, its transaction costs (e.g. administrative efforts, information needs, monitoring possibility), political feasibility as well as the secondary effects of and the existing legal framework for its implementation.[423]

The polluter pays principle, which is originally and primarily a maxim of neoclassical environmental economics that has been embraced by law,[424] stipulates that it is the polluter, *not the taxpayer*, who should pay for the environmental costs of pollution. There are very different definitions of 'environmental costs' in economic literature, ranging from the costs of pollution prevention *alone* to the costs of elimination and compensation for the remaining, non-avoided pollution (i.e. the degradation of the environment in its sink function) plus the costs of merely using the environment (in its resource function) *in addition to* those prevention costs.[425] Each conception leads to a different way of applying the polluter pays principle, but for the purposes of the discussion herein, environmental costs are understood broadly as comprising the costs of prevention of, elimination of, and compensation for the degradation of the environment in both its resource and sink functions.

This conceptual divergence aside, the polluter pays principle speaks briefly against the privatisation of (economic) benefits and socialisation of

---

421 This possibility is already present in the enunciation of the principle of rectification at source depicted above.

422 Within 'environmental protection measures' fall both command-and-control and economic instruments. Fundamentally, whilst the latter (also known as flexible, market-based and/or incentive-based instruments) *induce* behaviour towards the desired environmental policy goals, the former (also known as direct regulation) *prescribe* the behaviour to be adopted in order to reach such goals. The distinction – incentive creation versus standard setting – lies in the way state regulations operate (*Wirkungsweise*). Even though this is only one possible criterion to classify regulatory instruments, it is commonplace in both economic and legal literature. See Nusdeo, 2006, p. 363 *et seq*. See also Rehbinder, 2012b, p. 234, footnote 465.

423 See Rehbinder, 1973, p. 34; Oberhauser, 1974, p. 48-49.

424 See chapter 1, section B, *supra*.

425 See Oberhauser, 1974, p. 29-31, 45.

(environmental) disbenefits by the polluter, regardless of whether he or she is the direct or the indirect polluter. For, under the conditions of the market in which both polluters find themselves, the first-payer polluter, that is, the polluter that takes on the responsibility for meeting the costs of pollution through the adoption of the environmental protection measures imposed by law, may pass said costs on to the other polluter.[426] The cascading of costs through the market, be it downwards the consumer or upwards the producer, does not violate the polluter pays principle, after all both are polluters.

The polluter pays principle says nothing about the level of environmental protection to be achieved, which is ultimately a political question, nor does it automatically determine which of the various polluters should pay for pollution.[427] It only demands that a polluter pays instead of taxpayers. Having the indirect polluter pay is hence perfectly compatible with the polluter pays principle, which, however, does not mean that he or she will end up bearing the financial burden of pollution, in whole or in part, in a concrete case.

Environmental protection measures may, but need not necessarily, be imposed on the polluter. It is possible that persons other than the polluter are made responsible for coping with pollution, as long as the polluter bears the corresponding costs.[428] 'Material responsibility' is spoken of to refer to the adoption of measures directly and physically combating pollution. The polluter pays principle does not imply the material responsibility of the polluter, but does not exclude it either,[429] as epitomised by the duties of collecting and recovering/disposing of end-of-life products in EPR.[430]

The polluter pays principle is therefore to be understood *functionally*, that is, in an *instrumental* sense, as a means of achieving politically desired environmental goals.[431] Various instruments fall under the umbrella of the

---

426 If the "first payer" is a non-polluter, then the law must provide for institutional (i.e. not market-based) mechanisms that reallocate the environmental costs of pollution to the direct or indirect polluter. In this situation, it is spoken of as an indirect implementation of the polluter pays principle. See Rehbinder, 1973, p. 37.

427 See Rehbinder, 1973, p. 28 and 31.

428 See Bullinger, 1974, p. 71.

429 See Rehbinder, 1973, p. 34-37. See also Rehbinder, 2012b, p. 199; Webersinn, 2010, p. 267.

430 See section C.III.1, *infra*.

431 See Rehbinder, 1973, p. 33.

polluter pays principle, EPR being only one of them.[432] The polluter can be defined as anyone taking part in a consecutive causal chain (*in casu* that of production and consumption of products) that anyhow contributes to pollution.[433] It never hurts to repeat: both producers and consumers are polluters and they should pay for pollution, not the taxpayer.

In the case of EPR, pollution (i.e. waste generation) arises at the consumption stage upon the use of products and responsibility is assigned mostly to the indirect polluter, that is, the producer of the product, for the reasons outlined above.[434] It is precisely in respect of product-related environmental problems occurring during or at the end of the consumption phase, in contrast to those arising during production processes,[435] that most controversies around the application of the polluter pays principle are raised, including that of making the indirect polluter responsible. It is only in comparison with pollution taking place at the production stage, in which case the producer is responsible for it as the direct polluter, that responsibility in EPR is said to go beyond the factory walls.[436] Extension of the responsibility of producers to the post-consumer stage thus means a change in their role from direct to indirect polluters.[437]

II. Extended producer responsibility

It has been posited so far that EPR involves making producers, the indirect polluters, responsible for the management of certain end-of-life products

---

432 That EPR is grounded on the polluter pays principle is widely acknowledged in legal commentary. Explicit reference to the principle of rectification at source as justifying EPR is seldom, however. Two examples in this sense are Meßerschmidt, 2011, p. 307 as well as Macroy and Havercroft, 2004, p. 209.

433 See Rehbinder, 1973, p. 31 and 33.

434 See section A, *supra*. One additional reason is the diffuse character of post-consumer waste and the corollary greater ease to control the production – from manufacturing to distribution – of products than the use thereof. See Rehbinder, 1973, p. 111. See also Aragão, 2009, p. 59-60.

435 With reason, the same-point, stage-specific approach to environmental problems, which is clearly focused on the direct polluter, has its place in the context of the production-oriented, end-of-pipe environmental law described in chapter 1, section C, *supra*.

436 See Lifset, 1993, p. 164-165.

437 This understanding of extension should not be confused with Sachs' reference to EPR 'as an ecological extension of [consumer-protection-oriented] product liability law' (see Sachs, 2006, p. 53).

(i.e. post-consumer waste streams) in lieu of, or in addition to, consumers, the direct polluters. In anticipation of the next section, it has been also stated that responsibility means the bearing of pollution costs, although it may comprise the taking of the environmental protection measures required by law as well. The financial burden may be shifted from the producer to the consumer depending on market conditions. This section turns to the questions of whom exactly the producer is, after all it is on him or her that the duties composing EPR are imposed, as well as whether the producer always has responsibility alone or may share it with other stakeholders.

1. Who is the producer?

In EPR, the term 'producer' is basically defined in opposition to that of 'consumer'. This hints at the fact that, at least to a first approximation, the producer should be understood broadly as encompassing all the various economic agents participating in any of the stages of the product life cycle apart from – but usually upstream of – the product use phase.

The consumer is the user of products, regardless of the type of use (professional, private, governmental etc.).[438] European legislation on waste in general, and on EPR in particular, does not provide a legal definition of consumer as it does for producer. However, it regularly makes reference to 'consumers' and 'users' of products interchangeably[439] as well as distinguishes between professional and non-professional (i.e. private) use[440].

The Brazilian PNRS mentions the figure of the consumer but does not define it either. Unlike European waste legislation, though, it does not allude to the notion of user. Nor do most specific legal acts on EPR,

---

438 See Cipriano, in press.

439 Reference to both 'consumers' and 'users' – including the variants 'final user', 'end-user', 'users of packaging', 'user(s) of EEE', 'users other than private households' – is made by almost all of the pieces of European legislation on EPR analysed herein, namely by Directive 94/62/EC on packaging, Directive 2006/66/EC on batteries and accumulators, Directive 2011/65/EU (OJ L 174, 1 July 2011, p. 88) on the restriction of the use of certain hazardous substances in electrical and electronic equipment (hereinafter 'RoHS Directive'), Directive 2012/19/EU on WEEE, and Directive (EU) 2019/904 on single-use plastic products. Directive 2000/53/EC on end-of-life vehicles, by contrast, speaks only of 'consumers'.

440 The distinction is found in both Directive 2006/66/EC on batteries and accumulators and Directive 2012/19/EU on WEEE.

which speak of consumers only.[441] In Brazil, the conclusion that in EPR consumption is equivalent to product use follows only from a systematic and teleological reading of both the PNRS and specific legislation on EPR.[442]

---

441 See Conama Resolution No. 362/2005 on lubricating oils, Conama Resolution No. 401/2008 on batteries and accumulators, Conama Resolution No. 416/2009 on tyres, the Sectoral Agreement on Lubricant Packaging and the Sectoral Agreement on Packaging in General. Three exceptions are Federal Law No. 7.802/1989 on pesticides (referring to *users – instead of consumers –* of pesticides, pesticide packaging and/or pesticide components), the Sectoral Agreement on Fluorescent Mercury-Vapour, Sodium-Vapour and Mixed-Light Lamps (defining *consumers as* both household and professional *users* of lamps) and the Sectoral Agreement on Household Electrical and Electronic Equipment (defining consumers as household *users* of EEE). Finally, Conama Resolution No. 401/2008 contains one mention of *users* of batteries and accumulators (article 4) *in addition to* references to *consumers* of said products.

442 The lack of a legal definition of consumer in the PNRS has led most Brazilian jurists to inadvertently resort to the definition provided by Federal Law No. 8.078/1990 (DOU 176, Supplement, 12 September 1990, p. 1), known as the Consumer Defence Code (*Código de Defesa do Consumidor*, hereinafter 'CDC'), and, as a result, exclude professional users of products from the scope of EPR. Article 2 of the CDC defines consumer as 'any natural or legal person who acquires or uses a product or service as an end-user [*destinatário final*]'. Interpretation as to the meaning of the term 'end-user' has led to two diverging schools of thought. For the so-called 'maximalist school', which now represents the minority opinion, 'end-use' relates to the utility obtained from purchasing or using a product or service, so that consumer should be understood *broadly* as anyone enjoying the use and advantages of it. In this sense, the CDC would represent a general code of consumption, thus applicable to all economic agents. For the so-called 'finalist school', *which has prevailed*, 'end-use' means the removal of a product or service from the production chain by a non-professional for his or her own use (or for the use of those persons subjugated to him or her by domestic or protective ties). End-users should therefore be understood *restrictively* as private users, as opposed to professional users. Professionalism, which implies specialisation of market-based, profit-seeking, organised economic activity, is the criterion for distinguishing producers (professionals) from consumers (non-professionals), with the CDC applying only to the situations in which the latter engage with the former. Case law of the *Superior Tribunal de Justiça* (hereinafter 'STJ'), Brazil's highest federal court for all matters not related to constitutional, labour, electoral and/or military law, has supported the finalist viewpoint. Indeed, consumer protection law, as the very name suggests, is concerned with protecting the consumer (against the economic power of producers), and defining the consumer is important to determine who exactly deserves protection. Contrary to the maximalists, and in agreement with the finalists, consumer protection law in general, and the CDC in particular, cannot apply to all economic agents, but only to some of them (consumers) and in

As for the producer (of a product, not of waste[443]), Article 8(1) of the WFD defines it broadly as 'any natural or legal person who professionally develops, manufactures, processes, treats, sells or imports products'. This definition of producer *sensu lato* supports the idea that the concept of producer is to be understood in contraposition to that of consumer, for the economic activities engaged in by the producer must not only be undertaken on a professional basis (unlike the consumer, who can be either a professional or a non-professional person), but also *precede* the use of products. Whilst the definition of producer contained in Article 8(1) of the WFD is important for drawing attention to the fact that all agents upstream of the consumer may have extended responsibility, it does not elaborate on whom is responsible for what in the concrete case. This is done by specific legislation on EPR.

In Europe, EPR legislation, which now enjoys over two decades of regulatory experience if we consider the period between Directive 94/62/EC on packaging and packaging waste and Directive (EU) 2019/904 on single-use

---

some situations (when they engage with producers). The legal concept of consumer is therefore relational and can only be ascertained on a case-by-case basis. Controversy arises over the protection conferred to producers against other producers by article 29 of the CDC, which equates to consumers all persons exposed to the undesirable commercial practices addressed and counteracted by articles 30 to 45. On the one hand, it is argued that producers may be regarded as being consumers (and thus be protected under the CDC) provided that they acquire or use consumer goods (as opposed to capital goods) and face an imbalance of power – legal scholarship and the STJ speak of (socioeconomic, technical, informational and/or legal) vulnerability – when engaging with other producers. (Vulnerability of natural, non-professional persons is presumed in the finalist understanding of consumer). Since the mid-2000s, the STJ has relativised its 'pure' finalist standpoint so as to allow for the protection of vulnerable producers, the so-called 'intermediary consumers'. On the other hand, it is contended that this extension of protection of intermediary consumers is undue, for they are already – and more adequately – protected under civil law. Be the case as it may, the notion of consumer under consumer protection law is different from that of waste law. In consumer protection law, the concept of consumer serves to determine who deserves legal *protection* against the economic power of producers. In waste law, in contrast, it serves to determine who should bear legal *responsibility* for waste. While the former is excluding, the latter is inclusive. End-of-life products from professional users are therefore *not* by definition exempted from the EPR regime, even though post-PNRS sectoral agreements exclude professional users from the scope of take-back schemes, as epitomised by the case of fluorescent lamps. See Cipriano, in press.

443 In order to avoid confusion, producers of waste are herein referred to as waste *generators*.

plastic products, details which of the persons falling within the broad definition of producer given by the WFD shall have which duties. Of course, specification of the obliged persons and their respective obligations varies according to the product market. Yet, generally speaking, it is possible to identify a few common roles.

Firstly, there is the producer *sensu stricto*, understood as the manufacturer of the product. Close to the manufacturer is the importer, who is nothing but the manufacturer abroad. Because both of them place products on the market (i.e. introduce their products for the first time into the territory of a Member State), they usually have very similar, if not the same, duties under EPR and are together sometimes referred to as the producer.[444] The difference between manufacturers and importers lies in the fact that the former either themselves design and make their products (*de facto* manufacturer) or have these designed and/or manufactured under their own name or trademark (*de iure* manufacturer),[445] whereas the latter simply place on the market products manufactured outside the EU without any direct power or control over the process of the making thereof. A third figure is the distributor: anyone in the supply chain, other than the manufacturer and the importer, who makes products available on the market, that is, anybody channelling manufactured or imported products to or performing a commercial activity in the course of which goods are provided to consumers, whether in return for payment or free of charge, and regardless of the selling technique.[446] Wholesalers and retailers, who together could be referred to as sellers, are included in the notion of distributor.

Considering that the main purpose of EPR is to improve product design, it is comprehensible that the producer was originally and theoretically understood as the manufacturer or producer *sensu stricto*. However,

444 See, for instance, article 3, point 3, of Directive 2000/53/EC on batteries and accumulators and article 3, point 12, of Directive 2006/66/EC on end-of-life vehicles.

445 This comprehension of manufacturer as comprising both the *de facto* and the *de iure* manufacturer is obtained from the definitions of manufacturer and importer, on the one hand, and that of producer, on the other hand, provided respectively by the RoHS Directive and Directive 2012/19/EU on WEEE. These are the two most recent pieces of legislation on EPR and they somewhat refine the definitions of manufacturer found in previous directives on EPR. For a similar concept of manufacturer in Brazil, see footnote 453, *infra*.

446 Once again, the notion of distributor is best drawn from the RoHS Directive in conjugation with Directive 2012/19/EU on WEEE.

it may be impossible or disadvantageous to address the manufacturer in some cases. Impossibility is illustrated by imported products, which fall outside the jurisdiction of a country's laws on EPR, and the solution has been to equate the importer with the manufacturer. Disadvantageousness relates to situations in which it may be more practical to reach and control actors other than the manufacturer but who are nonetheless capable of effectively influencing him or her to make the desired changes in product design by virtue of business interdependencies existing between both agents. An often cited example is the original German EPR scheme for packaging introduced in 1991, which made retailers of packaged products, not the manufacturers thereof (packers or fillers), responsible for the return and recovery of secondary packaging[447] as well as for the return of primary packaging[448] on the grounds that distributors were much smaller in number in comparison to manufacturers of packaging and packaged products.[449] Retailers continue to be responsible for secondary packaging under the Packaging Act in force since 2019,[450] and this has been lauded as successful in pushing their suppliers (manufacturers, distributors and wholesalers) to cut off avoidable secondary packaging.[451] Adopting a broad concept of producer in general, and ascertaining the identity of the producer in the concrete case in particular, is a practical rather than semantic or moral issue.[452]

Specific EPR legislation in the EU sometimes imposes post-consumer duties also on persons other than the consumer and who are situated downstream of the consumption stage in the product life cycle. The term

---

447 Article 3(1)(a) of Directive 94/62/EC defines 'sales packaging or primary packaging' as 'packaging conceived so as to constitute a sales unit to the final user or consumer at the point of purchase'.

448 Article 3(1)(b) of Directive 94/62/EC defines 'grouped packaging or secondary packaging' as 'packaging conceived so as to constitute at the point of purchase a grouping of a certain number of sales units whether the latter is sold as such to the final user or consumer or whether it serves only as a means to replenish the shelves at the point of sale; it can be removed from the product without affecting its characteristics'.

449 See Lindhqvist, 2000, p. 126-127.

450 See the Gesetz über das Inverkehrbringen, die Rücknahme und die hoghwertige Verwertung von Verpackungen (Verpackungsgesetz – VerpackG) vom 5. Juli 2017 (BGBl. 45, 12 July 2017, p. 2234), which repealed the Verordnung über die Vermeidung und Verwertung von Verpackungsabfällen (Verpackungsverordnung – VerpackV) vom 21. August 1998 (BGBl. 56, 27 August 1998, p. 2379) and its successive amendments.

451 Flanderka *et al.*, 2015, p. 120-121.

452 See Lindhqvist, 2000, p. 127.

'economic operator' is often used to refer to the collectivity of obliged subjects in the product life cycle other than the consumer, including both the producer *sensu lato* and downstream agents. Article 3, point (15), of Directive 2006/66/EC on batteries and accumulators and Article 2, point 10, of Directive 2000/53/EC on end-of-life vehicles are two instances. But sometimes the term 'economic operator' encompasses only upstream agents, as is the case in Article 3, point (10), of the RoHS Directive 2011/65/EU or Article 3, point 11, of Directive 94/62/EC on packaging. In some cases, the term 'economic operator' embraces upstream agents that do not fit and go far beyond the definition of producer provided by the WFD. Examples include Article 2, point 10, of Directive 2000/53/EC on end-of-life vehicles, which mentions vehicle insurance companies, and Article 3, point 11, of Directive 94/62/EC on packaging, which mentions authorities and statutory organisations.

In Brazil, neither the PNRS nor EPR legislation know the broad, collective figures of producer *sensu lato* or economic operator. In imposing EPR duties, the PNRS refers to only four individual roles in the product life cycle upstream of the use phase, namely manufacturers, importers, distributors and sellers. As with the concept of consumer, it gives no legal definitions of any of such actors.[453] Nevertheless, in contrast to the PRNS, specific legal acts on EPR all make reference to agents both upstream and downstream of the consumer. When definitions are provided by those legal acts, they are worded in an *ad hoc* manner so as to best describe each of the individual roles played in the specific product market under regulation.

---

453 In Brazil, this lack of definition has raised doubt as to the concept of manufacturer in the personal hygiene, perfumery and cosmetic industries. In these sectors, it is common for manufacturers to outsource parts or all of the manufacture of their products, including the packing and/or filling thereof, or to manufacture products as a trademark licensee. The question that thus arises is whether those outsourced third parties and trademark licensors also fall within the concept of manufacturer. This question has been answered positively by one commentator on the grounds that 'manufacturer, for the purposes of the PNRS, is any economic agent (notably legal persons) that *de facto* manufactures a final product or participates in any of its manufacturing stages, including the manufacture of parts or accessories (intermediary or semi-finished products), or even has legal powers over production decisions so that he or she can control, both quantitatively and qualitatively, the result of the manufacturing process, that is, the product, and consequently also the future waste generated upon consumption thereof' (see Cipriano, 2017).

In light of the above, and for the sake of clarity, the terminology employed hereinafter should be made unambiguous. Firstly, producer of *waste*, better referred to as waste *generator*, is to be distinguished from the producer of the *product* subjected to the EPR regime. In EPR, the term 'producer' means the latter, not the former. Secondly, the concept of *producer* is best grasped as opposed to that of *consumer*, who is the user of the product (and happens to be the waste generator, incidentally). In this first, albeit not wholly accurate sense, a producer is anyone in the product life cycle *upstream or downstream of* the use phase, so that the term 'producer' is synonymous with 'economic operator'. Thirdly and more precisely, it is only those economic operators *upstream of* the consumer that have *extended* responsibility. They are collectively described as the producer *sensu lato*. Fourthly and lastly, within the producer *sensu lato* fall figures such as the manufacturer (or producer *sensu stricto*) as well as the importer, the distributor and the seller (wholesaler and/or retailer). Graphically:

<table>
<tr><td rowspan="6">Economic operator</td><td rowspan="4">Producer sensu lato</td><td>Manufacturer or producer sensu stricto</td></tr>
<tr><td>Importer</td></tr>
<tr><td>Distributor</td></tr>
<tr><td>Seller (wholesaler/retailer)</td></tr>
<tr><td colspan="2">Consumer</td></tr>
<tr><td>Down-stream operator</td><td>Collector, transporter, treater, recycler, landfill operator etc.</td></tr>
</table>

Figure 3 – Terminology of EPR as regards producer identity

2. Producer, product or shared responsibility?

Having in mind the distinction between the producer *sensu stricto* as the manufacturer of the product and the producer *sensu lato* as anyone in the product life cycle upstream of the consumer it is possible to adequately confront EPR with what is considered to be its main variant: shared responsibility.

The notion of shared responsibility originated in the early 1990s in Canada, gained momentum a few years later in the discussions on waste management held by the federal government of the United States[454], and has reverberated in the Brazilian PNRS.[455] It challenges the idea that the producer alone should be made responsible for waste management and instead calls for a cooperative model marked by a sum of efforts by all persons involved in the product life cycle, including the consumer, as well as by the government.[456] In a nutshell, everyone should share responsibility for the waste problem, and apportioning of responsibility amongst stakeholders depends on a number of factors, most notably on each party's ability to contribute to waste management improvement considering their historical individual roles and current practices, therefore in clear support of the *status quo*.[457]

The flaws of this reasoning are twofold. Firstly, it comprehends the producer restrictively as the manufacturer. Secondly, it presumes that post-consumer waste management-related duties are not and cannot be imposed on stakeholders other than the producer. As has been shown, in 'European EPR', the term 'producer' means the producer *sensu lato*, not the producer *sensu stricto*. Besides, to say that the producer has extended responsibility is not to exclude the possibility of other persons – economic operators, consumers and/or even waste management authorities – assuming obligations.[458] In this sense, to differentiate between EPR and shared responsibility according to the criterion of the obliged subjects (i.e. on whom duties may be imposed) is a sterile discussion.[459]

---

454 This is mostly evidenced in the workshop on EPR held by the President's Council on Sustainable Development in October 1996, the proceedings of which are available on the United States Environmental Protection Agency's website.

455 See Cipriano, 2016, p. 187-191.

456 Idem, ibidem.

457 Expressly in this sense, see the proposal formulated by the Ontario Waste Reduction Advisory Committee in 1992, titled "Resource Stewardship: A Shared Responsibility" and published by the Ontario Ministry of Environment, which is considered a precursor of the discussions on EPR and shared responsibility in Canada. Similarly, see Lifset and Lindhqvist, 2002, p. 9: 'In many cases, an appeal for shared responsibility is a call for the status quo, or at least an effort to ensure that the costs of any new environmental programs do not fall on industry.'.

458 Similarly, see Lifset and Lindhqvist, 1997, p. 7.

459 See Cipriano, 2016, p. 190. It might seem contradictory to state, on the one hand, that EPR involves making producers responsible for certain post-consumer waste streams instead of public authorities and consumers, and, on the other hand, that post-consumer waste-related obligations may be (and indeed are) imposed on other stakeholders, including those same authorities and consumers. Nonetheless, as shall be discussed in the following section, EPR consists

If attention is drawn to the apportionment of responsibility *vis-à-vis* the impetus to advance DfE, the differences between EPR and shared responsibility tend to be slightly more apparent. A telling criticism of the shared model is that making everyone responsible renders no one responsible in practice,[460] so that local governments (and thus taxpayers) end up incurring the expense of managing post-consumer waste, which contrasts with the idea of having polluters internalise costs as sought by EPR.[461]

It is true that the ability of EPR to achieve DfE cannot be taken for granted, after all it depends on the concrete allocation of duties to producers and other stakeholders, with special attention to the conjugation of the allotted physical and financial obligations, as well as on whether responsibility is implemented individually or collectively.[462] Yet, under shared responsibility, involvement of all actors in the product life cycle is frequently overpraised and this exaggeration diverts attention away from the focus on the role of producers in achieving upstream goals. In a few words, producer responsibility is much more easily, if not automatically, diluted under the shared model.

Finally, EPR is also often contrasted with product responsibility (*Produktverantwortung*) or product stewardship[463]. For many, EPR invariably involves some or other form of shared responsibility in the sense that, in practice, one or more product-related duties ends up being imposed on almost everyone in the product life cycle. For this reason, it is contended that it would be most accurate to speak of product responsibility.[464] This is, however, a mere terminological dispute, of no practical significance.

---

of various, interrelated duties. Producers may be charged with all or only part of these duties, with the other part being assigned to other stakeholders naturally taking part in the product life cycle (e.g. consumers, downstream operators) or not (e.g. public waste management authorities). In practice, multiple combinations are found. The concrete allocation of obligations to producers and other stakeholders determines not only the success of EPR policies but also the boundaries between EPR and alternative instruments. These considerations are addressed in the next section.

460 See Lifset and Lindhqvist, 1997, p. 7.

461 See McKerlie, Knight and Thorpe, 2006, p. 620.

462 See sections D and E, *infra*.

463 The word 'stewardship' is usually used when responsibility is voluntarily taken on by producers rather than mandated by law. See OECD, 2016, p. 22.

464 Expressly in this sense, see Roller and Führ, 2008, p. 278: 'More precise than "producer responsibility" is the term 'product responsibility', since the product and its 'design and production' is the object of the legal duties directed at the producer". Proponents of EPR rebut: '[…] making producer responsibility into product responsibility holds out the distinct possibility that no one will be

III. Extended producer responsibility

In legal terms, the word 'responsibility' in EPR means a plexus of diversified obligations (or duties), for the most part positive duties (i.e. duties to do something) as opposed to negative duties (i.e. duties to refrain from doing something), which are imposed upon the various participants in the product life cycle. Defining and apportioning responsibility is by far the most controversial aspect of EPR.

Before delving into the plethora of duties that make up the universe of responsibility, the very notion of responsibility must be distinguished from that of liability. For, in Brazil, presumably because both concepts are expressed by the same word (*responsabilidade*), a few scholars have incorrectly and anachronically described EPR, which the PNRS names 'shared responsibility for the product life cycle' (*responsabilidade compartilhada pelo ciclo de vida do produto*), as a form of civil liability for environmental damage.[465] Such misconception is in a less explicit fashion also present in recent Brazilian court decisions.[466]

Strictly legally speaking, liability (*Haftung*) is the consequence of failure to meet responsibility (*Verantwortung*):[467] if an obligation is not complied with, another one (i.e. a sanction) is imposed in its place. This latter, 'secondary' obligation arising from the non-observance of that former, 'primary' one varies in both nature (e.g. civil, criminal and/or administrative liability[468]) and content (e.g. if one is held liable, then he or she must, typi-

---

responsible. Ascribing responsibility to a product fundamentally misconstrues what is usually meant by the notion of responsibility' (Lifset and Lindhqvist, 1997, p. 7).

465 See Lemos, 2012; Moreira, 2008.

466 See STJ, Quarta Turma, Recurso Especial 684.753/PR, rel. Min. Antonio Carlos Ferreira, 4 February 2014 and TJPR, Oitava Câmara Cível, Apelação Cível 118.652-1, rel. Des. Ivan Bortoleto, 5 August 2002. Attention to this misconception in Brazilian case law has been drawn by Cipriano, 2016, p. 167.

467 See Lopes, 1992, p. 9.

468 In Brazil, by virtue of article 225, paragraph 3 of the Constitution and the predominant academic and court interpretation given thereto, environmental liability is said to be threefold, so that the same fact may give rise to sanctions at the civil, criminal and administrative levels, *each independent of one another*. German law, in contrast, in spite of acknowledging the same three types of liability, not only differentiates criminal offences (*Straftaten*) from administrative infractions (*Ordnungswidrigkeiten*), which is essentially a scholarly endeavour marked by a controversy about the qualitative and/or quantitative differences between both categories, but also – and rightly – forbids an action to be penalised simultaneously by a criminal and an administrative sanction: in case

cally and respectively, compensate for damage, face imprisonment or pay a fine). Such a variety of sanctions is explained by the different justifying principles of liability, that is, by the functions it serves, and is reflected in the different existing procedural enforcement remedies. A somewhat more concise notion of liability is the sanction for the breach of a legal duty, or for the violation of a legally protected interest.

Confusion between EPR and civil liability for environmental damage in Brazil exists essentially in two ways. In a first sense, it is wrongly argued that EPR would correspond to a manifestation of the deterrent function of liability: as producers are made responsible for waste management, future environmental damage resulting from the lack of waste management (or the mismanagement thereof) is avoided.[469] The flaws of this stance are striking and several-fold. Civil liability for environmental damage[470], whether grounded on private (i.e. tort) law or public (i.e. administrative) law, revolves around the *legal* idea of damage, which is defined as the *violation* of a legally protected interest. Such a violation *is absent in EPR*, as much as the effective implementation of EPR does prevent environmental damage from happening. Civil liability serves the purpose of prevention only indirectly because of the threat of a sanction – namely restoration of damage – and the certainty of its enforcement, in a way very similar to criminal liability. In addition, the limitations of liability as a deterrence mechanism when it comes to environmental damage have been acknowledged by economic-legal literature, which has long since shown that liability plays a subsidiary (i.e. complementary) role in relation to other *ex ante*

---

of coincidence, only criminal law is to apply (§ 21 I OWiG). However, if the criminal penalty is not imposed, then the administrative punishment is allowed (§ 21 II OWiG).

469 See Moreira, 2008, p. 147, 155, 161-162.

470 The expression 'environmental damage' is used in Brazil to refer indistinguishably to both damage *to* the environment (i.e. harm suffered by ecological goods) and damage *through* the environment (i.e. injury inflicted on legally protected goods other than the environment itself and/or its components). This distinction is a commonplace in Portuguese legal scholarship, which refers to the two categories more accurately as 'ecological damage' and 'environmental damage', respectively (see, for example, Sendim, 1998). At the European level, it is spoken of 'environmental damage (as such)' to refer to the former and 'traditional damage' to refer to the latter (see, for instance, Winter *et al.*, 2008, p. 164 and 168).

regulatory (i.e. public-law) instruments.[471] EPR is a clear example of *ex ante* regulation, in visible contrast to the *ex post* logic of liability.

In a less gross, but more blurred and equally mistaken point of view, it is contended that EPR would represent one instance of the so-called 'preventive civil liability' put forward by a small handful of French legal scholars. Based on an evolutionary critique of civil liability and its limitations in tackling risks[472], this strain of thought advocates a future-oriented liability regime whereby one could be held liable for (i.e. tasked with) avoiding potential future environmental damage on the grounds of the precautionary and preventive principles.[473] It is spoken of as 'liability without damage'.[474] In practice, this means that courts may order the adoption of all risk minimisation measures deemed necessary to prevent the damage from happening,[475] as exemplified by EPR: waste management duties are

471 See, for instance, Rose-Ackerman, 1996, p. 13-39, especially p. 16 (including footnote 8), 30 and 30-32.

472 The notion of risk (*Risiko*) can be understood only in relation and as opposed to that of danger (*Gefahr*). '"Danger" is considered to be a situation which, if not prevented from taking its course, can be expected with a sufficient degree of probability to lead to a violation of [legally protected] goods [i.e. damage]' (Huber, 2009, p. 25). Danger-averting action requires a prognosis of the degree of probability of damage based on objective circumstances (Krämer and Winter, 2015, 1566), that is, a forecast about the likelihood of damage according to the experience of a neutral observer (Huber, 2009, p. 25). The degree of probability is relative to the importance of the legally protected good at stake (or, relatedly, the extent and intensity of the damage), so that a higher-ranked good (or more severe damage) requires a lower degree of probability for action to be taken and vice versa (Rehbinder, 2012b, p. 149; Huber, 2009, p. 25; Hanschel, 2006, p. 184). When the information needed to make a prognosis is lacking but there are indications that damage may be caused, danger is suspected to exist and investigative action should be taken in order to secure information (Huber, 2009, p. 26). Risk, in turn, involves a situation in which "there is either insufficient probability of damage or insufficient scientific insight and experience to decide whether there is a suspected danger and the necessary information cannot be acquired in a predictable or reasonable time" (Huber, 2009, 26-27). Other attempts to define risk in opposition to danger refer to a lower probability (or potential) of danger or uncertainty as to the occurrence, extent, intensity or consequences of the damage (see Sparwasser, Engel and Voßkuhle, 2003, p. 70-71). The distinction between risk and danger as well as between risk and residual risk is not clear-cut (Sparwasser, Engel and Voßkuhle, 2003, p. 71), especially in the field of environmental law, where the probability of danger cannot always be calculated (Hanschel, 2006, p. 185).

473 See Lemos, 2012, p. 151, 159, 199.

474 See Lemos, 2o12, p. 204 *et seq.*, especially p. 205-206.

475 See Lemos, 2012, p. 187 and 199.

to be imposed with a view to reducing the risks that a lack of (or an insufficient) waste management may pose to the environment. Such a viewpoint not only broadens the conceptual and functional boundaries of liability in such a way that it loses its specificity,[476] but also violates the separation of powers[477] in that the judiciary, by being in charge of identifying, assessing and deciding upon the potential environmental risk(s) and the solution(s) thereto, unduly replaces the legislature and the executive in the processes of choosing and enforcing risk management instruments, respectively. As if it were not enough, supporters of this view themselves end up referring to other regulatory, non-liability mechanisms, such as the provision of information to consumers or the adoption of clean(er) technologies, as examples of measures (that courts could rule and enforce) for preventing waste-related risks,[478] which demonstrates that EPR is not about liability whatsoever.[479]

The common denominator of both interpretations of EPR as civil liability is that they are concerned more with non-compliance of the PNRS and the environmental damage resulting therefrom, than with enforcement of the obligations set forth by the PNRS, which is completely comprehensible in a scenario where waste management has only recently been governed by legislation. The fact that implementation of the PNRS in general, and of EPR in particular, does not happen overnight must be acknowledged instead of leaving it for the judiciary alone to regulate the issue.

Once responsibility is properly understood as a bundle of duties, attention is now turned to a more detailed examination of such duties. As already anticipated, under the rubric of EPR typically fall post-consumer obligations, that is, duties relating to products *at their end of life*. This notwithstanding, duties with reference to products *before they become waste* are sometimes also found in EPR legislation. This section deals with those

---

476 For one Brazilian commentator (Levy, 2012, p. 161-167), the so-called 'preventive civil liability' is an attempt to completely reconstruct liability as a legal discipline that has much more sketchy, philosophical than solid, practical value. He adds that the still undefined and rather abstract character of the idea makes it a very distant reality.

477 Similarly, see On, 2013, p. 142.

478 See Lemos, 2012, p. 188, 200-204.

479 Expressly in this sense also Aragão, 2009, p. 25. This finding does not prevent analogies between EPR and tort law. See, for instance, Kalimo *et al.*, 2012, p. 282-283. From a law and economics perspective, see also Lidgren and Skogh, 1996.

downstream duties only, with the *upstream* obligations being looked at later on.[480]

Based on the *content* of the duties that make up EPR, responsibility is said to be *physical*, *financial* or *informational*.[481] Each of these three categories are analysed below in light of both European and Brazilian legislation. Analysis does not focus on those duties imposed exclusively to ensure that this threefold responsibility is met, that is, on those duties intended only for monitoring and controlling compliance with EPR duties. Such 'accessory (or ancillary) duties' are only marginally addressed if relevant to the understanding of physical, financial and/or informational EPR obligations ('principal (or main) duties').[482]

1. Physical responsibility

Physical (or material) responsibility can be understood as the obligation to perform all actions necessary to ensure that post-consumer waste is managed properly. Strictly speaking, it comprises the duty to physically transfer the end-of-life products subjected to the EPR regime from the sphere of the consumer to the sphere of the producer (or to the sphere of third parties, usually downstream operators, acting on his or her behalf) plus the duty to subsequently manage (i.e. recover or dispose of) what has been transferred.[483] In between there are several activities, such as

---

480 See chapter 5, section A, *infra*. The RoHS Directive is examined in this section due to its closeness with Directive 2012/19/UE on WEEE as well as its heuristic value, after all, strictly speaking, it governs the (chemical) composition of products, which is clearly an upstream aspect.

481 See Lindhqvist, 2000, p. 38-39. See also the second part of article 8(1) of the WFD, which reads '[s]uch measures [i.e. EPR measures] may include an *acceptance of returned products and of the waste* that remains after those products have been used, as well as the *subsequent management of the waste* and *financial responsibility for such activities*. These measures may include the *obligation to provide* publicly available *information* as to the extent to which the product is re-usable and recyclable' (emphasis added).

482 The terminological distinction between accessories (ancillary) and principal (main) duties is also made by Cipriano, 2015, p. 287-288.

483 In Brazil, the combination of both duties is termed 'reverse logistics' (*logística reversa*) by the PNRS, which is the most common name to refer to EPR in general, and the physical responsibility embedded in it in particular. Article 3, point XII, of the PNRS defines reverse logistics as an 'instrument for economic and social development [that is] characterised by a set of actions, procedures and means aimed at enabling the collection and reclaim of waste to the en-

transport, sorting, and treatment, which are necessarily encompassed by physical responsibility.

The duty of transference can be fulfilled by way of *collection* by producers from consumers or *return* by consumers to producers[484], although it is often spoken of collection in a rather blurred way to refer indistinctly to both modalities. The wide use of the word 'collection' by EPR legislation sometimes obscures the distinction between what has herein been termed 'transference' – the so-called 'first-mile collection'[485], which refers to the end-of-life product's exit from the sphere of the consumer and entry into the sphere of producers – and the further movement of the transferred end-of-life products within the sphere of producers until they finally undergo a waste recovery/disposal operation.[486] The route from waste generation to actual waste management may be shorter or longer and logistic options are manifold. For this reason, the regulation of waste collection tends to be more complicated than that of waste recovery/disposal.[487]

a) Physical responsibility in the EU

In the EU, allocation of physical responsibility by EPR legislation has become increasingly detailed over time.

Directive 94/62/EC confines itself to demanding that systems for the collection and recovery of waste packaging be set up, without specifying who should do what (Article 7).

Directive 2000/53/EC goes a little bit further to stipulate that the setting up of systems for the collection, treatment and recovery of end-of-life vehicles is incumbent on economic operators (Article 5(1)). The word

trepreneurial sector for reuse in the same or other productive cycles or for other types of environmentally sound [recovery and/or disposal]'.

484 The return of end-of-life products by consumers to producers is often named 'take-back' in both literature and practice of EPR. It relates to the duty of consumers to deliver post-consumer waste back to producers as well as to the duty of producers to accept such delivery. Sometimes, however, the term 'take-back' is used in a broader, more blurred sense to refer to what has been here called 'transference'.

485 See Kalimo *et al.*, 2015, p. 47-48.

486 Hereinafter, the word 'collection', when used in isolation, shall mean 'first-mile collection', whether in the form of collection by producers from consumers or in the form of return by consumers to producers.

487 Besides, waste recovery/disposal operations are already covered by other specific regulations, so that they need not be governed by EPR legislation.

'collection' is used in a broad, imprecise way to embrace the transference of end-of-life vehicles from consumers to treatment facilities. 'First-mile collection' is not clearly regulated. The only provision in this regard demands "the adequate availability of collection facilities" (Article 5(1)). In practice, however, the consumer is required to return their end-of-life vehicles. Once returned, they must be transferred to treatment facilities (Article 5(2)), although delivery of end-of-life vehicles by the consumer directly to such facilities is also allowed (Article 5(4)).[488] Technical requirements for the storage and treatment of end-of-life vehicles are also provided (Article 6(1) and (3) combined with Annex I).

Under Directive 2006/66/EC, collection of waste batteries and accumulators varies depending on whether these are portable, industrial and/or automotive, as shown in the table below:[489]

Table 1 – Collection of batteries and accumulators under Directive 2006/66/EC

Collection of waste batteries and accumulators in the EU	Who?	How?
Portable	1. Manufacturers and importers (together referred to as 'producers' by Directive 2006/66/EC), with the possibility of other economic operators participating); and/or 2. Economic operators other than producers.	1. Consumers return to an accessible collection point in their vicinity; and/or 2. Consumers return to distributors (i.e. sellers); and/or 3. Collection in conjunction with WEEE systems
Industrial	Manufacturers and importers ('producers')	1. Consumers return to producers; and/or 2. Third parties acting on behalf of producers collect from consumers

488 In any case, a system must exist whereby a certificate of destruction is issued – by producers, treatment facilities or third parties (dealers or collectors) acting on behalf of either of them – to the consumer (last holder or owner) when end-of-life vehicles reach treatment facilities. Such a certificate must be a condition for deregistration of the end-of-life vehicle or notified to the relevant competent authority in case a deregistration system does not exist. See article 5(3) of Directive 2000/53/EC.

489 See article 8 of Directive 2006/66/EC.

Collection of waste batteries and accumulators in the EU	Who?	How?
Automotive	Manufacturers and importers ('producers')	1. Producers or third parties acting on their behalf collect from the consumer; and/or 2. Consumers return to a collection point in their vicinity (where collection systems for end-of-life vehicles under Directive 2000/53/EC are absent)

Manufacturers and importers[490] are responsible for the subsequent management, including recovery, of all waste batteries and accumulators collected, which as a rule must be treated[491] and recycled and only exceptionally landfilled or stored underground (Article 12(1))[492].

For the purposes of collection, Directive 2012/19/UE distinguishes between WEEE from private households[493] and WEEE from sources other than private households. While the latter must be collected by manufacturers, importers and some sellers[494] (or by third parties acting on their behalf),[495] the following collection options exist in relation to the former:

- consumers return WEEE to collection facilities, including public collection points[496], the availability and accessibility of which must take into account population density (Article 5(2)(a));

490 They are together referred to as 'producers' by Directive 2006/66/EC.

491 Article 12(2) of Directive 2006/66/EC prescribes that treatment must meet the minimum requirements set out in Annex III, Part A.

492 Article 14 of Directive 2006/66/EC allows only residues of any batteries and accumulators that have undergone both treatment and recycling to be disposed of in landfills or by incineration.

493 Point (h) of Article 3(1) of Directive 2012/19/EU stipulates that '"WEEE from private households" means WEEE which comes from private households and WEEE which comes from commercial, industrial, institutional and other sources which, because of its nature and quantity, is similar to that from private households. Waste from EEE likely to be used by both private households and users other than private households shall in any event be considered to be WEEE from private households'.

494 Namely, those who sell EEE the brand of which does not appear on the product as well as those who sell EEE by means of distance communication directly to the consumer (see article 3(1)(f)(ii) and article 3(1)(f)(iv) of Directive 2012/19/UE, respectively).

495 See article 5(5) of Directive 2012/19/UE.

496 See Recital 14 of Directive 2012/19/UE.

- consumers return WEEE to sellers and/or distributors upon the purchase of a new EEE on a one-to-one basis as long as the equipment is of equivalent type and fulfils the same functions (Article 5(2)(b));
- consumers may return very small WEEE to distributors and sellers either at retail shops with sales areas relating to EEE of at least 400 m² or in their immediate proximity (Article 5(2)(c)).

Responsibility for the subsequent management of WEEE lies with manufacturers, importers and some sellers (Article 8(3)). As with end-of-life vehicles as well as waste batteries and accumulators, minimum technical requirements for the storage and treatment of the WEEE collected before it undergoes recovery are foreseen (Article 8(2) combined with Annex VII and Article 8(3) combined with Annex VIII).

b) Physical responsibility in Brazil

In Brazil, the apportioning of physical responsibility amongst producers occurs differently for collection and subsequent management, including recovery/disposal.

The PNRS elaborates on the duty of collection in an illustrative rather than peremptory manner. Paragraph 3 of Article 33 offers a non-exhaustive list of collection options, to which paragraphs 4 and 5 add another one. The options are as follows:

- producers buy end-of-life products back from consumers (Article 33, paragraph 3, point I);
- producers establish drop-off centres for consumers to return end-of-life products (Article 33, paragraph 3, point II);
- producers act in partnership with cooperatives of *catadores* to collect (presumably door-to-door) end-of-life products from consumers (Article 22, paragraph 3, point III);
- consumers return end-of-life products to sellers and/or distributors (Article 33, paragraph 4), who, in turn, return said products to manufacturers and/or importers (Article 33, paragraph 5).

Article 33 of the PNRS has been so interpreted by legal practitioners that the last option is understood as prevailing over the others, presumably because it shares the duty of collection among specific producers in a somewhat clearer way than the first three. Nevertheless, there has been a dispute between manufacturers, on the one hand, and distributors and sellers, on the other hand, as to the meaning and extent of Article 33, paragraph 5, of the PNRS, which requires sellers and distributors to return to manufacturers the end-of-life products returned by the consumer. Whilst manufacturers insist on a literal reading of the legal command, sellers and distributors challenge it to contend that 'return' is meant not necessarily an active behaviour of sellers and distributors ('to deliver') and a passive behaviour of manufacturers ('to accept delivery'), but (also) the other way round, that is, an active behaviour of manufacturers ('to collect') and a passive behaviour of sellers and distributors ('to let collect'). Behind this dispute is the question about whom is to be responsible for carrying out (and paying for) sorting and transport activities once the consumer has returned the end-of-life products (i.e. post-consumer waste).

Specific legislation on EPR indeed reinforces the interpretation according to which the channel 'consumer – sellers/distributors – manufacturers/importers' should be regarded as the default option for collection, but it allows for small variations to accommodate product and market specificities. For instance, although consumers are almost unanimously required to return end-of-life products to sellers,[497] in some cases they are allowed to return said products directly to recyclers[498] or to have them collected by manufacturers and/or importers (or third parties on their behalf)[499]. Once end-of-life products have been returned by consumers, the transfer thereof from sellers/distributors to manufacturers/importers (or to recovery and/or disposal operators acting on behalf of the latter) usually goes through that which, despite terminological disparities, could be named 'aggregation centres' or 'consolidation points', that is, places maintained by either manufacturers/importers or sellers/distributors (or both) where the returned post-consumer waste is stored, sorted (if applicable) and scaled up before proceeding to recovery and/or disposal.

The duty of environmentally sound recovery/disposal of post-consumer waste, in contrast to that of collection, is clearly and *exclusively* imposed on

497 Sometimes consumers may also return their post-consumer waste to the authorised technical assistance (see article 4 of Conama Resolution No. 401/2008 on batteries and accumulators) or to drop-off centres maintained by either sellers/distributors or manufacturers/importers or both (see the Sectoral Agreement on Packaging in General).

498 See articles 9 and 12 of Conama Resolution No. 401/2008 as regards lead-acid, nickel-cadmium and mercuric oxide batteries and accumulators.

499 Conama Resolution No. 362/2005 stipulates that collectors acting on behalf of manufacturers and/or importers by virtue of a contract to which recyclers are intervening parties (article 19, point I) collect waste lubricating oils from consumers (article 18, point III) and/or from resellers (article 17, point IV).

manufacturers and importers under Article 33, paragraph 6 of the PNRS, with which EPR legislation also accords.

Finally, Article 33, paragraph 7 of the PNRS permits waste management authorities to take charge of the physical responsibility laid on producers. This is argued to offer producers the chance to take advantage of the already existing local public waste collection systems[500] instead of setting up their own private schemes, thereby avoiding duplication of efforts.

c) Targets

In both the EU and Brazil, the placing of physical responsibility on producers is almost always[501] accompanied by the setting of sector-specific, industry-wide quantitative collection and/or recovery targets, which may assume different forms.

Collection targets are set for batteries and accumulators as well as single-use plastic products in the EU[502], and for lubricating oils[503], fluorescent lamps[504] and lead-acid batteries[505] in Brazil in proportion (by mass) to sales or the number of products placed on the market. *Recovery* targets are found in relation to packaging[506] and end-of-life vehicles[507] in the EU as

500 Under the PNRS, such systems are to be run by local – municipal and/or district – authorities responsible for managing urban waste (domestic waste plus waste from public cleaning services; see footnote 200, *supra*) as well as waste from commercial establishments or service providers that is exceptionally equated to domestic waste, except for streams subjected to EPR. See footnote 376, *supra*.

501 In Brazil, no targets are set for pesticide packaging and batteries and accumulators. The collection and recovery/disposal rate of pesticide packaging is reported to have been 94% in 2014, of which 91% was recycled and 9% incinerated (see inPEV's 2014 sustainability report, available at <http://www.inpev.org.br/relatorio-sustentabilidade/2014/en/index.html>, last accessed on 1 May 2016). As for batteries and accumulators, targets exist only for lead-acid batteries as per clause six of the Sectoral Agreement on Lead-Acid Batteries.

502 See article 10 and Annex I of Directive 2006/66/EC and Article 9 of Directive (EU) 2019/904.

503 See article 7 of Conama Resolution No. 362/2005.

504 See clause seven, paragraph 4, of the Sectoral Agreement on Fluorescent Mercury-Vapour, Sodium-Vapour and Mixed-Light Lamps.

505 See clause six of the Sectoral Agreement on Lead-Acid Batteries.

506 See article 6 of Directive 94/62/EC.

507 See article 7(2) of Directive 2000/53/EC. Article 7(4): reuseable and recyclable/recoverable.

well as to lubricant packaging[508] and tyres[509] in Brazil. In all cases, recovery targets are calculated by weight, with rates being determined proportionally (by mass) to the amount of waste generated or the number of products placed on the market. In respect of WEEE in both the EU and Brazil, progressive targets are established for both collection and recovery.[510] Target rates are fixed by weight in both cases.[511] In the EU, they are proportional to the amount of EEE placed on the market or the amount of WEEE generated, as regards collection, and the amount of WEEE that has been collected, as concerns recovery. A separate collection target for WEEE from private households also exists. In Brazil, target rates regarding both collection and recovery are proportional to the amount of EEE placed on the market in the baseline year (2018). Lastly and much less commonly, targets can take the form of diversion targets, in a way akin to recovery targets. Examples include packaging in general[512] and steel packaging[513] in Brazil.

In order for government to monitor the achievement of targets, producers and other economic operators are usually required to report to public authorities the amount of end-of-life products collected and recovered/disposed of through EPR systems.

Targets are seen as pragmatically beneficial in that they induce economies of scale, which encourages producers to advance EPR after the burdensome start-up phase, and serve as measurable indicators.[514] But targets are also criticised for the drawbacks from which they suffer: firstly, target setting is a difficult task for policymakers and the determination of target percentages is ultimately arbitrary; secondly, targets are typically static since they are not habitually changed (i.e. raised) when costs decrease or new technologies emerge; thirdly, targets work only as a minimum,

---

508 See clause six, paragraph 3, of the Sectoral Agreement on Lubricant Packaging.

509 See article 3 of Conama Resolution No. 416/2009.

510 See article 7 and article 11 of Directive 2012/19/UE as well as clause sixteen combined with Annex VII of the Sectoral Agreement on Household Electrical and Electronic Equipment.

511 Mayers *et al.* (2011) note that specifying targets in mass terms leads to a focus on heavy items, which may not necessarily be the ones having the highest benefits from recycling.

512 Reduction, by 2018, of 22% in the amount of packaging that was landfilled in 2013. See clause seven of the Sectoral Agreement on Packaging in General.

513 Reduction, by 2018, of 28% in the amount of packaging that was landfilled in 2014. See clause nine, paragraph two, of the Sectoral Agreement on Steel Packaging.

514 See Dubois, 2016, p. 6.

after all producers have no incentives to go beyond the established percentages, that is, they do not collect and/or recover more than what the targets require; fourthly and lastly, targets do not lead to full cost internalisation in the sense that there will always be a certain amount of waste that will be disposed of, namely and precisely that amount of waste exceeding the target percentages.[515]

2. Financial (and economic) responsibility

Financial responsibility is the obligation to cover the costs of physical and informational responsibility. It can be distinguished from economic responsibility in the sense that the latter refers to the actual bearing of the financial burden. The distinction recalls the possibility of producers passing on the costs incurred to consumers via market mechanisms, which is in tune with the polluter-pays principle.

a) Financial responsibility in the EU

Article 8a(4) of the WFD, as amended by Directive (EU) 2018/851, sets forth general minimum requirements on financial responsibility for EPR schemes. Except for end-of-life vehicles, batteries and WEEE, it prescribes that for EPR schemes established under EU or national law producers must cover at least the costs of separate collection of waste and its subsequent transport and treatment, including treatment necessary to meet the Union waste management targets; the costs of providing adequate information to waste holders; and the costs of data gathering and reporting (point (c) of Article 8a(4)).

In the EU, Directive 94/62/EC on waste packaging has no rules on financial responsibility.

---

515 See Dubois, 2016, p. 6-7. As a means to overcome the drawbacks of target setting, the author puts forward the introduction of a tax on the fraction of end-of-life products exceeding the mandated take-back (i.e. collection and/or recovery) targets. He argues that if the proposed tax were levied per product put on the market and high enough to represent, on average, all external costs of waste management, producers would be incentivised to go beyond the minimum take-back targets and full cost internalisation would occur.

The issue is dealt with by Directive 2000/53/EC on end-of-life vehicles and Directive 2006/66/EC on waste batteries and accumulators, but limited to the collection aspect.

With reference to end-of-life vehicles, the following provisions apply:[516] firstly, the return of end-of-life vehicles by the consumer must occur without any cost to him or her;[517] secondly, manufacturers and importers must bear all, or significant part of, the costs of transferring the end-of-life vehicles returned by the consumer to treatment facilities (referred to as 'collection costs' by Directive 2000/53/EC); thirdly, treatment facilities or third parties acting on their behalf are not entitled to claim any financial reimbursement for issuing the certificate of destruction.

In the case of portable batteries and accumulators as well as automotive batteries and accumulators from private, non-commercial vehicles, consumers may not be charged for returning them, nor may any obligation to buy a new battery or accumulator be imposed.[518]

Directive 2012/19/EU on WEEE goes into more detail about financial responsibility than the aforementioned directives. Just as with physical responsibility, distinction is made between WEEE from private households and WEEE from users other than private households,[519] as shown in the table below:

Table 2 – Financial responsibility for WEEE under Directive 2012/19/UE

Financing in respect of...	... WEEE from private households ('B2C')	... WEEE from users other than private households ('B2B')
General rule	Producers must finance the collection, treatment, recovery and environmentally sound disposal of WEEE that has been deposited at collection facilities; each producer is financially responsible for his or her own products	Producers must finance the collection, treatment, recovery and environmentally sound disposal of WEEE

516 See article 5(3) and article 5(4) of Directive 2000/53/EC.

517 If the end-of-life vehicle returned does not contain the essential components of a vehicle, in particular the engine and the coachwork, or contains waste which has been added to it, then the free-of-charge rule may be waived (see article 5(4) of Directive 2000/53/EC).

518 See article 8(1)(b), article 8(1)(c) and article 8(4) of Directive 2006/66/EC.

519 See article 12 and article 13 of Directive 2012/19/EU, respectively.

Financing in respect of...	... WEEE from private households ('B2C')	... WEEE from users other than private households ('B2B')
Collection/return of WEEE from/by consumers	1. Return of WEEE by the consumer to collection facilities must occur free of charge; 2. Producers may be made responsible for bearing the costs of collection of WEEE from consumers to collection facilities.	n/a
Historical WEEE (waste from EEE placed on the market on or before 13 August 2005)	Producers existing on the market when the costs of collection, treatment, recovery and/or environmentally sound disposal of WEEE occur must provide for financing in proportion to their respective share of the market by type of equipment	1. Producers supplying consumers with new products that are either equivalent to or fulfil the same function of the end-of-life EEE must provide for financing (1.1), but consumers may be made partly or totally responsible as well (1.2); 2. Consumers must provide for financing in respect of other historical WEEE; 3. Producers and consumers may conclude agreements stipulating other financing methods
Other provisions	When placing EEE on the market, producers must provide a guarantee ensuring the financing of the collection, treatment, recovery and/or environmentally sound disposal of (future) WEEE	n/a

Article 8 of Directive 2019/904 on single-plastic products is the regulation with the most detailed provisions on the financial responsibility of producers in relation to the single-use products listed in Part E of the Annex. It mandates that, in addition to the minimum requirements of Article 8a(4) of the WDF, producers cover the following costs:

Table 3 – Financial responsibility for certain single-use plastic products under Directive (EU) 2019/904

Single-use plastic products	Costs to be covered by producers
Section I of Part E of the Annex[520] (Article 8(2))	The costs of awareness raising measures (Article 10 of Directive (EU) 2019/904)
	The costs of waste collection for those products that are discarded in public collection systems, including the infrastructure and its operation, and the subsequent transport and treatment of that waste
	The costs of cleaning up litter resulting from those products and the subsequent transport and treatment of that litter
Sections II[521] and III[522] of Part E of the Annex (Article 8(3))	The costs of awareness raising measures (Article 10 of Directive (EU) 2019/904)
	The costs of cleaning up litter resulting from those products and the subsequent transport and treatment of that litter
	The costs of data gathering and reporting (point (c) of Article 8a(1) of the WFD)
Section III of Part E of the Annex (Article 8(3))	The costs of waste collection for those products that are discarded in public collection systems, including the infrastructure and its operation, and the subsequent transport and treatment of that waste. The costs may include the setting up of specific infrastructure for the waste collection for those products, such as appropriate waste receptacles in common litter hotspots.

520 Namely (1) food containers, i.e. receptacles such as boxes, with or without a cover, used to contain food which: (a) is intended for immediate consumption, either on-the-spot or take-away, (b) is typically consumed from the receptacle, and (c) is ready to be consumed without any further preparation, such as cooking, boiling or heating, including food containers used for fast food or other meals ready for immediate consumption, except beverage containers, plates and packets and wrappers containing food; (2) packets and wrappers made from flexible material containing food that is intended for immediate consumption from the packet or wrapper without any further preparation; (3) beverage containers with a capacity of up to three litres, i.e. receptacles used to contain liquid such as beverage bottles including their caps and lids and composite beverage packaging including their caps and lids, but not glass or metal beverage containers that have caps and lids made from plastic; (4) cups for beverages, including their covers and lids; (5) lightweight plastic carrier bags as defined in point 1c of Article 3 of Directive 94/62/EC.

521 Namely (1) wet wipes, i.e. pre-wetted personal care and domestic wipes; (2) balloons, except balloons for industrial or other professional uses and applications that are not distributed to consumers.

522 Namely tobacco products with filters and filters marketed for use in combination with tobacco products.

Single-use plastic products	Costs to be covered by producers
Fishing gear containing plastic (Article 8(9))	The costs of the separate collection of waste fishing gear containing plastic that has been delivered to adequate port reception facilities in accordance with Directive (EU) 2019/883[523] or to other equivalent collection systems that fall outside the scope of that Directive and the costs of its subsequent transport and treatment.
	The costs of the awareness raising measures (Article 10)

b) Financial responsibility in Brazil

In Brazilian specific EPR regulations, there are very few provisions detailing financial responsibility.

Manufacturers and importers must pay for the collection of used or contaminated lubricating oils in proportion to the amount of oil they place on the market.[524]

No burdens should be imposed on consumers for returning end-of-life tyres to sellers.[525]

The Sectoral Agreement on Fluorescent Lamps, in establishing a collective EPR scheme[526], specifies that the funds needed to run the scheme be raised by means of financial contributions paid by manufacturers and importers to the producer responsibility organisation (hereinafter 'PRO') according to their market shares.[527] The amount of said contributions, which are presumably to be cascaded through the supply chain, may be displayed on the fiscal receipt upon the purchase of new lamps.[528] Although, strictly speaking, this rule governs informational responsibility (see the next section), it implicitly permits the costs of the EPR scheme to be passed on to the consumer.

Similarly, the Sectoral Agreement on Packaging in General, in establishing a collective EPR scheme, stipulates that the costs of the actions taken to reach the targets set are to be apportioned based on market share,

523 Directive (EU) 2019/883 on port reception facilities for the delivery of waste from ships, amending Directive 2010/65/EU and repealing Directive 2000/59/EC (OJ L 151, 7 June 2019, p. 116).

524 See article 7 of Conama Resolution No. 362/2005.

525 See article 9 of Conama Resolution No. 416/2009.

526 See section E, *infra*.

527 See clause seven, paragraph two.

528 See clause seven, paragraph three.

whereas the so-called 'governance costs' (i.e. the costs to run the scheme) are to be shared equally between producers (or, more precisely, between the signatory producer associations).[529]

The Sectoral Agreement on Lead-Acid Batteries contains a generic clause that places financial responsibility on both producers (i.e. manufacturers, importers, distributors, and sellers) and recyclers.[530] In turn, the financing of PRO activities shall be governed by the PRO's own rules.

The Sectoral Agreement on Household Electrical and Electronic Equipment regulates the issue of financial responsibility in a more detailed manner.[531] Consumers shall bear the costs of returning end-of-life EEE to drop-off centres, whereas producers (i.e. manufacturers, importers, distributors, and sellers) are responsible for financing all the subsequent end-of-life management operations – from maintenance of drop-off centres through second-mile collection to recovery/disposal – proportionally to their market share. Financial contributions (i.e. fees) paid by producers to PROs shall be product specific.

The PNRS itself is silent on the allocation of financial responsibility, except for Article 33, paragraph 7, which is by far one of its most controversial provisions. According to it, when local (i.e. municipal and/or district) waste management authorities undertake activities that comprise the physical responsibility of producers, they must be duly remunerated for their actions. Both the participation of local public waste management authorities and their remuneration must have been previously agreed on with producers, though.

Practice reveals a serious and still unresolved conflict between producers and public waste management authorities in this respect, as epitomised by the negotiations of the sectoral agreement on packaging in general.[532] On the one hand, local authorities contend that their participation in EPR is *de facto* inevitable, since, in practice, public waste systems invariably collect end-of-life products that should have otherwise been collected by producer

529 See clause three, paragraph five, item a).

530 See clause four.

531 See clause five.

532 In the EU, whether and the extent to which local authorities engage in EPR is decided upon at the national level and thence varies across Member States, ranging from industry-run schemes with no involvement of local authorities at all through coordination between producers and local authorities – whereby the former usually compensate the latter for their (exclusive or shared) physical role in the system – to local authorities having both physical and financial responsibility. See Cahill, Grimes and Wilson, 2010.

schemes. On the other hand, producers are extremely reluctant to accept the involvement of said authorities in EPR. They fear that local waste management authorities will use Article 33, paragraph 7 of the PNRS as an excuse to charge producers for the costs of managing not only the end-of-life products subjected to the EPR regime that are inevitably collected by public waste management systems, but also all other waste streams already legally falling within the responsibility of those authorities[533], after all both categories will be collected through one same (public) collection system.[534] In short, producers fear that local waste authorities will make them their 'hostage'[535].

This practical conflict is behind the legal dispute between producers and local waste management authorities as to the interpretation of the chapeau of Article 33 of the PNRS, which requires EPR schemes to be implemented *independently* from local public waste collection systems. Whilst local authorities rightly understand such independence as rendering producer schemes and public waste systems *mutually exclusive*, in the sense that wastes falling under the former scheme are *by definition* excluded from the latter system, producers conveniently see a *parallelism* between them: both producer schemes and public systems, so it is argued, are equally apt to collect and manage post-consumer waste, each one in its own way. It follows from the first interpretation that local waste management authorities are entitled to be remunerated (i.e. reimbursed) if they end up collecting and/or managing end-of-life subjected to the EPR regime, whereas this possibility does not exist under the second interpretation.

The correctness of the first interpretation derives from the very concept of EPR and the political decision made by the PNRS to have producers bear responsibility for certain waste streams. The second interpretation reflects mere resistance from producers to effectively take on responsibility. Nonetheless, their concerns are not unfound and must be addressed.

---

533 Namely domestic (or household) waste and waste from public cleaning services, together referred to as 'urban waste' (see footnote 200, *supra*), as well as waste from commercial establishments and service providers that has been equated with domestic waste (see article 13, sole paragraph, of the PNRS in conjunction with article 6 of Federal Law No. 11.445/2007 on national basic sanitation guidelines). See footnote 376, *supra*.

534 Cahill, Grimes and Wilson (2010, p. 478) also note a fear on the part of European industry about the costs associated with local authorities' engagement in EPR.

535 The expression is used by Dubois, 2016, p. 7.

Firstly, it is evident that collection and/or recovery targets represent a political limitation to the legal responsibility placed on producers, in the sense that all post-consumer waste beyond the set targets invariably escapes the EPR regime and falls back within the responsibility of generators (in the case of end-of-life products from professional sources) or local public waste management authorities (in the case of end-of-life products from non-professional sources). This fact points to the need to set targets that are not only legally binding (i.e. that give rise to sanctions in case of non-compliance) but also high enough as a means of stimulating producers to opt for the already existing infrastructure of public waste systems until they implement schemes of their own or if they fail to do so.

Secondly, even though participation of local public authorities in EPR avoids duplication of efforts and builds on local authority experience[536] as well as facilitates the collection/return of end-of-life products from/by consumers, especially when it comes to very diffuse waste streams such as packaging, it requires that the post-consumer waste subjected to EPR but exceptionally falling within public waste systems can be identified and separated from the other waste streams also collected by such systems but which are not subjected to EPR (e.g. organic waste). This is provided for by Article 19 of the PNRS, which states that municipal/district waste plans must *inter alia* establish a diagnosis of the current situation of waste generation within the municipal and/or district territory, including the source, volume, type of the wastes generated and options for the management thereof (point I), plus identify the waste subjected to the EPR regime (point III). If, on the one hand, demanding that producers previously and formally agree to the participation and remuneration of local public authorities may be seen as an obstacle to have producers make use of public waste systems, on the other hand, it must be ensured that municipal/district waste plans be established so that the portion of end-of-life products subjected to EPR that is collected by public waste systems can be calculated and hence producers are fairly charged only for that portion instead of unduly having to finance such systems integrally, including waste streams not subjected to the EPR regime.

One possible solution *de lege ferenda* would be to replace the entering into an agreement between producers and local public authorities with the effective drawing up of municipal/district waste plans as a condition of the

536 Similarly, see Cahill, Grimes and Wilson, 2010, p. 471.

participation and remuneration of said authorities in EPR.[537] Of course, this presupposes that producers have failed to meet their collection and/or recovery targets. Still, this would not circumvent the problem that there are almost six thousand municipalities in Brazil, so that any EPR scheme based on an involvement with each of them would be unwieldy. For this reason, another alternative would be to circumscribe the interaction between EPR (i.e. private) and public waste systems to inter-municipal and/or micro-regional waste management systems, that is, waste management systems involving a plurality of municipalities, which is already provided for and incentivised by the PNRS.[538]

3. Informational responsibility

Informational responsibility, as the name suggests, corresponds to the duty to provide information. Who must inform whom about what is a question the answers to which assume different formats both in the EU and Brazil.

In general, it is the producer who must provide information, but legislation sometimes also requires government to do so, for example by means of awareness campaigns.[539] Information is generally, but not exclusively, aimed at the consumer. Other receivers are downstream operators (i.e. post-consumer waste managers) and public enforcement authorities. The content of information depends closely on whom it is to be provided

537 Abolishing the agreement prerequisite is also advisable because municipalities, despite being affected by the national sectoral agreements entered into between producers and the federal government, are not parties thereto.

538 See article 14, points III and IV, article 16, paragraph 1, as well as article 18, paragraph 1, point I, of the PNRS.

539 In the EU, see the second paragraph of article 13 of Directive 94/92/EC on packaging. Article 14(5) of Directive 2012/19/EU on WEEE refers to public awareness campaigns, but these are to be run by the producer, not by Member States. In Brazil, see article 17 of Conama Resolution No. 401/2008. Also, sectoral and commitment agreements generically call on the federal government to participate in the communication programs aimed at making the EPR schemes known. In this regard, see clause four, paragraph two, point 'b)', of the Sectoral Agreement on Lubricant Packaging; clause ten, point II, of the Sectoral Agreement on Fluorescent Mercury-Vapour, Sodium-Vapour and Mixed-Light Lamps; clause three, point (iii), of the Sectoral Agreement on Packaging in General; clause five, point 'b)', of the Commitment Agreement on Steel Packaging; clause thirteen, points II and III, of the Sectoral Agreement on Lead-Acid Batteries.

to and the objectives for its provision. It can refer to either physical or financial responsibility.

Classically, consumers are to be given information that helps them best meet their duty of returning end-of-life products to producers, thereby contributing to the fulfilment of the physical responsibility borne by the latter. For this reason, producers are obliged to provide information to the consumers. Information normally includes the consumer's role in contributing to waste management, especially to waste recovery, the necessity to sort and dispose of end-of-life products subject to EPR separately from municipal waste,[540] the collection and/or return systems available,[541] the harms to the environment and human health arising from improper waste management, the presence of hazardous substances in products as well as the potential effects of such substances to the environment and human health.

Whilst European legislation does not elaborate on how information should be made available, Brazilian legislation tends to be quite illustrative in this respect. For instance, nearly all the sectoral and commitment agreements in force contain specific clauses on 'communication' that impose various measures to provide information.[542] In both jurisdictions labelling or marking requirements also exist to ensure that information, usually about the hazardous substances, is provided on the product itself. European and Brazilian EPR legislation on batteries and accumulators, the RoHS Directive in the EU, and Federal Law No. 7.802/1989 on pesticides[543] as well as Conama Resolution No. 362/2005 on lubricating oils in

540 Article 11 of Directive 2006/66/EC and article 15 of Conama Resolution No. 401/2008 determine that end-users of batteries and accumulators incorporated in appliances be informed on how to safely remove those batteries and accumulators.

541 In Brazil, this often encompasses the localisation of collection/drop-off centres, the necessity and importance of consumer participation in collection/return schemes etc.

542 See clause seven of the Sectoral Agreement on Lubricant Packaging; clause sixteen of the Sectoral Agreement on Fluorescent Mercury-Vapour, Sodium-Vapour and Mixed-Light Lamps; clause nine of the Sectoral Agreement on Packaging in General; clause ten of the Commitment Agreement on Steel Packaging; clause fifteen of the Sectoral Agreement on Household Electrical and Electronic Equipment. The agreements on fluorescent lamps and household EEE even speak of 'environmental education' in addition to 'communication'.

543 Because pesticides are nothing but (hazardous) chemicals, informational responsibility concerning them is regulated much more extensively than in the case of other products (including packaging) subject to EPR.

Brazil are particularly illustrative thereof. These statutes usually demand that information such as identification of the manufacturer, chemical symbols indicating the presence of heavy metals as well as symbols indicating the separate collection of or exhorting consumers to return end-of-life products be displayed on the product itself,[544] on its label and/or packaging or in its accompanying documentation.

In some cases, producers, mainly manufacturers and importers, are also required to disclose to downstream operators technical information about their products with a view to facilitating end-of-life management. This happens in relation to multi-material products or products containing hazardous substances, such as vehicles, EEE as well as batteries and accumulators, as opposed to mono-material products such as packaging.[545] In Europe, information must typically identify product components and/or materials as well as the localisation of hazardous substances and mixtures in products.[546] Article 15 of Directive 2012/19/EU on WEEE even determines information to be provided free of charge and by means of electronic media. Brazilian law, in turn, more vaguely requires manufacturers and importers to technically capacitate downstream operators regarding post-consumer waste management.[547]

As already mentioned, information is not limited to physical responsibility, but may relate to financial responsibility as well. More specifically, producers may have to make the costs of fulfilling their physical responsibility known to the public in general[548] or to consumers[549] in particular, especially upon purchase of new products.[550]

---

544 In this case, information must be visible, legible and indelible. See, for instance, article 21(2) of Directive 2006/66/CE and article 16, I of Conama Resolution No. 401/2008, both of which on batteries and accumulators.

545 Apart from material composition, the latter products also have much shorter life spans than the former ones.

546 See article 8(3) of Directive 2000/53/EC on end-of-life vehicles and article 15 of Directive 2012/19/UE on WEEE.

547 See article 18 of Conama Resolution No. 401/2008 and clause seven, point IV, of the Sectoral Agreement on Fluorescent Mercury-Vapour, Sodium-Vapour and Mixed-Light Lamps.

548 In Brazil, see clause sixteen, paragraph one, point V, of the Sectoral Agreement on Fluorescent Mercury-Vapour, Sodium-Vapour and Mixed-Light Lamps as well as clause nine, point (ii) of the Sectoral Agreement on Packaging in General.

549 In Brazil, see clause six, point 6.1, sub-point (iii) of the Sectoral Agreement on Packaging in General.

550 In Europe, see article 14(1) of Directive 2012/19/UE on WEEE. In Brazil, see clause seven, paragraph three of the Sectoral Agreement on Fluorescent Mer-

One last form of informational responsibility concerns the duty of producers to inform public enforcement authorities of the fulfilment of their physical and financial responsibility, which is done fundamentally by means of registration and reporting mechanisms. These accessory obligations are intended for governmental monitoring and evaluation of the implementation of EPR.[551]

D. *Conjugating physical and financial responsibility*

As a rule, physical responsibility entails financial responsibility, since those on whom physical responsibility is imposed incur the costs of fulfilling it. In other words, physical responsibility and financial responsibility normally go together.

In some cases, however, physical responsibility is placed on a party other than that having financial responsibility. For instance, consumers are often responsible for 'first-mile' collection in that they are required to return end-of-life products to producers at collection points/drop-off centres at their expense[552]. Another example is the possibility of downstream economic operators or even local public waste management authorities being charged with collecting and/or recovering end-of-life products subjected to EPR.[553]

---

cury-Vapour, Sodium-Vapour and Mixed-Light Lamps as well as clause 5.4 of the Sectoral Agreement on Household Electrical and Electronic Equipment. In all three cases, showing the costs to purchasers is *possible*, but *not mandatory*. Sometimes legislation prohibits costs to be shown to end-users at the time of sale, as illustrated by article 16(4) of Directive 2006/66/EC on batteries and accumulators.

551 On the challenges of enforcing and monitoring EPR as illustrated by the financial guarantee required from producer for the management of WEEE in the EU, see Führ, 2006.

552 Rules forbidding consumers from being charged, or having to buy a new product, for returning end-of-life products (see section C.III.2, *supra*) are intended to prevent additional disincentives to the efforts consumers must already make such as sort the end-of-life products covered by EPR separately from the other waste streams they generate and take them back to collection points/drop-off centres.

553 This is the case with batteries and accumulators in both the EU and Brazil, in relation to which downstream operators may be called to assume EPR duties *on their own behalves*. It differs from the situation in which physical responsibility is laid on producers and these delegate the carrying out of their duties to downstream operators. In this second case, it is the producers, not the (delegat-

It is often argued that physical and financial responsibility should be kept connected in order for producers to have full control of costs and thus the incentive structure of EPR to work.[554] Reasons for separating them should be then offsetting and clear.

Taking into account the possible separation of physical and financial responsibility, three arrangements deriving from the conjugation between them have been identified in the EU.[555]

Firstly, producer responsibility may be limited to financing waste collection and management systems operated by third parties, which in most cases are the already existing local public waste systems. Producers assume an exclusive financial role that is akin to that of taxpayers. Put briefly, producers have financial responsibility, but no physical responsibility.

Secondly, producers may have 'partial organisational' (i.e. physical) responsibility in addition to financial responsibility. In this situation, producers are called on to undertake some of the waste collection and/or subsequent management operations, whereas some other activities remain within the physical responsibility of third parties and are only financially supported by producers.

Thirdly, financial and 'full organisational' (i.e. physical) responsibility may be imposed on producers, so that the carrying out and financing of waste collection and/or subsequent management is incumbent exclusively on them. Sometimes, producers even own part of the waste collection and/or subsequent management infrastructure.

In the second and third scenarios, producers may play a role of either service requesters, if they contract out the execution of the activities that make up their physical responsibility, or service providers, if they themselves perform said activities. Their control over the functioning of EPR schemes as well as the costs arising therefrom, and hence their aptitude to (be incentivised to) improve both waste management systems and product design, tends to be much greater than in the first scenario.

Which of the possible configurations – ranging from mere financial responsibility to financial plus full organisational/physical responsibility – prevails on the concrete case depends on several factors, including, but not limited to, the product subject to EPR and its characteristics, both

---

ed) downstream operators, who are responsible under law and before public enforcement authorities for fulfilling EPR obligations.

554 See Kalimo *et al.*, 2012, p. 277-279 and 299.

555 The considerations of the following five paragraphs are based on Monier *et al.*, 2014, p. 78-83.

intrinsic (e.g. hazardousness) and extrinsic (e.g. positive or negative value at end of life[556]), as well as the existence or non-existence of other waste collection and/or management channels and/or infrastructure prior to the introduction of EPR. For instance, physical responsibility for potentially hazardous waste streams tends to be placed on producers to ensure that treatment occurs. For some streams arising from professional sources, especially those with a positive value such as lubricating oils, waste collection and management channels between consumers (waste generators) and downstream operators already exist, so producers tend to play a financial role only.

Unlike physical responsibility, financial responsibility always rests with producers. It is what characterises EPR as such and therefore cannot be delegated. Yet, shifting part or all of the costs of post-consumer collection and subsequent management away from producers to other stakeholders, notably consumers or taxpayers, is a reality in both theory and practice. This brings up the question about whom should ultimately bear the economic burden of environmental improvements and invariably touches upon the issue of alternative instruments to EPR.

As already discussed, making producers financially responsible for managing end-of-life products does not prevent them from passing on the costs incurred in meeting their EPR obligations to consumers through the pricing mechanism. On the one hand, there seems to be an implicit belief or hope among some EPR theorists that cost shifting will not necessarily take place, particularly in competitive markets, where producers would rather absorb costs by reducing their profit margins instead of raising prices and risk losing sales, or when demand is inelastic.[557] On the other hand, some experts observe that consumers always end up bearing the costs in practice.[558]

Whilst this last observation may be true, one thing is the *possibility* of having consumers pay for EPR because market conditions allow producers

556 The positive or negative value of end-of-life products relates to whether collection and/or management activities are self-financed by revenues from sales of the recovered materials or not, respectively.

557 See Kalimo *et al.*, 2012, p. 279-280. Self-financed EPR systems are another example.

558 See Tojo, Lindhqvist and Davis, 2001, p. 29. Even if costs are passed on to consumers, it is contended that competition would protect consumers from being overcharged, for products that are more difficult to manage at end of life would be more costly and therefore lose market against products that are better designed for end-of-life management (see Kalimo *et al.*, 2012, p. 279).

to pass on their costs, another thing is the *certainty* of making consumers financially responsible from the outset without any financial involvement on the part of producers, as it is the case with advance fees and deposit-return systems.[559]

Advance disposal fees or advance recycling fees, hereinafter simply 'advance fees', are payments made by consumers either when they purchase goods ('up-front fees') or discard them ('last-owner fees') to finance the collection and/or subsequent management of end-of-life products. They can be assessed per unit of the product sold or on a weight basis.[560] They may also vary according to product and/or material type. Up-front fees are charged upon sales of *new* goods to cover the costs of collecting and managing *old* products that are presently discarded. As a result, funding for future 'orphan products'[561] as well as for products that come to be legally banned is compromised.[562] In addition, funding for products with longer life spans faces financial uncertainties due to fluctuations in both waste collection and/or management costs and sales revenue.[563] In last-owner-pays systems, by contrast, producers announce in advance the fees that are charged for the current collection and subsequent management of end-of-life products, so that the amount paid is as close to the actual costs as possible and the problem of orphan products is eliminated.[564]

In deposit-return systems, consumers are charged a fee at the time of purchase of a good ('deposit') that is paid back once they return end-of-life

559 There are other policy instruments alternative to EPR (see, for instance, OECD, 2016, p. 17; Walls, 2006, p. 2-5), including, but not limited to, bans, standards, materials tax and subsidies, but they do not have consumers (in lieu of producers) as addressees, which is the focus of the argument being put forward.

560 See Walls, 2006, p. 3.

561 'Orphan products' are end-of-life products whose producer has exited the market or, in more legal terms, has ceased to exist as a legal entity. See Lindhqvist, 2000, p. 123-124.

562 See Tojo, Lindhqvist and Davis, 2001, p. 31.

563 See Tojo, Lindhqvist and Davis, 2001, p. 31.

564 See Tojo, Lindhqvist and Davis, 2001, p. 31. The authors mention a third option, in which fees are collected at time of purchase but set aside for future use when the product reaches end of life. As with the last-owner-pays model, incentives to DfE are greater since the fees collected cover the actual management costs. The problem with this approach is the delay in implementing collection and management for durable products. Moreover, orphan products might be an issue if the fees collected are not protected from creditors of no-longer-existing companies.

products to collection systems ('refund').[565][566] Such a financial incentive usually leads to high collection rates. Deposit-refund systems have been widely used for beverage packaging and, together with up-front advance fees, have some advantages over last-owner fees and pay-as-you-throw systems:[567] firstly, the problem of illegal dumping that arises whenever the discarding of waste is taxed (in an economic, Pigouvian sense) is circumvented; secondly and consequently, the need for administrative monitoring and control of non-point sources discarding post-consumer waste is reduced; thirdly, fee evasion is avoided, for payments are due upon sales.[568]

Whenever consumers must pay for waste collection and/or subsequent management, it is debated whether the costs borne should be shown to them or not. Put another way, whether costs are to be displayed separately from the product price or simply included in the posted price is a matter of discussion. The first merit of the so-called 'visible fees' is their 'educational effect'[569]: consumers become more aware and allegedly also more supportive of post-consumer waste management endeavours. Besides, assuming that fees truly reflect all actual costs of collecting and managing each product at end of life, consumers can compare between the eco-efficiencies of producers.[570] In collective EPR systems[571], just like up-front advance fees and deposit-return systems, making the costs known to consumers involves charging them a separate fee for the financing of collection and management activities on top of product price. By not being hidden in price, separate fees are immune to bargaining in distribution channels,[572] and thus constitute an own source of funding for PROs,

---

565 The deposit as such does not pay for waste management (see Lee, 2008, p. 304). Waste management costs as well as the administrative costs of deposit-return systems are covered by revenues from three sources: retained deposits (i.e. unredeemed deposits from non-returned products), sales of recovered materials, and notional interest gained from deposit payments until redeemed (see Tojo, Lindhqvist and Davis, 2001, p. 30; Lee, 2008, p. 304).

566 In some systems, deposits are rebated to downstream operators (e.g. authorised recyclers) instead of consumers as a means to incentivise materials recovery (see Walls, 2011). Strictly speaking, it is a combination of an up-front advance fee with a recovery (i.e. recycling) subsidy, not a deposit-refund system.

567 In pay-as-you-throw (hereinafter 'PAYT') systems, waste generators are charged by public waste management authorities for the waste they discard on a per-unit or weight basis.

568 See Walls, 2011, p. 1-2.

569 See Tojo, Lindhqvist and Davis, 2001, p. 30.

570 Kalimo *et al.*, 2012, p. 289.

571 See section E, *infra*.

572 Kalimo *et al.*, 2012, p. 289.

which can operate autonomously from decisions made by their corporate individual members.[573] Visible fees are also simple to apply and track.[574]

However, they are disadvantageous because consumers often (albeit wrongly) perceive them as a government-levied tax and this may have an 'anti-environmental effect'.[575] Furthermore, they do not eliminate the need for communication and/or consumer awareness campaigns. Most fundamentally, visible fees, just like the fees paid by producers to PROs, face the practical challenge of being differentiated only by very broad product groups, not by criteria associated with each product's characteristics or, more precisely, by aspects of design for end-of-life management such as ease or difficulty of reuse and/or material recycling. PRO independence derived from financing, the corollary exclusion of individual PRO members from EPR decision-making as well as poor fee differentiation undermine DfE incentives.[576] Ultimately, producers (via PROs) act as mere fee collectors and/administrators and producers end up being recompensed for the inconvenience of having their-end-of-life products returned for management.[577],[578]

E. Implementing EPR: individual versus collective responsibility

To say that producers have extended responsibility means that each producer is responsible for carrying out – and thus paying for – the collection and subsequent management of his or her own products at end of life. In practice, however, producers have massively fulfilled their obligations in a collective fashion. This means that producers in a given sector collect and subsequently manage their end-of-life products together, regardless of product type and/or brand, and share the respective costs. It is frequently spoken of as collective responsibility as opposed to individual responsibility.[579]

573 Bury, 2010, p. 935.
574 Bury, 2010, p. 937.
575 Clift and France, 2006, p. 5-6.
576 See Bury, 2010, p. 935-936, 943 and 945.
577 See Clift and France, 2006, p. 6.
578 Finally, not hiding fees exposes the problem of non-harmonised fees where EPR programmes are not run nationwide. See Bury, 2010, p. 15 and 17.
579 In fact, any of the three facets of responsibility – physical, financial and informational – may be implemented individually or collectively. When physical responsibility is individual, so is financial responsibility. If physical responsibility

Reference to both modalities is epitomised by the first German packaging ordinance, which placed individual responsibility for the collection and management of sales packaging on manufacturers and distributors but exempted them from their individual obligations if they participated in a (collective) system whereby said obligations were met.[580]

Despite the extensive resort to collective responsibility, legislation does not normally expressly state whether responsibility is individual or collective. The European WFD is illustrative in this sense. The same is true in relation to the Brazilian PNRS, although its emphasis on implementing EPR by means of sectoral agreements suggests clear preference for the collective variant.

In the EU, Directive 2012/19/EU on WEEE is the only piece of EPR legislation that explicitly addresses the issue of individual and collective responsibility.[581] With regard to physical responsibility, the following three obligations may be fulfilled either individually or collectively by producers:

- the setting up and operation of return systems for WEEE from private households (Article 5(2)(d));
- the setting up of recovery systems for WEEE (Article 8(3)); and
- the collection, treatment, recovery and/or environmentally sound disposal of WEEE from private households that has been deposited at collection facilities (first sentence of Article 12(3)).

Concerning the last-mentioned obligation, the second sentence of Article 12(3) states that financial responsibility must be individual for WEEE from products placed on the market later than 13 August 2005 (the so-called

---

is collective, then financial responsibility may be either individual or collective. Individual financial responsibility under a regime of collective physical responsibility means that the costs of collecting and subsequently managing a specific product, which is collected and subsequently managed together with other products, are separately identifiable and thus borne by the individual producer thereof. Whether this occurs in practice is discussed at the end of this section.

580 See § 6 of the *Verordnung über die Vermeidung von Verpackungsabfällen (Verpackungsverordnung – VerpackV) vom 12. Juni 1991*. To date, since the fifth amendment to the *Verordnung über die Vermeidung und Verwertung von Verpackungsabfällen (Verpackungsverordnung – VerpackV) vom 21. August 1998, now repealed by the Gesetz über das Inverkehrbringen, die Rücknahme und die hoghwertige Verwertung von Verpackungen (Verpackungsgesetz – VerpackG) vom 5. Juli 2017*, collective systems are the rule, whereas individual solutions are the exception. See, for instance, Flanderka and Stroetmann, 2012, p. 3-4.

581 A subtle, implicit reference to collective responsibility is found in article 7(1) of Directive 94/62/EC.

'waste from new products'), even if producers choose to meet their physical responsibility collectively.

In Brazilian EPR legislation, the sectoral agreements on fluorescent lamps, packaging in general, lead-acid batteries, and household EEE as well as the commitment agreement on steel packaging expressly refer to the collective implementation of both physical and financial responsibility. Other legal acts on EPR are silent in this respect.

Collective responsibility is preferred over individual responsibility mainly due to the economies of scale it creates, which reduces costs for producers.[582] By lowering the number of EPR schemes and simplifying operations, collective action also makes it easier for producers to set up and run waste collection and subsequent waste management systems, especially where these do not yet exist, as well as for consumers to participate in said systems and for public authorities to monitor and enforce EPR obligations. Moreover, it generates peer pressure amongst producers in order to combat free riders[583].[584]

Once the mutualisation of responsibility has been decided upon, several organisational issues arise. The first and most obvious question is how to collectively perform the activities intended to fulfil the responsibility placed on producers. The most frequent answer has been the establishment of the so-called PROs by producers[585] or independent third parties, including downstream operators. PROs may have different legal status-

582 Kalimo *et al.* (2012, p. 282) note that two particular kinds of producers tend to lose out under individual responsibility and therefore prefer collective responsibility. The first ones are environmentally inefficient producers, who, at least in theory, incur greater waste management costs than efficient competitors. The second ones are producers with large amounts of products placed on the market prior to the introduction of EPR and who are made responsible for such 'historical waste'. In this case, their financial burden may be disproportionately heavy in comparison to current sales, especially if their market shares have diminished over time.

583 Free riders are producers who do not comply with their EPR obligations by neither participating in a collective system nor fulfilling their responsibility individually. Under collective responsibility, products from non-compliant producers are collected and managed by compliant producers, who then face an unfair competitive disadvantage. In addition, free riders avoid the consequences of their own (and normally poor) DfE.

584 On the benefits of collective responsibility, see OECD, 2016, p. 23. See also Walls, 2006, p. 7.

585 In this case, PROs are entities with legal personality distinct from that of the producers creating them.

es.[586] They are typically non-profit organisations, usually taking the legal form of professional associations, and only occasionally for-profit firms.[587] Governmental or quasi-governmental formats also exist.

Which tasks are assigned to PROs evidently depends on the role assumed by producers in EPR.[588] In general, PROs are charged with governance of the collective system, including, but not limited to, monitoring and data reporting activities. Where producers have (partial or full) physical responsibility, PROs contract out waste collection and subsequent waste management activities, but PROs may also themselves provide said services, especially if they are owned by downstream operators or have these as members. Be the case as it may, PROs act on behalf – and not in place – of producers, which means that producers remain as the addressees of the EPR legal duties imposed by law in spite of transferring the execution thereof to PROs.

From an economic perspective, the collective implementation of EPR creates a market for the organisation of compliance with legal obligations, on which PROs are on the supply side and producers are on the demand side.[589] There are markets with only one single PRO, whereas in other markets several PROs are found, both competing and non-competing[590]. Collective EPR has raised numerous competition issues in the, so to speak, 'PRO market' as well as in both the market for the products subjected to EPR and the waste management market.[591]

In collective schemes, some typical problems associated with any EPR system are felt more acutely. The first one is the placing of responsibility for 'historical waste', that is, responsibility for the collection and management of end-of-life products placed on the market before EPR is made legally mandatory or implemented. Collective schemes have been regarded as being more appropriate than individual systems for tackling historical waste because, as shall be discussed below, under collective responsibility

586 See Monier *et al.*, 2014, p. 101-102. See also OECD, 2016, p. 64-66.

587 On the main arguments for and against non-profit and for-profit PROs, see OECD, 2016, p. 65-66.

588 See section D, *supra*.

589 See Monier *et al.*, 2014, p. 98; OECD, 2016, p. 102.

590 Strictly speaking, non-competing PROs are active on distinct 'relevant markets' (to use the terminology of competition law), for they differ in scope (e.g. coverage of different product subcategories, different geographical extent). See Monier *et al.*, 2014, p. 99.

591 For a balanced overview on this topic, see OECD, 2016, p. 101-145. See also Monier *et al.*, 2014, p. 98-106.

costs are customarily apportioned among the various producers based on their current market shares (i.e. present sales), so that once EPR is legally introduced and producers are made responsible for 'historical waste' competitive positions are less distorted and producers with heavy historical burdens do not face the risk of insolvency.[592] However, collectivisation of responsibility for 'historical waste' does not eliminate the legal problem of retroactivity.[593] Nor can it contribute to DfE, for the incentive logic of EPR is directed towards the future, not the past.[594] Furthermore, even where legislation mandates individual responsibility for 'waste from new products', such waste ends up being 'locked into' the collective responsibility regime established for 'historical waste', since it is difficult in practice to maintain parallel schemes for each stream, that is, to collect and subsequently manage 'historical waste' separately from 'waste from new products'.[595] This 'lock-in' effect tends to last as long as the amount of 'historical waste' remains large.[596]

The decision as to whom should bear responsibility for 'orphan products'[597], 'grey products' as well as illegal products is a second, related challenge. 'Orphan products' may be a specific case within 'historical waste' or relate to 'waste from new products'. In this latter situation, 'orphan products' pose a problem of free riding, for the responsible producer no longer exists when the collection and management costs of his or her products at end of life materialise. In order to avoid this in the case of WEEE from private households, as shown above,[598] EU legislation requires producers to provide a financial guarantee for the future management of their products when placing them on the market.[599] 'Grey products',

592 See Kalimo *et al.*, 2012, p. 283-284.

593 See Kalimo *et al.*, 2012, p. 283-284.

594 See Lindhqvist, 2000, p. 123; Lidgren and Skogh, 1996, p. 177.

595 See Kalimo *et al.*, 2012, p. 285.

596 Only when a producer's share of 'historical' waste has become so negligible that he or she can threaten to leave the collective scheme, thereby increasing everyone else's shares of the collective liability unless a return-share model is adopted, it is possible to escape the 'lock-in effect'. Of course, in order for the threat to work the producer must have a considerable market share and, most importantly, be able to run an individual system oh his or her own. See Kalimo *et al.*, 2012, p. 285.

597 For the notion of 'orphan products' see footnote 561, *supra*.

598 See section C.III.2.a, *supra*.

599 Article 12(3) of Directive 2012/19/UE states that 'the guarantee may take the form of participation by the producer in appropriate schemes for the financing of the management of WEEE, a recycling insurance or a blocked bank account'.

in turn, refer to end-of-life products the producer of which cannot be identified. Examples include unbranded products and, more typically, the so-called 'grey imports'[600].

Ultimately, deciding who should be made responsible for historical, orphan, grey and illegal products is a political task. Responsibility could even be placed on taxpayers in lieu of producers. This may be justified on three grounds: firstly, the incentive mechanism inherent to EPR cannot operate in relation to these product categories; secondly, the lock-in effect would be avoided; thirdly, lastly but somewhat less courageously, having taxpayers bear responsibility in the start-up phase after the introduction of EPR is based on the acknowledgement that changes do not happen overnight.

Probably the thorniest issue of collective EPR systems is the allocation of financial responsibility among producers.

Which costs are actually covered by EPR systems and whether coverage is full or partial varies in practice and evidently depends on the concrete apportioning of physical and informational responsibility between producers and other stakeholders. The European experience shows that most EPR systems meet the net[601] costs of collecting and/or managing the end-of-life products that have been separately collected plus the running expenses of the collective system itself, which comprise costs associated with the administration of the scheme, data management and reporting activities as well as communication with producers and other stakeholders.[602] Other costs such as those relating to the collection and management of end-of-life products entering collection channels other than EPR schemes (e.g.

Based on the first alternative, most Member States have interpreted membership in a collective system to be an adequate guarantee, while demanding a recycling insurance or a blocked bank account from producers fulfilling their responsibility individually (Sander *et al.*, 2007, p. 52-53). This creates at one and the same time competition-distorting effects as well as a lock-in effect in favour of collective responsibility. Other challenges include (the lack of) harmonisation of guarantees across Member States as well as devising guarantees so as to reflect investments in DfE. See Kalimo *et al.*, 2012, p. 287-288 and 291-293.

600 'Gray imports, also called parallel imports, refer to imports of goods through distribution channels which, while not illegal, are unintended, unofficial or unauthorized by the producer' (see Kalimo *et al.*, 2012, p. 287). That is the case, for instance, of a product purchased abroad by tourists from a given country to which the product is not exported.

601 Revenues deriving from the sale of the materials recovered are therefore subtracted.

602 See Monier *et al.*, 2014, p. 89-97.

public waste management systems) or even those to fulfil informational responsibility towards consumers (e.g. awareness campaigns) are dogged by controversy.

Besides the question of what producers must pay for is the issue of how costs are to be allotted to each PRO member. When systems are not self-financing, the aggregate costs of collecting and managing all end-of-life products subjected to EPR in a given sector are normally prorated amongst producers in that sector,[603] who then individually make a financial contribution to PROs.

Individual contributions (or fees) can be assessed on a per-unit or weight basis and may vary by product or material type. Under collective action, products of a given sector subject to EPR are collected separately from other waste streams[604] but then gathered and managed together. Each producer is then assigned a portion of the total costs of managing an undifferentiated mixture of products and/or materials based on current sales (or market) share (i.e. the quantity of products sold at the time recovery takes place) or return share (i.e. the number of products that is collected through the collective EPR system).[605]

The problem is that contributions set in this way are at best only proxies for the relative costs of product-specific management. The fee paid by a single producer does not reflect the actual costs of collecting and managing his or her own products. Investments in DfE, which cheapen waste management, are thus not perceived by collective EPR systems.

The inability of collective responsibility to promote DfE has led experts to call for the incorporation of elements of individual (financial) responsibility into collective EPR schemes.[606] 'Eco-modulation' of fees is

603 Costs could be also shared equally amongst producers, but this is less frequent in practice.

604 In practice, however, it is quite common for products or product categories not subjected to EPR to be collected by EPR systems. This exacerbates the practical challenges of implementing EPR.

605 See Kalimo *et al.*, 2012, p. 283-284 and 294; Roller and Führ, 2008, p. 279-280; Chancerel, Schill and Rotter, 2007, p. 269-270 and 276. The sales-share model is current practice for several reasons. Firstly, it is much easier to ascertain the quantity of products sold than collected at end-of-life. Secondly, in the return-share model, waste collection and management costs can be known only in hindsight. Thirdly, calculations made under the return-share model are based on statistical methods, which are themselves not problem-free, and involve a significant amount of work.

606 It is in this context that reference is made to 'individual producer responsibility' (hereinafter 'IPR'). See, for instance, Lifset and Lindhqvist, 2008, p. 145.

an attempt to advance towards collective EPR systems that are individual-friendly. It seeks to counteract the averaging of costs among producers by charging producers reduced fees for products abiding by ecodesign technical criteria and increased fees for products disturbing waste management processes or making these more difficult, thereby rewarding producers who have invested in DfE and penalising laggards.[607] In this sense, as proposed by the European Commission in the 2015 action plan for the circular economy,[608] point (b) of Article 8a(4) of the WFD, as amended by Directive (EU) 2018/851, stipulates that the financial contributions paid by producers to PROs

> 'in the case of collective fulfilment of extended producer responsibility obligations, are modulated, where possible, for individual products or groups of similar products, notably by taking into account their durability, reparability, re-usability and recyclability and the presence of hazardous substances, thereby taking a lifecycle approach and aligned with the requirements set by relevant Union law, and where available, based on harmonised criteria in order to ensure a smooth functioning of the internal market',

Of course, apart from the fact that establishing ecodesign criteria faces technical difficulties, fee differentiation requires that products can be individually identified after collection and that product-specific, ecodesign-related information can be readily made available to downstream operators. To do this in the simplest and least expensive way possible, the introduction of an automatised (i.e. machine-based) identification and information exchange system is discussed in the WEEE sector.[609]-[610] Improved financ-

607 See Monier *et al.*, 2014, p. 93-94 and 96-97; Kalimo *et al.*, 2012, p. 299-300.

608 See chapter 3, section D, *supra*.

609 See Roller and Führ, 2008, p. 280-282; Kalimo *et al.*, 2012, p. 294-295. Such a system evidently depends on the existing technologies and raises a series of other questions (e.g. product labelling and/or marking to ensure readability by machines, database development and standardisation, just to cite a few).

610 Still in the field of WEEE, a more elaborate regulation of recovery operations in general, and treatment requirements in particular, has been suggested as a means of combating material shredding and foster EEE dismantling as well as material recovery (see Kalimo *et al.*, 2012, p. 296-297). Interestingly, this proposal is in tune with the conclusions reached at section C, *supra*.

ing formulae are also necessary.[611] In the case of packaging, fees are diversified by material (sub-)type rather than by product (category) or brand.[612]

Eco-modulation initiatives have been introduced in some European countries, notably in France, but their implications are not known yet.[613]So far, it is a commonplace in literature that EPR, as it has been practised, fails to achieve upstream goals.[614] This finding leads one to not only acknowledge the trade-offs between individual and collective responsibility[615] – which have been best summarised as 'simplicity and flexibility coupled with minimal incentives for DfE [in collective systems] on the one hand, versus complexity and high administrative and monitoring costs combined with sharp DfE incentives [in individual systems] on the other'[616] – but also question the efficacy of EPR for DfE and hence search for alternative instruments that regulate product ecodesign in a more direct fashion.[617] These are dealt with in the next chapter.

---

611 See, for instance, Mayers *et al.*, 2012.

612 See Flanderka *et al.*, 2015, 132-133; Cahill, Grimes and Wilson, 2010, p. 465. The packaging sector is often lauded as successful in encouraging light-weighting and rewarding producers with easily recyclable packaging (see, for instance, Mayers *et al.*, 2012, p. 187; Bury, 2010, p. 932; Lifset and Lindhqvist, 2008, p. 144-145). Some observers note, however, that 'even long after the introduction of EPR, packaging that is difficult to recycle (or even not recyclable) is still widely used' (Monier *et al.*, 2014, p. 96). Moreover, according to a specialist's comment on Germany's 1991 packaging ordinance with hindsight, 'it is clear that over the past 20 years the total amount of packaging waste in Germany did not decrease and, despite the existence of EPR schemes, in many other countries it even increased' (see Rotter, 2011, p. 889).

613 See Monier *et al.*, 2014, p. 94 and 97. See also Kalimo *et al.*, 2012, p. 299-300.

614 See, for instance, Monier *et al.*, 2014, p. 23; Lifset, Atasu and Tojo, 2013, p. 162; Kalimo *et al.*, 2012, p. 281, 296, 298; Prelle, 2011, p. 43; Lifset and Lindhqvist, 2008, p. 146; Tojo, 2003, p. 67.

615 See, for instance, Kalimo *et al.*, 2012, p. 281; Sachs, 2006, p. 77; Lifset and Lindhqvist, 2003, p. 3.

616 See Palmer and Walls, 2002, p. 33.

617 Instead of resorting to alternative instruments, it has been suggested that binding targets for waste prevention (as opposed and in addition to waste recovery) be introduced, for example in the form of product reuse targets or targets for preparation for reuse as opposed and in addition to recycling of materials. (Article 11(2)(a) of the WFD confusingly does not distinguish between, and thus neither establishes separate targets for, the reuse of products, on the one hand, and the recycling of materials, on the other hand.) So far, this remains only wishful thinking. Lacking political will to set binding waste prevention targets is manifest in both Brazilian and EU legislation on EPR. In the EU, Article 29(3) of the WFD, which allowed – but did not require – Member States

F. Summary

EPR is the first instrument provided for by waste law in order to intervene in the ecodesign of products with a view to waste prevention. In a nutshell, EPR involves the placing of responsibility on producers for the management of the products they put on the market at end of life. By doing so, EPR aims at relieving local authorities from the burden of managing certain waste streams (downstream goal) while incentivising producers to improve the ecodesign of their products with a view to reducing the costs incurred with the management of said products at end of life (upstream goal). Producer responsibility is extended in that producers are made responsible because of their role as indirect polluters. Producer (*sensu lato*) is anyone upstream of the consumer in the life cycle of a product – namely, the manufacturer, the importer, the distributor and/or the seller (wholesaler and/or retailer), although EPR-related duties may also be imposed on persons downstream of the consumer. Responsibility means a set of diversified obligations (or duties), for the most part positive duties (i.e. duties to do something) as opposed to negative duties (i.e. duties to refrain from doing something). Responsibility may be physical, financial or informational. Physical (or material) responsibility means the obligation to perform all actions necessary to ensure that end-of-life products are managed properly. Financial responsibility is the obligation to cover the costs of physical and informational responsibility. Informational responsibility corresponds to the duty to provide information about aspects pertaining to both physical and financial responsibility. The success of EPR in reaching upstream goals depends on the conjugation of both physical and financial responsibility, on the one hand, and whether EPR is implemented individually or collectively, on the other hand. Physical and financial responsibility should be kept connected in order for producers to have full control of costs and thus the incentive structure of EPR to work. Reasons for separating them should be offsetting and clear. As for implementation, individual responsibility means that each producer is responsible for the management of his or her own products at end of life, whereas collective responsibility refers to producers managing their end-of-life products together, that is, regardless of product type and/or brand, thus sharing the respective costs. Collective implementation faces many organisational challenges and usually involves the creation of a PRO

---

to determine specific quantitative targets for waste prevention, has been deleted by Article 1(22)(d) of Directive 2018/851 amending the WFD.

to fulfil the obligations imposed on producers on their behalf. There are trade-offs between individual and collective responsibility, which can be summarised as high costs and sharp DfE incentives in individual responsibility versus lower costs and minimal incentives for DfE in collective responsibility. Considering that collective responsibility has been a default so far, it is commonplace that EPR has failed to achieve upstream goals. In order to overcome this drawback, two proposals stand out. The first one is the devising of a collective system in which the fees paid by individual producers to the PRO are product- and/or material-specific, so that they reflect the actual end-of-life management costs of specific products and/or materials, thereby being able to perceive investments in DfE and consequently rewarding front-runners as well as sanctioning laggards (eco-modulation). This requires that products and materials are individually identifiable even if collected and managed collectively, which in turn requires the existence of identification technologies and/or improved financing formulae. The second proposal concerns the search for alternative instruments regulating product ecodesign in a more direct fashion, which are explored in the following chapter.

Chapter 5 – Selected examples of direct ecodesign regulation in product-oriented environmental law

Given the impotence of EPR to advance DfE on an incentive basis, this chapter looks at alternative instruments regulating the ecodesign of products in a direct fashion. Four examples have been selected for analysis: the product design mandates found in both EU and Brazilian EPR legislation (section A, *infra*), the EC Ecodesign Directive (section B, *infra*), the regulation of plastics (section C, *infra*) and the requirement of a common charging solution for mobile chargers in the EU (section D, *infra*).

A. Direct ecodesign regulation in EU and Brazilian EPR legislation

Influenced by life cycle thinking and EPR's pursuit of upstream goals, waste legislation on EPR, or simply end-of-life product legislation, contains a few provisions attempting to regulate the ecodesign of products in a more direct fashion as opposed to the indirect, incentive-based rationale of EPR. Such attempts usually take place under the heading of 'waste prevention', although regulation is more product-related than waste-oriented.

I. EU EPR legislation

Article 8(2) of the WFD, as amended by Directive 2018/851, reads:

> 'Member States may take appropriate measures to encourage the design of products and components of products in order to reduce their environmental impact and the generation of waste in the course of the production and subsequent use of products, and in order to ensure that the recovery and disposal of products that have become waste take place in accordance with Articles 4 [waste hierarchy] and 13 [protection of human health and the environment].
>
> Such measures may encourage, inter alia, the development, production and marketing of products and components of products that are suitable for multiple use, that contain recycled materials, that are technically durable and easily reparable and that are, after having become

waste, suitable for preparing for reuse and recycling in order to facilitate proper implementation of the waste hierarchy. The measures shall take into account the impact of products throughout their life cycle, the waste hierarchy and, where appropriate, the potential for multiple recycling.'

In EU EPR legislation, Article 4 of the directives on packaging waste, end-of-life vehicles, waste batteries and accumulators as well as WEEE seek to intervene directly into the ecodesign of products.

Article 4(1) of Directive 94/62/EC on *packaging and packaging waste* calls on Member States to take waste prevention measures, including those referred to in Article 9. Under this provision, and in tune with the so-called 'new approach'[618], Member States are obliged to ensure that packaging

618 In essence, the 'new approach to harmonisation and standardisation' designates a change in the technique of regulating the technical aspects of products in the EU and is therefore to be understood in contrast to the preceding, so-to-speak 'old' approach, under which all product-specific details were legislated at the highest level of European politics. Pioneered by (now repealed) Directive 73/23/EEC on the harmonisation of the laws of Member States relating to electrical equipment designed for use within certain voltage limits (OJ L 77, 26 March 1973, p. 29), the so-called 'Low Voltage Directive', and institutionally supported by (now repealed) Council Directive 83/189/EEC which laid down a procedure for the provision of information in the field of technical standards and regulations (OJ L 109, 26 April 1983, p. 8), the so-called 'Information Directive', the 'new approach' was officially launched by Council Resolution of 7 May 1985 on a new approach to technical harmonisation and standards (OJ L 109, 26 April 1983, p. 8). Under the 'new approach', harmonisation of the technical characteristics of products by European legislation is to be limited to the setting down of essential requirements, with specifications being laid down by European standards bodies. The wording of essential requirements must be precise enough to create legally binding obligations that can be enforced as well as enable products to be certified as being in conformity even in the absence of standards. Products manufactured in accordance with (private) European standards enjoy a presumption of conformity with (public-law) essential requirements and thus freedom of movement within the EU market. Because standards are voluntary, producers that do not manufacture their products according to the applicable standards must provide proof of compliance with the relevant requirements. In order to ensure the quality of standards, not only is the reference-to-standards technique accompanied by standardisation mandates conferred by the European Commission on the European Committee for Standardisation (hereinafter referred to as 'CEN') and the European Committee for Electrotechnical Standardisation (hereinafter referred to as 'CENELEC'), but also safeguard procedures allowing Member States to challenge the conformity of a product or the quality of a standard are provided for in each piece of

be placed on the EU market only if it complies with the essential requirements imposed by the directive on the composition, reusability and recoverability of packaging, including those set out in Annex II.

In a nutshell, packaging must be so designed that, firstly, its volume and weight be limited to the minimum adequate amount to maintain the necessary level of safety, hygiene and consumer acceptance of the packed product, secondly, it can be reused and/or recovered, and, thirdly, the presence of noxious and other hazardous substances and materials as constituents of the packaging material or of any of the packaging components be minimised. In this latter respect, Article 11 of Directive 94/62/EC sets the maximum concentration levels of four heavy metals – namely lead, cadmium, mercury and hexavalent chromium – allowed to be present in packaging.

---

harmonising legislation (i.e. directive). On the new approach, see, for instance, Schepel, 2013; Schepel, 2005, p. 37-75 (notably p. 63-70); Joerges, Schepel and Vos, 1999; Falke, 1997; Pelkmans, 1987.

The new approach was complemented by (now repealed) Council Resolution of 21 December 1989 on a global approach to conformity assessment (OJ C 10, 16 January 1990, p. 1), which was followed by (now repealed) Council Decision of 13 December 1990 concerning the modules for the various phases of the conformity assessment procedures which are intended to be used in the technical harmonisation directives (OJ L 380, 31 December 1990, p. 13). A revision of both the new and global approaches took place in 2003 (see COM (2003) 240 final, 7 May 2003), which culminated in a package of measures improving the then existing legislative framework. This package of legislative acts is known as the 'new legislative framework' (hereinafter referred to as 'NLF') and consists of Decision No. 768/2008/EC on a common framework for the marketing of products (OJ 218, 13 August 2008, p. 82), Regulation (EC) 764/2008 laying down procedures relating to the application of certain national technical rules to products lawfully marketed in another Member State (OJ L 218, 13 August 2008, p. 21) as well as Regulation (EC) 765/2008 setting out requirements for accreditation and market surveillance relating to the marketing of products (OJ 218, 13 August 2008, p. 30). Since then, the so-called 'new-approach directives' have been and/or are being updated and aligned to the NLF. For a brief historical overview of the evolution from the old approach through the new approach to the NLF, see, for instance, European Commission, 2016.

To date, besides the legislative acts making up the NLF, the following pieces of legislation apply: Regulation (EU) 1025/2012 on European standardisation (OJ L 316, 14 November 2012, p. 12) and Directive (EU) 2015/1535 laying down a procedure for the provision of information in the field of technical regulations and of rules on Information Society services (codification) (OJ L 241, 17 September 2015, p. 1).

According to Article 9(2) of Directive 94/62/EC, and once again in obedience to the dictates of the 'new approach', compliance with the essential requirements is to be presumed if packaging conforms to either harmonised EU standards, the reference numbers of which have been published in the official journal of the EU, or national standards in so far as no harmonised standards exist. In this latter case, Member States must communicate to the European Commission the text of their national standards, the reference of which must also be published in the official journal of the EU (Article 9(3) of Directive 94/62/EC).

EU standards exist, and they have been prepared under mandates given to CEN by the European Commission pursuant to Article 10 of Directive 94/62/EC. They are the following:

Table 4 – Harmonised packaging standards under Directive 94/62/EC[619]

Reference	Title
CEN EN 13427:2004	Packaging – Requirements for the use of European Standards in the field of packaging and packaging waste'
CEN EN 13428:2004	Packaging – Requirements specific to manufacturing and composition – Prevention by source reduction'
CEN EN 13429:2004	Packaging – Reuse'
CEN EN 13430:2004	Packaging – Requirements for packaging recoverable by material recycling'
CEN EN 13431:2004	Packaging – Requirements for packaging recoverable in the form of energy recovery, including specification of minimum inferior calorific value'
CEN EN 13433:2000	Packaging – Requirements for packaging recoverable through composting and biodegradation – Test scheme and evaluation criteria for the final acceptance of packaging

Just like the essential requirements of Directive 94/62/EC, the specifications set forth by the above-listed standards are normally too general and this vagueness gives manufacturers enormous compliance flexibility. More specifically, the standards on packaging preventability, reusability and recyclability follow a quality management approach similar to that of the management system standards such as the ISO 9000 or the ISO 14000 series, which means that instead of laying down concrete, clear-cut and ver-

619 See Commission communication 2005/C 44/23 (OJ C 44, 19 February 2005, p. 23).

ifiable technical requirements, they only establish very loose and non-measurable performance criteria. In addition, they leave it to the judgement of the standard user – and ultimately to the discretion of industry – to determine, by means of a documented, albeit interpretative, assessment, whether the criteria have been met or not.[620]

In 2011, a study[621] commissioned by the European Commission found that most Member States do not have any formal procedures to implement or enforce the essential requirements laid down by Directive 94/62/EC other than resort to the CEN standards to prove compliance. Three main reasons were identified. Firstly, Member States often lack knowledge, staff, and/or finances. Secondly, except for the concentration limits on heavy metals, essential requirements are formulated in an insufficiently concrete way and without quantitative benchmarks, thereby preventing a clear assessment of whether packaging is compliant or not. Thirdly and lastly, several Member States assume not only that the industry has enough incentives to comply with the essential requirements but also that companies integrate considerations of the essential requirements in their businesses anyway (mainly for cost considerations).

The solutions proposed by the study include not only the introduction into Directive 94/62/EC of both a requirement to assess conformity to the essential requirements and benchmark indicators on the weight and size of packaging for various product categories but also the provision of guidance at the EU level covering implementation, inspections and producer responsibility systems. The study also identified best practices for the implementation and enforcement of the essential requirements.

More recently, Directive (EU) 2018/852[622] has amended Directive 94/62/EC and introduced Article 9(5), which requires the European Commission, by the end of 2020, to 'examine the feasibility of reinforcing the essential requirements with a view to, inter alia, improving design for reuse and promoting high quality recycling, as well as strengthening their enforcement'.

620 See ANEC-ECOS, 2005. This is not the case with the standards on energy recovery (CEN EN 13431:2004) and organic recovery (CEN EN 13433:2000): the former contains a clear, albeit not very demanding (see ANEC-ECOS, 2005, p. 7), calorific gain requirement of at least 5MJ/kg; the latter likewise sets quantitative limits on packaging substances known to be, or expected to become, harmful to the environment during the biological treatment process.

621 See Monier *et al.*, 2011.

622 OJ L 150, 14 June 2018, p. 141.

Article 4(1) of Directive 2000/53/EC on *end-of-life vehicles* requires Member States to ensure that vehicle manufacturers, sometimes in liaison with material and equipment manufacturers, design vehicles with reduced hazardous substances and increased recycled material content as well as vehicles that facilitate reuse and recovery at end of life.

With respect to hazardousness, Article 4(2)(a) of Directive 2000/53/EC forbids vehicles (or, more precisely, their components and materials) to contain lead, mercury, cadmium or hexavalent chromium, except for the cases listed in Annex II under the conditions specified therein. Article 4(2)(b) allows substance-, material- and/or component-specific amendments to Annex II.

Concerning reuse and recovery requirements, Article 7(2) of Directive 2000/53/EC sets quantitative targets to be attained by economic operators. More specifically, Article 7(2)(b) provides that, from 1 January 2015, for all end-of-life vehicles, recovery must be increased to a minimum of 95% by an average weight per vehicle and year, whereas recycling must be increased to a minimum of 85% by an average weight per vehicle and year. Directive (EU) 2018/852 has amended Directive 2000/53/EC and authorised the European Commission to establish detailed rules to control compliance of Member States with said targets.

In order to achieve the *recovery* and *recycling* targets, and in line with the idea that the environmental impacts of end-of-life vehicles, their materials and substances can be best reduced if vehicles are designed from the conception phase with a view to facilitating dismantling, reuse, and recovery, in particular recycling (Article 4(1)(b))[623], Article 7(4) requires the preparation of European standards relating to the dismantl*ability*, recover*ability* and recycl*ability* of vehicles so that recyclability and recoverability targets of 85% and 95% by weight per vehicle, respectively, are reached. Directive

623 'Reusability of component parts, recyclability and recoverability of materials constitute a substantial part of the Community strategy for waste management. Therefore, vehicle manufacturers and their suppliers should be requested to include those aspects *at the earliest stages of the development of new vehicles*, in order to facilitate the treatment of vehicles at the time when they reach the end of their life' (see recital 2 of Directive 2005/64/EC, OJ L310, 25 November 2005, p. 10, emphasis added).

2005/64/EC on the type-approval of motor vehicles[624] with regard to their reusability, recyclability and recoverability[625] has been thus enacted.

Point 1 of Annex I to Directive 2005/64/EC requires type-approved vehicles to be recyclable to a minimum of 85% by mass and recoverable to a minimum of 95% by mass. Manufacturers must demonstrate that these requirements are satisfied for vehicles to pass the type approval. To this end, manufacturers must provide the calculation of the recyclability and recoverability rates[626], which pursuant to point 3 of Annex I is to be made following the method prescribed in Annex B to the standard ISO 226228:2002 ('Road vehicles – Recyclability and recoverability – Calculation method').[627] Manufacturers are obliged to make available to the

---

624 The type-approval of vehicles and their trailers (as well as of systems, components and separate technical units intended for such vehicles) is regulated by Directive 2007/46/EC (OJ L 263, 9 October 2007, p. 1). This directive repeals Directive 70/156/EEC, which is referred to by Directive 2005/64/EC as regards the type-approval procedure. Under Directive 2007/46/EC, vehicles are classified into categories – carriage of persons and their luggage (category M), carriage of goods (category N), and trailers (category O) – and subcategories (M_1 to M_3, N_1 to N_3, and O_1 to O_4, respectively). For each (sub)category, a 'type vehicle' is defined according to certain features (see parts A and B of Annex II to the directive). For each type, certain technical requirements apply, as mandated by legislation. Among them are the reusability, recyclability and recoverability requirements discussed herein, which are applicable to the M_1 and N_1 categories only. Compliance with the mandated requirements must be tested either by the competent authority of a Member State, the so-called approval authority, or by a national technical service (i.e. testing laboratory) designated by that authority. Based on these tests, the approval authority must approve the type, that is, certify that is satisfies the relevant administrative provisions and technical requirements. It then issues the type-approval certificate. An application for approval must be submitted for each type to be approved. Manufacturers may submit the application to the approval authority in any EU country. All vehicles of the approved type may be placed on the market. Manufacturers must deliver a certificate of conformity to accompany each individual vehicle stating that it is manufactured in conformity with the approved vehicle type to which it belongs.

625 Recovery/recycling targets set by article 7(2) of Directive 2000/53/EC are not the same as recoverability/recyclability targets set by Directive 2005/64/EC. The latter refer to the *potentials* of vehicles for recovery/recycling and are therefore higher than the former.

626 The recyclability and/or recoverability rate of a vehicle means the percentage by mass of a new vehicle that can be potentially recycled and/or recovered. See article 4, points 16 and 17, of Directive 2005/64/EC.

627 Points 6 and 7 of Annex I to Directive 2005/64/EC contain other calculation rules.

approval authority detailed technical information necessary for the purposes of the required calculations and checks relating to the nature of the materials used in the construction of the vehicle and its component parts (Article 5(2), first sentence, of Directive 2005/64/EC). In order to fulfil this obligation, manufacturers must submit the data reporting form established by Annex A to the standard ISO 22628:2002, including the material breakdown[628], accompanied by a listing of the dismantled component parts (declared with respect to the dismantling stage) as well as the process recommended for their treatment (see point 2 of Annex I to Directive 2005/64/EC). In cases where the required information is covered by intellectual property rights or constitute specific know-how of manufacturers or of their suppliers, these must provide sufficient information to enable those calculations to be made properly (Article 5(2), second sentence of Directive 2005/64/EC).

'The manufacturer's calculations can be properly validated at the time of the vehicle type-approval only if the manufacturer has put in place satisfactory arrangements and procedures to manage all information he receives from his suppliers. Before any type-approval can be granted, the competent body[629] should carry out a preliminary assessment of those arrangements and procedures and should issue a certificate indicating that they are satisfactory'[630]. This additional obligation is imposed by Article 6 of Directive 2005/64/EC. Points 3 and 4 of Annex IV to the directive set forth the checks to be made by the competent body.

Directive 2006/66/EC on *waste batteries and accumulators* has two provisions on ecodesign. The first one is Article 4, which regulates the chemical composition of batteries and accumulators placed on the EU market by stipulating the maximum amount of mercury and cadmium they may contain. The second one is Article 5, which requires Members States to 'pro-

---

628 In accordance with section 5.2 of standard ISO 22628:2002, '[t]he materials breakdown of the vehicle is established by classifying the materials composing the vehicle into the following seven categories: a) metals; b) polymers, excluding elastomers; c) elastomers; d) glass; e) fluids; f) modified organic natural materials (MONM), such as leather, wood, cardboard and cotton fleece; g) others (components, materials or both, for which a detailed material breakdown cannot be established such as compounds, electronics, electrics)'.

629 Point 20 of Article 4 of Directive 2005/64/EC defines competent body as 'an entity, e.g. a technical service or another existing body, notified by a Member State to carry out preliminary assessment of the manufacturer and to issue a certificate of compliance [...]. The competent body may be the type-approval authority, provided its competence in this field is properly documented'.

630 See recital 7 of Directive 2005/64/EC.

mote research and encourage improvements in the overall environmental performance of batteries and accumulators throughout their entire life cycle as well as the development and marketing of batteries and accumulators which contain smaller quantities of dangerous substances or which contain less polluting substances, in particular as substitutes for mercury, cadmium and lead'.

Lastly, Article 4 of Directive 2012/19/UE on *WEEE*, which is captioned 'product design' (instead of 'waste prevention' as in the other directives), calls on Member States to have producers adopt ecodesign measures aiming at 'facilitating reuse, dismantling and recovery of WEEE, its components and materials' in addition to 'not prevent[ing], through specific design features or manufacturing processes, WEEE from being reused, unless such specific design features or manufacturing processes present overriding advantages, for example, with regard to the protection of the environment and/or safety requirements'.

Unlike packaging, end-of-life vehicles as well as batteries and accumulators, provisions governing the chemical composition of EEE are dealt with in a separate directive, the RoHS Directive. As per Article 4(1) of said directive, EEE, including cables and spare parts for its repair, its reuse, updating of its functionalities or upgrading of its capacity, shall not contain the substances listed in Annex II thereto (namely lead, mercury, cadmium, hexavalent chromium, polybrominated biphenyls and polybrominated diphenyl ethers, bis(2-ethylhexyl) phthalate, butyl benzyl phthalate, dibutyl phthalate, and diisobutyl phthalate).

Normally, the above-discussed ecodesign requirements found in the end-of-life product legislation of the EU are transposed literally into the national law of the Member States. The reigning opinion among specialists commenting on the national transposing legislation is that, except for the prohibitions and/or limits on hazardous substances, provisions on product design are of a rather programmatic nature and hence disregarded in practice, after all, not only are they worded vaguely, thereby hindering enforceability, but also no sanctions exist in case of non-compliance.[631] Recoverability and recyclability requirements for vehicles are a notable exception to this finding, even if verification of compliance with the quan-

631 See, for instance, Flanderka *et al.*, 2015, p. 227; van Calster, 2015, p. 153; Brinktrine, 2013, p. 940; Gattermann, 2013, p. 145; Prelle, 2013, p. 923-924; Prelle, 2010, p. 516 and 518.

titative targets 'is [...] mostly based on self-assessed/calculated information, indicators, and on supporting documentation and labelling'.[632]

II. Brazilian EPR legislation

In Brazil, Article 31, point I, of the PNRS obliges producers to invest in the development, manufacturing and placing on the market of products whose manufacture and use generate the least amount of waste possible and which can be reused, recycled or recovered and/or disposed of in an environmentally sound manner after consumption.

Article 32 of the PNRS has similar provisions for packaging. It prescribes that packaging must be made of materials that enable reuse or recycling (chapeau), restricted in volume and weight to the dimensions required for the protection and commercialisation of the product they contain (paragraph 1, point I), projected so that they can be reused in a manner that is technically viable and compatible with the requirements of the packed product (paragraph 1, point II) as well as recycled if reuse is not possible (paragraph 1, point III). Implementing acts may exempt certain types of packaging from the obligations above where compliance is technically or economically unviable (Article 32, paragraph 2).

Only two pieces of specific EPR legislation lay down product ecodesign requirements. The first one is Conama Resolution No. 362/2005 on lubricating oils, whose Article 4 prescribes that all lubricating oils used in Brazil must observe the principle of recyclability, although without elaborating on what that means.

The second one is Conama Resolution No. 401/2008 on batteries. It imposes limits for the maximum content of mercury, cadmium and lead in portable, button-cell and/or miniature batteries (Article 7) as well as of cadmium and mercury in lead-acid batteries (Article 8). It also requires manufacturers and importers to conduct studies into the replacement or reduction in the amount of hazardous substances contained in batteries (Article 26, chapeau). Such studies must be submitted to, and technically examined by, Ibama[633], which must then report on it to Conama[634] (Arti-

632 See Ardente *et al.*, 2011, p. 20.
633 Ibama is the Brazilian federal environmental protection agency.
634 Conama is the Brazilian National Environmental Council. See footnote 405, *supra*.

cle 26, sole paragraph). In practice, however, this requirement remains wishful thinking.

In 2018, Brazil's then-existing National Chemical Safety Commission set up a working group composed of government, industry and civil society representatives to draft a legislative proposal on the restriction of the use of certain hazardous substances in EEE, known as the Brazilian RoHS.[635] The working group came up with a draft resolution to be put forward to, and ultimately adopted by, Conama[636], which has, nonetheless, not happened yet.

It has been argued elsewhere[637] that the ecodesign mandates of Article 31, point I, and Article 32 of the PNRS apply indistinctly to all products and packaging, and not only to those subjected to the EPR regime, thereby forming a sort of 'general ecodesign clause (or duty)' in Brazilian environmental law. Nevertheless, the indeterminateness of both provisions and the lack of implementing acts elaborating on their application in addition to the absence of penalties for non-compliance render legal enforceability doubtful, a conclusion identical to that reached by European scholars.[638]

III. Appraisal

The preceding considerations show that the only aspect clearly and effectively addressed by both EU and Brazilian end-of-life product legislation when it regulates product ecodesign more directly is the chemical composition of products and packaging with a view to addressing their hazardousness. This finding accords with the evolution of product-oriented environmental law, as discussed above.[639] Regarding other aspects, especially quantitative concerns such as lightweighting or increasing recycled material content, to cite a few examples, ecodesign regulation attempts are usually stifled by the extreme vagueness in which provisions are worded, which hence cannot be applied, as well as by the absence of compliance

635 Further information available at <https://www.mma.gov.br/seguranca-quimica/gestao-das-substancias-quimicas/rohs-brasileira>, last accessed on 12 December 2019.

636 On Conama, see footnote 405, *supra*.

637 See Cipriano, 2016, p. 193.

638 Legal commentary on waste law in general, and on EPR in particular, is still extremely scarce in Brazil. Regarding product-oriented environmental law, it is completely inexistent.

639 See chapter 3, section D, *supra*.

mechanisms. It is precisely this drawback that the EC Ecodesign Directive proposes to surmount.

B. The EC Ecodesign Directive

I. Descriptive overview of the Ecodesign Directive

In the context of both the new approach to harmonisation and standardisation[640] and the IPP[641], Directive 2005/32/EC[642], which established a framework for the setting of ecodesign requirements for energy-using products (hereinafter 'EuPs'), was enacted on the grounds of Article 95 of the Treaty establishing the European Community (now Article 114 of the TFEU) as a means to harmonise the national law of the Member States on the ecodesign of EuPs and hence reduce barriers to trade within the European market.

Directive 2009/125/EC[643], hereinafter 'Ecodesign Directive', has recast Directive 2005/32/EC and extended its scope of application from EuPs to energy-*related* products (hereinafter 'ErPs'), except for means of transport for persons or goods (Article 1(3)[644]).[645] Article 2(1) defines ErPs as goods having an impact on energy consumption during use[646] and whose envi-

640 On the new approach, see footnote 618, *supra*.

641 See chapter 3, section D, *supra*.

642 OJ L 191, 22 July 2005, p. 29.

643 OJ L 285, 31 October 2009, p. 10.

644 Henceforth in this section, unless otherwise specified, the provisions (recitals and/or articles) mentioned in this section refer to the Ecodesign Directive.

645 Despite their sizeable impact on the environment, means of transport have been excluded from the scope of the Ecodesign Directive because, at least as regards motor vehicles, their environmental impact is already addressed by existing (or proposed, albeit not yet adopted) legislation, so that the benefits of applying the Ecodesign Directive to them would be limited. Concerning means of transport other than road transport, the application of the Ecodesign would not only bring comparatively smaller benefits, but also face difficulties. See SEC (2008) 2115, 16 July 2008, p. 23-24.

646 For Schomerus and Spengler (2010, p. 61), a literal interpretation of the definition makes it is hard to find a product that does not in any way have an impact on energy consumption. For this reason, they advocate that ErPs should be understood in a narrower sense, namely as products directly affecting energy consumption during use. Similarly, Mertens (2011, p. 239-330) explains that the Ecodesign Directive only applies 'to products having an impact on energy

ronmental performance[647] can be assessed independently. Parts intended to be incorporated into ErPs as well as those placed on the market and/or put into service as individual parts for end-users are also encompassed in the definition. Although not applicable to every single product, the recast directive is aimed at reducing environmental impacts in general, and achieving energy savings in particular, through improved design not only of products that use, generate, transfer and/or measure energy, but also of products that affect energy consumption (i.e. that contribute to energy conservation during their use[648]), including, for example, windows, insulation materials or even some water-using products such as shower heads or taps (see recital 4).

Just like its forerunner, the Ecodesign Directive does not itself lay down ecodesign requirements. Instead, it only provides for the framework within which such requirements may be imposed.

Among the ErPs to which the Ecodesign Directive applies, only those meeting the threshold criteria laid down in Article 15(2) qualify for being targeted by a measure establishing ecodesign requirements. In this sense, ErPs must, firstly, represent a *significant* volume of sales and trade, secondly, have a *significant* environmental impact within the EU, *and*, thirdly, present *significant* potential for improvement in terms of its environmental impact without entailing excessive costs.[649] The 'significance' of these three factors is to be assessed based on the parameters offered in Article 15(2), as follows:

- the volume of sales and trade is significant if it exceeds the *indicative* amount of more than 200,000 units a year within the EU according to the most recently available figures (Article 15(2)(a));

---

consumption during use', as opposed to 'products having an impact on energy consumption during manufacturing, packaging, transport, distribution, installation, maintenance, recycling, recovery or reuse'.

647 'Environmental performance' corresponds to 'the results of the manufacturer's management of the environmental aspects of the product, as reflected in its technical documentation file' (article 2, point 21). 'Environmental aspect', in turn, is defined as 'an element or function of a product that can interact with the environment during its life cycle' (article 2, point 11).

648 See Mertens, 2011, p. 330.

649 For Malcom (2011, p. 496), this 'significance requirement' is reminiscent of Directive 85/337/EEC (OJ L 175, 5 July 1985, p. 40), known as the Environmental Impact Assessment Directive, which is applicable only to 'those public and private projects [that] are likely to have *significant* effects on the environment' (emphasis added).

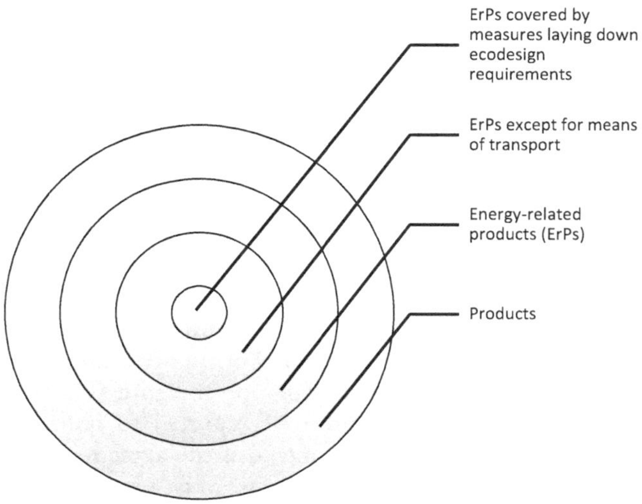

Figure 4 – Products the ecodesign of which may be regulated under the Ecodesign Directive

- environmental impacts are to be regarded significant considering the quantities of ErPs placed on the market and/or put into service as well as the strategic priorities set out in the Environment Action Programme[650] (Article 15(2)(b));
- the potential for improvement is all the more significant the greater the absence of other relevant EU legislation or the failure of market forces to address the issue properly as well as the wider the disparity in the environmental performance of products available on the market with equivalent functionality (Article 15(2)(c)).

The fact that the threshold criteria above must be satisfied cumulatively indicates a considerable restriction in the application of the Ecodesign Directive.

Based on the same threshold criteria, the European Commission must establish a three-year working plan containing an indicative list of product groups that are considered as priorities for the adoption of implementing

650 See Decision No. 1386/2013/EU (OJ L 354, 28 December 2013, p. 171) on a General Union Environment Action Programme to 2020 'Living well, within the limits of our planet' (7th Environment Action Programme).

measures.[651] Working plans may be set out only after the Consultation Forum[652] has been consulted.

Once the so-to-speak 'significance test' has been passed (and products and/or product groups have thus been included in the working plan), measures laying down ecodesign requirements may be adopted. Such measures may be of two types: *self-regulatory* measures or *implementing* measures.

Self-regulatory measures, including (and usually in the form of) voluntary agreements, are preferred alternatives to implementing measures,[653] but their admissibility as such must be evaluated according to the nine indicative criteria listed in a non-exhaustive fashion by Annex VIII (Article 17).[654] Industry proposals are presented to the European Commission and must be submitted for discussion by the Consultation Forum. The European Commission's decision to recognise the self-regulation measure as a valid alternative to an implementing measure must be reported to both the European Parliament and the Council and the text of the agreement, together with other relevant accompanying documents, must be published. So far, self-regulation under the Ecodesign Directive, in the form of vol-

651 Working plans are formulated based on preparatory studies commissioned by the European Commission. For the working plans adopted for the periods 2009-2011, 2012-2014 and 2016-2019, see, respectively, COM (2008) 660 final, 21 October 2008, SWD (2012) 434 final, 7 December 2012, as well as COM (2016) 773 final, 30 November 2016.

652 The Consultation Forum is a group of sixty experts representing EU Member States, EEA Member States and all interested parties concerned with the ErP or product group in question, including small and medium-sized enterprises (hereinafter referred to as 'SMEs') as well as craft industry, trade unions, traders, retailers, importers, environmental protection groups and consumer organisations. See article 18 of the Ecodesign Directive as well as Commission Decision 2008/591/EC on the Ecodesign Consultation Forum (OJ L 190, 18 July 2008, p. 222).

653 Recital 18 reads: 'Priority should be given to alternative courses of action such as self-regulation by the industry where such action is likely to deliver the policy objectives faster or in a less costly manner than mandatory requirements. Legislative measures may be needed where market forces fail to evolve in the right direction or at an acceptable speed'.

654 See Commission Recommendation (EU) 2016/2125 of 30 November 2016 on guidelines for self-regulation measures concluded by industry under Directive 2009/125/EC of the European Parliament and of the Council (OJ L 329, 3 December 2016, p. 109).

untary agreements recognised by the European Commission, exists for complex set-top boxes[655], imaging equipment[656] and games consoles[657].[658]

Implementing measures are legal acts (Article 291(2) and (4) of the TFEU) introduced by the European Commission and they have so far taken the form of regulations in the sense of Article 288 of the TFEU. For the preparation and the adoption thereof, a set of conditions of both *procedural* and *substantive* nature must be satisfied. This further 'filters' the imposing of ecodesign requirements on ErPs.

From a *procedural* perspective, implementing measures are adopted in accordance with the (comitology) regulatory procedure with scrutiny, which means that the European Commission is assisted (i.e. controlled) by a regulatory committee composed of representatives of the Member States in the law-making process.[659] Furthermore, the procedural requisites of Article 15(4) apply, which means that in preparing the implementing measure the European Commission must, in sum:

---

655 See 'voluntary industry agreement to improve the energy consumption of complex set-top boxes within the EU – proposal from the industry group, version 6.0' as of 2 April 2018, available at <http://cstb.eu/wp-content/uploads/2018/08/EU-VA-V6.pdf>, last accessed on 18 December 2019. See also COM (2012) 684 final, 22 November 2012.

656 See 'industry voluntary agreement to improve the environmental performance of imaging equipment placed on the European market', version 5.2 as of April 2015, available at <https://ec.europa.eu/energy/sites/ener/files/documents/VA%20Imaging%20Self-Regulatory%20Initiative-V-4-0.pdf>, last accessed on 18 December 2019. See also COM (2013) 23 final, 29 January 2013.

657 See 'self-regulatory initiative to further improve the energy efficiency of games consoles', version 2.6.3 as of 11 October 2018, available at <http://efficientgaming.eu/fileadmin/user_upload/2018_SCM/Final_Games_Consoles_SRI_v2.6.3_20181115.pdf>, last accessed on 18 December 2019. See also COM (2015) 178 final, 22 April 2015.

658 The voluntary agreements and their respective impact assessment are available at <https://ec.europa.eu/energy/sites/ener/files/documents/List_Eco-design-Voluntary%20Agreements.pdf>, last accessed on 18 December 2019.

659 Pursuant to article 15 of the Ecodesign Directive, implementing measures must be adopted in accordance with the regulatory procedure with scrutiny referred to in article 19(3) thereof, which states that article 5a (1) to (4) as well as article 7 of Council Decision 1999/468/EC laying down the procedures for the exercise of implementing powers conferred on the Commission (OJ L 184, 17 July 1999, p. 23) must apply. Even though Regulation (EU) 182/2011 (OJ L 55, 28 February 2011, p. 13) repeals Council Decision 1999/468/EC, article 12, second subparagraph, of Regulation (EU) 182/2011 provides that '[t]he effects of article 5a of [Council] Decision 1999/468/EC shall be maintained for the purposes of existing basic acts making reference thereto'.

- adopt a life cycle approach;
- carry out an impact assessment;
- consider existing national environmental legislation that Member States consider relevant;
- consult with stakeholders;
- prepare an explanatory memorandum of the draft regulation based on the impact assessment; and
- provide for a progressive implementation taking into account possible impacts on SMEs.

The procedure for preparing and adopting implementing measures that impose ecodesign requirements works as follows.[660] It starts with a preparatory study that is conducted by consultants commissioned by the European Commission. The study is carried out based on the 'methodology for the ecodesign of energy-related products' (hereinafter 'MEErP')[661]. After stakeholder input into the draft reports has been provided, a non-binding final report is prepared. The European Commission produces a working document with proposals for implementing measures that is discussed in the Consultation Forum. An impact assessment is then carried out and the European Commission drafts the implementing measure. The draft regulation is submitted to the regulatory committee for approval under the comitology procedure.

From a *substantial* viewpoint (Article 15(5)), implementing measures that lay down ecodesign requirements should, on the one hand, *not* adversely affect health, safety and the environment, while, on the other hand, have the least negative impact on some non-environmental concerns, including consumers' interests (e.g. functionality and affordability of the ErP) and producers' interests (e.g. industry's competitiveness). In addition, implementing measures should *not* impose excessive administrative burden on manufacturers or have the consequence of imposing proprietary technology on them either.

Implementing measures are thus to set out ecodesign requirements, which are defined as 'any requirement in relation to a product [i.e. an ErP], or the design of a product, intended to improve its environmental performance[662], or any requirement for the supply of information

660 See Dahalmmar, 2014, p. 159-160, and Siderius, 2012. More elaborately, see Peiró *et al.*, 2019, p. 5; Hinchliffe and Akkerman, 2017, p. 1604.

661 See Kemna *et al.*, 2011.

662 'Improvement of the environmental performance' is 'the process of enhancing the environmental performance of a product over successive generations, al-

with regard to the environmental aspects of a product' (Article 2, point 24).[663] Implementing measures may, however, stipulate that no ecodesign requirement is necessary for certain ecodesign parameters (Article 15(6), third subparagraph).

Ecodesign requirements may be *generic* or *specific*. The difference between them lies in the fact that the latter set limit values, whereas the former do not.[664]

Annex I specifies the method for setting *generic* ecodesign requirements, which are to focus on selected environmental aspects that have a *significant* environmental impact (Article 15(6), first subparagraph). The identification of the significant environmental aspects that must be specified in the implementing measure is incumbent on the European Commission when preparing the draft to be submitted to the committee (Annex I, first paragraph).

Annex I is divided into three parts. Part 1 deals with 'ecodesign parameters for products'. It contains a non-exhaustive list of parameters (point 1.3) that must be used for evaluating the potential for improving the environmental aspects (point 1.2) of ErPs for each life cycle phase (point 1.1). Part 2 concerns the kind of information consumers and downstream operators are to be provided with by manufacturers and how it is to be supplied. Member States may demand that information be given in their official language(s) (Article 5(5)). Part 3 requires manufacturers to establish the ecological profiles[665] of ErPs and to make use of them to evaluate alternative design solutions as well as the achieved environmental performance of the product against the benchmarks to be identified by the European Commission in the implementing measure on the basis of the information gathered in the preparation thereof.

---

though not necessarily in respect of all environmental aspects of the product simultaneously' (article 2(22)). For the definition of 'environmental performance' and 'environmental aspects', see footnote 647, *supra*.

663 Henceforth in this section, reference is made to 'performance standards' and 'information standards' to distinguish between the two types of ecodesign requirements.

664 See article 2(25) combined with Annex I for generic ecodesign requirements and article 2(26) combined with Annex III for specific ecodesign requirements.

665 Point 20 of Article 2 defines ecological profile as 'a description, in accordance with the implementing measure applicable to the product, of the inputs and outputs (such as materials, emissions and waste) associated with a product throughout its life cycle which are significant from the point of view of its environmental impact and are expressed in physical quantities that can be measured'.

The method for setting *specific* ecodesign requirements is foreseen in Annex II. Limit values are to be set for the ecodesign parameters referred to in Part 1 of Annex I and they are to be based on a technical, environmental and economic analysis, 'which is [...] commonly known as the [...] preparatory study'[666]. In the case of energy consumption, the level of energy efficiency must be set following a life cycle cost analysis and a sensitivity analysis. Furthermore, the date of entry into force of the requirement must take the redesign cycle for the product into account.

Regardless of the type of requirements laid down, implementing measures, as legal acts, must include the elements listed in Annex VII (Article 16(8)). In addition, they must be formulated so as to ensure that market surveillance authorities can verify the conformity of the product with the requirements of the implementing measure, with the implementing measure specifying whether verification can be achieved directly on the product or on the basis of the technical documentation (Article 16(7)).

Once an implementing measure setting down ecodesign requirements has been adopted, before placing the ErP covered by it on the market[667] and/or putting such a product into service[668], the manufacturer or its authorised representative is obliged to ensure that:

- an assessment of the ErP's conformity with the applicable implementing measure is carried out (Article 8(1)), which may be done in accordance with either the internal design control procedure established in Annex IV or the management system procedure established in Annex V[669] (Article 8(2));

---

666 Kemna *et al.*, 2011, p. 19.

667 As per article 2, point 4, placing on the market means 'making a product available for the first time on the [EU] market with a view to its distribution or use within the [EU], whether for reward or free of charge and irrespective of the selling technique'.

668 Putting into service means 'the first use of a product for its intended purpose by an end-user in the [EU] (article 2(5)).

669 There are two situations in which the management system of the organisation carrying out the conformity assessment may be presumed to comply with the requirements of Annex V on the management system procedure. Firstly, 'where a product covered by implementing measures is designed by an organisation registered in accordance with Regulation (EC) 761/2001 of the European Parliament and of the Council of 19 March 2001 allowing voluntary participation by organisations in a Community eco-management and audit scheme (EMAS) (OJ L 114, 24 April 2001, p. 1), repealed by Regulation (EC) 1221/2009 (OJ L 342, 22 December 2009, p. 1, and the design function is included within the scope of that registration' (article 8(2), third subparagraph). Secondly, 'if a product covered by implementing measures is designed by an organisation

- a CE marking, as specified in Annex III, is affixed to the ErP (Article 5(1) and (2));
- an EC declaration of conformity stating that the ErP complies with the provisions of the applicable implementing measure is issued, which must contain the elements referred to in Annex VII (Article 5(1) and (3)).

In the absence of the manufacturer or its authorised representative, the importer must ensure compliance of the ErP with the Ecodesign Directive and applicable implementing measure as well as keep and make available the declaration of conformity and the technical documentation (Article 4).

ErPs bearing the CE marking must be presumed to conform to the applicable implementing measure (Article 9(1))[670], and compliant ErPs enjoy free access to and movement within the EU market (Article 6). Market surveillance falls on Member States (Article 3), which, under the conditions and the procedure set out in Article 7, may impose sanctions in case of non-compliance. These sanctions range from obliging the manufacturer of a non-compliant ErP, or its authorised representative, to make the product comply with the implementing measure through the restriction or prohibition of the placing on the market and/or the putting into service of the non-compliant ErP to determining the withdrawal of the non-compliant ErP from the market. The burden of proof falls on Member States (Article 7 combined with Article 8(2), second subparagraph).

---

having a management system which includes the product design function, and which is implemented in accordance with harmonised standards, the reference numbers of which have been published in the *Official Journal of the European Union*' (article 8(2), fourth subparagraph).

670 In accordance with articles 9(2) to (4) as well as articles 10(2) to (4) of the Ecodesign Directive, conformity to the relevant ecodesign requirements of the applicable implementing measure may be presumed in two situations: firstly, in respect of products for which harmonised standards relating to and presumed to satisfy such requirements have been applied; secondly, in respect of products that have been awarded the EU Ecolabel pursuant to Regulation (EC) 66/2010 (OJ L 27, 30 January 2010, p. 1) – or other ecolabels that the European Commission considers to fulfil equivalent conditions to the EU Ecolabel – in so far as the ecodesign requirements are met by the ecolabel.

II. Discussion on the much-lauded potential of the Ecodesign Directive: is it the 'Super Directive'?

In that the Ecodesign Directive is built on a life cycle approach and allows for ecodesign aspects of products other than energy consumption during the use phase to be addressed, thereby covering all environmental issues, it has been lauded as the 'Super Directive'.[671] This section enquires into the real potential of the Ecodesign Directive in advancing product ecodesign regulation by discussing both its strengths and shortcomings. A closer inspection of the implementing and self-regulatory measures laying down ecodesign requirements offers some insights into the role of the Ecodesign Directive in advancing environmental product improvement.

1. Standard setting and regulatory unambitiousness: does the Ecodesign Directive provide impetus to eco-innovation?

The ecodesign requirements set out by implementing and self-regulatory measures under the Ecodesign Directive, apart from focusing on energy consumption reduction during the use phase of products, take the form of performance (as opposed to technology-based) standards.

In environmental economics[672] and environmental law[673] parlance, standards refer to regulations mandating certain environmental protection outcomes.[674]Seen from the perspective of the adverse effects of human activity on the environment, these outcomes may be set in relation to either the affected environment or the activities affecting it.

In the first case, the level of environmental quality – or, more precisely, the quality level of biotic and/or abiotic components of the environment – that is deemed necessary and/or adequate as a policy goal is determined. For this reason, reference is made to '(environmental) quality standards'. Quality standards have been typically resorted to with a view to combating pollution, that is, in order to protect the environment in its sink function.

---

671 See Schomerus and Spengler, 2010.

672 See, for instance, Jaffe, Newel and Stavins, 2003, p. 477-478; Pearce, 2002, p. 72-73.

673 See, for instance, Driesen, Adler and Engel, 2016, p. 127-278; Bell, McGillivray and Pedersen, 2013, p. 239-249; Sachs, 2012, p. 1640; Coglianese, Nash and Olmstead, 2003.

674 Standards are the epitome of the command-and-control approach to environmental regulation.

Standards prescribing the quality of environmental media[675] – namely air, water and soil – are the most characteristic type and they are habitually named 'ambient standards'.

In turn, when setting environmental protection outcomes based on the human activities affecting the environment rather than the affected environment, standards limit (i.e. put a ceiling on or require the reduction of) the amount of environmental degradation arising from particular sources, usually as a way to meet quality standards. Sources can be production processes or the products themselves. While environmental degradation may refer to either natural resource depletion or – more traditionally – pollution. In pollution-oriented environmental law, so-to-speak 'source-related standards' are called 'emission (or effluent) standards'[676].

Seen from the perspective of how to achieve the environmental protection outcomes, standards may be means-oriented or ends-oriented. The former, better known as 'technology-based standards'[677], specify by which means human activity – once again, production processes and/or products – is to reach the required environmental policy goals. Concerning production processes, technology-based standards normally dictate a particular method, technique and/or technology to be employed or sometimes even the actual equipment to be used.[678] As regards products, they may determine characteristics that goods must have, including the regulation of a product's composition (i.e. materials/input requirements), form, content, design, construction, finish, or packaging.[679] In turn, end-oriented standards, better known as 'performance standards', establish criteria for the functioning (hence 'performance') of production processes and/or products so that quality and/or source-related standards are met. In contrast to technology-based standards, performance standards allow some latitude in how to comply with regulation (flexibility) and are therefore preferred.

675 Of course, this can be done in a generic or specific way. For example, regulation may provide that a certain medium must, say, 'remain reasonably clean' (generic quality standard) or set the maximum allowed level of a certain pollutant in a certain medium (specific quality standard).

676 Emission standards refer to discharges into the air, whereas effluent standards refer to discharges into watercourses.

677 Technology-based standards are known by plenty of other names, including 'design standards', 'engineering standards', 'descriptive standards', and 'specification standards'.

678 Production-related, technology-based standards can also be generic, however, as in the case of the so-called 'best available technology standards'.

679 See, for instance, Asafu-Adjaye, 2005, p. 84; Klayman, 1982, p. 104.

Although not technology-prescriptive, the ecodesign requirements imposed so far by implementing and self-regulatory measures under the Ecodesign Directive, as performance standards, have rarely been technology forcing[680]. Product improvement has only been incremental for two main reasons.

Firstly, like any product standard, and in accordance with the principle of legal certainty, ecodesign requirements apply only to new products as they are placed on the market (i.e. non-retroactivity).[681]

Secondly and most fundamentally, implementation of ecodesign requirements occurs gradually.[682] Implementing and self-regulatory measures usually lay down ecodesign requirements under a staged, 'double-tiered' approach. Initially, a first set of more modest improvements is required to be in place at a certain point in time, normally one year after the entering into force of the measure onwards ('first-tier requirements'). Then another set of (more stringent) requirements, or an increased stringency of the ones already in force, is mandated to take effect at later date ('second-tier requirements').[683] This gives some time for manufacturers to make the necessary production adjustments and, in particular, allows them to align medium and long-term changes with product design cycles and investment decisions.[684]

The lack of stringency of the ecodesign requirements can be explained in part by the lengthy process of making and adopting implementing measures[685], which renders the setting and updating of standards cumber-

---

680 Technology-forcing standards are those which '[command] results beyond the capabilities of existing technology' (Sachs, 2012, p. 1645, especially note 47), in the case of performance standards, or which '[mandate] technologies that are not fully developed' (Jaffe, Newel and Stavins, 2003, p. 477), in the case of technology-based standards, thereby requiring technological innovation.

681 Similarly, see Sachs, 2009, p. 314.

682 See Dietrich and Akkerman, 2013, p. 275; Mertens, 2011, p. 347.

683 See Siderius and Nakagami, 2013, p. 7. See also Ballu and Toulouse, 2010, p. 24. 'Multi-tiered' approaches (i.e. implementation of ecodesign requirements in more than two stages) also exist.

684 See Dalhammar, 2014, p. 159. Ecodesign requirements are not immutable, however. Implementing measures must specify the date for their evaluation and possible revision taking into account the speed of technological progress (item 9 of Annex VII). The same applies to self-regulatory, voluntary agreements, which must contain a review clause (item 4.14 of the European Commission's draft 'Guidelines on self-regulation measures concluded by industry under the Ecodesign Directive 2009/125/EC').

685 The average duration of the legislative process is estimated at around five years (Oehlmann, 2017, p. 230; Dalhammar *et al.*, 2014, p. 35; Centre for Strategy &

some.[686] For example, it has been reported that '[t]he delays in the development of an implementing measure for boilers and water heaters have led to a missed opportunity in terms of energy saving'[687]. Delays can be attributed to various, albeit interdependent, factors, including extensive stakeholder participation, absence of strict deadlines, lack of cooperation by stakeholders, understaffing of the European Commission, low-quality preparatory studies, and complexity and/or contentiousness of the subject matter being regulated.[688]

Another factor contributing to the modesty of ecodesign requirements is whether upcoming technology is accounted for or not.[689] In the case of televisions, for instance, implementing measures failed to take into account the (then) emerging technological development, which allowed new televisions to easily comply with, and even surpass, the energy efficiency requirements set.[690] This meant that ecodesign requirements not only failed to trigger eco-innovation, but also were already out-dated when the implementing measure was adopted.[691]-[692]

Finally, the stringency of ecodesign requirements, at least with regard to energy efficiency, is further limited by the adoption of the *least* life cycle cost approach required by Article 15(5)(c) and elucidated by point 1, fifth paragraph, of Annex II to the Ecodesign Directive[693]. Behind these provi-

---

Evaluation Services, 2012, p. 122; Siderius, 2012, p. 2). The time span increases to almost seven years if one considers the period between the start of the preparatory study and the entering into force of the second-tier requirements (Siderius and Nakagami, 2013, p. 8).

686 See Dalhammar, 2014, p. 164. For this reason, it has been proposed that the legislative process be made more flexible by setting requirements in more than two tiers, with checkpoints along the way: standards may be tightened or loosened depending on technological development. See Dalhammar, 2015b, p. 36.

687 Centre for Strategy & Evaluation Services, 2012, p. 134.

688 For a more detailed account of the reasons for delays, including proposals to reduce them, see Siderius, 2012. See also Centre for Strategy & Evaluation Services, 2012, p. 122-125.

689 Dalhammar *et al.*, 2014, p. 36.

690 See Huulgaard and Remmen, 2012, p. 16, 18-19.

691 See Huulgaard and Remmen, 2012, p. 16, 18-19.

692 Not to mention the failure to account for the market trend of televisions having increasingly larger screens, which increases energy consumption and thus offsets the energy savings intended by the ecodesign requirements (see Huulgaard and Remmen, 2012, p. 17-18).

693 The latter provision reads: 'Concerning energy consumption in use, the level of energy efficiency or consumption must be set aiming at the life cycle cost minimum to end-users for representative product models, taking into account

sions is the idea that the imposition of ecodesign requirements should not make consumers worse off: an increase in product price as a result of the adoption of implementing measures should be offset by the decrease of other costs, especially energy costs, resulting from the mandated product (performance) improvement.[694] Calculations must therefore be made. Currently available technical saving options are identified based on the *status quo* and life cycle costs are simulated for each option.[695] This involves estimating purchase prices of best performing (i.e. most efficient) products, energy savings from these products as well as energy prices.[696] At least three problems can be identified in connection with this method: firstly, price and energy efficiency are not necessarily correlated; secondly, prices are not necessarily the best proxy for costs; thirdly and most importantly, the absence of 'learning (or experience) curves' in life cycle cost calculations showing how quickly prices of top performing products decrease over time leads to an overestimation of prices and therefore the setting of less strict standards.[697]

Because of this regulatory unambitiousness, the Ecodesign Directive is less a driver for eco-innovation than it has the effect of phasing out the worst performing products.[698] Particularly illustrative of this observation is the regulation of non-directional household lamps: Commission Regulation (EC) 244/2009[699] set down (gradual) technical performance require-

---

the consequences on other environmental aspects. The life cycle cost analysis method uses a real discount rate on the basis of data provided from the European Central Bank and a realistic lifetime for the product; it is based on the sum of the variations in purchase price (resulting from the variations in industrial costs) and in operating expenses, which result from the different levels of technical improvement options, discounted over the lifetime of the representative product models considered. The operating expenses cover primarily energy consumption and additional expenses in other resources, such as water or detergents.'.

694 See Siderius, 2013, p. 762.

695 See Jepsen *et al.*, 2011, p. 57-60, who point out to the fact that the *least* life cycle does not match the most stringent option.

696 See Siderius, 2013, p. 762.

697 See Dalhammar, 2014, p. 161-162; Siderius, 2013, p. 770; Jepsen *et al.*, 2011, p. 57-63.

698 See Dalhammar, 2014, p. 164; Sachs, 2012, p. 1649; Tholen, 2011, p. 480.

699 OJ L 76, 24 March 2009, p. 3. Commission Regulation (EC) 244/2009, as amended by Commission Regulation (EC) 859/2009 (OJ L 247, 19 September 2009, p. 3) and Commission Regulation (EU) 2015/1428 (OJ L 224, 27 August 2015, p. 1), has been repealed with effect from 1 September 2021 by Commis-

ments that incandescent and conventional halogen light bulbs could not satisfy,[700] which have consequently been removed from the market.[701]-[702]

2. From energy efficiency to non-energy environmental aspects

Energy and the use phase of products are, respectively, the environmental aspect and the product life cycle stage that unquestionably lie at the centre of the Ecodesign Directive's concerns.[703] Recitals 6 and 14 make it very clear that the policy focus lies on energy efficiency improvement, for example through savings in electricity consumption during the use phase of products, as a means to mitigate greenhouse gas emissions.

This notwithstanding, in the Ecodesign Directive there are explicit references to a life cycle approach[704] and to different environmental aspects along the product life cycle other than energy that are worth regulatory attention.

---

sion Regulation (EU) 2019/2020 on ecodesign requirements for light sources and separate control gears (OJ L 315, 5 December 2019, p.209).

700 See Brenncke, 2009, p. 247. See also European Commission, MEMO/09/368 (FAQ: phasing out conventional incandescent bulbs), Brussels, 1 September 2009, available at <http://europa.eu/rapid/press-release_MEMO-09-368_en.htm?locale=en>, last accessed on 5 September 2016.

701 This has been often regarded as a product ban (see, for instance, Wegener, 2009, p. 169). Of course, one may speak only of a *de facto* product ban. For, strictly legally speaking, what regulation does is to prescribe the performance of a certain product or product group (*Gebot*) rather than to proscribe it altogether (*Verbot*). In the case under consideration, 'household lamps' as regulated by Commission Regulation (EC) 244/2009 represent a whole product category and, as such, correspond to the 'relevant market' (to borrow the terminology of competition law), with only specific products from this group, namely incandescent and conventional halogen light bulbs, being forced off the market exclusively as a result of their being inefficient. Similarly, see Tölle, 2016, p.93; Brenncke, 2009, p. 249.

702 In Brazil, the phase-out of incandescent light bulbs has been mandated by a federal ordinance issued jointly by the Ministry of Mines and Energy, the Ministry of Science and Technology as well as the Ministry of Development, Industry and International Trade (*Portaria Interministerial* MME/MCT/MDIC No. 1,007/2010, DOU 4, Section 1, 6 January 2011, p. 44) in implementation of Federal Law No. 10,295/2001 (DOU 200, Section 1, 18 January 2001, p.), which governs the National Policy on the Conservation and Rational Use of Energy.

703 See Mertens, 2011, p. 334.

704 See, for instance, recitals 7 and 13, article 15(4)(a) as well as point 1.1 of part I of Annex I.

For instance, Annex I, part 1, point 1.2 of the Ecodesign Directive provides that generic ecodesign requirements may be set in respect of consumption of *inter alia* materials and other resources such as fresh water; emissions to air, water or soil; pollution through physical effects such as noise, vibration, radiation, electromagnetic fields; generation of waste material; reuse, recycling and recovery of materials.

With regard to specific ecodesign requirements, Annex II states that '[t]hey may take the form of requirements for reduced consumption of a given resource, such as a limit on the use of a resource in the various stages of an product's life cycle, as appropriate (such as a limit on water consumption in the use phase or on the quantities of a given material incorporated in the product or a requirement for minimum quantities of recycled material)'.

Therefore, despite the focus on energy consumption during the use phase of products (i.e. one environmental aspect at one specific life cycle stage), the Ecodesign Directive does allow for the setting of, as some implementing as well as self-regulatory measures have already laid down, requirements in connection with other non-energy environmental aspects, as shown below.

a) Ecodesign performance requirements

Given the distinction made between performance and information requirements,[705] this subsection looks at the former type of requirements imposed by both implementing and self-regulatory measures.

aa) Implementing measures

Regulation of environmental aspects other than energy efficiency by the implementing measures adopted so far is found in relation to several products and/or product groups, as summarised in the following table:

705 See footnote 663, *supra*.

Table 5 – Non-energy aspects regulated by implementing measures under the Ecodesign Directive

Product (group)	Non-energy aspect/requirements
Heaters[706], boilers[707] as well as air heating products, cooling products, high temperature process chillers and fan coil units[708]	Limit values for emissions of nitrogen oxides, particulate matter, organic gaseous compounds and carbon monoxide
Air conditioners[709]; vacuum cleaners[710]; space heaters, combination heaters, water heaters and hot water storage tanks[711]; ventilation units[712]	Noise

706 See point 4 of Annex II to Commission Regulation (EU) 813/2013 on ecodesign requirements for space heaters and combination heaters (OJ L 239, 6 September 2013, p. 136), point 1.5 of Annex II to Commission Regulation (EU) 814/2013 on ecodesign requirements for water heaters and hot water storage tanks (OJ L 239, 6 September 2013, p. 162), point 2 of Annex II to Commission Regulation (EU) 2015/1185 on ecodesign requirements for solid fuel local space heaters (OJ L 193, 21 July 2015, p. 1), as amended by Commission Regulation No. 2016/2282 (OJ L 346, 20 December 2016, p. 51), as well as point 2 of Annex II to Commission Regulation (EU) 2015/1188 on ecodesign requirements for local space heaters (OJ L 193, 21 July 2015, p. 83), as amended by Commission Regulation (EU) 2016/2282.

707 See points 1(c) to 1(f) of Annex II to Commission Regulation (EU) 2015/1189 on ecodesign requirements for solid fuel boilers (OJ L 193, 21 July 2015, p. 100), as amended by Commission Regulation (EU) 2016/2282.

708 See point 4 of Annex II to Commission Regulation (EU) 2016/2281 on ecodesign requirements for air heating products, cooling products, high temperature process chillers and fan coil units (OJ L 346, 20 December 2016, p. 1), as amended by Commission Regulation (EU) 2016/2282.

709 See tables 3 and 5 of point 2 of Annex II to Commission Regulation (EU) 206/2012 on ecodesign requirements for air conditioners and comfort fans (OJ L 72, 10 March 2012, p. 17), as amended by Commission Regulation (EU) 2016/2282.

710 See sixth indent of point 1(b) of Annex I to Commission Regulation (EU) 666/2013 on ecodesign requirements for vacuum cleaners (OJ L 192, 13 July 2013, p. 24), as amended by Commission Regulation (EU) 2016/2282.

711 See point 3 of Annex II to Commission Regulation (EU) 813/2013 and point 1.4 of Annex II of Commission Regulation (EU) 814/2013.

712 See the second indent of points 1 and 2 of Annex II to Commission Regulation (EU) 1253/2014 on ecodesign requirements for ventilation units (OJ L 337, 25 November 2014, p. 8), as amended by Commission Regulation (EU) 2016/2282.

Product (group)	Non-energy aspect/requirements
Electronic displays[713]	Prohibition of the use of halogenated flame retardants in the enclosure and stand of electronic displays
Washing machines and washer-dryers[714]	Water consumption
Household dishwashers[715]; washing machines and washer-dryers[716]	Provision of an eco-programme
Light sources [717]	Lifetime
Vacuum cleaners[718]	Durability of the hose (if any)
	Lifetime of the operational motor

713 See point 4 of section D of Commission Regulation (EU) 2019/2021 on ecodesign requirements for electronic displays (OJ L 315, 5 December 2012, p. 241), which shall apply from 1 March 2021 and repeals Commission Regulation (EC) 642/2009 on ecodesign requirements for televisions (OJ L 191, 23 July 2009, p. 42), as amended by Commission Regulation (EU) 801/2013 (OJ L 225, 23 August 2013, p. 1) and Commission Regulation (EU) 2016/2282.

714 See point 6 of Annex II to Commission Regulation (EU) 2019/2023 on ecodesign requirements for household washing machines and household washer-dryers (OJ L 315, 5 December 2019, p. 285), which shall apply from 1 March 2021 and repeals Commission Regulation (EU) 1015/2010 on ecodesign requirements for household washing machines (OJ L 293, 11 November 2010, p. 21), as amended by Commission Regulation (EU) 2016/2282.

715 See point 5(1) and 5(5) of Annex II to Commission Regulation (EU) 2019/2022 on ecodesign requirements for household dishwashers (OJ 315, 5 December 2019, p. 267).

716 See points 8(1), 8(2) and 8(5) of Annex II to Commission Regulation (EU) 2019/2023.

717 See Commission Regulation (EU) 2019/2020 on ecodesign requirements for light sources and separate control gears (OJ L 315, 5 December 2019, p.209), which shall apply from 1 September 2021 and repeals the following three regulations: Commission Regulation (EC) 244/2009 on ecodesign requirements for non-directional household lamps (OJ L 76, 24 March 2009, p. 3), as amended by Commission Regulation (EC) 859/2009 (OJ L 247, 19 September 2009, p. 3) and by Commission Regulation (EU) 2015/1428 (OJ L 224, 27 August 2015, p. 1); Commission Regulation (EC) 245/2009 on ecodesign requirements for fluorescent lamps without integrated ballast, for high intensity discharge lamps, and for ballasts and luminaires able to operate such lamps (OJ L 76, 24 March 2009, p. 17), as amended by Commission Regulation (EC) 347/2010 (OJ L 104, 24 April 2010, p. 20) and by Commission Regulation (EU) 2015/1428; Commission Regulation (EU) 1194/2012 on ecodesign requirements for directional lamps, light emitting diode lamps and related equipment (OJ L 342, 14 December 2012, p. 1), as amended by Commission Regulation (EU) 2015/1428.

718 See the seventh and eight indents of point 1(b) of Annex I to Commission Regulation (EU) 666/2013.

Product (group)	Non-energy aspect/requirements
Servers and data storage products[719]	Availability of the latest version of, and the latest available security update to, the firmware for a minimum period after the placing on the market of the last product of a certain product model, free of charge and/or at a fair, transparent and non-discriminatory cost
	Joining or sealing techniques are not to prevent the disassembly for repair or reuse purposes of certain components
Welding equipment[720]; refrigerating appliances[721]; household dishwashers[722]; washing machines and washer-dryers[723]; refrigerating appliances with a direct sales function[724]	Availability to professional repairers and end-users of spare parts (for a minimum period after placing the last unit of the product model on the market)
	Maximum delivery time of spare parts

719 See point 1.2 of Annex II to Commission Regulation (EU) 2019/424 on ecodesign requirements for servers and data storage products (OJ L 74, 18 March 2019, p. 46).

720 See points 2(a), 2(c) and 2(e) of Annex II to Commission Regulation (EU) 2019/1784 on ecodesign requirements for welding equipment (OJ L 272, 25 October 2019, p. 121).

721 See points 3(c), 3(c) and 3(d) of Annex II to Commission Regulation (EU) 2019/2019 on ecodesign requirements for refrigerating appliances (OJ L 315, 5 December 2019, p. 187), which shall apply from 1 March 2021 and repeals Commission Regulation (EC) 643/2009 on ecodesign requirements for household refrigerating appliances (OJ L 191, 23 July 2009, p. 53), as amended by Commission Regulation (EU) 2016/2282.

722 See point 5(1) and 5(5) of Annex II to Commission Regulation (EU) 2019/2022 on ecodesign requirements for household dishwashers (OJ 315, 5 December 2019, p. 267).

723 See points 8(1), 8(2) and 8(5) of Annex II to Commission Regulation (EU) 2019/2023.

724 See points 2(a), 2(b) and 2(c) of Annex II to Commission Regulation (EU) 2019/2024 on ecodesign requirements for refrigerating appliances with a direct sales function (OJ L 315, 5 December 2019, p. 313.).

Product (group)	Non-energy aspect/requirements
Welding equipment[725]; refrigerating appliances[726]; electronic displays[727]; household dishwashers[728]; washing machines and washer-dryers[729]; refrigerating appliances with a direct sales function[730]	Dismantling for material recovery and recycling while avoiding pollution: products are to be designed in such a way that the materials and components referred to in Annex VII to Directive 2012/19/EU on WEEE can be removed with the use of commonly available tools
Electronic displays[731]	Joining, fastening or sealing techniques are not to prevent the removal, using commonly available tools, of the components indicated in point 1 of Annex VII of Directive 2012/19/EU on WEEE or in Article 11 of Directive 2006/66/EC on batteries and accumulators, when present

bb) Self-regulatory measures

The voluntary agreements also contain ecodesign performance requirements not related to energy aspects, as shown in the table below:

725 See points 2(a), 2(c) and 2(e) of Annex II to Commission Regulation (EU) 2019/1784 on ecodesign requirements for welding equipment (OJ L 272, 25 October 2019, p. 121).

726 See points 3(c), 3(c) and 3(d) of Annex II to Commission Regulation (EU) 2019/2019 on ecodesign requirements for refrigerating appliances (OJ L 315, 5 December 2019, p. 187), which shall apply from 1 March 2021 and repeals Commission Regulation (EC) 643/2009 on ecodesign requirements for household refrigerating appliances (OJ L 191, 23 July 2009, p. 53), as amended by Commission Regulation (EU) 2016/2282.

727 See points 5(a) and 5(c) of section D of Commission Regulation (EU) 2019/2021 on ecodesign requirements for electronic displays (OJ L 315, 5 December 2012, p. 241), which shall apply from 1 March 2021 and repeals Commission Regulation (EC) 642/2009 on ecodesign requirements for televisions (OJ L 191, 23 July 2009, p. 42), as amended by Commission Regulation (EU) 801/2013 (OJ L 225, 23 August 2013, p. 1) and Commission Regulation (EU) 2016/2282..

728 See point 5(1) and 5(5) of Annex II to Commission Regulation (EU) 2019/2022 on ecodesign requirements for household dishwashers (OJ 315, 5 December 2019, p. 267).

729 See points 8(1), 8(2) and 8(5) of Annex II to Commission Regulation (EU) 2019/2023.

730 See points 2(a), 2(b) and 2(c) of Annex II to Commission Regulation (EU) 2019/2024 on ecodesign requirements for refrigerating appliances with a direct sales function (OJ L 315, 5 December 2019, p. 313.).

731 See section D of Commission Regulation (EU) 2019/2021.

Table 6 – Non-energy aspects regulated by self-regulatory measures under the Ecodesign Directive

Product (group)	Non-energy aspect/requirements
Complex set-top boxes[732] (requirements F.1 to F.9) and their packaging (requirements F.10 to F.12)	Prohibition/restriction of the use of certain substances/materials in the products and/or their components, including paraffins (F.1), flame retardants (F.2), brominated and chlorinated flame retardants (F.3), and PVC (F.4)
	Minimum recycled content: manufacturers must declare the minimum percentage of both post-consumer recycled plastic content (F.5) and bio-based plastic content (F.6), calculated as a percentage of total plastic (by weight) in each product
	Ease of disassembly (requirement F.7): products shall be designed so that authorised service centres and recyclers can easily access: (a) materials with special handling needs at end of life; (b) material, components and subassemblies that could potentially be reused; and (c) components and subassemblies that may need removal for repair or replacement.
	Plastics compatibility with recycling (F.8): each plastic part of greater than 25g shall consist of only one recyclable plastic type or types that are compatible for recycling
	Product upgradeability (F.9): products shall include means by which their functionality may be extended, which may include software upgrades or hardware interfaces
	Packaging requirements: elimination of the use of chlorine as a bleaching agent in packaging material (F.10), prohibition of bonding dissimilar packaging materials together (F.11), and identification by the universal recycling symbol and the resin identification code (F.12)

732 See 'Annex F – non-energy requirement[s]' to 'voluntary industry agreement to improve the energy consumption of complex set-top boxes within the EU', version 6.0 as of 2 April 2018, available at <http://cstb.eu/wp-content/uploads/2018/08/EU-VA-V6.pdf>, last accessed on 18 December 2019.

Product (group)	Non-energy aspect/requirements
Imaging equipment[733]	Availability of N-up printing (capability to print several pages of a document on one sheet of paper as a standard feature). For certain products, duplex-printing is to be set as default
	Design for recycling requirements, including (i) manual separability of plastic parts >100g into recyclable plastic streams, (ii) utilisation of commonly used fasteners for joining components, subassemblies, chassis and enclosures, (iii) avoidance of non-separable connections, (iv) marking of product plastics by material type
	Requirements on polymer composition of casing parts, including restrictions on the use of coatings
	Cartridges: design of cartridge shall not prevent reuse and recycling and design of the machine shall not prevent the use of non-OEM (original manufacturer equipment) cartridges
	Availability of spare parts (for a minimum period after the end of product manufacturing)
	Minimum percentage of postconsumer recycled plastic content, calculated as a percentage of total plastic (in weight) in each product
Games consoles[734]	Availability of refurbishment or out-of-warranty repair service by (i) making spare parts available to authorised repair or refurbishment centres for each games console; (ii) ensuring that maintenance and refurbishment are possible by non-destructive disassembly of key components (motherboard, hard disk drive, optical drive, and internal power supply); (iii) ensuring that joining or sealing techniques do not prevent the removal of the components listed in point 1 of Directive 2012/19/EU on WEEE; and (iv) enabling access to components by documenting dismantling operations needed to access the targeted components
	Consideration of the feasibility of ensuring that any plastic components >100g are removable and made of polymers compatible for recycling during the next review of the self-regulatory measure

733 See points 4 to 6 of 'Industry voluntary agreement to improve the environmental performance of imaging equipment placed on the European market', version 5.2 as of April 2015, available at <https://ec.europa.eu/energy/sites/ener/files/documents/VA%20Imaging%20Self-Regulatory%20Initiative-V-4-0.pdf>, last accessed on 18 December 2019.

734 See point 3.3 of the 'self-regulatory initiative to further improve the energy efficiency of games consoles', version 2.6.3 as of 11 October 2018, available at <http://efficientgaming.eu/fileadmin/user_upload/2018_SCM/Final_Games_Consoles_SRI_v2.6.3_20181115.pdf>, last accessed on 18 December 2019.

b) Ecodesign information requirements

In addition to the ecodesign performance requirements listed above, most implementing measures as well as self-regulatory measures contain information requirements pertaining to environmental aspects not related to energy consumption.

aa) Implementing measures

Information requirements of non-energy aspects laid down by implementing measures are presented in the table below:

Table 7 – Information requirements not related to energy aspects imposed by implementing measures under the Ecodesign Directive

What kind of information?	In relation to which product(s)?	To whom?	How?
Emissions of nitrogen oxides (if applicable)	Comfort chillers, air-to-air air conditioners (if engine driven), water/brine-to-air air conditioners (if engine driven) and heat pumps[735]; water heaters[736]	Installers and end users	In the instruction manual and on free-access websites of manufacturers, importers and/or authorised representatives

735 See tables 10 to 14 of point 5(a) of Annex II to Commission Regulation (EU) 2016/2281.

736 Point 1(6)(b) of Annex II combined with point 6(e) of Annex III to Commission Regulation (EU) 814/2013.

What kind of information?	In relation to which product(s)?	To whom?	How?
Global warming potential	Air conditioners[737]	Not specified	In the technical documentation of the product and on manufacturers' free-access website
	Professional refrigerated storage cabinets and blast cabinets (in relation to the refrigerant fluid contained in the cabinet)[738]	Installers and end users	In the instruction booklet and on free-access websites of manufacturers, importers and/or authorised representatives
	Comfort chillers, air-to-air air conditioners, water/brine-to-air air conditioners, heat pumps and high temperature process chillers[739]	Installers and end users	In the instruction manual and on free-access websites of manufacturers, importers and/or authorised representatives
Noise levels	Air conditioners and comfort fans[740]	Not specified, presumably to end users	In the technical documentation of the product and on manufacturer's free-access website
	Computers[741]	End users	In the technical documentation and publicly available on free-access websites
	Heat pump space heaters and heat pump combination heaters;	Installers and end users	In the instruction manual, on free-access websites of manufacturers, importers and/or authorised representatives as well as in the technical

737 See tables 1 to 3table 2 of point 3(d) of Annex I to Commission Regulation (EU) No. 206/2012.

738 See point 2(a)(x) of Annex II to Commission Regulation (EU) 2015/1095 on ecodesign requirements for professional refrigerated storage cabinets, blast cabinets, condensing units and process chillers (OJ L 177, 8 July 2015, p. 19), as amended by Commission Regulation (EU) 2016/2282.

739 See tables 10 to 15 of point 5(a) of Annex II to Commission Regulation (EU) 2016/2281.

740 See table 3 of point 3(d) and table 3 of point 3(e) of Annex I to Commission Regulation (EU) 206/2012.

741 See points 7.1.1(n) and 7.3.1(k) of Annex II to Commission Regulation (EU) 617/2013.

What kind of information?	In relation to which product(s)?	To whom?	How?
	water heaters[742]		documentation for the purposes of conformity assessment
	Domestic range hoods[743]	Not specified, presumably to end users	In the technical documentation of the product, in the booklet of instructions and on free-access websites of manufacturers, importers and/or authorised representatives
	Ventilation units[744]	Not specified	In the technical documentation of the product and on free-access websites of manufacturers, importers and/or authorised representatives
	Air heaters, comfort chillers, air-to-air conditioners, water/brine-to-air air conditioners, fan coil units, heat pumps and high temperature process chillers[745]	Installers and end users	In the instruction manual and on free-access websites of manufacturers, importers and/or authorised representatives
Water consumption	Household dishwashers[746]; washing machines and washer-dryers[747]	Users and installers	In the form of a user manual on free-access websites of manufacturers, importers and/or authorised representatives

742 See table 2 of point 5 of Annex II to Commission Regulation (EU) 813/2013 as well as point 1.6(b) of Annex II combined with point 6(c) of Annex III to Commission Regulation (EU) 814/2013.

743 See point 2.3 of Annex 1 to Commission Regulation (EU) 66/2014.

744 See point 1(j) of Annex IV and point 1(r) of Annex V to Commission Regulation (EU) 1253/2014.

745 See points 5(a)(1) to 5(a)(7) of Annex II to Commission Regulation (EU) 2016/2281.

746 See points 6(1) to 6(5) of Annex I Commission Regulation (EU) 2019/2022.

747 See point 9(2)(d) of Annex I to Commission Regulation (EU) 2019/2023.

What kind of information?	In relation to which product(s)?	To whom?	How?
Vacuum insulation panels (VIP)	Refrigerating appliances[748] and refrigerating appliances with a direct sales function[749] containing VIP are to be labelled with the letters VIP	Not specified	Labelling
Refrigerant gasses	Washing machines and washer-dryers[750] as well as household dishwashers equipped with a heat pump[751] ('the chemical name of the refrigerant gas used, or equivalent reference such as a commonly used and understood symbol, label or logo')	Not specified	Permanently displayed and in a visible and readable way on the exterior of the product, for example on the back panel
Presence/total content of hazardous substances	Computers[752] (mercury)	Not specified	In the technical documentation of the product and publicly available on free-access websites
	Light sources[753] (if the light source contains mercury, a warning of this, including the mercury content in mg rounded to the first decimal place)	Not specified, presumably to end users	Visibly displayed on the packaging, either in words or in the form of graphs, drawings or symbols
	Electronic displays[754] ('cadmium inside' logo for electronic displays with a screen panel in which concentration values of cadmium by weight	Not specified	Labelling with clearly visible, durable, legible and indelible logo
		Workers (presumably of end-of-life operations)	Additional 'cadmium inside' logo firmly attached internally on the display panel or

748 See point 2(d) of Annex II to Commission Regulation (EU) 2019/2019.

749 See point 2(c) of Annex II to Commission Regulation (EU) 2019/2024.

750 See points 8(1), 8(2) and 8(5) of Annex II to Commission Regulation (EU) 2019/2023.

751 See point 5(4) of Annex II to Commission Regulation (EU) 2019/2022.

752 See point 7.1.1(y) of Annex II to Commission Regulation (EU) 617/2013 on ecodesign requirements for computers and computer servers (OJ L 175, 27 June 2013, p. 13), as amended by Commission Regulation (EU) 2016/2282.

753 See point 3(b)(1)(m) of Commission Regulation (EU) 2019/2020.

754 See point 3 of section D of Commission Regulation (EU) 2019/2021.

What kind of information?	In relation to which product(s)?	To whom?	How?
	in homogeneous materials exceed 0,01% as defined in the RoHS Directive)		moulded clearly visible once the external back cover bearing the external logo is removed
Plastic components	Electronic displays[755] (marking of plastic components > 50g; additional marking requirement for components containing flame retardants)	Not specified	Marking
Critical raw materials	Servers and data storage products[756] (indicative weight range at component level of certain critical raw materials)	Third parties dealing with maintenance, repair, reuse, recycling and upgrading of servers (including brokers, spare parts repairers, spare parts providers, recyclers and third-party maintenance)	Upon registration of the interested third party on free-access websites of manufacturers, importers and/or authorised representatives and in the technical documentation of the product
	Welding equipment[757] ('a list of critical raw materials present in indicative amounts > 1 gram at component level, and an indication of the component(s) in which these critical materials are present')	Installers and end-users	In the instruction manuals and on free-access websites of manufacturers, importers and/or authorised representatives
Lifetime	Light sources (lifetime for LED and OLED light sources, expressed in hours)	Not specified, presumably to end users	Visibly displayed on the packaging, either in words or in the form of graphs, drawings or symbols
Use and/or maintenance	Fans driven by motors with an electric input power between 125 W and 500 kW ('information relevant to [...]	Not specified	In the technical documentation of the product and on free-access websites of manufacturers, im-

755 See point 3 of section D of Commission Regulation (EU) 2019/2021.
756 See point 1.2 of Annex II to Commission Regulation (EU) 2019/424.
757 See point 3(h) of Annex II to Commission Regulation (EU) 2019/1784.

What kind of information?	In relation to which product(s)?	To whom?	How?
	ensure optimal life expectancy as regards installation, use and maintenance)[758]		porters and/or authorised representatives
	Vacuum cleaners[759] ('information relevant for non-destructive disassembly for maintenance purposes, in particular in relation to the hose, suction inlet, motor, casing and cable')	Professionals	In the technical documentation and on free-access websites of manufacturers, importers and/or authorised representatives
	Domestic ovens, hobs and range hoods[760] ('information relevant for non-destructive disassembly for maintenance purposes')	Not specified	In the technical documentation of the product, the booklet of instructions and on free-access websites of manufacturers, importers and/or authorised representatives
	Professional refrigerated storage cabinets, blast cabinets, condensing units and process chillers[761] ('information relevant for non-destructive disassembly for maintenance purposes')	Installers and other professionals	On free-access websites of manufacturers, importers and/or authorised representatives
	Household dishwashers[762] ('access to repair	Professional repairers	on free-access websites of manufacturers, importers and/or autho-

758 See point 3.2(13) of Annex I to Commission Regulation (EC) 327/2011 on ecodesign requirements for fans driven by motors with an electric input power between 125W and 500kW (OJ L 90, 6 April 2011, p. 8), as amended by Commission Regulation (EU) 666/2013 (OJ L 192, 13 July 2013, p. 24) and Commission Regulation (EU) 2016/2282.

759 See the first indent of point 2(b) of Annex I to Commission Regulation (EU) 666/2013.

760 See the second paragraph of point 2 of Annex 1 to Commission Regulation (EU) 66/2014 on ecodesign requirements for domestic ovens, hobs and range hoods (OJ L 29, 31 January 2014, p. 33), as amended by Commission Regulation (EU) 2016/2282.

761 See points 2(b)(ii) of Annexes II, V and VII to Commission Regulation (EU) 2015/1095.

762 See point 5(3) of Annex II to Commission Regulation (EU) 2019/2022.

What kind of information?	In relation to which product(s)?	To whom?	How?
	and maintenance information')		rised representatives upon registration of the professional repairer
	Household dishwashers[763]; washing machines and washer-dryers[764] ('instructions to perform maintenance operations')	User	In the form of a user manual on free-access websites of manufacturers, importers and/or authorised representatives
	Refrigerating appliances[765] and refrigerating appliances with a direct sales function[766] ('instructions for the correct installation and end-user maintenance, including cleaning; information on access to professional repair; relevant information for ordering spare parts; the minimum period during which spare parts necessary for the repair of the product are available')	Installers and end-users	In the instruction manuals and on free-access websites of manufacturers, importers and/or authorised representatives
	Electronic displays[767] (information on the availability of software and firmware updates, free of charge or at a fair, transparent and non-discriminatory cost for a minimum period after the placing on the market of the last product of a certain product model)	Third parties dealing with professional repair and reuse of electronic displays (including third-party maintenance actors, brokers and spare parts providers)	Not specified
	Welding equipment[768]; refrigerating appli-	Professional repairers	List of spare parts and the procedure to ob-

763 See points 6(8) to 6(16) of Annex II to Commission Regulation (EU) 2019/2022.

764 See point 9(3) of Annex II to Commission Regulation (EU) 2019/2023.

765 See points 4(g), 4(j), 4(k) and 4(l) of Annex II to Commission Regulation (EU) 2019/2019.

766 See points 3(e), 3(g), 3(h) and 3(i) of Annex II to Commission Regulation (EU) 2019/2024.

767 See section E of Commission Regulation (EU) 2019/2021.

What kind of information?	In relation to which product(s)?	To whom?	How?
	ances[769]; electronic displays[770]; Washing machines and washer-dryers[771]; refrigerating appliances with a direct sales function[772] (list of spare parts and the procedure to obtain them as well as information on how to access repair and maintenance information)		tain them: on free-access websites of manufacturers, importers and/or authorised representatives Access to repair and maintenance information: on free-access websites of manufacturers, importers and/or authorised representatives upon registration of professional repairers
Warning that battery/ies cannot be accessed and replaced by a non-professional user (where applicable)	Notebook computers[773] ('The battery[ies] in this product cannot be easily replaced by users themselves')	End users	In the technical documentation of the product, on free-access websites and on the external packaging of the notebook computer (clearly visible and legible as well as in all official languages of the country)
Disassembly/dismantling, recycling and/or disposal at end of life: generic requirements ('relevant information')	Fans driven by motors with an electric input power between 125 W and 500 kW[774] ('information relevant for facilitating disassembly, recycling or disposal at end-of-life')	Not specified	In the technical documentation of the product and on manufacturer's free-access website
	Water pumps[775] ('information relevant for	Not specified	In the technical documentation of the

768 See point 2(b) of Annex II to Commission Regulation (EU) 2019/1784.

769 See points 3(a)(4), 3(a)(5) and 3(b) of Annex II to Commission Regulation (EU) 2019/2019.

770 See points 5(a)(4), 5(a)(5) and 5(b) of section D of Commission Regulation (EU) 2019/2021.

771 See points 8(1) and 8(3) of Annex II to Commission Regulation (EU) 2019/2023.

772 See point 2(a)(4), 2(a)(5) and 2(c) of Annex II to Commission Regulation (EU) 2019/2024.

773 See point 7.2 of Annex II to Commission Regulation (EU) 617/2013.

774 See point 3.2(12) of Annex I to Commission Regulation (EU) 327/2011.

775 See point 2(10) of Annex II to Commission Regulation (EU) 547/2012 on ecodesign requirements for water pumps (OJ L 165, 26 June 2012, p. 28), as amended by Commission Regulation (EU) 2016/2282.

What kind of information?	In relation to which product(s)?	To whom?	How?
	disassembly, recycling or disposal at end-of-life')		product and on manufacturers' free-access websites
	Vacuum cleaners[776] ('information for dismantling, in particular in relation to the motor and any batteries, recycling, recovery and disposal at end-of-life')	Professionals	In the technical documentation of the product and on free-access websites of manufacturers, importers and/or authorised representatives
	Space heaters, combination heaters, water heaters, hot water storage tanks, solid fuel local space heaters and local space heaters[777]	Installers and end-users	In the instruction manuals, on free-access websites of manufacturers, importers and/or authorised representatives as well as in the technical documentation for the purposes of conformity assessment
	Domestic ovens, hobs and range hoods[778] ('information relevant for dismantling, in particular in relation to the motor, if applicable, and any batteries, recycling, recovery and disposal at end-of-life')	Not specified	In the technical documentation of the product, the booklet of instructions and on free-access websites of manufacturers, importers and/or authorised representatives

776 See the second indent of point 2(b) of Annex I to Regulation (EU) 666/2013.

777 See the last indent of point 5(a) of Annex II to Commission Regulation (EU) 813/2013; point 1.6(f) and point 2.2(d) of Annex II to Commission Regulation (EU) 814/2013; point 3(a)(i)(3) of Annex II to Commission Regulation (EU) 2015/1185; and point 3(a)(i)(5) of Annex II to Commission Regulation (EU) 2015/1188.

778 See the second paragraph of point 2 of Annex 1 to Commission Regulation (EU) 66/2014.

What kind of information?	In relation to which product(s)?	To whom?	How?
	Professional refrigerated storage cabinets, condensing units (information relevant for disassembly and dismantling for disposal as well as for recycling and disposal at end-of-life')[779]	Installers and other professionals	On free-access websites of manufacturers, importers and/or authorised representatives
	Boilers[780] ('information relevant to disassembly, recycling and disposal at end-of-life')	Professionals	On free-access websites of manufacturers, importers and/or authorised representatives
	Air heating products, cooling products, high temperature process chillers and fan coil units[781]	End-users	In instruction manuals
		Professionals	In instruction manuals and on free-access websites of manufacturers, importers and/or authorised representatives
	Welding equipment[782] ('information relevant to recycling and disposal at end-of-life')	Installers and users	On free-access websites of manufacturers, importers and/or authorised representatives
	Separate control gears[783] (recommendations on how to dispose of it at the end of its life in line with Directive 2012/19/UE on WEEE)	Not specified, presumably to end users	Visibly displayed on free-access websites of manufacturers, importers and/or authorised representatives, either in words or in the form of graphs, drawings or symbols
	Light sources[784] (manufacturers, importers	Not specified	On a free-access website

779 See points 2(a)(xii) and 2(b)(ii) of Annex II, points 2(a)(viii) and 2(b)(iii) of Annex V and points 2(a)(xi) and 2(b)(iii) of Annex VII to Commission Regulation (EU) 2015/1095.
780 See point 2(b) of Annex II to Commission Regulation (EU) 2015/1189.
781 See point 5(b) of Annex II to Commission Regulation (EU) 2016/2281.
782 See point 3(g) of Annex II to Commission Regulation (EU) 2019/1784.
783 See point 3(c)(1)(f) of Commission Regulation (EU) 2019/2020.

What kind of information?	In relation to which product(s)?	To whom?	How?
	or authorised representatives of containing products shall ensure that light sources and separate control gears can be dismantled from containing products at end of life)		
	Household dishwashers[785]; washing machines and washer-dryers[786] (fulfilment of the obligations laid down in Article 15(1) of Directive 2012/19/EU on WEEE, namely provision of information free of charge about preparation for reuse and treatment, including the different product components and materials as well as the location of dangerous substances and mixtures in the product)	Centres which prepare for reuse as well as treatment and recycling facilities	In the form of manuals or by means of electronic media (e.g. CD-ROM, online services)
	Welding equipment[787], refrigerating appliances[788] and refrigerating appliances with a direct sales function[789] (fulfilment of the obligations laid down in Article 15(1) of Directive 2012/19/EU on WEEE, namely provision of information free of charge about preparation for reuse and treatment, including the different product components and	Centres which prepare for reuse as well as treatment and recycling facilities	In the form of manuals or by means of electronic media (e.g. CD-ROM, online services)

784 See Article 4(3) of Commission Regulation (EU) 2019/2020.
785 See point 5(3) of Annex II to Commission Regulation (EU) 2019/2022.
786 See point 8(5) of Annex II to Commission Regulation (EU) 2019/2023.
787 See point 2(e) of Annex II to Commission Regulation (EU) 2019/1784.
788 See point 3(d)(2) of Commission Regulation (EU) 2019/2019.
789 See point 2(d)(2) of Annex II to Commission Regulation (EU) 2019/2024.

What kind of information?	In relation to which product(s)?	To whom?	How?
	materials as well as the location of dangerous substances and mixtures in the product)		
Disassembly/dismantling, recycling and/or disposal at end of life: (somewhat more) specific requirements	Standalone circulators and circulators integrated into products[790] ('information concerning disassembly, recycling, or disposal at end-of-life of components and materials')	Treatment facilities	On manufacturers' free-access websites
	Ventilation units[791] ('detailed instructions, inter alia, identifying the required tools for the manual disassembly of permanent magnet motors, and of electronics parts (printed wiring boards/printed circuit boards and displays > 10g or >10cm2), batteries and larger plastic parts (>100g) for the purpose of efficient materials recycling, except for models of which less than 5 units per year are produced')	Not specified	In the technical documentation of the product and on free-access websites of manufacturers, importers and/or authorised representatives
	Servers and data storage products[792] (instructions on the disassembly operations in relation to certain components)	Third parties dealing with maintenance, repair, reuse, recycling and upgrading of servers (including brokers, spare parts repairers, spare parts providers, recyclers and	Upon registration of the interested third party on free-access websites of manufacturers, importers and/or authorised representatives and in the technical documentation of the product

790 See point 2.3 of Annex I to Commission Regulation (EC) 641/2009.

791 See point 3 of Annex IV and point 3 of Annex V to Commission Regulation (EU) 1253/2014.

792 See point 1.2 of Annex II to Commission Regulation (EU) 2019/424.

What kind of information?	In relation to which product(s)?	To whom?	How?
		third-party maintenance)	
	Light sources[793] (if the light source is within the scope of Directive 2012/19/Eu on WEEE or contains mercury: a warning that it shall not be disposed of as unsorted municipal waste)	Not specified, presumably to end users	Visibly displayed on the packaging, either in words or in the form of graphs, drawings or symbols
Relationship with other products/waste streams (i.e. food preservation/waste)	Refrigerating appliances with a direct sales function[794] (information as to the recommended setting of temperatures in each compartment or optimum food preservation and an estimation of the impact of temperature settings on food waste)	Installers and end-users	In the instruction manuals and on free-access websites of manufacturers, importers and/or authorised representatives
	Refrigerating appliances[795] ('clear guidance about where and how to store foodstuffs in a refrigerating appliance for best preservation over the longest period to avoid food waste'; information as to 'the recommended setting of temperatures in each compartment for optimum food preservation'; 'an estimation of the impact of temperature settings on food waste')		

793 See point 3(b)(1)(n) of Commission Regulation (EU) 2019/2020.
794 See points 3(a) and 3(b) of Annex II to Commission Regulation (EU) 2019/2024.
795 See points 4(b), 4(c) and 4(d) of Annex II to Commission Regulation (EU) 2019/2019.

What kind of information?	In relation to which product(s)?	To whom?	How?
Reduction of total environmental impacts/ minimisation of impact on the environment	Circulators[796] ('how to install, use and maintain the circulator in order to minimise its impact on the environment')	Not specified	On manufacturers' free-access websites
	Fans driven by motors with an electric input power between 125 W and 500 kW[797] ('information relevant to minimise impact on the environment')	Not specified	In the technical documentation
	Domestic ovens, hobs and range hoods[798] (information relevant to users in order to reduce total environmental impact of the cooking process)	End users	In the technical documentation of the product, in the booklet of instructions and on free-access websites of manufacturers, importers and/or authorised representatives

bb) Self-regulatory measures

Concerning self-regulatory measures, examples of non-energy information requirements are found in relation to games consoles and imaging equipment, as follows:

796 See the penultimate paragraph of point 2 of Annex I to Commission Regulation (EC) 641/2009 on ecodesign requirements for glandless standalone circulators and glandless circulators integrated in products (OJ L 191, 23 July 2009, p. 35), as amended by Commission Regulation (EU) 622/2012 (OJ L 180, 12 July 2012, p. 4), Commission Regulation (EU) 2016/2282 and Commission Regulation (EU) 2019/1781 (OJ L 272, 25 October 2019, p. 74).

797 See point 3.2(13) of Annex I to Commission Regulation (EC) 327/2011.

798 See point 2(b) of Annex I to Commission Regulation (EU) 66/2014.

Table 8 – Information requirements not related to energy aspects imposed by self-regulatory measures under the Ecodesign Directive

Product (category)	What kind of information?	To whom?	How?
Complex set-top boxes[799] and their packaging	Plastic parts > 25g shall be marked with the universal recycling symbol and the resin identification code in accordance with 94/62/EC	Not specified	Marking
	All plastic parts weighing > 10g or with a surface area of < 25cm2 shall be identified by the universal recycling symbol and the resin identification code in accordance with ISO11469, unless it is not technically feasible to apply the mark		
Imaging equipment[800]	Resource efficiency when using imaging equipment: - Suitability of recycled as well as virgin paper certified under environmental stewardship initiatives or carrying recognised eco-labels; - For electrophotography printers, indication that these can print on 64 g/m^2 paper and that this paper contains less raw material per print,	End-users	The information shall be provided in the form of compact statements on pop-up screen on the end-user's computer during the initial installation of software (preferred); on a CD or publicly available website; on an insertion sheet provided in/on the box of the product; on an information sheet provided at the time of sale of the product.

799 See points F.8 and F.12 of 'Annex F – non-energy requirement[s]' to 'voluntary industry agreement to improve the energy consumption of complex set-top boxes within the EU', version 6.0 as of 2 April 2018.

800 See points 5 and 6 of 'Industry voluntary agreement to improve the environmental performance of imaging equipment placed on the European market', version 5.2 as of April 2015.

Product (category)	What kind of information?	To whom?	How?
	thus saving significant resources; - Description of the benefits of printing in duplex mode; - The environmental benefits of printing in duplex mode		
	Availability of spare parts and replacement instructions		Either online or in the product manual
	Suitable end-of-life management options for used cartridges		Via a company website
	Paper recyclability (and its environmental benefits)		Website or other means
	Product environmental characteristics, including information on: - The environmental performance of product models; - Inkjet and toner cartridge		Not specified
	Minimum percentage of post-consumer recycled plastic content		Not specified
Games consoles[801]	Product life extension, including: - Explanation on how to keep the consoles in good working condition (e.g. how to keep the product dust free, how to install system updates, how to remove trapped disks); - How to delete personal data (e.g. if the consumer wishes to send the console for reuse); - Options available (if any) to consumers to upgrade the performance of their consoles (e.g.	Consumers	With the console itself, onscreen, in hardcopy or online

801 See point 3.3 of the 'Self-regulatory initiative to further improve the energy efficiency of games consoles', version 1.0 as of 22 April 2015.

Product (category)	What kind of information?	To whom?	How?
	installing a bigger hard drive)		
	Repair or refurbishment of each games console	Authorised repair centres	Technical documentation
	End-of-life processing, refurbishment and out-of-warranty repair options available within the operating instructions of each game consoles	Consumers	With the console itself, onscreen, as a hard copy or online)
	Console plastics parts >25g must be marked indicating their material composition to improve recycling at end-of-life	Not specified, presumably to recyclers	Marking on the product
	Information about whether plastic casing contains brominated flame retardants in order to improve end-of-life recyclability	Repair and recycling operators	Within product disassembly instructions

c) Appraisal

Analysis of implementing and self-regulatory measures as concerns non-energy aspects shows that ecodesign performance requirements are fewer than information requirements, which, in turn, can be very generic or more specific.

Non-energy aspects covered by the *performance* requirements introduced by both implementing and self-regulatory measures may be categorised as follows:

Table 9 – Categories of non-energy aspects covered by performance requirements under the Ecodesign Directive

Requirement on product use or the product itself?	**Qualitative or quantitative aspect?**	**Categories of non-energy aspects**
Product use	Qualitative	Emissions/output (e.g. pollutants, noise)
	Quantitative	Consumption of resources/input (e.g. water, paper)
Product itself (i.e. composition)	Qualitative	Hazardousness (e.g. ban of chemicals use)
	Quantitative	Minimum recycled content (e.g. post-consumer plastic)
		Durability (e.g. lifetime, updatability)
		Repairability (e.g. availability of spare parts and repair service, disassemblability)
		End-of-life concerns (e.g. dismantlability, removability/separability of components, use of materials compatible with recycling)

Comparing such categorisation with the five-step model proposed in the previous chapter,[802] which focuses on quantitative as opposed to qualitative aspects of the product itself rather than of its use, performance requirements already address steps 3 (material composition), 4 (longer use through increased durability and repairability) and 5 (end-of-life/waste phase), highlighted in grey in the figure above.

Requirements on *repairability* stand out. They have existed for game consoles since the first version of the voluntary agreement (version 1.0 as of 22 April 2015)[803], which requires *inter alia* availability of a refurbishment or out-of-warranty repair service, including availability of spare parts, and for imaging equipment since version 5.2 of the voluntary agreement as of April 2015, when industry incorporated requests made by several

802 See chapter 3, section D, above.

803 Available at <http://efficientgaming.eu/fileadmin/user_upload/VA_1.0__22_April_2015_.pdf>, last accessed on 28 December 2019.

stakeholders in the Consultation Forum to add a number of additional non-energy requirements, including on availability of spare parts.[804]

With respect to imaging equipment, resource, as opposed to energy, efficiency standards during the use phase, as illustrated by requirements on the availability of N-up printing and (re)usability of cartridges, had already been existent before the introduction of repairability requirements. This is explained by a conjugation of factors.[805] Firstly, the preparatory study identified resource efficiency (alongside energy efficiency) in the use phase as an area for improvement.[806] Secondly, the voluntary agreement was concluded at a time when resource efficiency was put on the political agenda.[807] Thirdly, pressure to address this issue was exerted by the stakeholders involved in the agreement-making process, notably in the Consultation Forum, including a threat of regulation by the European Commission.[808] Fourthly and lastly, the voluntary agreement builds on some already existing (and equally voluntary) initiatives adopted by parts of industry, including the duplexing requirement deriving from the Energy Star[809] version 1.1 as well as other requirements from the Electronic

---

804 See the European Commission's endorsement of the revised voluntary agreement on imaging equipment (version 5.2) submitted by industry on 30 April 2015, available at <http://www.eurovaprint.eu/fileadmin/eurovaprint_files/pdfs/Reply_on_Imaging_equipment_VA_version_5.2_for_endorsement.pdf>, last accessed on 28 December 2019.

805 See Bundgaard, Remmen and Zacho, 2015, p. 35-36.

806 'The use of consumables, especially paper, was identified as a major contribution to the total energy use, supporting requirements such as duplex availability, duplex printing as default and possibility for N-up printing. For many of the base-cases, the manufacturing phase had the second largest total energy use, and for ink jet printers, it had the largest total energy use. This supports requirements on design for recycling, polymer composition and recycled plastic content. However, durability was not approached in the voluntary agreement, even though the short lifetime of inkjet printers was used to explain the high impact from the production phase' (see Bundgaard, Mosgaard and Remmen, 2017, p. 368.).

807 See chapter 3, section D, *supra*.

808 See also Bundgaard, Mosgaard and Remmen, 2017, p. 369-370.

809 Energy Star is a U.S. Environmental Protection Agency (hereinafter referred to as 'EPA') voluntary labelling programme designed to identify and promote energy efficient products to reduce greenhouse gas emissions since 1992. To date, it covers major appliances, office equipment, lighting, home electronics, new homes as well as commercial and industrial buildings and plants. The label is awarded if the energy efficiency specifications laid down by the EPA are met, which is verified by accredited third parties. Further information on the Energy Star is available at <https://www.energystar.gov>. At the end of 2000, the (then)

Product Environmental Assessment Tool (known as 'EPEAT')[810] and the Blue Angel[811]. 'The introduction of resource efficiency requirements into the Ecodesign Directive is facilitated by the existence of standards defining test methods and verification procedures'[812].

Requirements on repairability (e.g. ease of disassembly) are also found in the latest version of the voluntary agreement on complex set-top boxes (version 6.0 as of 2 April 2018). Most recently, amendments to already existing, and adoption of new, implementing measures at the end of 2019,[813] have introduced repairability requirements such as availability

---

European Community entered into an (now superseded) agreement with the U.S. Government on the coordination of energy-efficient labelling programmes for office equipment, from which followed the EU Energy Star programme covering office equipment not carrying a EU energy efficiency label. Further information on the EU Energy Star is available at <https://www.eu-energystar.org>.

810 Managed by Green Electronics Council, a non-profit organisation whose mission is 'to inspire and catalyse environmental leadership throughout the life cycle of electronic technologies' (see information available at <http://greenelectronicscouncil.org>), EPEAT is a system whereby manufacturers of electronics self-declare that their products fulfil certain required and optional environmental criteria. EPEAT criteria address the full product life cycle and they are based on public standards approved by the American National Standards Institute. Depending on the number of criteria satisfied devices are rated bronze (all the required criteria in each EPEAT product category are met), silver (all the required criteria plus at least 50% of the optional criteria are met) or gold (all the required criteria plus at least 75% of the optional criteria are met). Manufacturers' claims of compliance are subject to ongoing verification by qualified certification bodies. Further information on EPEAT is available at <http://www.epeat.net>. EPEAT criteria for imaging equipment are available at <http://www.epeat.net/resources/criteria/#tabs-1=imagingequipment>.

811 The Blue Angel (*Blauer Engel*) is the German voluntary ecolabel scheme. The so-called Environmental Label Jury, an independent and impartial decision-making body, determines which product groups and service sectors should be awarded the label as well as discusses and ratifies the award criteria developed for each individual product or service by the Federal Environmental Protection Agency (*Umweltbundesamt*). Criteria are reviewed every three to four years. The label is owned by the Federal Ministry for Environment, Nature Protection, Building and Nuclear Safety (*Bundesministerium für Umwelt, Naturschutz, Bau und Reaktorsicherheit*) and is always awarded for a limited period of time by RAL gGmbH, the state-authorised awarding body. The use of the label is not free of charge and is regulated by contracts entered into with RAL gGmbH. Further information on the Blue Angel is available at <https://www.blauer-engel.de>.

812 See Bundgaard, Mosgaard and Remmen, 2017, p. 370.

813 Most – but not all – of them are to take effect from 2020 or 2021.

and maximum delivery time of spare parts for several categories of EEE, thereby reinforcing those already laid down by self-regulatory measures, in a movement known as the 'right to repair'[814].

Requirements on *durability* are also noteworthy. They exist for light sources (i.e. lighting products) and vacuum cleaners (in relation to the hose and the motor).

Regarding vacuum cleaners,[815] although the preparatory study concluded that product durability should be addressed only at a later stage, namely after the adoption and effecting of the other proposed energy-related requirements,[816] it paved the way for the insertion of durability requirements into the implementing measure. This only happened late in the (quite long) law-making process due to a demand from the European Commission, more specifically due to pressure from the Directorate-General for Environment.[817] Furthermore, industry standards for (measuring) the durability of both the motor and the hose already existed.[818]

Concerning light sources, regulation of durability is much more complex, not only due to the rapid technological development of the lighting manufacturing sector and the corollary launching of new products with new functions, but also because durability in the case of lighting is a concept that has functional (i.e. quality) dimensions, such as lumen main-

814 See, for instance, Svensson *et al.*, 2018.

815 See Bundgaard, Remmen and Zacho, 2015, p. 36-40.

816 Maitre-Ekern and Dalhammar (2016), reviewing the preparatory study on vacuum cleaners, note that '[t]he issue of durability was considered to be complex. There were vacuum models with poor performance on the market, and the optimal approach was considered to be the pushing of durability, but not until the worst performers had been removed from the market' (p. 383).

817 See Bundgaard, Mosgaard and Remmen, 2017, p. 368.

818 See, for instance, the harmonised standards referred to in Commission communication in the framework of the implementation of Commission Delegated Regulation (EU) 665/2013 supplementing Directive 2010/30/EU of the European Parliament and of the Council with regard to energy labelling of vacuum cleaners and of Commission Regulation (EU) 666/2013 implementing Directive 2009/125/EC of the European Parliament and of the Council with regard to ecodesign requirements for vacuum cleaners (OJ C 272, 20 August 2014, p. 5), most notably EN 60312-1:2013. ASTM International, an international organisation that develops consensus-based technical standards, has published since mid-1990s standards concerning test methods for motor life evaluation of vacuum cleaners as well as for the durability of vacuum cleaner hoses. Finally, see also Blue Angel's 'RAL UZ 188 – Basic Criteria for Award of the Environmental Label – Vacuum Cleaners,' as of 1 August 2013 and now superseded by the 1 January 2015 version (point 3.8).

tenance (i.e. remaining amount of light output), which go beyond the mere idea of time during which a light source operates.[819]

In turn, software *upgradeability* for complex set-top boxes and firmware *updatability* for servers and data storage products are examples of requirements that may be regarded as an intermediate category between repairability and durability standards in that they are aimed at enabling changes to, and improvement of, an existing product, like requirements on repairability, while at the same time extending the functionality – and hence the lifetime – of the product.

As for the material composition of products (step 3), which is the focus of the present study, the self-regulatory measure on complex set-top boxes is the only regulation that touches on this aspect by requiring manufacturers to declare the minimum bio-based and post-consumer recycled plastic content.[820]

Interestingly, complex set-top boxes represent a product category for which the most wide-ranging non-energy requirements have been imposed. Requirements address aspects of both the devices and their packaging, from bans of chemicals use through the aforementioned material composition, upgradeability and repairability standards to end-of-life concerns (e.g. plastics' compatibility with recycling). A technical standard for resource efficiency covering these and other issues has been drafted by the Institute of Electrical and Electronics Engineers (IEEE) Standards Association[821],[822] which, along with pressure from Member States and the European Commission, explains the comprehensiveness of the non-energy requirements adopted.

---

819 See Maitre-Ekern and Dalhammar, 2016, p. 384-385. See also Peiró *et al.*, 2019, p. 2: 'In lamps, durability aspects are measured by lumen maintenance factor as well as a number of other factors such as the number of switching cycles before failure, premature failure rate, and for some lighting products, colour rendering'.

820 Strictly speaking, unlike lightweighting miniaturisation requirements, minimum recycled content mandates do not promote the reduction of material intensity in products themselves, but rather replace the use of virgin materials with secondary ones. For this reason, one may speak of quantitative prevention of materials used and waste generated only in a broader sense.

821 IEEE is a technical professional association for electronic engineering and electrical engineering. Further information available at <https://www.ieee.org/>. IEEE Standards Association (IEEE SA) is a consensus-building organisation within IEEEE that develops global standards. Further information available at <https://standards.ieee.org/>.

822 See the IEEE's draft standard for environmental assessment of complex set-top boxes (P1680.6/D19), as of January 2017.

In respect of resource efficiency standards, the European Commission, noting that '[o]ne of the reasons for the relative lack of ecodesign requirements related to material efficiency in the implementing measures adopted so far is the absence of adequate metrics'[823], and with a view to contributing to the implementation of the EU action plan for the circular economy,[824] made a request to CEN, CENELEC and the European Telecommunications Standards Institute (hereinafter ETSI) to draft European standards and European standardisation deliverables on material efficiency aspects for ErPs in support of the implementation of the Ecodesign Directive (M/543). Three material efficiency aspects fall within the scope of the standardisation mandate: product lifetime extension; ability to reuse components or recycle materials from products at end-of-life; and use of reused components and/or recycled materials in products.[825]

The table below summarises the standards that are being, or already have been, drafted by CEN following the request made by the European Commission:[826]

Table 10 – Standards resulting from European Commission's standardisation mandate M/543

Reference	Title	Status (as of December 2019)
EN 45550	Definitions related to material efficiency	Under drafting
EN 45552	General method for the assessment of the ability to repair, reuse and upgrade energy-related products	Under approval
EN 45553	General method for the assessment of the ability to remanufacture energy-related products	Under approval
EN 45554:2020	General methods for the assessment of the ability to repair, reuse and upgrade energy-related products	Approved

823 See C(2015) 9096 final, 17 December 2005, p. 2.

824 Idem, p. 3. See also chapter 3, section D, and footnote 341, *supra*.

825 See point 1 of Annex I to M/543 Commission Implementing Decision C(2015) 9096 final, 17 December 2005.

826 See the information available at <https://standards.cen.eu/dyn/www/f?p=204:7:0::::FSP_ORG_ID:2240017&cs=146F3F0C3434E2342477B7A2945D5E308>, last accessed on 29 December 2019.

Reference	Title	Status (as of December 2019)
EN 45555:2019	General methods for assessing the recyclability and recoverability of energy-related products	Published
EN 45556:2019	General method for assessing the proportion of reused components in energy-related products	Published
EN 45557	General method for assessing the proportion of recycled content in energy-related products	Under approval
EN 45558:2019	General method to declare the use of critical raw materials in energy-related products	Published
EN 45559:2019	Methods for providing information relating to material efficiency aspects of energy-related products	Published

The need for technical standards allowing for measurements is not the only obstacle to imposing non-energy requirements, though. As some experts observe,

> 'Establishing compulsory minimum requirement[s] on material efficiency has been a challenge for several reasons, including: the lack of discussion of material efficiency concepts during the policy debate, the absence of appropriate metrics (commonly accepted material efficiency assessment methods, e.g., in standards)', and the related problems of verifying requirements, the variability between product groups, and diverging interest of stakeholders along the value chain'[827].

Finally, information requirements also cover non-energy aspects and, despite being more numerous and wide-ranging than performance requirements, the same categorisation applies to them: information may refer to product use or the product itself and address qualitative or quantitative concerns. As already delimited, focus is given on quantitative aspects of product themselves.[828]

827 See Peiró et al., 2019, p. 2.

828 Refrigerating appliances and imaging equipment are product categories that offer interesting examples of information requirements addressing quantitative aspects of product use. Regarding refrigerating appliances, clear guidance about where and how to store foodstuffs for best preservation over the longest period

Information requirements are instrumental in bringing about the product improvements that performance requirements seek to achieve. For example, requirements for the provision of information to end users on product utilisation such as cleaning instructions (e.g. refrigerating appliances, game consoles) contribute to product lifetime optimisation (i.e. durability).

As with performance standards, information requirements on maintenance and repairability stand out. They include, for instance, instructions to perform maintenance operations (e.g. household dishwashers, washing machines and washer-dryers) and information on access to professional repair as well as on the availability and the ordering of spare parts (e.g. electronic displays, refrigerating appliances, welding equipment).

Requirements on information relevant for end-of-life management also abound. The vast majority are very generic (i.e. information relevant to disassembly, dismantling, treatment, recovery, including recycling, and /or disposal), but more specific requirements also exist, such as detailed instructions identifying the required tools for disassembly of components in the case of ventilation units. For EEE, some requirements are made in reference to obligations already laid down by Directive 2012/19/UE on WEEE.

As for product composition, requirements concern information not only on the presence of hazardous chemicals (e.g. computers, light sources) but also on the presence and amount of critical materials (e.g. servers and data storage products as well as welding equipment) in addition to the marking of plastic components (e.g. electronic displays, complex set-top boxes).

3. Methodological challenges

The so-called MEErP methodology can be regarded as being the very first step in the decision-making process of setting ecodesign requirements, for it guides the formulation of the preparatory studies on which the drafting of implementing measures are based.[829] The MEErP methodology is comprised of seven tasks, two of which 'require an environmental

---

to avoid food waste is to be provided to end users. Concerning imaging equipment, end users are to be informed *inter alia* about the environmental benefits of printing in duplex mode and paper recyclability.

829 See Kemna *et al.*, 2011, p. 15.

impact assessment [also known as] life cycle assessment (LCA)[830] of the product and its improvement options'[831]. In connection with the life cycle assessment carried out within the MEErP:

> '[A] reporting tool called [...] EcoReport [has been] developed that facilitates the necessary calculations [made within the life cycle assessment] to translate product-specific characteristics into environmental impact indicators *per product*. The intended audience for this tool consists of policy makers, consultants and stakeholder experts involved in the preparatory stages and final decisions regarding implementing ecodesign measures; it might also be used by manufacturers for a preliminary analysis of the environmental performance resulting from the implementation of various design options'[832].

Despite the comprehensiveness of parameters, life cycle stages and environmental aspects that must be considered for the adoption of ecodesign requirements pursuant to Annexes I and II to the Ecodesign Directive, not all of them are really considered in practice,[833] with focus lying on energy consumption during use, as already mentioned above. This has been explained by the fact that preparatory studies in general, and the MEErP methodology on which they rest in particular, tend to 'steer' regulatory attention towards the energy aspect,[834] arguably because 'energy use in the product use phase has theoretically the least uncertainty in terms of measurement and testing protocols for product performance assessment'[835]:

> 'Whilst energy is a standardised parameter amongst products which can be entered into an LCA, materials used in different product models may vary substantially and data relating to this is very difficult to obtain, making resource inputs for a standard product to the LCA highly challenging.'[836]

830 On LCA, see, for instance, Klöpffer and Grahl, 2014; Baumann and Tillman, 2005; Chehebe, 1997; SETAC, 1993. On LCA and (environmental) law, see Rehbinder and Schmihing, 2001. See also Dalhammar, 2015a.

831 See Kemna *et al.*, 2011, p. 87. See also Hinchliffe and Akkerman, 2017, p. 1609.

832 See Kemna *et al.*, 2005, p. 8-9.

833 See Mertens, 2011, p. 334-335; Tölle, 2016, p. 75-77.

834 See Dalhammar, 2014, p. 167. Van Rossem, Dalhammar and Toulouse (2010, p. 25) speak of an overestimation of the energy aspect, which is sometimes unduly identified as the most important environmental issue.

835 See van Rossem, Dalhammar and Toulouse, 2010, p. 40.

836 Hinchliffe and Akkerman, 2017, p. 1610. Nevertheless, the authors note that '[...] consultants carrying out preparatory studies still tend to face a number

In addition, for non-energy aspects to be considered in the preparatory study, importance to them needs to be assigned by the MEErP and the associated EcoReport tool,[837] as was the case with servers.[838] Recommendations for including material/resource-related considerations into the MEErP have been proposed by several studies.[839]

An important methodological concern involving the imposition of ecodesign requirements relates to possible trade-offs and the need for balancing them, as provided for Article 15(10) of the Ecodesign Directive: '[w]here appropriate, an implementing measure laying down ecodesign requirements shall include provisions on the balancing of various environmental aspects'. Trade-offs, which can be dealt with on a case-by-case basis only, may occur between the same environmental aspects, different environmental aspects, and/or environmental and non-environmental aspects, as illustrated by the following examples:

- trade-off between the same environmental aspects:[840] '[R]educing the quantity of material used in the product (without substituting the material) can affect the solidity of the product and thus reduce its durability'; '[R]eplacing metal with plastics can reduce the overall quantity of materials used but decrease its recyclability';
- trade-off between different environmental aspects: incandescent lamps, which have been phased out under the Ecodesign Directive, consume more energy, but they do not contain mercury, in contrast to their more energy-efficient alternatives;[841] '[I]n the example of boilers and air heaters, lightweight can be an option improving material efficiency of a product, but this could hinder its energy efficiency if the material reduced is part of the insulation of the heater and that drives to higher energy consumption during the use phase'[842];

of challenges, particularly in product groups which are highly complex, heterogeneous or have been subject to limited investigation of efficiency parameters until the Ecodesign preparatory study. For such products it can be difficult to set an appropriate scope, find meaningful product data, align to suitable energy efficiency measurement methods (if these exist) and avoid overlaps with other environmental policy' (p. 1604).

837 Bundgaard, Mosgaard and Remmen, 2017, p. 369.

838 See Peiró *et al.*, 2019, p. 4 *et seq.*

839 See, for instance, Mudgal *et al.*, 2013a, 2013b and 2013c.

840 Examples taken from Mudgal *et al.*, 2013a, p. 24.

841 See Dalhammar, 2014, p. 149.

842 See Mudgal *et al.*, 2013a, p. 25.

- trade-off between environmental and non-environmental aspects: instructions for dismantling of a product containing hazardous substances may threaten the health and decrease the safety of users if they are able to dismantle products themselves.[843]

The existence of trade-offs and the need for balancing rules are particularly interesting because they pinpoint the limits of scientific (i.e. objective) knowledge in providing definite policy answers and accentuate the informative rather than determinative nature of LCA in general and the MEErP in particular.

4. Regulatory context and legislative coordination: fine-tuning environmental legislation or simply shifting the burden?

Recital 2 of the Energy Labelling Directive[844] correctly states that the Ecodesign Directive forms part of a broader legal framework consisting

843 See Mudgal *et al.*, 2013a, p. 25.

844 Directive 2010/30/EU (OJ L 153, 18 June 2010, p. 1), known as the 'Energy Labelling Directive', establishes a framework for the harmonisation of national measures on information for end-users about the consumption of energy and other resources by energy-related products during use, particularly by means of labelling and standard product information. Unlike the Energy Star (see footnote 809, *supra*), EPEAT (see footnote 810, *supra*) and Blue Angel (see footnote 811, *supra*) programmes, the Energy Labelling Directive establishes a mandatory rather than voluntary scheme (see its recital 12). As per its article 1(2), the Energy Labelling Directive applies to energy-related products (see definition in article 2(a)) that have a significant direct or indirect impact (see definitions in article 2(e) and (f), respectively) on the consumption of energy and, where relevant, on other essential resources (see definition in article 2(c)). The scope of application of the Energy Labelling Directive is therefore very similar to that of the Ecodesign Directive (see Mertens, 2011, p. 329-330). The framework provided by the Energy Labelling Directive is also very similar to that of the Ecodesign Directive. Under the provisions of the Energy Labelling Directive, the European Commission, in accordance with the procedural requirements of article 10(3), lays down delegated acts (in the sense of article 290 of TFEU) relating to the label and the fiche – a standard table of information – of ErPs meeting the criteria listed in article 10(2). Delegated acts must contain the specifications listed in article 10(3). Just like the Ecodesign Directive, the Energy Labelling Directive also prioritises energy concerns over non-energy aspects. For instance, article 10(1) third sub-paragraph provides that, '[W]here a delegated act lays down provisions with respect to both energy efficiency and consumption of essential resources of a product, the design and content of the label shall emphasise the energy efficiency of the product'.

of different EU regulatory instruments working together to bring about energy savings and environmental gains. This recalls that legal instruments are indeed to be understood not in isolation, but rather in their policy context, and this observation automatically leads to a discussion about their regulatory function.

As discussed above, the Ecodesign Directive serves to remove the worst performing products from the market, which is explained fundamentally by the low stringency of the requirements set thereunder. As an instrument relying on minimum product standards, from a policy perspective, the Ecodesign Directive works by 'pushing' laggards towards improved environmental performance.

Yet, while the ecodesign requirements imposed under the directive's framework establish only a minimum level of environmental performance, better or best performing products do exist on the market and they ought not escape regulatory attention. On the contrary, in that they go beyond the minimum standards required by law, front-runners are to be rewarded as a means to 'pull' the market towards environmental advancements. For this reason, they are usually covered by incentive-based (i.e. economic), informational and/or voluntary (as opposed to command-and-control) legal instruments, of which the aforementioned labelling schemes are only one example.

Over time, adjustments at both ends of this 'push-and-pull' mechanism – forcing eco-innovation amongst the laggards and stimulating eco-innovation amongst front-runners – should raise the overall stringency of environmental regulation.[845] One way of doing this is to make use of the experience gained from the regulation of top-runners when setting the requirements for laggards. For example, as seen above, voluntary legal instruments – for the most part labelling schemes, but also green procurement programmes – already addressing non-energy aspects of ErPs not only exist, but they have also played an important role in the setting of ecodesign requirements under the Ecodesign Directive, as best illustrated by the case of imaging equipment. This is particularly important in relation to those products to which the application of the Ecodesign Directive is still challenging or of limited contribution, as shall be discussed in the following section. A few studies have explored the possibility and the challenges of incorporating the criteria and requirements developed with-

845 See Dalhammar *et al.*, 2014, p. 116-117. Of course, a bolder alternative would be the establishment of technology-forcing standards from the outset.

in these voluntary initiatives into the Ecodesign Directive framework,[846] and this merits further investigation that goes beyond the scope of this dissertation.

Besides the possibility of learning from the avant-gardism of other product-specific (and usually voluntary) regulations covering better-performing products, another interesting way the Ecodesign Directive may interact with other legal instruments is as a complement to existing (mandatory) product-specific or horizontal (i.e. cross-sectorial) rules dealing with other environmental aspects or other life cycle phases of so-to-speak 'average-performing' products. As a rule, even though the Ecodesign Directive allows for the regulation of various environmental aspects of products at different life cycle stages, this does not always occur. For instance, when existing legislation already addresses an environmental aspect at a certain life cycle stage that preparatory studies deem worth tackling, these same studies often assume that compliance with the existing legislation just happens, so that improvement via the Ecodesign Directive framework, that is, the setting of requirements that are additional to or more stringent than the ones already mandated, is regarded unnecessary or at least faces political resistance.[847]

Another situation regarding the abstention of implementing measures from imposing ecodesign requirements concerns the idea that certain environmental aspects that have been identified as meriting regulatory attention should be dealt with under regulatory frameworks other than the one provided by the Ecodesign Directive. In this case, instead of filling possible gaps in existing environmental legislation, implementing measures simply refer to the relevant statute, as illustrated by the case of light sources: recital 10 of Commission Regulation (EU) 2019/2020 refers to the RoHS Directive as the appropriate piece of legislation to address the mercury content of this product category.[848]

---

846 See, for instance, Dalhammar *et al.*, 2014, p. 135-174; Bundgaard, Remmen and Zacho, 2015, p. 47-58.

847 See Maxwell *et al.*, 2011, p. 282; van Rossem, Dalhammar and Toulouse, 2010, p. 26.

848 Recital 10 of Commission Regulation (EU) 2019/2020 reads: 'The use of hazardous substances, including mercury in light sources, is governed by Directive 2011/65/EU of the European Parliament and of the Council (RoHS). *No specific ecodesign requirements on mercury content should therefore be set in this Regulation*' (emphasis added). Pursuant to article 4 combined with Annex II of the RoHS Directive, the maximum concentration value (by weight in homogeneous mate-

There are two possible ways of looking at this evasive approach, one positive and one negative. On the one hand, it can be lauded for avoiding legislative overlaps.[849] On the other hand, it misses the chance of complementing existing environmental legislation, an attitude that has been described as a 'passing-the-buck strategy'.[850] Examples of the potential complementary role of the Ecodesign Directive include the provision of information (i) about chemicals in products to actors not encompassed by Article 33 of the REACH Regulation[851], (ii) in relation to substances or products not covered by the RoHS Directive and/or (iii) that is more specific than the requirements of Article 15 of the WEEE Directive (Directive 2012/19/EU).[852]

5. Scope expansion

A frequently mentioned shortcoming of the Ecodesign Directive is its restricted scope of application. Even though it has been broadened from EuPs to ErPs, and in spite of the fact that the regulation of environmental aspects beyond energy efficiency is not only possible but has also already taken place under the Ecodesign Directive,[853] it still does not apply indistinctively to all products.

Hope to overcome this limitation was pinned on the review of the effectiveness of both the Ecodesign Directive and the implementing measures deriving therefrom, followed by an assessment of the appropriateness of extending the scope of the Ecodesign Directive to non-ErPs, as provided

rials) tolerated for mercury in EEE, including lighting equipment (Annex I, point 5), is 0,1%. Points 1 to 4(g) of Annex III contain many exceptions, though.

849 See Schomerus and Spengler, 2010, p. 59.

850 See van Rossem, Dalhammar and Toulouse, 2010.

851 Regulation (EC) 1907/2006. See footnote 149.

852 See Dalhammar *et al.*, 2014, p. 123-126.

853 This notwithstanding, the European Parliament's Committee on the Environment, Public Health and Food Safety, in a report dated 7 May 2018 on the implementation of the Ecodesign Directive, criticising the lack of political support for the Ecodesign Directive even at the highest decision-making levels, noted that 'since the 2009 extension of the scope of the Ecodesign Directive to include energy-related products (ErP), not one of these products [had] actually been the subject of an implementing measure'. See A8-0165/2018, Rapporteur Frédérique Ries, available at <https://www.europarl.europa.eu/doceo/document/A-8-2018-0165_EN.html>, last accessed on 30 December 2019.

for in Article 21.[854] However, at the end of 2012, based on an evaluation study,[855] the European Commission decided that such extension was still premature.[856]

The evaluation study found, among other things, that for a large number of non-ErPs the main environmental impacts occur at earlier stages of the life cycle, which are better addressed by targeting inputs and production processes rather than through product conformity testing. In this sense, apart from the compliance difficulties in connection with the control of upstream impacts that would arise in complex, internationalised supply chains as well as in markets dominated by SMEs, the setting out of ecodesign requirements for non-ErPs faces data and methodological challenges, thereby requiring an update (i.e. improvement or replacement) of the MEErP,[857] especially regarding those products in relation to which life cycle assessment is still considered problematic. Other corollaries of the scope expansion would be the involvement of an even greater number of stakeholders and increased workload. Finally, concerning the non-ErPs for which ecodesign requirements would be more suitable, not only are they fewer in number, but the expected improvement of their environmental performance is also either limited or already provided for by existing regulatory framework.[858]

Whilst there are plausible reasons for not extending the scope of the Ecodesign Directive, this may change over time as experience is gained. However, Article 21 of the directive provides for a one-time revision only (in lieu of a periodic review, for instance), thereby leaving the question of future reviews completely open to the discretion of the European legislature in general, and the European Commission in particular.[859]

---

854 See, for instance, Schomerus and Spengler, 2010, p. 61.

855 See Centre for Strategy & Evaluation Services, 2012.

856 See COM (2012) 765 final, 17 December 2012.

857 See section B.II.3, *supra*.

858 It should be noted, however, that analysis was based on a somewhat arbitrary choice of non-ErPs for which some, at times limited, life cycle information was available, including products covered by eco-labels schemes and those examined in a study report (Tukker *et al.*, 2006) made on behalf of the Institute for Prospective Technological Studies (hereinafter referred to as 'IPTS) of the Joint Research Centre (hereinafter referred to as 'JRC'), a Directorate-General of the European Commission. See Centre for Strategy & Evaluation Services, 2012, p. 159-164.

859 In the 2012 review, the European Commission proposed to reassess specific aspects of the Ecodesign Directive when revising the Energy Labelling Directive (see COM (2012) 765 final, 17 December 2012, p. 5). This took place in 2015.

6. Room for national ecodesign requirements?

This section discusses whether the Member States are authorised to lay down national ecodesign requirements in the face or lack of European requirements, that is, in those cases where EU requirements are inexistent or regarded by the Member States as being insufficient.

As regards the absence of EU requirements, one might consider the need for national requirements in relation to: (i) products not covered by the Ecodesign Directive, that is, non-ErPs; (ii) products covered by the Ecodesign Directive (i.e. ErPs), but for which no implementing measure has been adopted; (iii) ErPs for which an implementing measure has been adopted but it expressly provides that no ecodesign requirement is necessary for certain specified ecodesign parameters referred to in part 1 of Annex I to the Ecodesign Directive[860]; and (iv) ErPs for which an implementing measure has been adopted but the requirements imposed do not address a certain environmental aspect.

A different, fifth situation concerns ErPs in relation to which there is an implementing measure imposing ecodesign requirements for certain environmental aspects. The issue, in this case, is whether the Member States are allowed to introduce national standards that are more stringent than the ones set at the European level.

The answer to these questions involves a discussion on the distribution of competence between the European Union (henceforth in this section referred to as the 'Union') and the Member States, the so-called vertical distribution of competence, as well as on the legal basis of the Ecodesign Directive, the so-called horizontal distribution of competence.[861]

Based on the evaluation study (Molenbroek *et al.*, 2014), which reached the same conclusions of the evaluation study supporting the 2012 review regarding scope expansion, most notably the inadequacy of the MEErP to address the environmental impacts of non-ErPs (Molenbroek *et al.*, 2014, p. 73-74), the European Commission decided that no legislative changes to the Ecodesign Directive in respect of the issues (re-)evaluated were necessary (see COM (2015) 345 final, 15 July 2015, p. 6).

860 See article 15(6), third sub-paragraph of the Ecodesign Directive.

861 On the allocation of competence in European law in general, see, for instance, Craig and de Búrca, 2015, p. 73-104; König, 2015, p. 83-144. On the allocation of competence in European environmental law in particular, see, for instance, Krämer, 2015, p. 97-139; Krämer and Winter, 2015, p. 1555-1559; de Sadeleer, 2014, p. 126-174; Epiney, 2013, p. 138; Meßerschmidt, 2011, p. 61-261.

Unlike the Member States, the Union is allowed to act only if and in so far as European primary law[862] explicitly or implicitly confers competence upon it (Article 5(1) and Article 5(2) of the TEU).[863]

Union competence is essentially threefold. The first category concerns exclusive competence. In accordance with Article 2(1) of the TFEU, only the Union may legislate and adopt legally binding acts, with the Member States being able to do so themselves only if so empowered by the Union or for the implementation of Union acts. In the second category, the Union shares competence with the Member States. Pursuant to Article 2(2) of the TFEU, both may legislate and adopt legally binding acts. The Member States may exercise their competence to the extent that the Union has not exercised, or has decided to cease exercising,[864] its competence. The third category deals with the powers conferred by Article 2(5) of the TFEU to the Union to carry out actions to support, coordinate or supplement the actions of the Member States, without thereby superseding their competence in these areas.

As per Article 4(1) of the TFEU, shared competence is the default option. It applies to areas[865] such as 'internal market' and 'environment' (Articles 4(2)(a) and 4(2)(e) of the TFEU, respectively). As shall be discussed below, it can be debated whether the Ecodesign Directive falls within one or the other of these two areas, with the consequence that the possibility of the Member States deviating from European legislation may be more or

862 In European law, primary law, since the Treaty of Lisbon, has consisted of the international treaties establishing and governing the European Union (former European Communities), namely the TEU and the TFEU, including the annexes and protocols to them (article 51 of the TEU), as well as the Charter of Fundamental Rights of the European Union (article 6(1) of the TEU) and general principles of law. See, for instance, Frenz, 2016, p. 1-2; Streinz, 2016, p. 2; König, 2015, p. 85.

863 Pursuant to article 4(1) and article 5(2) of the TEU, competences not conferred upon the Union remain with the Member States.

864 On this second modality (cessation), which is not focused upon herein, see Declaration No. 18 in relation to the delimitation of competences annexed to the TEU and the TFEU.

865 The competence rules contained in European primary legislation grant powers not only over certain subject matters, but also in connection with objectives of the Union. Put another way, allocation of competence occurs not only materially, but also functionally. An example of this goal-oriented conferral of competence is article 114(1) of the TFEU, which gives the Union powers to harmonise the national law of the Member States in order to achieve the objectives set out in article 26 of the TFEU, more precisely the functioning of the internal market.

less limited. Yet, regardless of its legal basis, the directive does come under the category of shared competence. This being so, the Member States are only allowed to legislate to the extent that the Union has not made use of its powers. Protocol No. 25 on the exercise of shared competence, which is annexed to the TEU and the TFEU, clarifies that, '[W]hen the Union has taken action in a certain area, the scope of this exercise of competence only covers those elements governed by the Union act in question and therefore does not cover the whole area'.

In this sense, in situations (i) to (iv) above, it must be determined to what extent the Union has (not) exercised its competence. All of them involve a lack of ecodesign requirements, but for different reasons. Situations (i) and (ii) concern the absence of European secondary and tertiary legislation[866] covering a given product, respectively. By contrast, in situations (iii) and (iv) products are indeed covered by European legislation but their ecodesign is left unregulated, in whole or in part, intentionally or unintentionally. The figure below shows this gradation:

	Situation (i)	**Situation (ii)**	**Situation (iii)**	**Situation (iv)**
Secondary legislation (i.e. Ecodesign Directive)	O	X	X	X
Tertiary legislation (e.g. implementing measure)	$O(-)_t$	$O(-)_t$	$X(+)_t$	$X(+)_p$ or $X(-)_p$

Figure 5 – Situations in which national ecodesign requirements may be necessary

Legend:
O (legislation exists)
X (legislation does not exist)
– (unintentional non-regulation)
+ (intentional non-regulation)
$_t$ (no ecodesign regulation)
$_p$ (partial ecodesign regulation)

866 In European law, secondary law refers to the legal acts enacted by the institutions of the European Union on the basis of primary law (see footnote 862, *supra*). Tertiary law, in turn, designates abstract-general legal acts enacted under the authorisation of secondary law on the grounds of article 290 or article 291 of the TFEU. See, for instance, Frenz, 2016, p. 1-2; Streinz, 2016, p. 2; König, 2015, p. 85.

The non-exercise by the Union of its competence is least disputable in situations (i) and (ii), less straightforward in situation (iii) and more controversial in situation (iv).

In situations (i) and (ii), there is complete inaction on the behalf of the European legislature and this omission clearly should leave room for national action.[867] In situation (i), the setting of ecodesign requirements for non-ErPs falls outside the scope of the Ecodesign Directive. In situation (ii), the Union has not made use of its 'implementing competence', that is, the powers conferred to it by the Ecodesign Directive to regulate concrete products and/or product groups.

Situation (iii) differs from the former two in that it deals with existing European legislation, which nonetheless deliberately and expressly decides not to regulate the ecodesign of a given ErP. In this case, Member State action should be pre-empted because, by stipulating the unnecessity of any ecodesign requirement whatsoever, Union action has covered the whole area, only negatively. Of course, such a decision must be justified, otherwise it would constitute a way for the Union to annihilate the powers of the Member States in this area.

The issue of partial regulation, as is the case of situation (iv), is less simple since it is possible to argue, on the one hand, an omission in relation to the environmental aspects for which no ecodesign requirements have been laid down by the relevant implementing measure,[868] like situations (i) and (ii), or, on the other hand, a deliberation to leave said aspects unregulated, like situation (iii). The latter case should be considered to occur only if the intention not to regulate is explicit, as advocated by some specialists.[869]

In the absence of Union legislation, which comprises situations (i) and (ii) as well as situation (iv) in the first interpretation, the national law of the Member States must not conflict with European primary law. In other words, the exercise by the Member States of their competence is restricted to the limits posed by European primary law.[870] Although conflicts may arise in different areas, the most illustrative example is the conflict

867 Similarly, see Toporek, 2010, p. 17-18.

868 See, for instance, Schulze, 2015, p. 12 and Herrmann *et al.*, 2012, p. 530. After noting the focus of the implementing measures adopted so far on the energy efficiency of ErPs, the authors argue that in the absence of European product requirements addressing (non-energetic) resource aspects relevant requirements may be adopted at the national level.

869 See Jepsen *et al.*, 2011, p. 112.

870 On this topic, see Krämer, 2015, p. 99-121; Epiney, 2013, 179-192; Meßerschmidt, 2011, p. 136-156.

between national product-related environmental legislation, which is precisely the case under consideration, with the freedom of movement of goods within the European internal market foreseen in Article 26(2) of the TFEU.[871]

At the centre of this conflict lies the prohibition imposed by Article 34 of the TFEU of measures having equivalent effect as quantitative restrictions on imports between member States. Exceptions to this prohibition – or, put another way, trade restrictions as a result of national (legislative) measures – are permitted under both Article 36 of the TFEU[872] and the so-called 'rule of reason'[873] developed by the case law of the ECJ[874]. Whilst Article 36 of the TFEU allows exceptional national measures that differentiate – but do not discriminate – between domestic and imported products, under the rule of reason said measures must be applicable to both domestic and imported products without distinction.[875] An attenuation of

---

871 See Epiney, 2013, p. 179; Meßerschimdt, 2011, p. 137. Examples of other possible conflicts are found in Krämer and Winter, 2015, p. 1555.

872 Environmental protection is not listed in article 36 of the TFEU among the grounds on which an exception to article 34 of the TFEU may be justified. 'The protection of health and life of humans, animals or plants,' is nevertheless an admissible justification. Therefore, environmental concerns may thus legitimate trade restrictions under article 36 of the TFEU only if and in so far as they connect with health issues.

873 See Jans and Vedder, 2012, p. 275.

874 Two rulings are worth pointing out. The first one is the *Cassis de Dijon* case (Case C-120/1978, *Rewe v Bundesmonopolverwaltung für Branntwein* [1979] ECR, p. 649), in which the court found that in the absence of European legislation ('common rules') governing the production and marketing of certain products (*in casu* alcohol and alcoholic beverages) it is for the Member States to regulate all matters relating to it in their own territories. The ECJ further decided that, '[o]bstacles to movement within the [then] Community resulting from disparities between the national laws relating to the marketing of the products in question must be accepted in so far as being necessary in order to satisfy *mandatory requirements* relating in particular to the effectiveness of fiscal supervision, the protection of public health, the fairness of commercial transactions and the defence of the consumer,' (p. 662, emphasis added). The second one is the *Danish bottles* case (Case C-302/86, *Commission v Kingdom of Denmark* [1988] ECR, p. 4607), in which the court confirmed the *Cassis de Dijon* decision and held that, '[…] the protection of the environment […] may […] justify certain limitations of the principle of the free movement of goods' (p. 4630), that is, that, '[…T]he protection of the environment is a *mandatory requirement* which may limit the application of Article 30 of the Treaty [now article 34 of the TFEU]' (p. 4630, emphasis added).

875 Explicitly in this sense, see Case C-302/86, *Commission v Kingdom of Denmark* [1988] ECR, p. 4629, para. 6, emphasis added.

this differentiation has nevertheless been noted in both legal commentary and the case law of the ECJ.[876] Be the case as it may, in order to be permissible, exceptions must satisfy some conditions. For the purposes of this dissertation, suffice it to say that they are justified only if they serve non-economic purposes and are non-discriminatory as well as proportional.[877]

A different question concerns the exercise by the Member States of their competence not in the absence of European secondary legislation, but in the face of it, as illustrated by the fifth situation described above: are national ecodesign requirements more stringent than the existing European ones legally possible? The answer depends on both the content and the legal basis of the European legislative measure, *in casu* the Ecodesign Directive.

Once European secondary legislation has been enacted, the admissibility of national legislation as well as its compatibility with European law, including the possibility of derogation by the Member States, depends primarily on the text (i.e. content) of the relevant European statute.[878] If the statute itself does not allow deviation from its rules, then the Member States may exercise their residual powers only if, and to the extent that, these residual powers are conferred by the primary-law provision on which the secondary-law legislative measure rests.

In terms of environmental protection, European secondary legislation may be based on different provisions of primary law. This is explained by the cross-sectorial nature (*Querschnittscharakter*) of the environmental issues,[879] as reinforced by Article 11 of the TFEU. The first option is Article 192 of the TFEU, which deals with the Union's powers to take action in connection with environmental matters in order to achieve the objectives set out in Article 191 of the TFEU. A second possibility is Article 114(1) of the TFEU, which governs the Union's competence to adopt measures for the harmonisation of the national law of Member States with a view to the functioning of the internal market. Thirdly, action motivated by environmental concerns can take place in the context of other (sectorial) policy areas for which the Union is competent under the TFEU, including

876 See Jans and Vedder, 2012, p. 276-279; Meßerschmidt, 2011, p. 144.

877 See Krämer, 2015, p. 101-114; Epiney, 2013, p. 185-192; Jans and Vedder, 2012, p. 280-294; Meßerschmidt, 2011, p. 149-155.

878 See Jans and Vedder, 2012, p. 97; Meßerschmidt, 2011, p. 137.

879 This feature is repeatedly stressed by de Sadeleer (2014, p. 127, 135, 148, and 171, for example).

agriculture (Article 43), transport (Article 100), energy (Article 194) and international trade (Article 207), to cite a few examples.[880]

According to the prevailing opinion and the case law of the ECJ,[881] the choice of the legal basis is an objective rather than subjective task, which means that it depends on criteria that are amenable to judicial review, in particular the stated aim and the content of the legislative act, instead of being left to the discretion of the European legislature. If a legislative measure pursues two or more purposes, the so-called centre-of-gravity theory applies: the main purpose is to be determined by looking at the measure as a whole as well as at its different provisions.

The importance of defining the legal basis of European statutes relates not only to the determination of the applicable legislative process, but also – and most importantly for the purposes of the present discussion – to the possibility and extent of national legislation. As the residual powers of the Members States vary considerably depending on the primary-law provision on which the piece of European secondary legislation is grounded,[882] a single legal basis is necessary. The ECJ exceptionally allows recourse to a dual legal basis if a legislative act pursues more than one objective having exactly the same weight, that is, where it is not possible to determine which of the stated policy aims is the predominant one.[883] The court finds that the decision-making procedures for each of the legal bases must not be incompatible with each other, though. However, the question as to the residual powers of the Member States in case of combination of legal bases remains unaddressed and this has been regarded as problematic due to the legal uncertainty arising from the disparities in the regulation of such powers by each legal basis.[884]

Regulation (EC) 842/2006 on certain fluorinated greenhouse gases[885], repealed by Regulation (EU) 517/2014,[886] attempted to offer an option to

880 Examples are given by Krämer and Winter, 2015, p. 1557 and, more extensively, by Epiney, 2013, p. 107-109 as well as by Jans and Vedder, 2012, p. 85-94.

881 See, for instance, Krämer, 2015, p. 76-86; Epiney, 2013, p. 109-118; Jans and Vedder, 2012, p. 77-79. See also the rulings of the ECJ cited therein.

882 See, for instance, de Sadeleer, 2014, p. 150.

883 See, for instance, Case C-300/89, *Commission v Council* [1991] ECR, p. I-2867 and Case C-178/03, *Commission v Parliament and Council* [2006] ECR, p. I-107. For Epiney (2013, p. 112), the ECJ does not always emphasise the exceptional nature of a double legal basis with sufficient clarity.

884 See Krämer, 2015, p. 77.

885 OJ L 161, 14 June 2006, p. 1.

886 OJ L 150, 20 May 2014, p. 195.

solving this problem: different legal bases for different provisions within the same legal act. As stated in the preamble, the general legal basis of the regulation was Article 175(1) of the TEC (now Article 192(1) of the TFEU), except for Articles 7, 8 and 9, which were particularly based on Article 95 of the TEC (now Article 114 of the TFEU). Accordingly, pursuant to Article 14 of now-repealed Regulation (EC) 842/2006, the maintenance or introduction by the Member States of more stringent protective measures in relation to the mentioned Articles 7, 8 and 9 had to occur in accordance with Article 95 of the TEC (now Article 114 of the TFEU), whereas in relation to the other provisions of the regulation it had to occur in accordance with Article 176 of the TEC (now Article 193 of the TFEU). This solution has been lauded as 'elegant' by some commentators,[887] while others are more sceptical.[888] In any case, Regulation (EU) 517/2014, which has repealed Regulation (EC) 842/2006, is based solely on Article 192 of the TFEU.

In environmental law, product-related legislation, as in the case of the Ecodesign Directive, is the most typical example of legal acts having a twofold purpose – namely environmental protection, on the one hand, and the free circulation of goods and hence the functioning of the market, on the other hand – in relation to which the definition of the centre of gravity is least clear-cut. The difficulty results from the mobility of products (and hence of their environmental impacts during and/or after use) and the need of uniformity in order to achieve the free movement of goods. In European law, this is reflected in the discussion on whether to base product-related environmental measures on Article 192 of the TFEU or on Article 114(1) of the TFEU. Whilst for some scholars either of these two provisions is a possible legal basis, with the choice, of course, depending on the primary objective of the legal act,[889] others argue that Article 114(1) is the only possibility.[890]

The two legal bases under consideration differ in regard to the residual powers of the Member States: these are allowed to maintain existing or introduce new national provisions deviating from the European legislative

887 See Jans and Vedder, 2012, p. 78.
888 See Krämer, 2015, p. 78.
889 See Epiney, 2013, p. 115-117.
890 See Krämer, 2015, p. 78, 80-81; Meßerschmidt, 2011, p. 105-106.

measure under Article 114(4)[891] and (5)[892] of the TFEU if the measure is grounded on Article 114(1) thereof or under Article 193 of the TFEU[893] if the measure is grounded on Article 192 thereof.[894] The possibility of derogation is much stricter in the former than in the latter situation.

The Ecodesign Directive has two objectives. One the one hand, it aims at reducing the environmental impacts of ErPs in general, and improving their energy efficiency in particular, through the setting of ecodesign requirements.[895] On the other hand, it seeks to approximate the laws of Member States in relation to the ecodesign of energy-related products as a means of avoiding barriers to trade and competition distortion and therefore ensure the functioning of the European internal market.[896] Proposals to have the directive rest on the environmental legal base, at least partially, were made during the drafting and the related policy discussions of its predecessor but they were eventually rejected:[897] the Ecodesign Directive is based on now Article 114(1) of the TFEU and is undisputed in legal commentary.[898]

---

891 Article 114(4) of the TFEU reads: 'If, after the adoption of a harmonisation measure by the European Parliament and the Council, by the Council or by the Commission, a Member State deems it necessary to maintain national provisions on grounds of major needs referred to in Article 36, or relating to the protection of the environment or the working environment, it shall notify the Commission of these provisions as well as the grounds for maintaining them.'.

892 Article 114(5) of the TFEU reads: 'Moreover, without prejudice to paragraph 4, if, after the adoption of a harmonisation measure by the European Parliament and the Council, by the Council or by the Commission, a Member State deems it necessary to introduce national provisions based on new scientific evidence relating to the protection of the environment or the working environment on grounds of a problem specific to that Member State arising after the adoption of the harmonisation measure, it shall notify the Commission of the envisaged provisions as well as the grounds for introducing them.'.

893 Article 193 of the TFEU reads: 'The protective measures adopted pursuant to Article 192 shall not prevent any Member State from maintaining or introducing more stringent protective measures. Such measures must be compatible with the Treaties. They shall be notified to the Commission.'.

894 On this topic, see, for instance, Krämer, 2015, p. 122-137; Jans and Vedder, 2012, p. 97-135; Meßerschmidt, 2011, p. 156-175.

895 See recitals 3 to 10 and 14 of the Ecodesign Directive.

896 See recitals 2 and 41 of the Ecodesign Directive.

897 See van Rossem, Dalhammar and Toulouse, 2010, p. 23; Valsecchi, n.d., p. 3.

898 See, for instance, Tölle, 2016, p. 94; Dalhammar, 2014, p. 156 (who nonetheless notes that giving legislative latitude to the Member States is beneficial to the dynamics of environmental law making in that the adoption of national rules has often triggered new EU laws where these did not yet exist); de Sadeleer,

In this context, once an implementing measure lays down ecodesign requirements for a given environmental aspect (situation (iv)) or provides that no ecodesign requirement is necessary (situation (iii)), Article 6 of the Ecodesign Directive prevents Member States from prohibiting, restricting or impeding the placing on the market and/or putting into service, within their territories, of ErPs complying with the applicable implementing measure. This provision indicates the intention of the directive in achieving harmonisation and thus precluding any derogation by the Member States.[899] Deviating national measures are therefore exceptionally permissible only on the grounds of Article 114(4) and (5) of the TFEU, as expressly foreseen in recital 11 of the Ecodesign Directive.

Lastly, the question as to whether national ecodesign requirements are allowed in the presence of European ecodesign requirements may also be posed in relation to self-regulatory measures. Point 9 of Annex VIII to the Ecodesign Directive exhorts the Member States not to send contradictory signals to participants in self-regulatory initiatives, highlighting the importance of consistency between national legislation and the voluntary initiative to the effectiveness of self-regulation. This notwithstanding, because of the non-binding character of self-regulatory measures, it is contended that they should not pre-empt stricter (i.e. additional and/or different) action by the Member States.[900]

7. Concluding remarks on the Ecodesign Directive

To assert that the Ecodesign is or may be a 'super directive' is an overstatement, as properly acknowledged by a commentator.[901] Many factors speak against its potential to solve all environmental problems.

Firstly, it does not apply to all products indistinctively, let alone to all ErPs. Even in relation to the ErPs to which the Ecodesign Directive is

2014, p. 159; Dietrich and Akkerman, 2013, p. 274; Jepsen *et al.*, 2011, p. 83-84; Schomerus and Spengler, 2010, p. 55; Toporek, 2010, p. 5; van Rossem, Dalhammar and Toulouse, 2010, p. 23; Brenncke, 2009, p. 247; Misonne, 2005, p. 17-18.

899 See, for instance, Langner and Klindt, 2014, Rn. 143, for whom the Member States may not impose Ecodesign requirements that are either additional to (*zusätzlich*) to or divergent from (*abweichend*) the ones laid down at the European level.

900 See Jepsen *et al.*, 2011, p. 116-117; Toporek, 2010, p. 19.

901 See Rehbinder, 2012a, p. 38.

applicable, 'no non-energy using products have [as] yet been covered by ecodesign requirements'[902]. In addition, several substantive and procedural conditions must be met in order for ecodesign requirements to be laid down.

Secondly, the stringency of ecodesign requirements has been modest and they have been imposed gradually, i.e. in a 'tiered' fashion, thereby serving more to phase out worst performing products than as a diver for eco-innovation.

Thirdly, despite the comprehensiveness of the Ecodesign Directive as regards the parameters, environmental aspects and life cycle phases to be considered for the setting out of ecodesign requirements, these have thus far concentrated on energy consumption during the use phase. Non-energy, resource-related requirements already exist in both implementing and self-regulatory measures adopted under the Ecodesign Directive, but they are fewer and seldom address the material composition of products. Most recently, a wave of implementing measures have introduced repairability requirements, the effects of which are yet to be perceived. The adoption of non-energy, resource-related requirements so far is explained by several factors, including consideration of non-energy aspects already in preparatory studies, pressure from stakeholders, and the fact that the applicable self-regulatory and implementing measures build on already existing industry technical standards. There are highly challenging methodological problems to address resource-related aspects, which also explain the hesitation to expand the scope of the Ecodesign Directive.

Another way the potential of the Ecodesign Directive is underused lies in its interaction with environmental legislation. Whenever a given environmental aspect is regarded by the preparatory study as being worth tackling but is thematically already covered by existing legislation (e.g. chemicals), implementing measures limit themselves to referring to the applicable piece of legislation as the appropriate *locus* to deal with the relevant aspect instead of supplementing it. The opportunity to fill in regulatory gaps is missed on the grounds of avoiding legislative overlaps.

The Member States may 'push' the EU legislator towards more ambitious ecodesign regulations by laying down national ecodesign requirements. This is legally possible in some situations – namely in relation to

902 See European Parliament resolution of 31 May 2018 on the implementation of the Ecodesign Directive (2009/125/EC), available at <https://www.europarl.europa.eu/doceo/document/TA-8-2018-0241_EN.html>, last accessed on 31 December 2019.

non-ErPs, ErPs for which no implementing measure has been adopted, and ErPs for which an implementing measure has been adopted but the ecodesign requirements imposed unintentionally do not address a certain environmental aspect – but less so in other situations – namely in relation to ErPs for which an implementing measure has been adopted but it expressly provides that no ecodesign requirement is necessary for a given ecodesign parameter as well as ErPs for which an implementing measure has been adopted but the ecodesign requirements imposed are deemed insufficient (i.e. not stringent enough). In these latter two situations, the introduction of deviating national standards is exceptional and must occur in accordance with Article 114(4) and (5) of the TFEU.

C. *Product ban/phase-out and product composition: the case against plastic carrier bags and single-use plastic products in the EU and Brazil*

Due to their significant contribution to waste streams in general and marine litter in particular, plastics have been increasingly receiving regulatory attention worldwide, usually in the form of bans or phase-outs on the use of plastic products, but legislation governing the design and the material composition of said products also exists. This section examines how the EU and Brazil have been regulating plastic products.

I. The EU

In 2015, Directive (EU) 2015/720 amended Directive 94/62/EC on packaging and packaging waste as regards reducing the consumption of lightweight plastic carrier bags.[903] Despite the focus on consumption, the amended regulation also targets the production (in a broad sense, ranging from manufacturing through distribution to sales) of lightweight plastic carrier bags. For example, Article 4(1a) on prevention requires Member States to take measures such as marketing restrictions, including instruments ensuring that lightweight plastic carrier bags are not provided free of charge at the point of sale of goods or products. In addition, Article 8a provides for the adoption of an implementing act on the specifications of labels or marks of biodegradable and compostable plastic carrier bags.

---

903 OJ L 115, 6 May 2015, p. 11.

As part of the 2018 circular economy package,[904] the European Commission launched an 'EU strategy for plastics in the circular economy', which has been described in a later report following up on the implementation of the 2015 circular economy action plan as 'the first EU-wide policy framework adopting a material-specific lifecycle approach to integrate circular design, use, and recycling activities into plastics value chains'[905].

The strategy strives *inter alia* for the design of plastics and products containing plastics to allow for greater durability, reuse and high-quality recycling; the replacement or phasing-out of substances hampering recycling processes; a greater integration of the plastics value chain so that the chemical industry works closely with plastics recyclers to help them find wider and higher value applications for their output; a revision of the essential requirements for placing packaging on the market to ensure that all plastics packaging placed on the EU market is reusable or easily recycled; the establishment of a clear regulatory framework for plastics with biodegradable properties, including the proposal of harmonised standards clarifying which plastics can be labelled 'compostable' or 'biodegradable' and how they should be handled after use, as well as the development of LCA to identify the conditions under which the use of biodegradable or compostable plastics is beneficial, and the criteria for such applications.

More recently, Directive (EU) 2019/904 on the reduction of the impact of certain plastic products on the environment was enacted. As per its Article 2(2), Directive (EU) 2019/904 shall prevail in case of conflicts with the WFD and Directive 94/62/EC on packaging and packaging waste.

As with lightweight plastic carrier bags, under Article 4 of Directive (EU) 2019/904 Member States shall take measures to achieve an ambitious and sustained reduction in the consumption of the single-use plastic products listed in Part A of the Annex[906], which may include measures affecting production such as those ensuring not only that those single-use plastic products are not provided free of charge, but also that re-usable alterna-

---

904 See chapter 3, section D, *supra*.

905 COM (2019) 190 final, 4 March 2019, p. 6.

906 Namely (1) cups for beverages, including their covers and lids; (2) food containers, i.e. receptacles such as boxes, with or without a cover, used to contain food which: (a) is intended for immediate consumption, either on-the-spot or take-away, (b) is typically consumed from the receptacle, and (c) is ready to be consumed without any further preparation, such as cooking, boiling or heating, including food containers used for fast food or other meal ready for immediate consumption, except beverage containers, plates and packets and wrappers containing food.

tives are made available at the point of sale to the final consumer. Marketing restrictions aimed at substituting single-use plastic products with alternatives that are re-usable or do not contain plastic are also allowed.

Article 5 requires Member States to prohibit the placing on the market of the single-use plastic products listed in Part B of the Annex[907] and of products made from oxo-degradable plastic[908].

In turn, Article 6 lays down requirements on product design and composition. Single-use plastic products listed in Part C of the Annex[909] that have caps and lids made of plastic may be placed on the market only if the caps and lids remain attached to the containers during the products'

---

907 Namely (1) cotton bud sticks, except if they fall within the scope of Council Directive 90/385/EEC on the approximation of the laws of the Member States relating to active implantable medical devices (OJ L 189, 20.7.1990, p. 17) or Council Directive 93/42/EEC concerning medical devices (OJ L 169, 12.7.1993, p. 1); (2) cutlery (forks, knives, spoons, chopsticks); (3) plates; (4) straws, except if they fall within the scope of Directive 90/385/EEC or Directive 93/42/EEC; (5) beverage stirrers; (6) sticks to be attached to and to support balloons, except balloons for industrial or other professional uses and applications that are not distributed to consumers, including the mechanisms of such sticks; (7) food containers made of expanded polystyrene, i.e. receptacles such as boxes, with or without a cover, used to contain food which: (a) is intended for immediate consumption, either on-the-spot or take-away, (b) is typically consumed from the receptacle, and (c) is ready to be consumed without any further preparation, such as cooking, boiling or heating, including food containers used for fast food or other meal ready for immediate consumption, except beverage containers, plates and packets and wrappers containing food; (8) beverage containers made of expanded polystyrene, including their caps and lids; (9) cups for beverages made of expanded polystyrene, including their covers and lids.

908 Article 3(3) of Directive (EU) 2019/904 defines 'oxo-degradable plastic' as 'plastic materials that include additives which, through oxidation, lead to the fragmentation of the plastic material into micro-fragments or to chemical decomposition'. Recital 15 acknowledges that this 'type of plastic does not properly biodegrade and thus contributes to microplastic pollution in the environment, is not compostable, negatively affects the recycling of conventional plastic and fails to deliver a proven environmental benefit'.

909 Namely beverage containers with a capacity of up to three litres, i.e. receptacles used to contain liquid, such as beverage bottles including their caps and lids and composite beverage packaging including their caps and lids, but not: (a) glass or metal beverage containers that have caps and lids made from plastic, (b) beverage containers intended and used for food for special medical purposes as defined in point (g) of Article 2 of Regulation (EU) No 609/2013 of the European Parliament and of the Council on food intended for infants and young children, food for special medical purposes, and total diet replacement for weight control (OJ L 181, 29.6.2013, p. 35) that is in liquid form.

intended use stage (Article 6(1)). To this end, and in accordance with Article 6(3), the European Commission has made a standardisation request to the European Committee for Standardisation as regards certain single-use plastic beverage containers with a capacity of up to three litres that have caps and lids made of plastic (M/563).[910] Beverage bottles listed in Part F of the Annex[911] which are manufactured from polyethylene terephthalate as the major component ('PET bottles') shall from 2025 contain at least 25% recycled plastic and from 2030 at least 30% recycled plastic, calculated as an average for all PET bottles placed on the market (Article 6(5)).

Finally, article 7 introduces marking requirements. Single-use plastic products listed in Part D of the Annex[912] placed on the market are to bear a conspicuous, clearly legible and indelible marking on their packaging or on the products themselves informing consumers of, firstly, appropriate waste management options for the product or waste disposal means to be avoided for that product, in line with the waste hierarchy,[913] and, secondly, the presence of plastics in the product and the resulting negative impact of littering or other inappropriate means of waste disposal of the product on the environment. Harmonised marking specifications shall be established.

II. Brazil

International attention to marine litter in general, and EU regulatory efforts to tackle plastics in particular, have had spill-over effects in Brazil,

910 See C (2019) 8624 final, 28 November 2019. Article 6(3) prescribes that those standards shall in particular address the need to ensure the necessary strength, reliability and safety of beverage container closures, including those for carbonated drinks.

911 Namely beverage bottles with a capacity of up to three litres, including their caps and lids, but not: (a) glass or metal beverage bottles that have caps and lids made from plastic, (b) beverage bottles intended and used for food for special medical purposes as defined in point (g) of Article 2 of Regulation (EU) No 609/2013 that is in liquid form.

912 Namely (1) sanitary towels (pads), tampons and tampon applicators; (2) wet wipes, i.e. pre-wetted personal care and domestic wipes; (3) tobacco products with filters and filters marketed for use in combination with tobacco products; (4) cups for beverages.

913 See chapter 3, section A, *supra*.

where local authorities constitutionally[914] and legally[915] in charge of waste management have, with the support of courts, been banning or phasing out certain plastic products, at times also regulating their composition. Plastic products targeted by regulations typically include plastic carrier bags and single-use plastic products such as straws, cups and cutlery. This section focuses on plastic carrier bags but first presents an overview on the constitutional distribution of legislative powers since it is based on that distribution that courts have been supporting municipal regulations against those products.

1. Environmental federalism and powers to legislate in Brazil

Brazil is a republic federation comprised of the inseparable union of the Federal States, Municipalities and the Federal District (Article 1, chapeau, of the Brazilian Federal Constitution, hereinafter simply 'the Constitution'). This union of all federal entities constitutes itself another federal entity, hereinafter 'the Union'.

From a legal perspective, one of the major issues surrounding federalism is the division of political powers among the federal entities.

Firstly, powers may be *enumerated* or *remaining* depending on whether they are explicitly stated in the Constitution or not, respectively.

Secondly, powers can be divided horizontally or vertically. In *horizontal* distribution, conferral of powers to one federal entity *excludes* all other federal entities from the exercise thereof. For this reason, 'exclusive powers' are spoken of. In *vertical* distribution, the *same* powers are granted concurrently to more than one federal entity and they may be exercised in a *limited* or *unlimited* manner. 'Unlimited concurrent powers' means that each federal entity has full powers, but rules are established in case of conflict between federal entities.[916] 'Limited concurrent powers', in turn, refers to the existence of constitutionally *predetermined* limits to the extent to which powers may be exercised by each federal entity. One could

914 See Article 175 of the Brazilian Constitution.

915 See Article 7 of Federal Law No. 11,445/2007 on sanitation (DOU 5, Section 1, 8 January 2007, p. 3) combined with Article 10 of the PRNS.

916 The most well-known example of such a rule is Article 31 of Germany's *Grundgesetz*, according to which federal legislation shall prevail over state legislation ('*Bundesrecht bricht Landesrecht*').

say that in the latter situation federal entities share the same powers, the reason for which reference is hereinafter made to *shared* powers.

Thirdly, a distinction must be made between powers of legislation and powers of execution. The former, also known as 'legislative powers', relates to the powers vested in parliaments to pass legislation, whereas the latter, also known as 'administrative (or executive) powers', refers to the powers to execute the enacted statutes.

For the purposes of this study, focus is given to the distribution of powers to legislate on environmental matters.

As regards legislative powers, the Constitution confers *exclusive* powers to the Union (Article 22) as well as to Municipalities (Article 30, point I), on the one hand, and *shared* powers to the Union, the Federal States and the Federal District (Article 24), on the other hand. Municipalities are further given the power to supplement existing federal and state legislation (Article 30, point II). The remaining powers rest exclusively with the Federal States (Article 25, paragraph 1). Finally, the Federal District has the legislative powers that are granted to both the Federal States and Municipalities (Article 32, paragraph 1). The subsequent paragraphs explain the distribution of legislative powers in some more depth.

Article 22 of the Constitution lists the *matters* on which the Union has *exclusive* powers to legislate, including, but not limited to, 'water' and 'energy' (point IV), 'world and interstate trade' (point VIII), 'transport' (point XI), '[mineral] deposits, mines, other mineral resources and metallurgy' (point XII), 'indigenous population' (point XIV) as well as 'nuclear activities' (point XXVI). Under Article 22, sole paragraph, of the Constitution, the Union may, by means of a national supplementary law[917] (*lei complementar*), *delegate* to the Federal States powers to legislate on specific aspects of the matters listed in Article 22.

As per Article 30, point I, of the Constitution, Municipalities have *exclusive* powers to legislate on all *matters of local interest*.

917 Under the Brazilian Constitution, legislative powers at the national level are exercised by the National Congress, which comprises the Chamber of Deputies (*Câmara dos Deputados*), the lower legislative house, and the Federal Senate (*Senado Federal*), the upper legislative house. Supplementary laws must be adopted by an absolute majority of the voting members in the National Congress (Article 69), as opposed to ordinary laws, which may be adopted by a simple majority of the votes cast so long as the absolute majority of the voting members in each of the two legislative houses are present at the voting session (Article 47). Unlike ordinary laws, the Brazilian Constitution specifies which matters shall be regulated by means of supplementary laws.

The *matters* for which legislative powers are *shared* among the Union, the Federal States and the Federal District (but not by Municipalities) are listed in Article 24 of the Constitution. The list includes, but is not limited to, the following subject matters: 'urban law' (point I), 'production and consumption' (point V), 'forests, hunting, fishing, nature conservation, soil and natural resources protection, environmental protection, and pollution control' (point VI), 'protection of historical, cultural, artistic, touristic and/or landscape heritage' (point VII), 'liability for damage to the environment, consumers or to goods and/or rights of artistic, aesthetic, historical, touristic and/or landscape value' (point VIII), and 'health protection' (point XII).

Division of shared legislative powers occurs as follows: firstly, the Union's powers are limited to the establishment of general rules (Article 24, paragraph 1); secondly, the Union's powers to enact general rules do not exclude the Federal States' powers to supplement national legislation (Article 24, paragraph 2); thirdly, where the Union has not made use of its powers, the Federal States have full (i.e. unlimited) powers (Article 24, paragraph 3), the exercise of which is evidently circumscribed to their respective territories; fourthly and lastly, where the Union has not, but decides to, make use of its powers, the supervening national legislation suspends the effect of any already existing state legislation to the extent that the two are contrary to each other (Article 24, paragraph 4).

The way the Constitution distributes legislative powers among federal entities is fraught with several interpretational difficulties. The first one arises from the disparity of criteria to confer exclusive powers to the Union (Article 22) and shared powers to the Union, the Federal States as well as the Federal District (Article 24), on the one hand, and exclusive powers to Municipalities (Article 30, point I), on the other hand. Whilst in the former two situations there is a list of *subject matters* on which one or more federal entities are authorised to legislate, in the latter situation legislative powers are granted according to the *scope of interest*. In other words, the Constitution resorts to two criteria that are *not mutually exclusive*.[918] Graphically:

Table 11 – Distribution of legislative powers in Brazil

Powers	Exclusive	Shared
Enumerated	The Union (Article 22):	The Union, the Federal States and the Federal District

918 See Afonso da Silva, 2010, p. 559.

Powers	Exclusive	Shared
	list of subject matters	(Article 24): list of subject matters
	Municipalities (Article 30, point I): matters of local interest	
Remaining	The Federal States (Article 25, paragraph 1)	—

This poses a problem because environmental protection is a subject matter that is listed in Article 24 of the Constitution[919] while at the same time is an issue of local interest,[920] from which follows a still unresolved dispute as to the possibility of Municipalities legislating on environmental matters and the extent of such powers, if any.

Opinions about Municipalities having legislative powers in connection with environmental issues range from acknowledging no such powers whatsoever to recognising the unlimited exercise thereof. On one extreme, it is argued that environmental protection is not a subject matter of local interest *only*, so that Article 30, point I, of the Constitution would not apply to environmental matters, thereby barring municipal action. This view is further reinforced by a restrictive interpretation of Article 30, point II, of the Constitution, as shall be explained in the following two paragraphs. Supporters of the opposite opinion, despite admitting that environmental protection is *not exclusively* local in scope, stress the local character of such an interest, in excessive reliance on Article 30, point I, of the Constitution.

In tandem with this debate lies a controversy about whether Municipalities would also participate in the sharing of powers set forth by Article 24, paragraphs 1 and 2, of the Constitution despite not being mentioned by said provision. Those who answer this question positively associate Article 30, point II, of the Constitution, which gives Municipalities powers to supplement both national and state legislation, with Article 24, paragraph 2, of the Constitution, which gives Federal States powers to supplement national legislation. For them, 'to supplement' means the same thing in both cases: 'to add normative content to already existing national and/or state legislation (in order to provide for state and/or municipal particularities)'.[921] This is a broader interpretation of Article 30, point II, of the Con-

919 Not to mention that subject matters directly related to environmental protection such as water and mineral resources fall within the list of exclusive powers of the Union under article 22 of the Constitution.

920 Although environmental protection is not a subject matter of purely local interest, its local character cannot be ignored.

921 Zago, 2016, p. 240 and 261.

stitution. Those against this viewpoint contend that the supplementary powers granted to Municipalities are of an 'implementing' (i.e. executive or administrative) rather than a 'complementary' (i.e. legislative) nature as is the case with the supplementary powers conferred to the Federal States.[922] This is a more restrictive interpretation of article 30, point II, of the Constitution.

In between the aforementioned two extreme, dissenting opinions on the (im)possibility of Municipalities legislating on environmental matters is the broader interpretation of article 30, point II, of the Constitution, which includes Municipalities in the sharing of the powers set forth by article 24, paragraphs 1 and 2, of the Constitution. According to such an interpretation, which is espoused herein, Municipalities may legislate on environmental matters indeed, *albeit in a limited fashion*. To be sure, case law of Brazil's Supreme Court for constitutional matters (*Supremo Tribunal Federal*, hereinafter 'STF') holds that municipal law must be compatible with both federal and state law.[923]

Besides the mismatch of criteria for dividing legislative powers among federal entities (list of subject matters versus scope of interest) and the related controversy as to whether and the extent to which Municipalities are allowed to exercise such powers in respect of environmental protection, there is the challenge of defining the terms used by articles 22 and 24 of the Constitution to list the subject matters on which legislative powers are conferred, so that one can determine which real life situations are to be subsumed under which of the subject matters listed.[924] In the EU, this is an issue of 'choosing the legal basis', as discussed above.[925] In German law, this subsumption task – which, legal-technically speaking, consists of referring a statute to a constitutional power-conferring (i.e. competence) rule – is known as 'qualification' (*kompetenzielle Qualifikation eines Gesetzes*).[926]

Qualification is particularly important in those cases where legislation governs real life situations that can fall within more than one of the subject matters listed by constitutional rules of competence. For instance, does a statute on water protection or the exploitation of mineral resources con-

---

922 Ferraz Júnior, 1995, p. 19-20.

923 See STF, RE 586.224/SP, rel. Min. Luiz Fux, 5 March 2015.

924 Of course, the expression 'of local interest' found in article 30, point I, of the Constitution is also open to interpretation. Yet, the discussion around it is of a different kind, for it concerns the territorial scope of a subject matter rather than the subject matter itself.

925 See section B.II.6, *supra*.

926 Zago, 2016, p. 423-424.

cern, respectively, 'water' or '[mineral] deposits, mines, other mineral resources and metallurgy' (article 22, points IV and XII, of the Constitution), thereby falling within the exclusive legislative powers of the Union, *or* '[...] soil and natural resources protection, [and] environmental protection [...]' (article 24, point VI, of the Constitution), thereby falling within the shared legislative powers of all federal entities? To give an example more directly related to the present study, do *product*-related, waste-prevention measures have to do with 'world and interstate trade' (article 22, point VIII, of the Constitution), hence falling under the exclusive remit of the Union, or '[...] environmental protection, and pollution control', hence falling under the powers shared by all federal entities (article 24, point VI, of the Constitution)?

Under German law, these questions would be answered by looking at the subject matter (*Gegenstand*), purpose (*Zweck*) and/or effects (*Wirkungen*) of the statute under scrutiny, although the prevailing opinion lays emphasis on the latter two criteria, the reason for which 'functional qualification' is spoken of.[927] In the EU, the ECJ applies the centre-of-gravity theory, as discussed above.[928] Unlike EU and German jurists, however, legal scholars in Brazil rarely address the problem of qualification.[929] No single court has ever developed a coherent set of criteria for undertaking such a task either. Case law of the STF in particular leaves a lot to be desired in this respect.[930]

Last, but by no means least, there is the equally challenging issue of ascertaining the meaning and reach of the expression 'general rules' in Article 24, paragraph 1, of the Constitution. The term must be determined because it delimits the extent to which the Union, on the one hand, and the other federal entities, on the other hand, are to exercise their shared powers. As with the problem of qualification, the lack of a definition in the Constitution leaves it for both legal scholarship and case law, notably that of the STF, to develop the contours of the notion of 'general rules'. So far, however, none of them has succeeded in providing a satisfactory answer to this question.

---

927 See Zago, 2016, p. 429-430. Cases involving legislation with more than one subject matter, purpose and/or effect are decided by examining where the focus (*Schwerpunkt*) lies (see Zago, 2016, p. 436).

928 See section B.II.6, *supra*.

929 Two exceptions are Afonso da Silva, 2010, p. 558-559, and Tavares, 2010, p. 166.

930 For an overview of the criteria that can be worked out from the rulings of the STF, see Tavares, 2010, p. 180-188.

One commentator[931] notes that defining 'general rules', which is to be done by contrasting the term with 'specific rules', is a difficulty inherent to the study of federalism from a legal perspective. For him, scholars' efforts to elucidate the distinction between 'general' and 'specific' have been limited to replacing the two words with synonyms, which obviously does not solve the problem. He adds that there seems to be no additional (i.e. more concrete) criterion to explain the difference between 'general' and 'specific' and that this dichotomy is of a relative rather than absolute nature (i.e. something can be regarded as being 'general' or 'specific' only in relation – or comparison – to alternatives). He then presents at least two possible solutions. The first one would be to acknowledge that the definition of 'general rules' is a matter of legislative policy: the Union decides what 'general rules' are and lays them down by way of national legislation, leaving it for the other federal entities to pass legislation on what it believes to be 'specific'. The main objection to this proposal is the fact that, in practice, shared powers disappear and are instead replaced by a mechanism of exclusive powers, for the decision as to the meaning of 'general rules' is left to only one federal entity, namely the Union. Alternatively, criteria can be obtained inductively, that is, based on case law, notably that of the STF. Once again, however, case law of the STF is helpless, not to say schizophrenic.[932]

For another commentator, the absence of further criteria to clearly distinguish between 'general' and 'specific' rules is explained by the fact that, from a pure logical point of view, the distinction may be made according to either the subjects to whom a rule is addressed or the situations determined by it.[933] Regarding its addressees, a rule can be 'universal' if it applies to absolutely everyone, 'generic' if it applies to subjects who 'are members of an open class (or genus) defined by certain properties'[934], or 'individual' or 'singular' if it applies to '[...] a closed class, that is, a class whose membership cannot logically vary with time'[935], so that one (or a very few persons) can be identified. As for its content, a rule can be

931 See Afonso da Silva, 2010, p. 559-563.

932 For an overview of the STF's interpretation of 'general rules', see Tavares, 2010, p. 167-180. See also Afonso da Silva, 2010, p. 562-563.

933 See Ferraz Júnior, 1995, p. 18-19, whose claims rely on Ross, 1968 (especially p. 108-112). Ross (1968) notes that 'the distinction between the subject and the situation which a norm [i.e. what has been here termed 'rule'] determines is vague and must be drawn somewhat arbitrarily' (p. 110).

934 See Ross, 1968, p. 110.

935 Idem, p. 109.

'universal' if it is to be applied under all circumstances, 'generic' if '[...] the situation in which a norm [i.e. rule] is to be applied is defined as an open class [...]', or 'individual' if '[...] the situation in which a norm [i.e. rule] is to be applied is defined as a closed class [...]'.[936] Graphically:

Table 12 – Possible classification of rules from a logical viewpoint[937]

A rule may be classified...					
... according to its addressees (i.e. to whom it applies) as ...			... according to its content (i.e. the situations to which it applies) as ...		
... **universal** (it applies to everyone)	... **generic** (it applies to some persons)	... **individual** or singular (it applies to one person only)	... **universal** (it applies to all situations)	... **generic** (it applies to some situations)	... **individual** (it applies to one situation only)

In this sense, it is contended that reference to 'general rules' in article 24, paragraph 1, of the Constitution may relate to either universal rules according to the addressees *or* universal rules according to the content. Accordingly, the Federal States, the Federal District and Municipalities would have powers to enact legislation containing generic and/or individual rules (again, according to either addressees or content). Logical analysis therefore helps explain the difference between 'general' and 'specific' rules but does not solve the problem. This calls for a teleological interpretation, so it is argued.[938]

The reigning opinion among scholars advocating such a purposive reading is that 'general rules' are to be distinguished from 'specific rules' – and therefore shared powers are to be delimited among federal entities – by determining the federal entity whose interest should prevail in a concrete case,[939] that is, by deciding in which cases an issue should be dealt with at the national level instead of being handled at the state, municipal and/or district levels.[940] The discussion is normally framed as a matter of allowing for regional and/or local diversity, thus respecting the autonomy of federal entities, particularly in a country of continental dimensions like Brazil,

936 Idem, p. 111.

937 See Ferraz Júnior, 1995, p. 18.

938 For the considerations of this paragraph, see Ferraz Júnior, 1995, p. 18-19. In favour of the finalistic approach, see also Krell, 2009, p. 638.

939 See Afonso da Silva, 2015, p. 482.

940 Of course, this is just one reformulation of, but not an answer to, the question. Be the case as it may, it invariably touches the broader discussion of federalism models, which goes beyond the focus of this study.

versus the need for uniformity (or, less rigorously, homogeneity),[941] hence with no room for differentiated legal regimes across the country, especially in those fields:
- where all federal entities have the same interest;[942]
- involving typologies and concepts that may create conflicts or difficulties to national (i.e. interstate) trade (*intercâmbio nacional*) if particularised in the ambit of any autonomous federal entity other than the Union;[943]
- of the economy and society that, in a Welfare State like Brazil, require unity of planning and direction;[944]
- involving issues that are new (i.e. that have never been regulated) or complex, in respect of which legislation enacted by the Union serves as a parameter for the other federal entities ('inducing character').[945]

With regard to environmental problems, the debate on centralisation versus decentralisation of legislative powers is virtually inexistent in Brazil. Both in legal scholarship and case law, it is frequently and simply stated that all federal entities have powers to legislate on environmental matters and, in case of conflicting legislation, the regulation providing for the highest level of environmental protection should *prima facie* prevail, regardless of whether it is national, state, district or municipal.[946] This is too simplistic a view, for it not only avoids the discussion of the advantages and disadvantages of vesting legislative powers with one federal entity rather than the other ones, but also ignores the diversity of environmental problems.

In contrast, the international literature on federalism and environmental regulation, including waste law, has long addressed the debate.[947] Considerations *in favour of centralisation and against decentralisation*, include, but are not limited to, the following: the cross-border nature of many environmental problems; the fear that competition amongst federal entities to attract businesses might lead to the so-called 'race to the bottom' in terms of environmental protection; the existence of interstate externalities; the need to guarantee a nationwide minimum level of environmental protection;

941 See Krell. 2009, p. 637.
942 See Ferraz Júnior, 1995, p. 19.
943 Idem, ibidem.
944 See Bercovici, 2004, p. 56.
945 See Krell, 2009, p. 638, 646.
946 See, for instance, Sarlet and Fensterseifer, 2013.
947 See, for instance, Revesz, 2000; Kloepfer, 1999; von Lersner, 1999.

and the benefits of uniformity in environmental regulation for businesses (e.g. no distortions of competition).

Conversely, several arguments speak *in favour of decentralisation and against centralisation*: some environmental problems are confined to the borders of a single federal entity; competition amongst federal entities might lead to innovation in terms of environmental regulation; innovative regulations are more easily experimented, and citizens' interests are less difficultly represented, at the regional and/or local level, so that chances to advance environmental policy are higher; centralisation entails greater informational costs and a lack of flexibility.

Given that the focus of this section is not to delve into federalism in general, nor its relationship with environmental regulation in particular, but rather to introduce to the reader not familiar with Brazilian law, firstly, how legislative powers over environmental matters are distributed among the federal entities and, secondly, what the main legal, interpretational challenges surrounding said distribution are, *especially because this issue pervades the discussions on product-related, waste prevention-oriented instruments in Brazil*, it shall suffice to make some concluding remarks to this section.

A common observation in support of centralising environmental regulation is that the environment knows no borders. While this is true, it is also true that some ecological issues are confined to – or at least more prominently perceived and/or better tackled within – clear geographical boundaries. The 'borderlessness' argument does not hold for all ecological issues, especially because it rests on a very specific problem, namely that of cross-border degradation of the environment. For instance, it seems straightforward that interstate externalities or biome protection as required by article 225, paragraph 4, of the Constitution, should be addressed by national legislation, whereas the protection of species that are endemic to a particular region or locality should be governed by state, district and/or municipal legislation. Of course, one could maintain that the protection of endemics goes beyond regional and/or local interests due to the interconnectedness of the environment, but this would ultimately require all ecological problems to be regulated at the global level, which reveals the impracticability of total centralisation.

Less obvious, but much more typical, is the disparity in the level of protection among federal entities. Indeed, the overwhelmingly majority of court cases involving conflicts in the exercise of legislative powers over environmental matters concern legislation with a narrower territorial scope increasing the stringency of legislation with a wider territorial scope, that is, state, district or municipal legislation that is stricter than national legislation *or* municipal legislation that is stricter than state legislation. Conflicts arise when legislation having a narrower territorial scope outlaws an impacting production activity and/or product allowed by legislation having a wider territorial scope[948] or sets higher environmental protection standards. This poses the question of competition among federal entities arising from diverging preferences for environmental protection across the country.[949]

Generally and traditionally, the STF has had a centralised stance on environmental federalism[950] and thus ruled in favour of the prevalence of legislation with a wider territorial scope over legislation with a narrower territorial scope, particularly in cases where the latter prohibits what the former permits or vice versa[951] or where uniformity is required *inter alia*

948 Well-known examples include, respectively, the *immediate* prohibition of sugarcane straw burning by the Municipality of Paulínia in the State of São Paulo despite the *progressive* phase-out at the state level and the *ban* on chrysotile asbestos by some Federal States and Municipalities despite the *permission* at the national level.

949 It should be noted that diversification of the level of environmental protection is sometimes imperative. In the field of contaminated land, for example, the setting of soil quality standards must take into account the presence of naturally occurring substances in soil, below or at the levels of which a site is not to be qualified as being contaminated. These levels are known as 'normal background concentrations' or 'background values'. Because normal background concentrations vary according to soil type, uniformity of standards is impossible. With reason, article 8 of Conama Resolution No. 420/2009 (DOU 249, Section 1, 30 December 2009, p. 81) requires the Federal States as well as the Federal District to set their own soil quality standards (*valores de referência de qualidade*).

950 Similarly, see Antunes, 2015.

951 In the case of sugarcane straw burning (see footnote 948, supra), the STF upheld the decision made by the São Paulo State Court of Justice (*Tribunal de Justiça do Estado de São Paulo*, hereinafter 'TJSP') to declare the municipal statute unconstitutional on the grounds that it ran counter to state legislation (see STF, RE 586.224/SP, rel. Min. Luiz Fux, 5 March 2015). Likewise, two state statutes that had banned chrysotile asbestos in Mato Grosso do Sul and São Paulo were rendered unconstitutional because they ran counter to federal legislation (see STF, ADI 2.396-9/MS, rel. Min. Ellen Gracie, 8 May 2003, and STF, ADI 2.656-9/SP, rel. Min. Maurício Corrêa, 8 May 2003). This notwithstanding, state and municipal laws forbidding the use of chrysotile asbestos were enacted after the two 2003 rulings. Lawsuits challenging the constitutionality of the state and municipal statutes were thus filed with the STF. But so was another lawsuit challenging the constitutionality of the federal statute allowing chrysotile asbestos. In a shift of opinion, the STF decided that the federal statute is unconstitutional on the grounds that permitting chrysotile asbestos violates the constitutional right to health, thereby maintaining the state and municipal legislation prohibiting the

because international or interstate trade may be affected. However, as one STF Justice notes, the court's movement towards centralisation/decentralisation is rather 'pendular' and recent case law has been favouring state and municipal autonomy, especially in the fields of health, consumer, and environmental protection.[952]

The distinction between facility and product-related regulation of environmental problems[953] offers an insight into the centralisation/decentralisation dilemma. Uniformity is much more compelling in the regulation of products due to their mobility and the corollary potential to affect interstate trade, which is a subject matter on which the Union has exclusive powers to legislate under Article 22 of the Constitution. For this reason, where the Union has exercised its powers, state, municipal and district action should be pre-empted or at least compatible with federal law.

Yet, the dilemma remains unresolved in those situations where federal product-related environmental legislation is inexistent or considered insufficient. Particularly in this latter scenario, unlike the primary law of the EU, most notably Articles 114(4) to (7) and of the TFEU,[954] the Brazilian Constitution does not provide for a mechanism whereby the Federal States, Municipalities or the Federal District may 'push' the Union to take action towards higher stringency of environmental regulations. What should then prevail: uniformity or autonomy?

While simple to ask, the question is difficult to answer. Not to mention that answers must be justified on a case-by-case basis. Practically and ultimately, they will be given by the erratic *iuris dictio* of the STF. As shall be discussed in the following section, recent precedents of the STF have allowed Municipalities to ban plastic bags because they pose a problem to waste management, which is a purely local matter.

---

use of chrysotile asbestos. See STF, ADI 3937/SP, rel. Min. Marco Aurélio, 24 August 2017. See also ADI 3356/PE, rel. Min. Eros Grau, 30 November 2017; ADI 3357/RS, rel. Min. Ayres Britto, 30 November 2017; ADPF/SP 109, rel. Min. Edson Fachin, 30 November 2017; ADI 3406/RJ and ADI 3470/RJ, rel. Min. Rosa Weber, 29 November 2017.

952 See Lewandowski, 2013.

953 See chapter 1, section D, and chapter 3, section B, *supra*.

954 See section B.II.6, *supra*.

2. Plastic carrier bags

In Brazil, plastic carrier bags (hereinafter in this section simply 'plastic bags') have usually been, and in most places across the country still are, provided to consumers free of charge at shops and then later used in households as bin liners. Recent concerns about the environmental impacts of plastic bags have led a few states and many municipalities to regulate their supply by retailers to consumers. No federal legislation on the matter exists, but a myriad of bills has been introduced before both the Chamber of Deputies (the lower legislative house) and the Senate (the upper legislative house).

Despite the differences among state and municipal regulations as well as the federal bills, generally speaking, they all address the following three interrelated questions: firstly, whether to use *plastic* bags at all as opposed to using bags made of other materials such as paper or even carrying shopping by other means such as cardboard boxes; secondly, *if plastic bags are the option*, whether to use *single-use* bags as opposed to using reusable and more durable bags; thirdly, *if single-use bags are decided upon*, whether to use *conventional* plastic carrier bags as opposed to using (oxo-)biodegradable bags.

In terms of regulatory technique, regulations and bills offer different answers to these questions. Whilst some ban or place a Pigouvian tax on the supply of less environmentally friendly bags, others mandate the supply of environmentally friendlier bags, at times free of charge. In many instances, there is a combination of both alternatives. The most typical solution offered by existing regulations and the proposed bills is to prohibit the provision to consumers of single-use, conventional plastic bags altogether, whether free of charge or not, *while at the same time* to mandate their replacement with bags that are (oxo-) biodegradable, reusable/more durable and/or made of materials other than plastic. Normally, a phase-out period ranging from a few months to a couple of years is provided for the replacement to take effect. In any case, the legal commands are always addressed to retailers, which means that the focus of the regulation is the *supply* of bags to consumers, not the *manufacture* thereof.[955]

The case against plastic bags in Brazil is best illustrated by Law No. 15,374/2011[956] from São Paulo City, which not only forbids all commer-

955 Of course, it is assumed that distributors will then push their suppliers for environmentally friendlier bags.

956 DOCSP 92, 19 May 2011, p. 1.

cial establishments to sell, or provide free of charge, plastic bags to consumers but also calls on them to stimulate the use of reusable bags instead. The municipal statute provoked a huge political and legal uproar for allegedly violating consumer rights and being enacted in breach of the provisions of the Brazilian Constitution on the powers to legislate on environmental matters,[957] from which followed a long-lasting judicial war that merits consideration.

In light of the various bills to regulate plastic bags that had been brought before municipal parliaments all across the State of São Paulo as well as the São Paulo State legislature itself, a letter of intent[958] was signed between the São Paulo State Secretary of Environment (*Secretaria do Meio Ambiente*, hereinafter 'SMA') and the São Paulo State Supermarket Association (*Associação Paulista de Supermercados*, hereinafter 'APAS') with a view to mounting a consumer awareness campaign to replace single-use, petroleum-based plastic bags with alternative, less environmentally impacting ways of carrying shopping, including the use of returnable bags. The supermarkets affiliated to APAS committed themselves *inter alia* to substitute single-use, petroleum-based plastic bags from January 2012 as well as to provide consumers with information about the environmental impacts of such bags at their shops. SMA should *inter alia* give its opinion about the informational material to be used by supermarkets in their campaigns.

About ten days after the letter of intent was signed, Municipal Law No. 15,374/2011 was enacted. Less than a month later, a lawsuit challenging its constitutionality was filed with TJSP, which granted a provisional order to suspend the effect of the statute,[959] thereby allowing the supply of conventional plastic bags.

---

957 See the previous section.

958 See 'Protocolo de intenções que celebram entre si o Estado de São Paulo, por intermédio da Secretaria do Meio Ambiente, e a APAS – Associação Paulista de Supermercados, para realização de estudos e adoção de ações sobre a viabilidade de substituição do uso de sacola plástica à base de petróleo descartável, em supermercados estabelecidos no Estado de São Paulo', as of 9 May 2011 (DOESP 86, 10 May 2011, p. 1).

959 A legal complaint against this provisional order was filed with STF. The claimants argued that judicial review of Municipal Law No. 15,374/2011 should take place with the STF, and not the TJSP, because the case would involve a violation of the Federal Constitution rather than of the São Paulo State Constitution. The STF dismissed the complaint on the grounds that deciding otherwise would mean to bar state courts from exercising their powers of judicial review. See STF, Complaint (*Reclamação*) 13.818/SP, rel. Min. Ricardo Lewandowski, 22 May 2012 (provisional ruling) and 28 April 2014 (final ruling).

In early February 2012, APAS and three other large supermarket chains entered into conduct adjustment agreements (*termo de ajustamento de conduta*, hereinafter 'TAC')[960] with the São Paulo State Prosecution Office (*Ministério Público do Estado de São Paulo*, hereinafter 'MPSP')[961] and committed themselves to the following:

- widely inform consumers at shops that single-use plastic bags would no longer be provided, not even for a charge (clauses 1 and 1.2); this should be done also, and in particular, at the checkout counter for a period of one year from the signing of the TAC (clause 5);
- for a period of 60 days from the signing of the TAC, provide consumers who would not bring their own shopping bags with appropriate packaging to transport their shopping, free of charge (clause 1.1);
- for a period of six months from the signing of the TAC, provide consumers with returnable bags at a price no higher than R$0,59 per unit (clause 2);
- on 15 March 2012 (celebration of Consumer's Day), provide consumers who would buy at least 5 items at any price with reusable bags, free of charge (clause 3);
- for a period of six months from 15 March 2012, exchange the bags that would be provided on Consumer's Day and that would have been damaged due to wear and tear for new ones upon request by the consumer and free of charge (clause 4).[962]

Under Brazilian civil procedural law, once a TAC has been signed, the civil inquiry within which it has been concluded is to be terminated and thus archived. The Superior Council of each State's public prosecution

960 As per article 5, paragraph 6, of Federal Law No. 7,347/1985 (DOU 140, Section 1, 25 July 1985, p. 10,649) on civil class actions seeking liability for damage to the environment, consumers, and/or to goods and/or assets of artistic, aesthetic, historic, touristic and/or landscape value, TACs are agreements by means of which natural or legal persons not complying with legal requirements commit themselves to do so – hence the idea of adjusting one's conduct to legal standards – before the public bodies who have legal standing to file a class action. TACs must set forth what the committed parties shall do or refrain from doing as well as impose penalties in case they do not abide by what has been stipulated. Finally, and most importantly, TACs have the legal nature of out-of-court (i.e. extrajudicial) enforcement orders.

961 TACs are typically concluded within the civil inquiries that public prosecution offices open to investigate non-compliance with legislation.

962 See MPSP Civil Inquiry 14.0161.0000981/2011. The TACs stipulated a daily fine of R$25,000.00 in case of non-compliance.

office (*Conselho Superior do Ministério Público*, hereinafter 'CSMP')[963] must homologate the termination and archiving of civil inquiries (article 9, paragraph 2, of Federal Law No. 7,347/1985 combined with article 30 of Federal Law No. 8,625/1993 on the organisation of public prosecution in Brazil[964]). For this reason, in the State of São Paulo, TACs take effect only after the homologation by the CSMP (article 112, sole paragraph, of State Supplementary Law No. 734/1993 on the organisation of public prosecution in the State of São Paulo[965]).

The CSMP did *not* homologate the TACs on plastic bags due to consumer protection reasons. For the CSMP, before the execution of the TACs, consumers used to be provided with conventional, single-use plastic bags *free of charge* as the costs of providing those bags were built into the price of the purchased goods. By contrast, as a result of the TACs, supermarkets started to sell environmentally friendlier bags without deducting the built-in costs of conventional, single-use bags from the price of the products they sell. In this sense, the solution arrived at by the TACs was argued to have led to a situation in which the burden of environmental protection fell exclusively and excessively on consumers, in violation of consumer protection law. In the CSMP's view, not only the environment, but also the consumer should be protected, the reason for which it did not homologate the TACs and decided in early June 2012 that the civil inquiries that had been initiated should continue in order for the committed parties to find a better alternative to protecting the consumer while at the same time banning conventional, single-use plastic bags.

Few days after the CSMP's decision, a consumer protection association filed a class action against APAS and the supermarkets that had concluded the TACs with the MPSP seeking the supply of carrier bags, preferably biodegradable or paper ones, *free of charge*.[966] On 25 June 2012, based on the same reasoning of the CSMP, the judge granted a provisional order requiring that the respondents should resume providing consumers with plastic bags *free of charge* and, within thirty days from the resumption, start to provide biodegradable or paper bags, *also free of charge*.

An interlocutory appeal against the interim first-instance injunction was then lodged with the TJSP. Initially, in early August 2012, the second-in-

---

963 CSMPs are an administrative body of public prosecution offices. Their powers are laid down in article 15 of Federal Law No. 8,625/1993.

964 DOU 31, Section 1, 15 February 1993, p. 1.

965 DOESP 221, Section I, 27 November 1993, p. 1.

966 See TJSP, 1ª Vara Cível, ACP 0155391-22.2012.8.26.0100.

stance reporting judge[967], *inspired by the TACs that had been executed with the MPSP*, issued an equally provisional order requiring the respondents to continue providing conventional, single-use plastic bags free of charge until 15 September 2012 as well as to start providing reusable bags *at a price no higher than R$0,59* per unit until 15 April 2013.

At the end of April 2014, the TJSP delivered its final ruling, which confirmed the reporting judge's initial decision and overturned the first-instance provisional injunction.[968] Firstly, the court held that the case is more about environmental protection than consumer protection. Secondly, it found that the provision of conventional, single-use plastic bags to consumers *free of charge* does not constitute customary law.[969] Thirdly, the court noted that there is *no* legislation mandating the provision of carrier bags *free of charge*, regardless of type or material. Fourthly, it rejected the argument that the *sales* of environmentally friendlier carrier bags would represent a heavy burden on the consumer. In fact, according to the TJSP, supplying environmentally friendlier carrier bags free of charge would not protect all consumers, but rather only a group of them, namely consumers who are 'environmentally unaware', to the disadvantage of another group, namely 'environmentally aware' consumers who already bring their own shopping bags. As the costs of providing environmentally friendlier bags 'free of charge' would too be built into the price of products, 'environmentally aware' consumers would end up paying for 'environmentally unaware' consumers.[970] Lastly, charges for bags not only

967 In Brazil, cases at second instance are normally decided by three judges, with one of them being in charge of reporting the proceedings to the other two before a decision is reached.

968 See TJSP, 1ª Câmara Reservada ao Meio Ambiente, AI 0165606-66.2012.8.26.0000, 24 April 2014.

969 Even if it did, the court hinted at the fact that, at least in a civil-law legal system like Brazil's, statutory law (e.g. legislation banning or taxing conventional, single-use plastic carrier bags) overrides customary law (e.g. the supply of said bags free of charge).

970 One of the judges expressed a dissenting opinion. For him, the case concerns consumer, not environmental, protection. He pointed out *inter alia* that paper bags used to be provided before the widespread use of plastic bags and added that the replacement of paper bags with plastic ones took place to meet the convenience of retailers, as consumers have never been asked about their preference. This fact is reinforced, he contends, by the excessive amount of secondary packaging found on supermarket shelves, which reveals no concern for environmental protection whatsoever.

are inexpensive, but can also be avoided if consumers use their own shopping bags.

It should not be forgotten that the ruling above, though final, was made by the TJSP when it decided the interlocutory appeal against the interim relief granted by the first-instance judge. In other words, it does not constitute a judgement on the merits. So much so that the lawsuit is still ongoing in the first-instance court. In fact, the first-instance judge suspended the class action to await a decision from the STF on a constitutional appeal (*recurso extraordinário*) addressing the issue of the constitutionality of a municipal statute[971] that requires commercial establishments to have their employees pack customers' goods.[972-973]

At the beginning of October 2014, the TJSP declared Municipal Law No. 15,374/2011 constitutional,[974] which had until then been barred from taking effect. At the core of the debate held by the court on the (un)constitutionality of the municipal statute is the distribution of legislative powers on environmental matters, as discussed in the previous section. The TJSP found that Law No. 15,374/2011 not only pursues the protection of the *local* environment, thus authorised by Article 30, point I, of the Brazilian Constitution (exclusive powers of Municipalities to legislate on matters of local interest), but also runs counter to neither federal[975] nor state law, therefore in line with Article 24 of the Constitution (shared powers to legislate on environmental matters).

An appeal was filed with the STF, which upheld the TJSP's declaration of constitutionality.[976] Based on precedents that acknowledge the constitutional powers of Municipalities powers to legislate on environmental

---

971 Namely Law No. 5.690/2010 from Pelotas City (Sate of Rio Grande do Sul).

972 See STF, RE 839.950/RS, rel. Min. Luiz Fux, 24 October 2018. Although the judgement was delivered at the end of 2018 and Municipal Law No. 5.690/2010 was declared unconstitutional for violating economic freedom (Article 1, point IV, and Article 170 of the Constitution), the final, *written* decision (*acórdão*) still has not been made available.

973 Strictly speaking, requiring commercial establishments to have their employees pack customers' goods has nothing to do with requiring them to provide carrier bags, whether free of charge or not, and regardless of material composition.

974 See TJSP, Órgão Especial, ADI 0121480-62.2011.8.26.0000, rel. Min. Arantes Theodoro, 1 October 2014. Two dissenting opinions were given.

975 On the contrary, the municipal statute accords with Article 9 of the PNRS, which establishes the waste hierarchy. See chapter 3, section A, above.

976 See STF, Ag. Reg. no RE 901.444/SP, rel. Min. Roberto Barroso, 4 June 2018.

matters[977] and that the ban on plastic bags is a matter of local interest,[978] the STF found that Municipal Law No. 15,374/2011 is not only aimed at the non-generation of waste but also allows for the use of reusable bags, which is unquestionably in tune with the PNRS (i.e. federal law).

While this finding is true, it disregards that the mobility of products speaks for centralisation of regulation by reason of both the impacts on interstate trade and environmental protection concerns: in *waste*-related issues, products are the problem themselves because of their bulk and the potential harmfulness of the materials and substances they contain and/or are made from.

After Municipal Law No. 15, 374/2011 was declared constitutional by the TJSP, it finally started to take effect. Implementing Decree No. 55,827/2015 was then issued in early January 2015 with a view to elaborating on the municipal statute. The decree recalls that commercial establishments should stimulate the use of reusable bags, which are defined as bags intended for the separate collection of the dry fraction of household waste and whose specifications are to be defined by the municipal waste management authority. It further prohibits reusable bags to be used for the conventional collection of unsorted household waste.

On the heels of Implementing Decree No. 55,827/2015, the waste management authority of São Paulo City (*Autoridade Municipal de Limpeza Urbana*, hereinafter 'Amlurb) issued Resolution No. 55/2015,[979] which 'lays down the technical specifications of the reusable, bioplastic bags to be used by commercial establishments in São Paulo City'.

Amlurb Resolution No. 55/2015 makes clear that 'reusable bags' are reusable in the sense that they are to be reused by consumers for discarding household waste (article 3, chapeau). Secondly, it distinguishes between 'green' and 'grey' bags. Whilst green bags are intended for the discarding/separate collection of the dry fraction of household waste, grey bags are intended for the discarding/conventional collection of unsorted

977 See footnote 923, *supra*.

978 See STF, RE 729.726/SP, rel. Min. Dias Toffoli, 8 June 2017 (finding that a municipal statute that requires the replacement of plastic bags with biodegradable ones is a matter of local interest since it relates to the management of the waste generated in the municipal territory) and STF, Ag. Reg. nos ED 729.731/SP, rel. Min. Dias Toffoli, 6 October 2017 (finding not only that a municipal statute that bans plastic bags is a matter of local interest but also that the PNRS does not establish any specific plastic bags policy to be developed by Municipalities, which reaffirms their powers to regulate the issue).

979 DOC 9, 15 January 2015, p. 29.

household waste, i.e. presumably the waste that is not collected separately in green bags (article 3, points I and II). Thirdly, it lays down the technical specifications of both green and grey bags, including requirements on pigmentation, material composition, size, thickness, area, and load withstand capability (articles 4 and 5) as well as visual identity (article 8 combined with Annexes I and II). Bags must also meet the technical specifications laid down by ABNT[980] NBR[981] 14.937:2010[982] (article 7).

Regarding material composition, both green and grey bags are to be made from at least 51% raw materials from sustainable technologies such as bioplastics. In addition, bags made from oxo-biodegradable and oxo-degradable materials are proscribed (article 6). Finally, non-reusable bags smaller than the size specified for the reusable, bioplastic bags must be manufactured from materials other than plastic (article 10).

Bearing the regulation of bags in mind, APAS and the São Paulo State Consumer Protection Foundation (*Fundação de Proteção e Defesa do Consumidor de São Paulo*, hereinafter 'PROCON/SP') signed a letter of intent at the end of April 2015, by means of which the supermarkets affiliated to APAS committed themselves *inter alia* to the following:

- between 11 May 2015 and 10 July 2015 (two months), provide consumers with a maximum of two bags per shop free of charge (clause 2, item 1);
- between 11 May 2015 and 10 November 2015 (six months), give a R$0,03 discount for every five products purchased or R$30,00 spent, or offer any alternative advantage/benefit, to consumers who bring their own shopping bags or any other means to carry their shopping (clause 2, item 2);
- between 11 May 2015 and 10 November 2015 (six months), have special offers on eco-bags (clause 2, item 5);
- between 11 May 2015 and 10 November 2015 (six months), inform consumers of the costs of the bags and, together with PROCON, the importance of using reusable bags (clause 2, items 3 and 4).

To date, virtually all plastic carrier bags are provided at a charge of a few cents per unit and conform to the specifications laid down in Amlurb Resolution No. 55/2011.

980 ABNT stands for *Associação Brasileira de Normas Técnicas*, the Brazilian Technical Standards Association.

981 NBR stands for 'norma(s) brasileira(s)', i.e. Brazilian technical standard.

982 ABNT NBR 14.937:2010 is a Brazilian technical standard on the requirements and test methods for T-shirt style plastic bags.

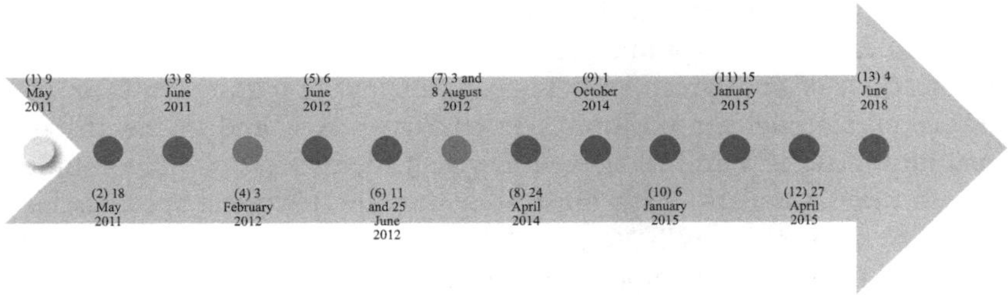

Figure 6 – Evolution of plastic bags regulation in São Paulo City[983]

Legend:
(**1**) Execution of the letter of intent between SMA and APAS. (**2**) Enactment of Municipal Law No. 15,374/2011. (**3**) Filing of a constitutional complaint against Municipal Law No. 15,374/2011 and suspension of its effect. (**4**) Execution of TACs between the MPSP and APAs/supermarket chains. (**5**) Non-homologation of the TACs by the CSMP. (**6**) Filing of a class action seeking the supply of plastic bags free of charge. Interim relief granted. (**7**) Filing of an interlocutory appeal against, and provisional overturning of, the first-instance interim injunction. (**8**) Interlocutory appeal decided. First-instance interim injunction overturned. (**9**) Constitutional complaint decided. Municipal Law No. 15,374/2011declared constitutional. (**10**) Enactment of Municipal Decree No. 55,827/2015 elaborating on Municipal Law No. 15,374/2011. (**11**) Publication of Amlurb Resolution No. 55/2015 in the DOC. (**12**) Execution of letter of intent between the PROCON and APAS. (**13**) Declaration of constitutionality of Municipal Law No. 15,374/2011 uphold by the STF.

The case against plastic bags in São Paulo allows for several conclusions.

Firstly, banning or phasing out a product is faced with different, often conflicting, interests, as epitomised by the debate on consumer versus environmental protection. Behind it lies an implicit discussion as to whom should bear the financial burden of providing environmentally friendlier bags. Resistance was mounted not only by the plastics industry, which sought judicial review of Municipal Law No. 15,374/2011, but also by the State Public Prosecution Office in charge of protecting diffuse interests such as the environment (Article 129, point III, of the Constitution).

Secondly, it confirms the thesis that waste *prevention* is best promoted by *product*-related measures taken at upstream stages in the product life

983 Green dots: plastic bags permitted. Red dots: plastic bags prohibited. Yellow dots: voluntary agreement to replace conventional plastic bags with environmentally friendlier ones. Orange: binding agreement to replace conventional plastic bags with environmentally friendlier alternatives.

cycle. It was based on the connection between waste management, on the one hand, and waste prevention (i.e. non-generation) and reusability of bags, on the other hand, that the STF has declared the constitutionality of Municipal Law No. 15,374/2011. In practice, this has led the local *waste management* authority to regulate the ecodesign, including material composition, of the *product* category plastic carrier bags.

Thirdly, however, allowing local authorities to regulate products not only hinders interstate trade, a matter on which the Union has exclusive legislative powers, but also poses questions as to the need for uniformity (and hence centralisation of product-related environmental law-making) due to the high mobility of products, which are the problem themselves.

D. Excursus: the case of mobile phone chargers in the EU

In the third chapter, a five-step model looking at waste prevention strategies through changes in the production and consumption of products before they are discarded has been outlined and a decision to focus on the design decisions made by producers as to the material composition of the products they place on the market ('step 3') has been made. This notwithstanding, a legislative attempt to tackle the question of superfluous needs for services and/or products ('step 1') by targeting product design decisions made by producers has been made in the EU. It deserves consideration precisely because it addresses the most important, albeit the most difficult, step without involving a prohibition of production and/or consumption.

It is widely known that mobile phones have normally been compatible only with very specific mobile phone chargers. This specificity has been such that there has been a typical incompatibility of mobile phone chargers not only amongst brands, but also amongst models from the same brand. Mobile phone chargers also long outlive the mobile phones they are designed for, so that new, *redundant* chargers are placed on the market as mobile phones are replaced. Considering the diversity of mobile phones, this not only causes considerable inconvenience for consumers, including a flood of superfluous phone mobile chargers, but also leads to unnecessary waste of materials.

In order to tackle the incompatibility of mobile phone chargers and the problems arising therefrom, in March 2009 the European Commission threatened to pass legislation on the matter if mobile phone manufacturers did not address the issue by providing a common charging solution.[984] The threat worked and, in June 2009, a Memorandum of Understanding (hereinafter 'MoU') was signed whereby mobile phone manufacturers committed themselves to take measures aiming at the harmonisation of a charging capability for mobile telephones.[985]

More specifically, the solution agreed upon was to equip chargers with a micro-USB connector as a common charging interface, with an adapter being mandated in relation to those mobile phones not having the micro-USB interface. To that end, the signatories agreed to develop a set of technical specifications on the charging capability with the micro-USB interface as well as to propose them for formal standardisation. On the heels of the MoU, the European Commission issued a 'standardisation mandate to CEN, CENELEC and ETSI on a common charging capability for mobile telephones',[986] which resulted in the publication of EN 62684:2010 ('Interoperability specifications of common external power supply (EPS) for use with data-enabled mobile telephones') in December 2010. In January 2011, the International Electrotechnical Commission (hereinafter 'IEC') released its version of the European standard as IEC 62684:2011. The international and European standards are essentially identical.

The MoU terminated on 31 December 2012. The European Commission asked the signatories to extend the agreement, but most of them disagreed to do so on the grounds that it was not adequate for new needs, including wireless charging and compatibility of specifications with more powerful smartphones.[987] In April 2013, only eight of the signatories signed a letter of intent declaring their intention to supply the EU market in 2013 with chargers meeting the standards set within the scope of the 2009 MoU standards. In March 2014, five of these eight mobile phone manufacturers signed another letter of intent with the same purpose for the year of 2014.

An evaluation of the impact of the MoU on the mobile phone market as well as on the markets for other portable rechargeable devices took place in 2014.[988] The study found a substantial decline in the number of different charging connectors over the period of the MoU, which has

---

984 See European Commission, 2011.

985 See 'MoU regarding harmonization of a charging capability for mobile phones' dated 5 June 2009, available at <http://ec.europa.eu/DocsRoom/documents/2417/attachments/1/translations/en/renditions/native>, last accessed on 15 September 2016.

986 See European Commission, M/455 EN, Brussels, 1 October 2009.

987 See Tajani, 2013, p. 3.

988 See Risk & Policy Analysts, 2014.

been achieved through a modest increase in cost per handset. Another finding was the apparent adoption of MoU-compliant solutions by non-signatories, arguably due to the ability to make use of an adaptor to effect compliance. Finally, spill over effects on non-European countries have been minor.

Regarding the environmental impacts of the MoU,[989] the study concluded that the number of sales of standalone chargers has declined because of the adoption of micro-USB solutions not only to mobile phones but also to other devices. This decline is explained by the fact that consumers do not need to buy additional chargers (when these break down, for example) since they can reuse their old chargers and/or use other people's chargers. In contrast, the decoupling of handsets as well as of other devices from their chargers has been very limited, that is, these products continue to be sold with a charger, thereby undermining the intended goal of resource saving. There are two likely reasons for this. Firstly, manufacturers believe that consumers expect to receive a charger with new devices unless there is a noticeable financial saving, which is not the case at stake: the production cost of a micro-USB charger has been estimated to be around €1.25, so that any cost reduction from not including a charger would be miniscule. Secondly, some manufacturers continue to supply mobile phones with chargers on the grounds that they can only guarantee the safety of their own charger.

Following the 2014 letter of intent, the issue of common chargers for mobile phones has been addressed by Directive 2014/53/EU on the harmonisation of the laws of the Member States relating to the making available on the market of radio equipment and repealing Directive 1999/5/EC[990]. Recital 12 recalls that 'interoperability between radio equipment and accessories such as chargers simplifies the use of radio equipment and reduces unnecessary waste and costs' and sets forth that 'mobile phones that are made available on the market should be compatible with a common charger'. In this regard, Article 3(3)(a) of Directive 2014/53/EU requires radio equipment within certain categories or classes to interwork with accessories, in particular with common chargers. Said categories or classes of radio equipment are to be specified by delegated acts adopted by the European Commission.

No such delegated acts have been adopted so far, but between May and August 2019 the European Commission held a public consultation to

989 See Risk & Policy Analysts, 2014, p. 48-50 and 125-126.
990 OJ L 153, 22 May 2014, p. 62.

gather evidence and stakeholders' views on a possible legislative initiative aimed at standardising chargers for mobile phones to guarantee full interoperability and consequently reduce e-waste.[991]

E. Summary

Efforts to regulate the ecodesign of products in a direct fashion as opposed to an indirect, incentive-based approach exist both in Brazil, albeit very timidly, and especially in the European Union.

Product ecodesign requirements are firstly and usually found in both Brazilian and EU (waste-related) legislation on EPR. These ecodesign mandates in end-of-life legislation fall under the heading of waste prevention, but they are product-related. They cover either qualitative or quantitative environmental aspects. Qualitative-related mandates concern the hazardousness of products and take the form of substance bans or restrictions in order to not only facilitate recovery, especially recycling, at end of life and hence avoid the disposal of hazardous waste but also prevent the release of hazardous substances into the environment, including during waste management operations. Quantitative-related mandates are more diversified and relate not only to the physicochemical composition of products with a view to reducing their material content, such as 'lightweighting' (e.g. packaging) or recycled content requirements (e.g. vehicles), but also to the construction of products so that they need not be disposed at end of life, such as reusability and recoverability (especially recyclability) requirements, respectively. Quantitative-related mandates usually lack enforceability due to the fact that they are worded too vaguely and are not accompanied by compliance mechanisms. Recoverability and recyclability requirements in connection with end-of-life vehicles in the EU are a conspicuous exception, for compliance occurs within an already existing (product-related) mechanism for controlling the technical aspects of vehicles, namely the type approval. The predominance of hazardousness concerns over quantitative ones is in tune with the evolution of product-related environmental law.

In the EU, hope to overcome the shortcomings above is pinned on the Ecodesign Directive, which is at present a key piece of product-related environmental law. It provides a framework for the adoption of self-regu-

991 Further information available at <https://ec.europa.eu/info/law/better-regulation/initiatives/ares-2018-6427186_en>, last accessed on 12 December 2019.

latory (i.e. voluntary) and implementing (i.e. binding) measures that lay down ecodesign requirements. In that such requirements may be imposed in relation to all environmental aspects of a product throughout its life cycle, thereby addressing all environmental problems, the Ecodesign Directive has been lauded as the 'super directive'. Yet, this is an overstatement for many reasons. Firstly, it does not apply to all products indistinctively, let alone to all ErPs. Even in relation to the ErPs to which the Ecodesign Directive is applicable, there has been a lack of political will to regulate the ecodesign of these products. Moreover, several substantive and procedural conditions must be met in order for ecodesign requirements to be laid down. Secondly, ecodesign requirements have been unambitious, thereby serving more to phase out the worst performing products than as a diver for eco-innovation. Thirdly, despite the comprehensiveness of the Ecodesign Directive, focus has been on energy consumption during the use phase. Non-energy, resource-related requirements already exist in both implementing and self-regulatory measures adopted under the Ecodesign Directive, but they are fewer and seldom address the material composition of products. Requirements on repairability represent a notable and important novelty, though. There are scientifically methodological problems to address resource-related aspects, which also explain the hesitation to expand the scope of the Ecodesign Directive. Fourthly, in order to avoid legislative overlaps, implementing measures have hesitated to fill in regulatory gaps found in existing environmental legislation. Finally, room for national requirements 'pushing' the EU legislators towards more ambitious ecodesign regulations is legally possible only in some situations.

Plastic carrier bags and single-use plastic products have been increasingly receiving regulatory attention worldwide, including in the EU and Brazil. In the EU, packaging regulations allowing for the adoption of measures affecting production such as marketing restrictions to reduce the consumption of lightweight plastic carrier bags have existed since 2015. In 2019, as part of the EU's circular economy strategy, a directive on single-use products was adopted, which provides for measures that also affect the production of those products, ranging from product bans through marketing restrictions to product design, material composition, and marking requirements. The EU's efforts against plastics and single-use plastic products has had a spill-over effect on Brazil, where local authorities have been striving to ban or phase out plastic carrier bags and single-use plastic products, and at times also to regulate their material composition. As illustrated by the case of plastic carrier bags, municipal efforts not only face resistance due to consumer protection concerns but they have only been possible with the help of courts and their decentralised interpretation of constitutional rules on the distribution of legislative powers on environmental matters. Such an interpretation is questionable if one considers that in São Paulo City it has allowed the local *waste management* authority to regulate the design of a *product* category.

In the EU, the case of mobile phone chargers illustrates a regulatory attempt to eliminate the very need for a product and hence avoid the use of materials as well as the generation of waste ('step 1' of the five-step model presented in chapter 3). It does so not by banning the product or by prescribing its design (means-oriented requirement), but by mandating that it performs a certain function, (result-oriented requirement), namely interoperability through charging compatibility. It builds on the pre-existing voluntary efforts of the industry to reach a common charging solution, albeit not a spontaneous one such as the self-voluntary measures under the Ecodesign Directive, after all, the devising of the micro-USB interface has occurred only due to a threat of regulation. Just as resource-related requirements for imaging equipment and vacuum cleaners under the Ecodesign Directive, arriving at a common charging solution has been influenced by, not to say dependent on, the existence of technical standards. While the MoU on a harmonised charging capability for mobile telephones has led to a reduction in the number of sales of standalone chargers, handsets continue to be sold with a charger due to consumer expectation and product safety reasons. This corroborates the finding that both producer and consumer decisions must be addressed if needs are to be questioned with a view to preventing material use and waste generation ('step 1').

CONCLUSION (THESES)

The purpose of the present dissertation has been to study both Brazilian and European environmental law in connection with waste prevention. The study has been based, on the one hand, on a dialogue between law and economics that considers not only the intrinsic relationship between the two disciplines in the context of environmental policy but also that interdisciplinarity is essential for the comprehension and tackling of environmental problems. The economic-legal approach has been instrumental in finding an answer to the research question of waste prevention means and how it is to be achieved in the wider context of environmental law. On the other hand, the study has consisted of a comparative dogmatic legal analysis of both Brazilian and European environmental as well as waste law with the aim of answering the research question of whether these legal orders adequately address the issue of waste prevention. The initial hypothesis has answered this latter question negatively in relation to Brazil and positively in relation to the European Union (EU). Analysis has confirmed the initial hypothesis in relation to Brazil but relativized it as concerns the EU.

The overall conclusion of this study is that Brazilian environmental law does not currently address the issue of waste prevention at all, the reason for which it should look up to the initiatives taken by EU environmental law. This neglect has to do less with the relative novelty of Brazilian waste law than with the fact that material and product-related environmental law in Brazil is still to be developed. (Quantitative) waste prevention, which is best understood as changes to the production and consumption of products throughout the economic circuit with a view to reducing the overall use of materials, requires coherent material and product-related legislation dealing with the life cycle environmental impacts of specific materials and products on a case-by-case basis. The case against plastic carrier bags and certain single-use plastic products may be regarded as an incipient exception, though.

Waste prevention is not yet an everyday reality in the EU either. Despite its protagonism in the regulation of waste, EU environmental law still does not tackle consumer waste prevention adequately enough, at least concerning the quantitative prevention of materials. Product- and resource-related environmental concerns are high on the political agenda of the EU, but this is not reflected in, or at least has not fully crystallised into, environmental legislation. As much as end-of-life legislation is an attempt to, and the Ecodesign Directive has paved the way for, a life cycle tackling of all environmental aspects of products, there is still much to do. Recent regulatory developments to foster repairability and tackle plastics are exceptions the actualisation of which deserves future research.

Brazil should pass a framework statute on the environmental impacts of products in general, one enabling the imposition of duties on producers and its suppliers of concrete products, for example on the basis of life cycle assessments. By the same token, the EU should take advantage of the experience gained by the Ecodesign Directive and, based on already existing proposals to improvements to the MEErP, expand the scope of the Ecodesign Directive to all products. The setting of reuse targets in the context of EPR could be an interesting complementary strategy, as already provided for by point (b) of Article 5(1) and Article 5(5) of Directive 94/62/EC on packaging and packaging waste, as amended by Directive (EU) 2018/852. This should constitute a sensible step towards the implementation of sustainable development as recommended by ecological economists.

That being said, the theses of the present study are enunciated below:

Theses in relation to chapter 1 ('The traditional economic-legal approach to the environmental and waste problems').

A. There is a clear parallel between the traditional economic and legal approaches to the environmental problem in general and the waste problem in particular. Environmental law has been informed and has served as a means of implementing the environmental protection measures proposed by economics.
B. Environmental economics, which is the branch of neoclassical economics dealing with environmental issues, corresponds to the traditional economic approach.
C. The traditional legal approach consists in a managerial (i.e. end-of-pipe), single-point, pollution-oriented, production-related regulation of environmental problems.
D. Both traditional economic and legal approaches provide an insufficient account of, and inadequate solutions to, environmental problems, including the waste problem. The insufficiency lies fundamentally in the methodological split that marks both approaches: environmental problems are addressed and treated separately and differently depending on whether they affect the environment in its source or sink function. The

waste problem puts this division at stake because it is both a pollution *and* resource problem.

Theses in relation to chapter 2 ('Theoretical reconstruction: sustainable development and its legal implementation').

A. Responses to the insufficiency of the traditional economic and legal approaches to the environmental and waste problems are found in the context of the debate on a sustainable development. Such a debate is originally and *par excellence* an economic one, for it builds on the discussions about economic development.

B. In environmental economics, sustainable development is treated as a matter of ensuring current and future utility and is based on the admissibility of compensation between those items providing utility, including the environment. Accordingly, the environment need not be protected at all (weak sustainability), or at least not in its entirety (strong sustainability), for economic development to be sustainable provided that something else compensates for the (total or partial) loss of environmental resources and/or quality.

C. In contrast, ecological economics in general, and the work of economist NICHOLAS GEORGESCU-ROEGEN in particular, identifies sustainable development as a resource conservation agenda. The acknowledgement of the entropic nature of the economic process is one of GEORGESCU-ROEGEN's main contributions to economic theory. The entropic predicament, however pessimistic it is, pinpoints the relationship between the economic and ecological systems in general, and the limits posed by the latter on the former in particular, thereby shedding light on environmental problems and pointing to more unorthodox, courageous solutions thereto, including, but not limited to, quantitative regulations to combat resource depletion, the elimination of fashion, and the need for durable and repairable products, as put forward by the author.

D. The legal implementation of a sustainable development requires the adoption of an integrated approach to environmental law. Integration consists of combining the metabolic perspective underlying the entropic analysis provided by ecological economics with a life cycle perspective. In practical terms, this means that facility and media-related regulations typical of traditional environmental law need to be complemented by materials and product-related regulations. An approach looking at the life cycle of materials and products requires much more from jurists, including interdisciplinary dialogues with other branches of (economic) law and non-legal disciplines.

Theses in relation to chapter 3 ('Integrated waste management as the protagonist of integrated environmental law').

A. Integrated waste management, understood as the life cycle management of materials from cradle to grave, illustrates the protagonism of waste law towards an integrated environmental law, as epitomised by the waste hierarchy laid down in both EU and Brazilian waste law: unless otherwise specified by a life cycle assessment, waste management should be carried out in a predetermined order whereby waste prevention takes precedence over waste recovery, and waste recovery, in turn, takes precedence over waste disposal (*presumptio iuris tantum*).
B. Waste law is law on materials, more specifically materials following a path on which their potential to cause damage increases or by virtue of which resources are prematurely depleted. It serves a dual purpose, namely human health and environmental protection (waste law as law on harmful materials), on the one hand, and resource conservation (waste law as law on scarce materials), on the other hand. The two functions of waste law are complementary rather than conflicting.
C. Waste is a legal creation. Both the concept of waste and its associated legal regime are dispensable in a truly integrated environmental law. The more materials/substances and products are addressed by facility-, media-, materials/substance- and/or product-related regulations, the less they need to be covered by waste law, except for when their secondary use is unknown. Since in a diversified economy this is the default situation, waste is broadly defined as 'anything that anyone destines or intends to destine or is required to destine for a purpose' and removal of the waste status occurs on an exceptional, case-by-case basis. Economic production and consumption activities should be more, and not less, regulated *vis-à-vis* their environmental impacts.
D. Waste prevention is best grasped positively, that is, by changes into the production and consumption of materials/substances and products so that fewer materials/substances and products are used (materials prevention) and therefore less waste is generated (waste prevention). Waste prevention law is, by definition, material- and product-related environmental law, at least as regards consumer waste. Modifications may be made at different 'steps' preceding the discarding of things ('step 5') – from making products repairable, more durable and/or apt to be used collectively as well as having them repaired and used longer

and collectively ('step 4') through reducing their material intensity or increasing their recycled content ('step 3') to eliminating the need for a product by providing a service ('step 2') or eliminating the need altogether ('step 1') – and they entail concrete materials/substance- and product-related duties imposed on both producers and consumers with regard to their decisions as to whether, what, how much and how to produce and consume. Decisions made by producers about the design of the products they place on the market are central to the attainment of materials and waste prevention and should therefore be regulated by law. In the EU, aspirations for an integrated product policy and a resource-efficient Europe have long been high on the political agenda but they have not yet been translated into coherent legislative action. Product-related environmental regulation in the EU occurs in a patchwork fashion and a systematic legal approach to resource protection is mostly a theoretical endeavour made by German scholars. This is not consistent with the lessons taken from ecological economics, in particular those by economist NICHOLAS GEORGESCU-ROEGEN.

Theses in relation to chapter 4 ('Indirect product design regulation: extended producer responsibility').

A. Extended producer responsibility (EPR) may be defined as the placing on agents upstream of the consumer in the economic circuit of positive duties to manage the products those agents place on the market at end of life (physical responsibility) as well as to bear the costs of said management (financial responsibility). It is a waste-related instrument aimed at incentivising producers to improve the ecodesign of their products and hence achieve materials and waste prevention.
B. Whilst EPR (just like waste law) is a relatively recent element of Brazilian environmental law, European legislation on EPR has now over two decades of regulatory experience.
C. In order for EPR to reach the goal of product ecodesign improvement, not only should both physical and financial responsibility be kept connected but responsibility should also take the form of individual responsibility. This means making producers responsible for their own products or making collective schemes individual-friendly. The latter option involves the introduction of mechanisms allowing the individualisation of materials and/or products managed collectively by the so-called producer responsibility organisations (PROs), including identification technologies and improved financing formulae, so that investments in ecodesign can be rewarded (through reduced fees to

PROs) and laggards penalised (through increased fees to PROs). This is known as eco-modulation, which is nonetheless still in its infancy in a very few Member States of the EU. Another proposal to advance materials and waste prevention through EPR is the establishment of quantitative reuse targets. Both topics merit further attention by future research.

Theses in relation to chapter 5 ('Selected examples of direct ecodesign regulation in product-oriented environmental law').

A. In parallel to EPR, both Brazilian and EU end-of-life (i.e. waste) legislation contains product-related ecodesign mandates. These attempt to regulate product ecodesign in a more direct fashion as opposed to the incentive-based logic of EPR. Two types of requirements exist. The first type tackles product hazardousness. Requirements take the form of substance bans and/or restrictions with a view to preventing the release of hazardous substances into the environment and facilitating recovery, especially recycling, of products at end of life. The second type addresses quantitative rather than qualitative aspects. Requirements of this second type are more diverse and relate to either the physicochemical composition of products or their construction with a view to reducing their material intensity/increasing their recycled content or enabling reusability/recoverability, respectively. Quantitative mandates lack enforceability because, unlike hazardousness requirements, they are worded vaguely and are not accompanied by compliance mechanisms. One exception in this sense concerns recoverability/recyclability requirements for end-of-life vehicles, which are dealt with by product-related regulations establishing mechanisms for controlling the technical aspects of vehicles. This once again points to the need for more, and not less, regulation, especially quantitative ones if we are to take the recommendations of ecological economists seriously.
B. In the EU, the Ecodesign Directive is to date the central piece of product-related environmental legislation. It provides a framework for the setting out of ecodesign requirements for products by self-regulatory and/or implementing measures. In that the Ecodesign Directive establishes a comprehensive list of parameters for the adoption of self-regulatory and/or implementing measures laying down ecodesign requirements for all environmental aspects of all life cycle stages of products, it has been praised for its potential to solve all environmental problems. Yet, this potential has been underused. Not only is the scope of application of the Ecodesign Directive very restricted, a fact that

is aggravated by the many substantive and procedural conditions for the adoption of measures setting down ecodesign requirements, but the statute is also focused on energy aspects during product use. Non-energy, resource-related requirements are exceptional and have been imposed on very few products in respect of which industry standards covering the requirements introduced already existed, which reinforces the importance of the 'methodology for ecodesign of energy-related products' (MEErP) in shaping the content of implementing measures. Hazardousness aspects aside, no ecodesign (quantitative) requirements on the material composition of products exist, which once again does not accord with the tenets of ecological economics.

C. The case against plastic carrier bags and single-use plastic products in both the EU and Brazil confirms that waste *prevention* is best promoted by *product*-related measures taken at upstream stages in the product life cycle. Product ban or phase-out, marketing restrictions as well as product design, material composition, and marking requirements are very illustrative examples of measures that impact on the decisions made by producers as to the production of plastic products and that have been adopted in the two jurisdictions studied herein.

D. As much as focus of this study is on 'step 3' (material input of products), the case of mobile phone chargers in the EU represents a pioneering regulatory attempt to address 'step 1' (needs) through product ecodesign regulation, albeit not a very successful one. It shows that legislation, or more precisely the threat of regulation, may push producers to improve the ecodesign of their products.

'Cross-sectoral' theses, including in relation to the need for further research.

A truly integrated approach to environmental regulation depends on material- and product-specific analyses of their life cycle environmental impacts. Integrated environmental law, including the law on integrated waste management, also known as waste prevention law, relies heavily on scientific knowledge, as illustrated by the limitations of the MEErP and the imposition of non-energy requirements under the Ecodesign Directive, to cite a few examples. Further research is needed as to the relationship between LCA and environmental law.

LIST OF REFERENCES

A

Afonso da silva, José Afonso da Silva, *Curso de direito constitucional positivo*, 38.ed., São Paulo, Malheiros, 2015.

Afonso da silva, Luís Virgílio, "Federalismo e articulação de competências no Brasil", in Peters, B. Guy; Pierre, Jon (org.), *Administração pública: coletânea*, vol. 1, Brasília/São Paulo, ENAP/UNESP, 2010, 549-570.

Amazonas, Maurício de Carvalho, *Valor e meio ambiente: elementos para uma abordagem evolucionista*, Tese de doutorado, Instituto de Economia da Universidade Estadual de Campinas, Campinas, Universidade Estadual de Campinas, 2001.

Anderson, David, *Environmental economics and natural resource management*, 3.ed., London, Routledge, 2010.

Anker, Helle Tegner, "Integrated resource management – lessons for Europe?", *European Environmental Law Review* 11 (2002), 199-209.

Antunes, Paulo de Bessa, *Federalismo e competências ambientais no Brasil*, 2.ed., São Paulo, Atlas, 2015.

Aragão, Maria Alexandra de Sousa, "Principe d'intégration: évolution vers une nouvelle étape législative", in Born, Charles-Hubert; Jongen, François (coord.), *D'urbanisme et d'environnement: liber amicorum de Francis Haumont*, Bruxelles, Bruylant, 2015, 401-412.

——, "Desmaterialização: uma mudança de paradigma?", *Revista CEDOUA* 29 (2012), 161-172.

——, "Direito administrativo dos resíduos", in Otero, Paulo; Gonçalves, Pedro, *Tratado de direito administrativo especial*, vol. I, Coimbra, Almedina, 2009, 1-147.

——, *O princípio do nível elevado de protecção e a renovação ecológica do direito do ambiente e dos resíduos*, Coimbra, Almedina, 2006.

——, *O princípio do poluidor-pagador: pedra angular da política comunitária do ambiente*, Coimbra, Coimbra Editora, 1997.

Ardente, Fulvio; Wolf, Marc-Andree; Mathieux, Fabrice; Pennington, David, *Integration of resource efficiency and waste management criteria in the implementing measures under the Ecodesign Directive: review of resource efficiency and end-of-life requirements*, European Union, Institute for Environment and Sustainability of the Joint Research Centre of the European Commission, 2011.

Asafu-Adjaye, John, *Environmental economics for non-economists: techniques and policies for sustainable development*, 2. ed., New Jersey, World Scientific, 2005.

Ayres, Robert U., "The second law, the fourth law, recycling and limits to growth", *Ecological economics* 29 (1999), 473-483.

——, "Comments on Georgescu-Roegen", *Ecological economics* 22 (1997), 285-287.

——, "Industrial metabolism: theory and policy", in Ayres, Robert U.; Simonis, Udo E. (eds.), *Industrial metabolism: restructuring for sustainable development*, Tokyo, United Nations University Press, 1994, 3-20.

——; Kneese, Allen V., "Externalities: economics and thermodynamics", in Archibugi, Franco; Nijkamp, Peter (eds.), Economy *and ecology: towards sustainable development*, Dordrecht, Springer, 1989, 89-118.

B

Ballu, Matthieu; Toulouse, Edouard, *Energy savings in practice: potential and delivery of EU ecodesign measures*, Cool products for a cool planet, 2010, available at <http://www.eeb.org/index.cfm/library/energy-savings-in-practice-potential-and-delivery-of-eu-ecodesign-measures/?LinkServID=9752FE1D-B396-3C0E-9B3380E32EC94147>, last accessed on 5 September 2016.

Bandeira de Mello, Celso Antonio, *Curso de direito administrativo*, 30.ed., São Paulo, Malheiros, 2013.

Bauman, Henrikke; Tillman, Anne-Marie, *The Hitch Hiker's guide to LCA: an orientation in life cycle assessment methodology and application*, Lund, Studentlitteratur, 2004.

Baumgärtner, Stefan, "Thermodynamics of waste generation", in Bisson, Katy; Proops, John (eds.), *Waste in ecological economics*, Cheltenham, Edward Elgar, 2002, 13-37.

Begon, Michael; Townsend, Colin R.; Harper, John L., *Ecology: from individuals to ecosystems*, 4.ed., Oxford, Blackwell, 2006.

Beinhocker, Eric D., *The origin of wealth: evolution, complexity, and the radical remaking of economics*, Boston, Harvard Business School Press, 2003.

Bell, Stuart; McGillivray, Donald; Pedersen, Ole W., *Environmental law*, 8. ed., Oxford, Oxford University Press, 2013.

Bercovici, Gilberto, *Dilemas do Estado federal brasileiro*, Porto Alegre, Livraria do Advogado, 2004.

Birn, Helmut, "Rechtliche Instrumente zur Steuerung der Abfall- und Reststoffströme", *NVwZ* 11 (1992), 419-425.

BMU, *Umweltgesetzbuch (UGB-KomE). Entwurf der unabhängigen Sachverständigenkommission zum Umweltgesetzbuch beim Bundesministerium für Umwelt, Naturschutz und Reaktorsicherheit*, Berlin, Duncker & Humblot, 1998.

Bortoleto, Ana Paula, *Waste prevention and policy behaviour – new approaches to reducing waste generation and its environmental impacts*, Oxford, Routledge, 2014.

Brandt, Edmund; Röckeisen, Susana, *Konzeption für ein Stoffstromrecht*, Berlin, Erich Schmidt, 2000.

Brandt, Edmund; Kotulla, Michael; Leitzke, Claus; Röckeisen, Susana; Schoeneck, Stefan; Schulz, Claudia Undine, *Stoffstromrecht. Ausgangslage und Entwicklungslinien*, Cottbus, Fakultät Umweltwissenschaften und Verfahrenstechnik der Brandenburgischer Technischen Universität Cottbus, 1996.

BREEN, Barry, "Environmental law from resource to recovery", in CAMPBELL-MOHN, Celia; BREEN, Barry; FUTRELL, J. William (eds.), *Environmental Law: From resources to recovery*, Saint Paul (Minnesota), West Publishing, 1993, 51-70.

BRENNCKE, Martin, "Die Zulässigkeit des europarechtlichen Verbots der Glühlampe nach Art. 95 EG", *Europäische Zeitschrift für Wirtschaftsrecht* 20 (2009), 247-250.

BREUER, Rüdiger, "Umweltschutzrecht", in SCHMIDT-ASSMANN, Eberhard; SCHOCH, Friedrich (Hrsg.), *Besonderes Verwaltungsrecht*, 14. ed., Berlin, de Gruyter, 2008, 591-774.

BRINKTRINE, Ralf, "Altfahrzeug-Verordnung (AltfahrzeugV)", in SCHMEHL, Arndt (Hrsg.), *Gemeinschaftskommentar zum Kreislaufwirtschaftsgesetz (KrWG) sowie zur Verpackungsordnung (VerpackV), zur Altfahrzeugverordnung (AltfahrzeugV), zum Elektro- und Elektronikgesetz (ElektroG), zum Batteriegesetz (BattG), zur Bioabfallverordnung (BioAbfV), zur Abfallverzeichnisverordnung (AVV) und zur EU-Abfallverbringungsverordnung (VVA)*, Köln, Carl Heymanns, 2013, 932-940.

BULLINGER, Martin, "Rechtsfragen des Verursacherprinzips beim Umweltschutz", in BULLINGER, Martin; RINCKE, Günther; OBERHAUSER, Alois; SCHMIDT, Ralf-Bodo, *Das Verursacherprinzip und seine Instrumente: Eine interdisziplinäre Untersuchung*, Berlin, Erich Schmidt, 1974, 69-108.

BUNDGAARD, Anja Marie; MOSGAARD, Mette Alberg; REMMEN, Arne, "From energy efficiency towards resource efficiency within the Ecodesign Directive", *Journal of Cleaner Production* 144 (2017), 358-374.

BUNDGAARD, Anja Marie; REMMEN, Arne; ZACHO, Kistrina Overgaard, *Ecodesign Directive 2.0: from energy efficiency to resource efficiency*, Copenhagen, Miljøstyrelsen, 2015.

BURY, Duncan R. W., "Should Extended Producer Responsibility Programs Use Eco-Fee-Included Pricing?", *Canadian Tax Journal* 58 (2010), 927-950.

C

CAHILL, Rachel; GRIMES, Sue M.; WILSON, David C., "Extended producer responsibility for packaging wastes and WEEE – a comparison of implementation and the role of local authorities across Europe", *Waste management & Research* 29 (2010), 455-479.

CAVALCANTI, Clóvis, "Concepções da economia ecológica: suas relações com a economia dominante e a economia ambiental", *Estudos avançados* 24 (2010), 53-67.

CENTRE FOR STRATEGY & EVALUATION SERVICES, *Evaluation of the Ecodesign Directive (2009/125/EC) Final Report*, 2012, available at <http://cses.co.uk/ecodesign_evaluation>, last accessed on 10 August 2016.

CHALMERS, Damian, "Community policy on waste management – managing environmental decline gently", in ETTY, Thijs; SOMSEN, Han (eds.), *Yearbook of European Law* 14 (1994), 257-312.

CHANCEREL, Perrine; SCHILL, Wolf-Peter; ROTTER, Susanne, "Praktische Aspekte der individuellen Herstellerverantwortung für Elektro- und Elektronikaltgeräte", in THOMÉ-KOZMIENSKY, Karl J.; VERSTEYL, Andrea; BECKMANN, Michael (Hrsg.), *Produktverantwortung – Verpackungsabfälle, Elektro- und Elektronikaltgeräte, Altfahrzeuge*, Neuruppin, TK, 2007, 267-283.

CHEHEBE, José Ribamar Brasil, *Análise de ciclo de vida de produtos: ferramenta gerencial da ISO 14000*, Rio de Janeiro, Qualitymark, 1997.

CHERTOW, Marian R., "Waste, industrial ecology, and sustainability", *Social Research* 65 (1998), 31-53.

CHEYNE, Ilona; "The definition of waste in EC law", *JEL* 14 (2002), 61-73.

——; PURDUE, Michael, "Fitting definition to purpose: the search for a satisfactory definition of waste", *JEL* 7 (1995), 149-168.

CIPRIANO, Tasso Alexandre Richetti Pires, "O conceito de consumidor no direito brasileiro dos resíduos", in press.

——, "O conceito de fabricante na Política Nacional de Resíduos Sólidos", *Revista de Direito Ambiental* 86 (2017), 239-258.

——, "Juridificação dos resíduos no Brasil", in PHILIPPI JR., Arlindo; PASSOS DE FREITAS, Vladimir; SPÍNOLA, Ana Luiza Silva (eds.), *Direito ambiental e sustentabilidade*, Barueri, Manole, 2016, 155-205.

——, "Logística reversa: produção e consumo sustentáveis?", BENJAMIN, Antônio Herman; LEITE, José Rubens Morato (org.), *20º Congresso Brasileiro de Direito Ambiental: ambiente, sociedade e consumo sustentável*, São Paulo, Instituto O Direito por um Planeta Verde, 2015, 278-291, available at <http://www.planetaverde.org/arquivos/biblioteca/arquivo_20150602200928_5210.pdf>, last accessed on 10 May 2016.

——, "O conceito econômico-jurídico de desenvolvimento sustentável", *Cadernos O Direito* 6 (2011), 337-360.

CLIFT, Roland; FRANCE, Chris, "Extended producer responsibility in the EU: a visible march of folly", *JIE* 10 (2006), 5-7.

COASE, Ronald Harry, "The problem of social cost", *Journal of Law and Economics* 3 (1960), 1-44.

COGLIANESE, Cary; NASH, Jennifer; OLMSTEAD, Todd, "Performance-based regulation: prospects and limitations in health, safety, and environmental protection", *Administrative Law Review* 55 (2003), 705-730.

COMPARATO, Fábio Konder, "A proteção do consumidor: importante capítulo do direito econômico", *Revista de Direito Mercantil, Industrial, Econômico e Financeiro* 15/16 (1974), 89-105.

CONRAD, Jon M., *Resource economics*, 2. ed., Cambridge, Cambridge University Press, 2010.

Craig, Paul; de Búrca, Gráinne, *EU Law: text, cases, and materials*, 6. ed., Oxford, Oxford University Press, 2015.

D

Dalhammar, Carl, "Industry attitudes towards ecodesign standards for improved resource efficiency", *Journal of Cleaner Production* 123 (2016), 155-166.

——, "The application of 'life cycle thinking' in European environmental law: theory and practice", *JEEPL* 12 (2015a), 97-127.

——, "The setting of progressive energy efficiency performances standards for products through the Ecodesign Directive", *Nordic Environmental Law Journal* (2015b), 21-41.

——, "Promoting energy and resource efficiency through the Ecodesign Directive", *Scandinavian Studies in Law* 59 (2014), 147-179.

——, "Product and life cycle issues in European environmental law: a review of recent developments"', in Etty, Thijs; Somsen, Han (eds.), *Yearbook of European environmental law*, vol. 7, Oxford, Oxford University Press, 2007b, 76-124.

——, *An emerging product approach in environmental law: incorporating the life cycle perspective*, Doctoral dissertation, The International Institute for Industrial Environmental Economics (IIIEE), Lund, Lunds Universitet, 2007a.

——; Machacek, Erika; Bundgaard, Anja; Overgaard, Kristina; Remmen, Arne, *Addressing resource efficiency through the Ecodesign Directive: a review of opportunities and barriers*, Copenhagen, Norden, 2014.

Daly, Herman Edward, "Toward some operational principles of sustainable development", *Ecological Economics* 2 (1990), 1-6.

de Sadeleer, Nicolas, *EU environmental law and the internal market*, Oxford, Oxford University Press, 2014.

——, "EC waste law or how to juggle with legal concepts. Drawing the line between waste, residues, secondary materials, by-products, disposal and recovery operations", in *JEEPL* 6 (2005), 458-477.

Dhondt, Nele, *Integration of environmental protection into other EC policies: legal theory and practice*, Groningen, Europa Law, 2003.

Dieckmann, Martin; Reese, Moritz, "Kreislaufwirtschafts- und Abfallrecht", in Koch, Hans-Joachim (Hrsg.), *Umweltrecht*, 4.ed., München, Franz Vahlen, 2014, 359-416.

Dietrich, Sascha; Akkerman, Floris, "EU-Ökodesign-Richtlinie. Implementierung - Umsetzung - Überwachung", *ZUR* 24 (2013), 274-278.

Di Fabio, Udo, "Integratives Umweltrecht – Bestand, Ziele, Möglichkeiten", *NVwZ* 17 (1998), 329-337.

D'Oliveira, Rafael Lima Daudt, *O princípio da integração ambiental e a simplificação do Estado*, Coimbra, Instituto Jurídico da Faculdade de Direito da Universidade de Coimbra, 2015, available at <http://www.ij.fd.uc.pt/publicacoes/estudos_serie M/pub_3/M_numero3.pdf>, last accessed on 10 April 2017.

Drews, Bill; Wacke, Gerhard; Vogel, Klaus; Martens,Wolfgang,*Gefahrenabwehr. Allgemeines Polizeirecht (Ordnungsrecht) des Bundes und der Länder*, 9.ed., Köln, Carl Heymanns, 1986.

Driesen, David M.; Adler, Robert W.; Engel, Kirsten H., *Environmental law: a conceptual and pragmatic approach*, 3.ed., New York, Wolters Kluwer, 2016.

Dubois, Maarten, "Extended producer responsibility with a tax on non-collected waste", *JIE* 20 (2016), 6-7.

E

Earp, Henrique N. Sá; Romeiro, Ademar R., "The entropy law and the impossibility of perpetual economic growth", *Open Journal of Applied Sciences* 5 (2015), 641-650.

Edbring, Emma Gullstrand; Lehner, Matthias; Mont, Oksana, "Exploring consumer attitudes to alternative models of consumption", *Journal of Cleaner Production* 123 (2016), 5-15.

Ehrenfeld, John R., "Industrial ecology: a framework for product and process design", *Journal of Cleaner Production* 5 (1997), 87-95.

Engel, Christoph, *Abfallrecht und Abfallpolitik*, Baden-Baden, Nomos, 2002.

Epiney, Astrid, *Umweltrecht der Europäischen Union*, 3.ed., Baden-Baden, Nomos, 2013.

European Association for the Coordination of Consumer Representation in Standardisation; European Environmental Citizens Organisation for Standardisation, *ANEC-ECOS position paper on the revised packaging standards prepared under the second standardisation mandate M317*, ANEC2005/ENV/001, Brussels, 2005, available at <http://www.anec.org/attachments/env001-05.pdf>, last accessed on 20 September 2016.

European Commission, *The 'Blue Guide' on the implementation of product rules 2016*, C (2016) 1958 final, 5 April 2016.

——, *A common mobile phone charger – questions and answers*, MEMO/11/75, dated 8 February 2011, available at <http://europa.eu/rapid/press-release_MEMO-11-75_en.htm>, last accessed 15 September 2016.

F

Faber, Malte; Manstetten, Reiner; Proops, John, *Ecological economics: concepts and methods*, Cheltenham/Northampton (Massachusetts), Edward Elgar, 1996.

Faber, Malte; Niemes, H.; Stephan, G., *Entropy, environment and resources: an essay in physic-economics*, 2. ed., Springer, Dordrecht, 1995.

FALKE, Josef, "Konkretisierung von Anforderungen des integrierten Umweltschutzes an Anlagen und Produkte durch untergesetzliche Regelungen, insbesondere durch technische Normen", BRAUNSCHWEIGISCHE WISSENSCHAFTLICHE GESELLSCHAFT, *Jahrbuch 2000 der Braunschweigischen Wissenschaftlichen Gesellschaft*, Braunschweig, Cramer, 2001, 199-242.

——, "Achievements and unresolved problems of European standardisation: the ingenuity of practice and the queries of lawyers", in JOERGES, Christian; LADEUR, Karl-Heinz; VOS, Ellen (eds.), *Integrating scientific expertise into regulatory decision-making: national traditions and European innovations*, Baden-Baden, Nomos, 1997, 187-224.

FAURE, Michael, "The harmonization, codification and integration of environmental law: a search for definitions", *European Environmental Law Review* 9 (2000), 174-182.

——; DALHAMMAR, Carl, "Principles for the design of a policy framework to address product life cycle impacts" in MAITRE-EKERN, Eléonore; DALHAMMAR, Carl; BUGGE, Hans Christian (ed.), *Preventing environmental damage from products: an analysis of the policy and regulatory framework in Europe*, Cambridge, Cambridge University Press, 2018, 57-86.

FERRAZ JUNIOR, Tercio Sampaio, *Introdução ao estudo do direito: técnica, decisão, dominação*, 4.ed., São Paulo, Atlas, 2003.

——, "Normas gerais e competência concorrente: uma exegese do art. 24 da Constituição Federal", *Revista da Faculdade de Direito da Universidade de São Paulo* 90 (1995), 245-251.

FLANDERKA, Fritz; KERI, Christian; QUODEN, Joachim; STROETMANN, Clemens, *Verpackungsverordnung: Kommentar unter vollständiger Berücksichtigung der 6. und 7. Änderungsverordnung mit Darstellungen zur Entwicklung in Deutschland, Österreich und Europa*, 4.ed., Heidelberg, Rehm, 2015.

FLANDERKA, Fritz; STROETMANN, Clemens, "Von der Verpackungsverordnung zum Wertstofssgesetz", *AbfallR* 11 (2012), 1-11.

FRENZ, Walter, *Europarecht*, 2.ed., Berlin/Heidelberg, Springer, 2016.

——, "Grundlagen und Grenzen abfallrechtlicher Produktverantwortung", in HENDLER, Reinhard; MARBURGER, Peter; REIFF, Peter; SCHRÖDER, Meinhard (Hrsg.), *Abfallrecht in Bewegung: Zur Neuordnung des Rechts der Verpackungsentsorgung*, Berlin, Erich Schmidt, 2008, 25-61.

FRIEGE, Henning, "Auf dem Weg zum Stoffrecht. Überlegungen zur Reform des Umweltrechts auf der Grundlage des Konzepts zum Management von Stoffströmen", *ZUR* 5 (1995), 241-248.

——; Engelhardt, Claudia; Henseling, Karl Otto (Hrsg.), *Das Management von Stoffströmen: geteilte Verantwortung – Nutzen für alle*, Berlin, Springer, 1998.

Frosch, Robert A., "Toward the end of waste: reflections on a new ecology of industry", *Daedalus* 125 (1996), 199-212.

Führ, Martin, "Stoffbezogenes Umweltrecht: Vom Gefahrstoffrecht zum produktorientierten Stoffstrommanagement", in Dolde, Klaus-Peter (Hrsg.), *Umweltrecht im Wandel*, Berlin, Erich Schmidt, 2001, 685-699.

——, *Stoffstromsteuerung durch Produktregulierung*, Baden-Baden, Nomos, 2000.

G

Gattermann, Jana, *Produktverantwortung nach dem Elektrogesetz und der Altfahrzeugverordnung: Wirkungen auf eine innovative Produktgestaltung*, Kassel, Kassel University Press, 2013.

Gebers, Betty; Führ, Martin; Wollny, Volrad, *Ökologische Stoffwirtschaft: Grundanforderungen an eine Stoffflußregulierung*, Darmstadt, Öko-Institut, 1993.

Georgescu-Roegen, Nicholas, "Looking back", in Dragan, J. C.; Seifert, E. K.; Demetrescu, M. C. (eds.), *Entropy and bioeconomics: proceedings of the First International Conference of the EABS*, Milano, Nargard, 1991a, 11-21.

——, "Thermodynamics and we, the humans", in Dragan, J. C.; Seifert, E. K.; Demetrescu, M. C. (eds.), *Entropy and bioeconomics: proceedings of the First International Conference of the EABS*, Milano, Nargard, 1991b, 184-201.

——, "The entropy law and the economic process in retrospect", *Eastern Economic Journal* 12 (1986), 3-25.

——, "Matter: a resource ignored by thermodynamics – renewable resource economics", in St.-Pierre, L. E.; Brown, G. R. (eds.), *Future sources of organic raw materials – CHEMRAWN I*, Oxford, Pergamon, 1980, 79-87.

——, "The steady state and ecologic salvation: a thermodynamic analysis", *BioScience* 27 (1977), 266-270.

——, "Energy and economic myths", *Southern Economic Journal* 41 (1975), 347-381.

——, *The entropy law and the economic process*, London/Cambridge (Massachusetts), Harvard University Press, 1971.

Gillespie, Alexander, *The illusion of progress: unsustainable development in international law and policy*, Sterling, Earthscan, 2001.

Goddard, Haynes C., "The benefits and costs of alternative solid waste management policies", *Resources, Conservation and Recycling* 13 (1995), 183-213.

Gopalakrishnan, Chennat, "Classic papers in natural resource economics: an overview", in Gopalakrishnan, Chennat (ed.), *Classic papers in natural resource economics*, Basingstoke, Palgrave Macmillan, 2000, 1-10.

Götz, Volkmar, *Allgemeines Polizei- und Ordnungsrecht*, 15.ed., München, C. H. Beck, 2013.

GROSZ, Mirina, *Sustainable waste trade under WTO law: chances and risks of the legal frameworks' regulation of transboundary movements of wastes*, Leiden, Martinus Nijhoff, 2011.

H

HANSCHEL, Dirk, "Progress and the precautionary principle in administrative law - country report on Germany", in RIEDEL, Eibe; WOLFRUM, Rüdiger (eds.), *Recent trends in German and European constitutional law*, Berlin, Springer, 2006, 179-209.

HARDIN, Garrett, "The tragedy of the commons", *Science* 162 (1968), 1243-1248.

HARSCH, Bradley A., "Consumerism and environmental policy: moving past consumer culture", *Ecology Law Quarterly* 26 (1999), 534-610.

HARTWICK, John M.; OLEWILER, Nancy D., *The economics of natural resource use*, New York, Harper & Row, 1986.

HERRMANN, Friederike; SANDEN, Joachim; SCHOMERUS, Thomas; SCHULZE, Falk, "Ressourcenschutzrecht – Ziele, Herausforderungen, Regelungsvorschläge", *ZUR* 23 (2012), 523-531.

HINCHLIFFE, Daniel; AKKERMAN, Floris, "Assessing the review process of EU Ecodesign regulations", *Journal of Cleaner Production* 168 (2017), 1603-1613.

HOTELLING, Harold, "The economics of exhaustible resources", *The Journal of Political Economy* 39 (1931), 137-175.

HUBER, Peter M., "Risk decisions in German constitutional and administrative law", in WOODMAN, Gordon R.; KLIPPEL, Diethelm (eds.), *Risk and the law*, Abingdon, Routledge, 2009, 23-35.

HUULGAARD, Rikke Dorothea; REMMEN, Arne, *Eco-design requirements for televisions: how ambitious is the implementation of the Energy-using Product Directive?*, Copenhagen, Miljøstyrelsen, 2012.

J

JAFFE, Adam B.; NEWELL, Richard G.; STAVINS, Robert N., "Technological change and the environment", in MÄLER, Karl-Göran; VINCENT, Jeffrey R. (eds.), *Handbook of environmental economics*, vol. 1, Amsterdam, Elsevier, 2003, 461-516.

JANS, Jan H.; VEDDER, Hans H. B., *European environmental law: after Lisbon*, 4.ed., Groningen, Europa Law Publishing, 2012.

JEPSEN, Dirk; REINTJES, Norbert; FRIEDER, Rubik; STECKER, Rebecca; ENGEL, Florian; EISENHAUER, Patrik; SCHOMERUS, Thomas; SPENGLER, Laura, *Grundkonzeption eines Top-Runner-Modells auf der EU-Ebene*, UBA Texte 36/2011, Dessau-Roßlau, UBA, 2011.

JOERGES, Christian; SCHEPEL, Harm; VOS, Ellen, *The law's problem with the involvement of non-governmental actors in Europe's legislative processes: the case of standardisation under the 'new approach'*, EUI Working Paper LAW No. 99/9, available at <http://cadmus.eui.eu/bitstream/handle/1814/154/law99_9.pdf>, last accessed on 17 August 2016.

K

Kalimo, Harri; Lifset, Reid; van Rossem, Chris; van Wassenhove, Luk; Atasu, Atalay, "What roles for which stakeholders under producer responsibility?", *RECIEL* 24 (2015), 40-57.

——, Mayers, Kieren, "Greening the economy through design incentives: allocating extended producer responsibility", *European Energy and Environmental Law Review* 21 (2012), 274-305.

Kemna, René; van Elburg, Martjin; Li, William; van Holsteijn, Rob; Brisaer, André, *Methodology study eco-design of energy-using products (MEEUP). Methodology report*, Delft/Brussels, 2005, available at <http://bookshop.europa.eu/en/methodology-for-ecodesign-of-energy-related-products-meerp-2011--pbNB0313617/downloads/NB-03-13-617-EN-C/NB0313617ENC_002.pdf?FileName=NB0313617ENC_002.pdf&SKU=NB0313617ENC_PDF&CatalogueNumber=NB-03-13-617-EN-C>, last accessed on 30 April 2017.

Kemna, René; Azaïs, Nelly; van Elburg, Martjin; van der Voort, Maaike; Li, William, *Methodology for ecodesign of energy-related products (MEErP 2011). Methodology report. Part 1: methods*, Brussels/Delft, 2011, available at <http://bookshop.europa.eu/en/methodology-for-ecodesign-of-energy-related-products-meerp-2011–pbNB0313617/downloads/NB-03-13-617-EN-C/NB0313617ENC_002.pdf?FileName=NB0313617ENC_002.pdf&SKU=NB0313617ENC_PDF&CatalogueNumber=NB-03-13-617-EN-C>, last accessed on 30 April 2017.

Klayman, Elliot, "Standard setting under the Consumer Product Safety Amendments of 1981 – a shift in regulatory philosophy", *The George Washington Law Review* 51 (1982), 96-112.

Kloepfer, Michael, "Zur Entwicklung des Kreislaufwirtschafts- und Abfallrechts in der Bundesrepublik Deutschland", *AbfallR* 11 (2012), 261-268.

——, *Produktverantwortung für Elektrogeräte: Rechtsprobleme der Entsorgung von Altprodukten unter besonderer Berücksichtigung des Entwurfs einer Elektroaltgeräte-Verordnung*, Berlin, Duncker & Humblot, 2001.

——, "Abfallrecht im Bundestaat: Eine Einführung", in Kloepfer, Michael (Hrsg.), *Abfallrecht und Föderalismus*, Berlin, Duncker & Humblot, 1999, 13-35.

Klöck, Oliver, "Abfall ohne Ende? – Bericht über die 9. Kölner Abfalltage", *UPR* 3 (2001), 100-102.

Klöpffer, Walter; Grahl, Birgit, *Life cycle assessment (LCA): a guide to best practice*, Weinheim, Wiley-VCH, 2014.

Koch, Hans-Joachim; Reese, Moritz, *Novellierung der EU-Abfallrahmenrichtlinie: Änderungsbedarf und Änderungsvorschläge für eine Weiterentwicklung des europäischen Abfallrechts*, Berlin, Erich Schmidt, 2006.

——, "Revising the Waste Framework Directive. Basic deficiencies of European waste law and proposals for reform", *JEEPL* 6 (2005), 441-457.

——, "Abfallrechtliche Regulierung der Verwertung – Chancen und Grenzen", *DVBl.* 115 (2000), 300-312.

KÖNIG, Doris, "Gesetzgebung", in SCHULZE, Reiner; ZULEEG, Manfred; KADELBACH, Stefan (Hrsg.), *Europarecht: Handbuch für die deutsche Rechtspraxis*, 3.ed., Baden-Baden, Nomos, 2015, 83-144.

KRÄMER, Ludwig, *EU Environmental Law*, 8.ed., London, Sweet & Maxwell, 2015.

——, *Überlegungen zu Ressourceneffizienz und Recycling*, Research Papers in Law 6/2003, Brugge, Collège d'Europe, 2003, available at <https://www.coleurope.eu/sites/default/files/research-paper/researchpaper_6_2003_kramer.pdf>, last accessed on 29 April 2017.

——, "The distinction between product and waste in Community law", in KLETT, Wolfgang; SCHMITT-GLESER, Gerhard; SCHNURER, Helmut (Hrsg.), *Abfall ohne Ende? Oder: Ende der Abfalleigenschaft durch Umwandlung zu Rohstoff*, Köln, Gutke, 2001, 253-276.

——; WINTER, Gerd, "Umweltrecht", in SCHULZE, Reiner; ZULEEG, Manfred; KADELBACH, Stefan (Hrsg.), *Europarecht: Handbuch für die deutsche Rechtspraxis*, 3.ed., Baden-Baden, Nomos, 2015, 1548-1639.

KRELL, Andreas Joachim, "A necessária mudança de foco na implantação do federalismo cooperativo no Brasil: da definição de competências legislativas para o desenho de formas conjuntas de execução administrativa", in DE SOUZA NETO, Cláudio Pereira; SARMENTO, Daniel; BINEBOIM, Gustavo (org.), *Vinte anos da Constituição Federal de 1988*, Rio de Janeiro, Lumen Juris, 2009, 635-660.

KRIEGER, Stephan, "Wozu wird das Abfallrecht gebraucht?", *UPR* 15 (1995), 408-412.

KUNIG, Philip, "Do direito do lixo para o direito da correcta gestão dos ciclos dos materiais? Comentários acerca da legislação alemã sobre os resíduos e a sua evolução", *Revista Jurídica do Urbanismo e do Ambiente* 1 (1994a), 95-108.

——, "Von der Wegwerfgesellschaft zur Kreislaufwirtschaft: Überlegungen zum Stoffstromrecht, in BREUER, Rüdiger; KLOEPFER, Michael; MARBURGER, Peter; SCHRÖDER, Meinhard (Hrsg.), *Jahrbuch des Umwelt- und Technikrechts*, Heidelberg, R. v. Decker, 1994b, p. 277-295.

L

LADEUR, Karl-Heinz, "Das Kreislaufwirtschafts- und Abfallgesetz als Schritt auf dem Weg zu einem 'ökologischen Stoffflußrecht'? Zu den Anforderungen an die Koordination öffentlichen und privaten Entscheidens unter Komplexitätsbedingungen", *ZfU* 21 (1998), 279-315.

LANGNER, Dirk; KLINDT, Thomas, "Technische Sicherheitsvorschriften und Normen", in DAUSES, Manfred A. (Hrsg.), *Handbuch des EU-Wirtschaftsrechts*, Band 1, 40.ed., München, C.H. Beck, 2016, Rn. 1-160.

LEA, Anne, "The scrapping of end of life vehicles: is new European legislation necessary?", *Environmental Law Review* 65 (2000), 65-73.

LEE, Maria, *EU environmental law: challenges, changes and decision-making*, Oxford, Hart Publishing, 2005.

LEE, Robert G.; STOKES, Elen, "Rehabilitating the definition of waste: is it fully recovered?", in ETTY, Thijs F. M.; SOMSEN, Han (eds.), *Yearbook of European Environmental Law*, vol. 8, Oxford, Oxford University Press, 2008, 162-181.

LEMOS, Patricia Faga Iglecias, *Resíduos sólidos e responsabilidade civil pós-consumo*, 2.ed., São Paulo, Revista dos Tribunais, 2012.

LEVY, Daniel de Andrade, *Responsabilidade civil: de um direito dos danos a um direito das condutas lesivas*, São Paulo, Atlas, 2012.

Lewandowski, Enrique Ricardo, "Considerações sobre o federalismo brasileiro", *Justiça & Cidaadania* 157 (2013), 13-17.

LIDGREN, Karl; SKOGH, Gorän, "Extended producer responsibility: recycling, liability, and guarantee funds", *The Geneva Papers on Risk and Insurance* 21 (1996), 170-181.

LIFSET, Reid J., "Industrial ecology in the age of input-output analysis", in Suh, Sangwon (ed.), *Handbook of input-output economics in industrial ecology*, Dordrecht *et al.*, Springer, 2009, 3-21.

——, "Take it back: extended producer responsibility as a form of incentive-based environmental policy", *Journal of Resource Management and Technology* 21 (1993), 163-175.

——; GRAEDEL, T. E., "Industrial ecology: goals and definitions", in AYRES, Robert U.; AYRES, Leslie W. (eds.), *A handbook of industrial ecology*, Cheltenham, Edward Elgar, 2002, 3-15.

LIFSET, Reid J.; LINDHQVIST, Thomas, "Producer responsibility at a turning point?", *JIE* 12 (2008), 144-147.

——, "Can we take the concept of individual producer responsibility from theory to practice?", *JIE* 7 (2003), 3-6.

——, "Trust, but verify", *JIE* 5 (2002), 9-11.

——, "Getting the goal right: EPR and DfE", *JIE* 2 (1998), 6-8.

——, "What's in a name: producer or product responsibility?", *JIE* 1 (1997), 6-7.

——; ATASU, Ataly; TOJO, Naoko, "Extended producer responsibility: national, international, and practical perspectives", *JIE* 17 (2013), 162-166.

LINDHQVIST, Thomas, *Extended producer responsibility in cleaner production: policy principle to promote environmental improvements of product systems*, Doctoral dissertation, The International Institute for Industrial Environmental Economics (IIIEE), Lund, Lunds Universitet, 2000.

——; Lidgren, Karl, "Modeller för förlängt producentansvar", in Miljödepartementet, *Från vaggan till graven – sex studier av varors miljöpåverkan*, Stockholm, Allmäanna, 1991, 7-44.

Lopes, José Reinaldo de Lima, *Responsabilidade civil do fabricante e a defesa do consumidor*, São Paulo, Revista dos Tribunais, 1992.

LUECK, Dean, "The rule of first possession and the design of the law", *Journal of Law and Economics* 38 (1995), 393-436.

M

Macroy, Richard; Havercroft, Ian, "Environmental principles in the United Kingdom", in Macroy, Richard; Havercroft, Ian; Purdy, Ray (eds.), *Principles of European environmental law*, Groningen, 2004, 195-214.

Maitre-Ekern, Eléonore; Dalhammar, Carl, "Regulating planned obsolescence: a review of legal approaches to increase product durability and reparability in Europe", *RECIEL* 25:3 (2016), 378-394.

——; Bugge, Hans Christian (ed.), *Preventing environmental damage from products: an analysis of the policy and regulatory framework in Europe*, Cambridge, Cambridge University Press, 2018a.

——, "Developing legislation to prevent environmental damage from products: a Herculean but necessary task", in Maitre-Ekern, Eléonore; Dalhammar, Carl; Bugge, Hans Christian (ed.), *Preventing environmental damage from products: an analysis of the policy and regulatory framework in Europe*, Cambridge, Cambridge University Press, 2018b, 1-20.

Malcom, Rosalind, "Ecodesign laws and the environmental impact of our consumption of products", *JEL* 23 (2011), 487-503.

——, "Integrated product policy – a new regulatory paradigm for a consumer society?", *European Environmental Law Review* 14 (2005), 134-144.

Masing, Johannes, "Kritik des integrierten Umweltschutzes", *DVBl.* 113 (1998), 549-559.

Maxwell, Dorothy; McAndrew, Laure; Schischke, Karsten; Stobbe, Lutz; Nissen, Nils F.; White, Owen, "Non-energy related policy options to foster eco-design of electronics products", *Proceedings of the 1st IEEE International Conference on Consumer Electronics*, New York, IEEE, 2011, 281-285, available at <http://ieeexplore.ieee.org/stamp/stamp.jsp?arnumber=6031846>, last accessed on 12 September 2016.

Mayers, Kieren; Lifset, Reid; Bodenhoefer, Karl; van Wassenhove, Luk N., "Implementing individual producer responsibility for waste electrical and electronic equipment through improved financing", *JIE* 17 (2012), 186-198.

Mayers, Kieren; Peagam, Richard; France, Chris; Basson, Lauren; Clift, Roland, "Redesigning the camel: the European WEEE Directive", *JIE* 15 (2011), 4-8.

Mayumi, Kozo, *The origins of ecological economics: the bioeconomics of Georgescu-Roegen*, London/New York, Routledge, 2001.

McDonough, William; Braungart, Michael, *Cradle to cradle: remaking the way we make things*, New York, North Point, 2003.

McDougall, Forbes R.; White, Peter R.; Franke, Marina; Hindle, Peter, *Integrated solid waste management: a life cycle inventory*, 2.ed., Oxford, Blackwell Sciences, 2001.

McKerlie, Kate; Knight, Nancy; Thorpe, Beverly, "Advancing extended producer responsibility in Canada", *Journal of Cleaner Production* 14 (2006), 616-628.

Meadows, Donella H.; Meadows, Dennis L.; Randers, Jørgen; Behrens III, William W., *The limits to growth: a report for The Club of Rome's project on the predicament of mankind*, Washington, D.C., Potomac, 1972.

Mertens, Kathleen, "The energy efficiency framework for energy-related products – is it really the story of a life cycle?", in Delvaux, Bram; Hunt, Michaël; Talus, Kim (eds.), *EU Energy law and policy issues*, vol. 3, Brussels, Intersentia, 2011, 327-349.

Messerschmidt, Klaus, *Europäisches Umweltrecht*, München, C. H. Beck, 2011.

Misonne, Delphine, "The Directive on ecodesign, the way forward regarding IPP?", *elni Review* 1 (2005), 16-28.

Mitchell, Brian S., *An introduction to materials engineering and science for chemical and materials engineers*, New Jersey, John Wiley & Sons, 2004.

Molenbroek, Edith; Smith, Metthew; Groenenber, Heleen; Waide, Paul; Attali, Sophie; Fischer, Corinna; Krivošik, Juraj; Fonseca, Paula; Santos, Bruno; Fong, João, *Evaluation of the Energy Labelling Directive and specific aspects of the Ecodesign Directive – final technical report*, Utrecht, Ecofys, 2014, available at <http://www.ecofys.com/files/files/final_technical_report-evaluation_eld_ed_june_2014.pdf>, last accessed 25 April 2017.

Monier, Véronique; Hestin, Mathieu; Cavé, Jérémie; Laureysens, Ilse; Watkins, Emma; Reisinger, Hubert; Porsch, Lucas, *Development of guidance on extended producer responsibility (EPR)*, Final report for the European Commission – DG Environment, 2014, available at <http://ec.europa.eu/environment/waste/pdf/target_review/Guidance%20on%20EPR%20-%20Final%20Report.pdf>, last accessed on 15 May 2016.

Monier, Véronique; Hestin, Mathieu; Schuster, Rita; van Acoleyen, Mike; Lauyrensens, Ilse, *Awareness and exchange of best practices on the implementation and enforcement of the essential requirements for packaging and packaging waste*, Final report for the European Commission – DG Environment, 2011, available at <http://ec.europa.eu/environment/waste/packaging/pdf/packaging_final_report.pdf>, last accessed on 15 August 2016.

Mont, Oksana, "Institutionalisation of sustainable consumption patterns based on shared use", *Ecological Economics* 50 (2004), 135-153.

Moreira, Danielle de Andrade, *Responsabilidade ambiental pós-consumo: da prevenção à reparação de danos*, Tese de doutorado, Faculdade de Direito da Universidade Estadual do Rio de Janeiro (UERJ), Rio de Janeiro, UERJ, 2008.

Mudgal, Shailendra; Tinetti, Benoît; Trigo, Alvaro de Prado; Faninger, Thibault; Schischke, Karsten; Proske, Marina; von Geibler, Justus; Teubler, Jens, *Material-efficiency ecodesign report and module to the methodology for the ecodesign of energy-related products (MEErP). Part 1: material efficiency for ecodesign*, n.p., BIO Intelligence, 2013a, available at <http://ec.europa.eu/DocsRoom/documents/105/attachments/1/translations/en/renditions/pdf>, last accessed on 2 May 2017.

——, *Material-efficiency ecodesign report and module to the methodology for the ecodesign of energy-related products (MEErP). Part 2: enhancing MEErP for ecodesign*, n.p., BIO Intelligence, 2013b, available at <http://ec.europa.eu/DocsRoom/documents/106/attachments/1/translations/en/renditions/native>, last accessed on 2 May 2017.

——, *Material-efficiency ecodesign report and module to the methodology for the ecodesign of energy-related products (MEErP). Part 2: test reports TV and washing machine*, n.p., BIO Intelligence, 2013c, available at <http://ec.europa.eu/DocsRoom/documents/107/attachments/1/translations/en/renditions/native>, last accessed on 2 May 2017.

Mueller, Charles C., *Os economistas e as relações entre o sistema econômico e o meio ambiente*, Brasília, Editora UnB/Finatec, 2007.

N

Nash, Hazel Ann, "The revised Directive on waste: solving legislative tensions in waste management?", *JEL* 21 (2009), 139-149.

Neumayer, Eric, *Weak versus strong sustainability: exploring the limits of two opposing paradigms*, 4.ed., Cheltenham, Edward Elgar, 2013.

Nusdeo, Ana Maria de Oliveira, "Desenvolvimento e ecologia revisitado. Evolução do debate e perspectivas atuais", in Nusdeo, Fábio (ed.), *O direito econômico na atualidade*, São Paulo, Revista dos Tribunais, 2014, 227-250.

——, "O uso de instrumentos econômicos nas normas de proteção ambiental", *Revista da Faculdade de Direito da Universidade de São Paulo* 101 (2006), 357-378.

Nusdeo, Fábio, *Curso de economia: introdução ao direito econômico*, 6.ed., São Paulo, Revista dos Tribunais, 2010.

——, "Desenvolvimento econômico – um retrospecto e algumas perspectivas", in Salomão Filho, Calixto (coord.), *Regulação e desenvolvimento*, São Paulo, Malheiros, 2002.

——, *Desenvolvimento e ecologia*, São Paulo, Saraiva, 1975.

O

Oberhauser, Alois, "Abgrenzung des Verursacherprinzips und seine Einordnung in die Umweltpolitik", in Bullinger, Martin; Rincke, Günther; Oberhauser, Alois; Schmidt, Ralf-Bodo, *Das Verursacherprinzip und seine Instrumente: Eine interdisziplinäre Untersuchung*, Berlin, Erich Schmidt, 1974, 27-49.

OECD, *Extended producer responsibility – updated guidance*, ENV/EPOC/WPRPW(2015)16/FINAL, 12 April 2016, available at <http://www.oecd.org/officialdocuments/publicdisplaydocumentpdf/?cote=ENV/EPOC/WPRPW(2015)16/FINAL&docLanguage=En>, last accessed 15 May 2016.

——, *Strategic waste prevention: OECD reference manual*, ENV/EPOC/PPC(2000)5/FINAL, 1 August 2000, available at <http://www.oecd.org/officialdocuments/publicdisplaydocumentpdf/?doclanguage=en&cote=env/epoc/ppc(2000)5/final>, last accessed on 10 April 2017.

Oehlmann, Claas, *Vom Abfall als Problem zum Abfall als Ressource. Das europäische Abfallrecht als Baustein einer europäischen Kreislaufwirtschaft*, Baden-Baden, Nomos, 2017.

On, Alexandru-Daniel, *Prevention and the pillars of a dynamic theory of civil liability: a comparative study on preventive remedies*, LL.M. Paper, Baton Rouge, Louisiana State University Law Center, 2013, available at <http://digitalcommons.law.lsu.edu/cgi/viewcontent.cgi?article=1001&context=studpapers>, last accessed on 25 March 2016.

Onida, Marco, "Products and the environment", in Macroy, Richard (ed.), *Reflections on 30 years of EU environmental law: a high level of protection?*, Groningen, Europa Law, 2006, 233-269.

——, "Environmental protection by product policy: focus on dangerous substances", in Onida, Marco (ed.), *Europe and the environment: legal essays in honour of Ludwig Krämer*, Groningen, Europa Law, 2004.

Oosterhuis, Frans; Rubik, Frieder; Scholl, Gerd, *Product policy in Europe: new environmental perspective*, Dordrecht *et al.*, Kluwer, 1996

Ormond, Thomas, "Der Kreislauf des Abfallrechts", *historiae iuris* (1998), available at <http://www.forhistiur.de/1998-10-ormond/>, last accessed 18 March 2017.

Ostrom, Elinor, "Private and Common Property Rights", in Bouckaert, Boudewijn; de Geest, Gerrit (eds.), *Encyclopedia of Law and Economics, Volume II: Civil Law and Economics*, Cheltenham, Edward Elgar, 2000, 332-379.

——; Ostrom, Vincent, "Public goods and public choices", in McGinnis, Michael D., *Polycentricity and local public economies: readings from the workshop in political theory and policy analysis*, Ann Arbor, The University of Michigan Press, 1999, 75-103.

——; SCHLAGER, Edella, "The formation of property rights", in HANNA, Susan S.; FOLKE, Carl; MÄLER, Karl-Göran (eds.), *Rights to nature: ecological, economic, cultural, and political principles of institutions for the environment*, Washington, D.C., Island Press, 1996, 127-156.

P

PACKARD, Vance, *The waste makers*, London, Longmans, 1960.

PALMER, Karen; WALLS, Margaret, *The product stewardship movement: understanding costs, effectiveness, and the role for policy*, RFF Report, Washington, Resources for the Future, November 2002, available at <https://media.rff.org/archive/files/sharepoint/WorkImages/Download/RFF-RPT-prodsteward.pdf>, last accessed on 28 December 2019.

PEARCE, David W., "An intellectual history of environmental economics", *Annual Review of Energy and the Environment* 27 (2002), 57-81.

——; TURNER, R. Kerry, "Packaging waste and the polluter pays principle: a taxation solution", *Journal of Environmental Planning and Management* 35 (1992), 5-15.

PEIRÓ, Laura Talens; POLVERINI, Davide; ARDENTE, Fulvio; MATHIEUX, Fabrice, "Advances towards circular economy policies in the EU: the new Ecodesign regulation of enterprise servers", *Resources, Conservation & Recycling*, in press, available online on 28 September 2019 at <https://doi.org/10.1016/j.resconrec.2019.104426>, last accessed on 29 December 2019.

PELKMANS, Jacques, "The new approach to technical harmonization and standardization", *Journal of Common Market Studies* 25 (1987), 249-269.

PERMAN, Roger; MA, Yue; COMMON, Michael; MADDISON, David; McGilvray, James, *Natural resource and environmental economics*, 4. ed., Harlow (England), Pearson, 2011.

PIGOU, Arthur Cecil, *The economics of welfare*, London, McMillan, 1920.

PLEPYS, Andrius; HEISKANEN, Eva; MONT, Oksana, "European policy approaches to promote servicizing", *Journal of Cleaner Production* 97 (2015), 117-123.

PORTER, Richard, *The economics of waste*, Washington D. C., Resources for the Future (RFF), 2002.

POWERS, Charles W.; CHERTOW, Marian R., "Industrial ecology: overcoming policy fragmentation", in ESTY, Daniel C.; CHERTOW, Marian R. (eds.), *Thinking ecologically: the next generation of environmental policy*, New Haven, Yale University Press, 1997, 19-36.

PRELLE, Rebecca, "Verpackungsverordnung (VerpackV)", in SCHMEHL, Arndt (Hrsg.), *Gemeinschaftskommentar zum Kreislaufwirtschaftsgesetz (KrWG) sowie zur Verpackungsordnung (VerpackV), zur Altfahrzeugverordnung (AltfahrzeugV), zum Elektro- und Elektronikgesetz (ElektroG), zum Batteriegesetz (BattG), zur Bioabfallverordnung (BioAbfV), zur Abfallverzeichnisverordnung (AVV) und zur EU-Abfallverbringungsverordnung (VVA)*, Köln, Carl Heymanns, 2013, p. 869-931.

——, "Bilanz und Perspektiven der Produktverantwortung", in FASSBENDER, Kurt; KÖCK, Wolfgang (Hrsg.), *Auf dem Weg in die Recyclinggesellschaft? – Aktuelle Entwicklungen im Kreislaufwirtschaftsrecht*, Baden-Baden, Nomos, 2011, 43-55.

——, "Abfallrechtliche Produktverantwortung: Rechtliche Zielsetzungen und Auswirkungen in der Praxis am Beispiel der AltfahrzeugV und des ElektroG", *ZUR* 21 (2010), 512-520.

——, "Begriff und Bedeutung der (Vorbereitung zur) Wiederverwendung im Abfallrecht", *AbfallR* 5 (2008), 220-225.

R

REDCLIFT, Michael R., *Wasted: counting the costs of global consumption*, London, Earthscan, 1996.

REESE, Moritz, "Grundprobleme des europäischen Abfallrechts und Lösungsbeiträge der neuen Abfallrahmenrichtlinie", *NVwZ* 28 (2009a), 1073-1079.

——, "Konzeptionelle Herausforderungen und Lösungsbeiträge der novellierten EG-Abfallrahmenrichtlinie", in Gesellschaft für Umweltrecht, *Dokumentation zur 32. Wissenschaftlichen Fachtagung der Gesellschaft für Umweltrecht e.V. Leipzig 2008*, Berlin, Erich Schmidt, 2009b, 131-162.

——, *Kreislaufwirtschaft im integrierten Umweltrecht: Eine Studie zu den begrifflichen, instrumentellen und funktionalen Grenzen des Abfallverwertungsrechts*, Baden-Baden, Nomos, 2000.

REHBINDER, Eckard, "Sustainable resource management – new legal approaches needed?", *JEEPL* 9 (2012a), 34-62.

——, "Ziele, Grundsätze, Strategien und Instrumente", in HANSMANN, Klaus; SELLNER, Dieter (Hrsg.), *Grundzüge des Umweltrechts*, 4.ed., Berlin, Erich Schmidt, 2012b, 135-310.

——, "Konzeption eines in sich geschlossenen Stoffrechts", in KLETT, Wolfgang; SCHMITT-GLESER, Gerhard; SCHNURER, Helmut (Hrsg.), *Vom Investitionserleichterungs- und Wohnbaulandgesetz zum Umweltgesetzbuch*, Köln, Gutke, 1995a, 391-413.

——, "Konzeption eines in sich geschlossenen Stoffrechts", in ENQUETE-KOMMISSION "SCHUTZ DES MENSCHEN UND DER UMWELT DES DEUTSCHEN BUNDESTAGES" (Hrsg.), *Studienprogramm Umweltverträgliches Stoffstrommanagement*, Band 2 (Instrumente), Bonn, Economica Verlag, 1995b.

——, "Abfall in der Ordnung von Mensch und Umwelt", in HOSEMANN, Gerhard (Hrsg.), *Abfall: Schicksal oder Herausforderung*, Erlangen, Universitätsbibliothek Erlangen-Nürnberg, 1994, 15-26.

——, *Politische und rechtliche Probleme des Verursacherprinzips*, Berlin, Erich Schmidt, 1973.

——; SCHMIHING, Christoph, *Ökobilanzen als Instrument des Umweltrechts*, Berlin, Erich Schmidt, 2001.

REIMER, Franz (Hrsg.), *Ressourceneffizienz – Leitbild für das Umweltrecht?*, Baden-Baden, Nomos, 2016.

——; TÖLLE, Susanne, "Ressourcenbegriff als Problembegriff", *ZUR* 24 (2013), 589-598.

RISK & POLICY ANALYSTS, *Study on the impact of the MoU on harmonisation of chargers for mobile telephones and to assess possible future options*, dated 22 August 2014, available at <http://ec.europa.eu/DocsRoom/documents/7432/attachments/1/translations/en/renditions/pdf>, last accessed on 15 September 2016.

REVESZ, Richard L., "Federalism and environmental regulation: an overview", in REVESZ, Richard L.; SANDS, Philippe; STEWART, Richard B. (ed.), *Environmental law, the economy, and sustainable development: the United States, the European Union and the international community*, Cambridge, Cambridge University Press, 2000, 37-79.

ROBBERS, Gerhard, *Einführung in das deutsche Recht*, 6.ed., Baden-Baden, Nomos, 2017.

RÖCKINGHAUSEN, Marc, *Integrierter Umweltschutz im EG-Recht: Der Begriff des integrierten Umweltschutzes in der Rechtsordnung der Europäischen Gemeinschaft*, Berlin, Erich Schmidt, 1998.

ROLLER, Gerhard; FÜHR, Martin, "Individual producer responsibility: a remaining challenge under the WEEE Directive", *RECIEL* 17 (2008), *277-283.*

ROSE, Ian; KNIGHTON, George, "Integrated product policy: the new approach to environmental regulation", *European Environmental Law Review* 8 (1999), 266-270.

ROSE-ACKERMAN, Susan, "Public law versus private law in environmental regulation: European Union proposals in the light of United States and German experience", in EIDE, Erling; VAN DEN BERGH, Roger (eds.), *Law and economics of the environment*, Oslo, Juridisk Forlag, 1996, p. 13-39.

ROSS, Alf, *Directives and norms*, New York, Humanities Press, 1968.

ROTTER, Vera Susanne, "Waste management and producer responsibility: a score behind – a new ahead", *Waste Management & Research* 29 (2011), 889-890.

S

SCHALL, John, *Does the solid waste management hierarchy make sense? A technical, economics and environmental justification for the priority of source reduction and recycling,* Working paper #1, School of Forestry and Environmental Studies, Yale University, 1992.

SACHS, Noah, "Can we regulate our way to energy efficiency? Product standards and climate policy", *Vanderbilt Law Review* 65 (2012), 1631-1678.

——, "Greening demand: energy consumption and U.S. climate policy", *Duke Environmental Law & Policy Forum* 19 (2009), 295-319.

——, "Planning the funeral at the birth: extended producer responsibility in the European Union and the United States", *Harvard Environmental Law Review* 30 (2006), 51-98.

SALOMÃO FILHO, Calixto, "Regulação, desenvolvimento e meio ambiente", in SALOMÃO FILHO, Calixto (org.), *Regulação e desenvolvimento: novos temas*, São Paulo, Malheiros, 2012, 15-59.

SANDEN, Joachim; SCHOMERUS, Thomas; SCHULZE, Falk, *Entwicklung eines Regelungskonzepts für ein Ressourcenschutzrecht des Bundes*, Berlin, Erich Schmidt, 2012.

SANDER, Knut; SCHILLING, Stephanie; TOJO, Naoko; VAN ROSSEM, Chris; VERNON, Jan; GEORGE, Carolyn, *The producer responsibility principle of the WEEE Directive: final report*, n.p., 2007.

SARLET, Ingo Wolfgang; FENSTERSEIFER, Tiago, "A competência constitucional legislativa em matéria ambiental à luz do 'federalismo cooperativo ecológico' consagrado pelo ordenamento jurídico brasileiro", *Revista de Direito Ambiental* 71 (2013), 55-116.

SCHENKE, Wolf-Rüdiger, *Polizei- und Ordnungsrecht*, 9.ed., Heidelberg, C. F. Müller, 2016.

SCHENKEL, Werner, "Visionen einer integrierten Stoffflusspolitik", in KLETT, Wolfgang; SCHMITT-GLESER, Gerhard; SCHNURER, Helmut (Hrsg.), *Abfall ohne Ende? Oder: Ende der Abfalleigenschaft durch Umwandlung zu Rohstoff*, Köln, Gutke, 2000, 391-413.

——, *Recht auf Abfall? Versuch über das Märchen vom süßen Brei*, Berlin, Erich Schmidt, 1993.

——; REICHE, Jochen, "Stoffpolitik und Umweltrecht – zur Diskussion über die 5. Novelle des Abfallgesetzes", *ZAU* 6 (1993), 184-196.

SCHEPEL, Harm, "The new approach to the new approach: the juridification of harmonized standards in EU law", *Maastricht Journal of European and Comparative Law* 12 (2013), 521-533.

——, *The constitution of private governance – product standards in the regulation of integrating markets*, Oxford, Hart, 2005.

SCHLAGER, Edella; OSTROM, Elinor, "Property-rights regimes and natural resources: a conceptual analysis", *Land Economics* 68 (1992), 249-262.

SCHLIESSNER, Ursula, "Integrated product policy: where is the EU heading?", *European Environmental Law Review* 10 (2001), 86-88.

SCHOMERUS, Thomas; SPENGLER, Laura, "Die Erweiterung der Ökodesign-Richtlinie – auf dem Weg zur 'Super-Umweltrichtlinie'?", *EurUP* 2 (2010), 54-61.

SCHRÖDER, Meinhard, "Europarecht und integriertes Umweltrecht", *NuR* 22 (2000), 481-486.

SCHULZE, Falk, *Kurzanalyse 22: Ressourceneffizienzvorgaben in der Ökodesign-RL*, PolRess (Ressourcenpolitik) AP 2 – Wirkungsanalysen Politikansätze, 2015, available at <http://edocs.fu-berlin.de/docs/servlets/MCRFileNodeServlet/FUDOCS_derivate_000000005875/KAx22xRessourceneffizienzvorgabenxxkodesign.pdf>, last accessed on 22 August 2016.

SCOTFORD, Eloise, "Trash or treasure: policy tensions in EC waste regulation", *JEL* 19 (2007), 367-388.

SENDIM, José de Sousa Cunhal, *Responsabilidade civil por danos ecológicos: da reparação do dano através da restauração natural*, Coimbra, Coimbra Editora, 1998.

SIDERIUS, Hans-Paul, "The role of experience curves for setting MEPS for appliances", *Energy Policy* 59 (2013), 762-772.

——, *The ecodesign and energy labelling process – challenges and solutions*, 2012, available at <http://www.eup-network.de/fileadmin/user_upload/Produktgruppen/Lots/Working_Documents/2012_19-04_horizontal_assessment_120227pdf__EN_1.pdf>, last accessed on 5 August 2016.

——; NAKAGAMI, Hidetoshi, "A MEPS is a MEPS is a MEPS: comparing Ecodesign and Top Runner schemes for setting product efficiency standards", *Energy Efficiency* 6 (2013), 1-19.

SMEDDINCK, Ulrich, "Von Trümmern zu Ressourcen – das Abfallrecht in Deutschland von der Nachkriegszeit bis heute", in SMEDDINCK, Ulrich; KLUG, Ann Christin (Hrsg.), *Vom Abfallrecht zur Kreislaufwirtschaft. Untersuchungen zur Entwicklung des Abfallrechts und zu Abfallvermeidungsprogrammen nach § 33 KrWG*, Halle an der Saale, Universitätsverlag Halle-Wittenberg, 2016, 9-32.

——, "Die Entwicklung des Ressourcenschutzrechts – Schlaglichter: Von den Ursprüngen zur globalen Governance", *Verwaltungsarchiv* 103 (2012), 183-2016.

SOCIETY OF ENVIRONMENTAL TOXICOLOGY AND CHEMISTRY (SETAC), *Guidelines for life-cycle assessment: a "code of practice"*, Pensacola (Florida), SETAC, 1993.

SOLER, Fabricio Dorado; SILVA FILHO, Carlos Roberto, *Gestão de resíduos sólidos: o que diz a lei*, 2.ed., São Paulo, Trevisan, 2013.

SPARWASSER, Reinhard; ENGEL, Rüdiger; VOSSKUHLE, Andreas, *Umweltrecht: Grundzüge des öffentlichen Umweltschutzrechts*, 5. ed., Heidelberg, C.F. Müller, 2003.

STREINZ, Rudolf, *Europarecht*, 10. ed., Heidelberg, C. F. Müller, 2016.

SUNDFELD, Carlos Ari, *Direito administrativo ordenador*, São Paulo, Malheiros, 1993.

SVENSSON, Sahra; RICHTER, Jessika Luth; MAITRE-EKERN, Eléonore; PIHLAJARINNE, Taina; MAIGRET, Aline; DALHAMMAR, Carl, "The emerging 'right to repair' legislation in the EU and the U.S", *Pre-print of the paper presented at Going Green CARE INNOVATION 2018*, Vienna, 2018, available at https://portal.research.lu.se/portal/files/63585584/Svensson_et_al._Going_Green_CARE_INNOVATION_2018_PREPRINT.pdf>, last accessed on 27 December 2019.

T

TAJANI, Antonio, "Common charger for small electronic devices", *Enterprise & Industry Magazine* 16 (2013), 3.

TAVARES, André Ramos, "Aporias acerca do 'condomínio legislativo' no Brasil: uma análise a partir do STF", in TAVARES, André Ramos; LEITE, George Salomão; SARLET, Ingo Wolfgang (org.), *Estado constitucional e organização do poder*, São Paulo, Saraiva, 2010, p. 161-191.

TCHOBANOGLOUS, George; KREITH, Frank, *Handbook of solid waste management*, 2.ed., New York *et al*, McGraw-Hill, 2002.

THOLEN, Lena, "Die Ressourcenfrage innerhalb der Ökodesign-Richtlinie. Aspekte einer neuen Schwerpunktsetztung im Zuge der Weiterentwicklung der Richtlinie auf nicht-energiebetriebene Produkte", *ZfU* 4 (2011), 469-495.

THOMPSON, Michael, "Waste and fairness", *Social Research* 65 (1998), 55-73.

——, *Rubbish theory: the creation and destruction of value*, Oxford, Oxford University Press, 1979.

THOMSEN, Silke, *Produktverantwortung: Rechtliche Möglichkeiten und Grenzen einer Kreislaufwirtschaft*, Baden-Baden, Nomos, 1998.

TIETENBERG, Tom; LEWIS, Lynne, *Environmental and resource economics*, 10.ed., Harlow (England), Pearson, 2015.

TOJO, Naoko, *EPR programmes: individual versus collective responsibility. Exploring various forms of implementation and their implication to design change*, IIIE Reports 2003:8, The International Institute for Industrial Environmental Economics, Lund University, Lund, 2003.

——; LINDHQVIST, Thomas, *Product-oriented environmental interventions. Building policy instruments,* The International Institute for Industrial Environmental Economics, Lund University, Lund, 2010.

——; Thomas; DAVIS, Gary A., "EPR programme implementation: institutional and structural factors", in ORGANISATION FOR ECONOMIC CO-OPERATION AND DEVELOPMENT, *Seminar on extended producer responsibility, EPR: programme implementation and assessment*, 13-14 December 2001.

TÖLLE, Susanne, *Der Rechtsrahmen für den Erlass von Ökodesign-Anforderungen*, Baden-Baden, Nomos, 2016.

TOPOREK, Marta, *Legal briefing: The potential for EU Member States to adopt national measures stricter than those established in the EU legislation based on Article 114 of the Treaty on the Functioning of the European Union (ex. Article 95 of the EC Treat) – study of the Ecodesign and Energy Labelling Directives*, n.p., ClientEarth, 2010, available at <http://www.clientearth.org/reports/climate-energy-art-114-1-tfeu-ecodesign-and-energy-labelling-directives-briefing.pdf>, last accessed on 25 October 2016.

TROMANS, Stephen, "EC waste law – a complete mess?", *JEL* 13 (2001), 133-156.

Tufet-Opi, Enrique, "Life after end of life: the replacement of end of life product legislation by a European integrated product policy in the EC", *JEL* 14 (2002), 33-60.

Tukker, Arnold; Huppes, Gjalt; Guinée, Reinout Heijungs; de Koning, Arjan; van Oers, Lauran; Suh, Sangwon; Geerken, Theo; van Holderbeke, Mirja; Jansen, Bart; Nielsen, Per, *Environmental impacts of products (EIPRO): analysis of the life cycle environmental impacts related to the final consumption of the EU-25*, European Communities, European Commission/JRC, 2006, available at <http://ec.europa.eu/environment/ipp/pdf/eipro_report.pdf >, last accessed 25 April 2017.

Turner, R. Kerry; Powell, Jane C., "Towards an integrated waste management strategy", *Environmental Management and Health* 2 (1991), 6-12.

U

UBA, *Kolloquium zur Konzeption des Stofffflußrechts. Bedeutung – Sachstand – Perspektiven für eine rechtliche Steuerung von Stoffströmen*, UBA Texte 18/95, Berlin, UBA, 1995.

V

Valsecchi, Carolina, *Energy efficiency in the EU: an introduction*, n.p., IEEP, n.d., available at <http://www.ieep.eu/minisite_assets/briefings-on-climate/pdfs/Energy%20Efficiency%20in%20the%20EU%20An%20Introduction.pdf>, last accessed on 25 October 2016.

van Calster, Geert, *EU waste law*, 2.ed., Oxford, Oxford University Press, 2015.

van Rossem, Chris; Dalhammar, Carl; Toulouse, Edouard, *Designing greener electronic products: building synergies between EU product policy instruments or simply passing the buck?*, Report for the EEB, 2010, available at <http://www.eeb.org/?LinkServID=66030392-BF80-2CAC-B5335569F1526F90&showMeta=0>, last accessed on 12 August 2016.

van Rossem, Chris; Kogg, Beatrice; Mont, Oksana, "Throwing out the baby with the bathwater?", *Ökologisches Wirtschaften* 19 (2004), 11-13.

von Lersner, Heinrich Freiherr, "Vor- und Nachteile föderalistischer Strukturen im Abfallrecht", in Kloepfer, Michael (Hrsg.), *Abfallrecht und Föderalismus*, Berlin, Duncker & Humblot, 1999, 37-44.

——, "Abfall als Wirtschaftsgut – Zur rechtlichen Problematik des Abfallbegriffs", *Natur und Recht* 3 (1981), 1-5.

Versmann, Andreas, "Artikel 4 – Abfallhierarchie", in von Lersner, Heinrich; Wendenburg, Helge (Hrsg.), *Recht der Abfallbeseitigung des Bundes, der Länder und der Europäischen Union*, Band 5, Berlin, Erich Schmidt, 2015, 1-15.

von Bertalanffy, Ludwig, *General system theory: foundations, development, applications*, New York, George Braziller, 1968.

W

Wagner, Erika, "Integratives Umweltrecht auf nationaler und europäischer Ebene", *Recht der Umwelt* (1999), 3-21.

Walls, Margaret, *Deposit-refund systems in practice and theory*, Discussion paper 11-47, Washington, Resources for the Future, 2011, available at <http://www.rff.org/files/sharepoint/WorkImages/Download/RFF-DP-11-47.pdf>, last accessed on 10 May 2016.

——, *Extended producer responsibility and product design: economic theory and selected case studies*, Discussion paper 06-08, Washington, Resources for the Future, 2006, available at <https://media.rff.org/documents/RFF-DP-06-08-REV.pdf>, last accessed on 29 July 2019.

——, *The role of economics in extended producer responsibility: making policy choices and setting policy goals*, Discussion paper 03-11, Washington, Resources for the Future, 2003, available at <http://www.rff.org/files/sharepoint/WorkImages/Download/RFF-DP-03-11.pdf>, last accessed on 10 March 2016.

Webersinn, Michael, "Produktverantwortung – Eine ordnungspolitische Standbestimmung anlässlich der Umsetzung der EU-Abfallrahmenrichtlinie in deutsches Recht", *AbfallR* 6 (2010), 266-275.

Wegener, Bernhard W., "Die Freiheit stirbt mit der Glühbirne (wieder ein Stück)", *ZUR* 20 (2009), 169-170.

Wicke, Lutz, *Umweltökonomie*, 4.ed., München, Vahlen, 1993.

Wilts, Henning, *Ausweitung der Produzentenverantwortung mit Fokus auf Rücknahmeverpflichtungen*, 2013, available at <http://www.ressourcenpolitik.de/wp-content/uploads/2013/04/PolRess_ZB_AP2-Kurzanalyse-5_Produzentenverantwortung_final.pdf>, last accessed on 29 July 2019.

Winter, Gerd, "Ecological proportionality: an emerging principle of law for nature?", in Voigt, Christina (ed.), *Rule of law for nature: new dimensions and ideas in environmental law*, Cambridge, Cambridge University Press, 2013, 111-129.

——; Jans, Jan H.; Macroy, Richard; Krämer, Ludwig, "Weighing up the EC environmental liability directive", *JEL* 20 (2008), p. 163-191.

——; BLAZEK, John R., "Perspectives for environmental law – entering the fourth phase", *JEL* 1 (1989), 38-47.

Z

Zago, Mariana Augusta dos Santos, *Federalismo no Brasil e na Alemanha: estudo comparativo de competências legislativas e de execução*, Tese de doutorado, Faculdade de Direito da Universidade de São Paulo, São Paulo, Universidade de São Paulo, 2016.

Zundel, Stefan; Bunke, Dirk; Schramm, Engelbert; Steinfeld, Michael, "Stoffstrommanagement: Zwischenbilanz einer Diskussion", *ZfU* 21 (1998), 317-339.